Interviews with Spanish Writers

Fernando Arrabal (*photo courtesy of the author*)

Marie-Lise Gazarian Gautier

Interviews with Spanish Writers

Dalkey Archive Press

To Nathalie, my mother,
who, at the death of Gabriela Mistral, imparted to me this message:

"I have accomplished my mission on this earth. My body could do no more.
I have gone back to the Source, without a murmur... I saw the Gate of Truth
and understood I had triumphed over Death. You, keep up the good work!"

and

In memory of María Mora Molares

Library of Congress Cataloging in Publication Data
Gazarian-Gautier, Marie-Lise.
    Interviews with Spanish writers / Marie-Lise Gazarian Gautier.
    Includes bibliographical references and index.
1. Authors, Spanish—20th century—Interviews. I. Title.
PQ6051.G39   1991   860'.9'006—dc20   90-14055
ISBN: 0-916583-72-4

First Edition

Partially funded by grants from The National Endowment for the Arts and
The Illinois Arts Council.

Dalkey Archive Press
1817 North 79th Avenue
Elmwood Park, IL 60635 USA

Printed on permanent/durable acid-free paper and bound in the United
States of America.

Contents

Foreword

Conversation is a difficult art. It is not an empty, meaningless babble, but an expression of the spirit in all its complexity and light. This is why a conversation where insight and elegance prevail is so unusual. As a positive example of this, I would mention the conversations of Ricardo Gullón with Juan Ramón Jiménez; on the negative side, interviews held with prominent political figures. In the first instance, both parties discourse, and run an etymological race through the thousand stages that the questioner opens up before the eyes of the interviewee. We assume, of course, that the interviewer knows how to select the right person, agile and eloquent, like the athlete in the arena. We also assume that the questioner is talented. If these two positive conditions are met, there is no doubt that through the relevance of the subjects discussed, the insight of the information revealed and the vitality reflected in the answers, a literary genre of singular merit has been achieved. A spontaneous confession or a letter written from the bottom of the heart is invaluable. The same thing does not occur when the journalist is deprived of freedom. Stiff questions, self-censorship, trivial or evasive responses. We prefer the first type of questions; if directed at representative writers, they also give us a feeling of life that is absent in manuals and provide us with the other necessary face of criticism. The various positive elements are thus blended, as in a collage, to obtain a subtle all-embracing multicolored painting, with numerous old vessels traveling the waterways.

A conversation is pleasant if it is spontaneous, when that small spark of wit does as it pleases and is not chained to the thwart of the galiots. This is why it is hard to come upon a good conversationalist. Some, no matter how intelligent they are, think too much about what they are going to say, so what is said to them is of little use; others swim with their clothes on. We could say there is an air of insincerity about them. On the other hand, there are those that plunge into the waters that have been prepared for them, and like shrewd divers bring to the surface hidden treasures. Intelligence is reinforced by sincerity and freedom.

These are not bad ingredients for the making of a good conversation. Not a painfully slow moving of pieces on a chessboard, but the rapid turns of the bullfighter before the attack. The conversation, then, is not only the peaceful haven for serenity, but also a ground for fragile luck. Knowledge is not just experience, it is also the unleashing of intuition. Thanks to this, conversing cannot be reduced to walking through the gardens of Akademos; it entails as well accompanying Ulysses on each of his journeys. That is why there are sluggish dialogues and nervous chats. The value of people lies in what they are, not in what they appear to be. And being is not an authoritarian imposition, but an act of coexistence. We speak so that others may arrive at truths by themselves or discover by surprise pearls they were not seeking. The son of a midwife, whom other men called Socrates, was a teacher who practiced the art of maieutics. Socrates never wrote a single book, but he was a great conversationalist. Better than anyone else, as history has it, he entertained his disciples and made them love the spirit that lay dormant at the heart of their own consciousness. He was their stimulus: the youths who would have spoken worthless thoughts traveled the trail blazed by the master. There was no need for them to hurry, for they followed what their interlocutor was expounding; and later came the self-discovery of the mind. Socrates was several centuries ahead of Samuel Beckett: waiting for Godot. Let us try to converse without getting carried away, since we are incapable of keeping silent. We ask for wise answers, but let the interlocutor speak, let us interrupt him as little as possible and not behave like those poor conversationalists on talk shows. To harrass is a form of hindrance, to overwhelm is an undignified way of silencing the other. Tirso de Molina and Jean Grenier may have said very different things, but they ended coinciding with Socrates or is it with Beckett? The pomegranate opens, you rip its skin and the seeds pop out, shiny and transparent. This image helps us define what a conversation should truly be.

The conversation is over, but we now have it in written form. We possess something that cannot be measured in commercial terms: it is not a group of people who speak like books, but a book that speaks like people. No longer soliloquies, but conversations. To speak about what one likes is a form of love. This is what these authors are doing as they unclothe their souls to speak their thoughts without tricking the starry-eyed reader. As I said at the beginning, conversation is a difficult art. We must learn to listen and discern. That is why I think the present book is so important. Marie-Lise Gazarian Gautier knows how to select people who have something to say and she leads the conversation where she set her goal. All of the remarks I have made on the art of conversation are but deductions of the art she practices.

MANUEL ALVAR
President, Spanish Royal Academy

Introduction

Culture should always open the way to
freedom and to man's dignity.
—King Juan Carlos I

Spanish writers have played an especially important role in the culture,
politics and development of their nation. They took an active part in the
formation of the Republic in 1931 and, with the death of Franco in 1975, in
the shaping of a democratic monarchy. In 1977, for instance, Camilo José
Cela was called upon by King Juan Carlos to serve as senator during the
political transition period. Along with others, Cela helped in the drafting of
the Spanish Constitution and spared no effort to ensure that its text represent the purest form of Castilian Spanish.

Spanish writers fought on both sides of their divided country torn by the
Civil War. Some were executed, like Federico García Lorca; others went
into a forced exile, like Rafael Alberti, to return at the onset of democracy
some forty years later, or like Ramón Sender, never to resettle in his
country. The majority chose to remain in Spain, enduring another form of
exile, the isolation from the rest of the world in a stifling atmosphere
imposed by a forty-year-long dictatorship.

Both writers of the pre–Civil War generation, such as Antonio Buero
Vallejo and Miguel Hernández, and writers born during the Civil War
years, such as Lidia Falcón and Manuel Vázquez Montalbán, were sub-
jected to the horrors of political imprisonment. In some cases, those years
completely changed the direction of their lives. When Buero Vallejo was
arrested shortly after the Civil War, he was a promising young painter; when
he came out of jail six years later, he turned to the theater. As for the poet
Hernández, he did not survive his incarceration. Buero Vallejo showed me a

ix

copy of a portrait he had made of his friend Hernández in 1940, when they were detained in the jail of Conde de Toreno. It bore the following inscription: "In remembrance of our friendship in jail." Falcón would never have written *En el infierno: Ser mujer en las cárceles de España,* a heartbreaking account of the brutality inflicted on women in Spanish jails during the dictatorship, had she not spent those months in Madrid's Yeserías prison. She wrote that testimony from her jail cell in a diminutive handwriting on onionskin paper which was passed on clandestinely to her family and friends. These bitter experiences strengthened her dedication to the cause of battered women. Others, like Fernando Arrabal and Juan Goytisolo, left Spain in the 1950s because there was no room for their voices to be heard and they felt like outcasts in their own country. They moved to Paris in 1955 and 1957, respectively, where they reside to this day.

Lives had been cut short in the most unexpected way. A mother who had gone out for a moment to buy presents for her children never came back; she was killed in an air raid. Those children were the three Goytisolo brothers and their sister. Juan Goytisolo recounts in his memoirs, *Forbidden Territory,* how this traumatic loss shook the structure of his life to its foundation. Countless are the names of the men and women of both factions in the war who disappeared from their homes never to come back and who left behind broken families. In a gesture of solidarity, Gabriela Mistral, the Chilean 1945 Nobel Prize winner, offered the proceeds of her book *Tala* to the children made homeless by the Spanish Civil War.

It is not surprising, then, that to many Spaniards there were two Spains, that of the conquered and that of the victors. Nor is it surprising, for both those who experienced the Civil War and those who only experienced the postwar years, that fratricidal war remained alive in their memories. Only now, in the decade of the 1990s, are writers beginning to turn away from these memories and seek other topics as material for their novels. Juan Benet, for instance, confided that he was about to put an end to his cycle of novels related to the Civil War.

The writers included in this book are men and women whose ages range from thirty-five to eighty-nine. In spite of the striking age difference between some of them, they all have been marked, directly or indirectly, by that war and have felt the pangs of hunger, whether spiritual or physical. Rafael Alberti, Antonio Buero Vallejo, Camilo José Cela, Carmen Conde, José Luis Sampedro and Gonzalo Torrente Ballester experienced as young men and women the tragic Civil War years. Juan Benet, José Luis Castillo Puche, Miguel Delibes, Carmen Laforet, Carmen Martín Gaite, and Ana María Matute belong to that "wounded generation," born in the twenties, that saw the war break out when they were in their teens. Fernando Arrabal, José María Carrascal, Lidia Falcón, Juan Goytisolo, Juan Marsé, Francisco Umbral, and Manuel Vázquez Montalbán, born during the decade of the thirties, were small children during those horrid years.

Eduardo Mendoza, Justo Jorge Padrón, and Julián Ríos, born in the forties, belong to a more internationally oriented generation. Rosa Montero and Antonio Muñoz Molina are the youngest writers included in this book; born in the fifties, they are representative of a very prolific young generation of writers in today's Spain: when Montero was twenty-nine, she won the 1980 National Prize for journalism; with Muñoz Molina's second novel, at age thirty-two, he received the 1988 National Literature Prize.

Interviews with Spanish Writers is a collection of twenty-four interviews with the giants, the veterans, and some of the newcomers of Spanish literature. Most of these writers are novelists, although there are some poets and playwrights. It is the first book of its kind, totally devoted to Spain, to appear in English. I have followed the advice of Gonzalo Torrente Ballester who, before I could interview him, told me that I should include some young writers in the book. "Leave no stone unturned" were his exact words, "get in touch with young writers like Muñoz Molina." In a similar way, Juan Goytisolo suggested that I get in touch with Julián Ríos and, to make sure I did, gave me his novel *Larva: Midsummer Night's Babel.* When I asked Goytisolo whether he considered himself a Spanish Joyce, his answer was, "Julián Ríos is the man who deserves that title."

With Franco's death in 1975, a new page was turned in the history of Spain. The transition period from dictatorship to one of the most advanced forms of democracy was a remarkable achievement. In a very moving statement, José Antonio Soler (of *El País,* one of Spain's foremost newspapers) said: "When in June 1977 more than three-fourths of the electorate voted for the first time in their lives, we felt like children with new shoes. To deposit this ballot was like the day of our First Communion."

In the last fifteen years, Spain has distinguished itself on many accounts. In 1976, the Miguel de Cervantes Prize, considered to be the Nobel Prize for literature of the Hispanic world, was created in Madrid. Such prominent figures from Spain and Latin America as Rafael Alberti, Antonio Buero Vallejo, Carlos Fuentes, Juan Carlos Onetti, and Ernesto Sábato are among its recipients. Another prize, the Príncipe de Asturias Prize, was created in 1980 by the King and Queen of Spain, bearing the name of their son, the Prince of Asturias, who presides over the award. Spaniards and Latin Americans have been granted this honor on an equal basis, among them being Camilo José Cela, Miguel Delibes, Carmen Martín Gaite, Juan Rulfo, Gonzalo Torrente Ballester and Mario Vargas Llosa. In 1978, the Spanish Royal Academy, the prestigious institution that has been watching over the language for over two hundred years, officially recognized the importance of women by electing Carmen Conde as its first female member. Five years later, Elena Quiroga became the second woman to enter the Royal Academy. The Nobel Prize was granted to two Spaniards in that same period of time: first in 1977, to Vicente Aleixandre, and in 1989 to Cela. In May 1990, the Spanish government agreed to the establishment of the Cervantes Institute to promote the Spanish language and culture on a worldwide scale.

Spain has joined the European Community and has opened its doors to the rest of the world. Spanish writers have conquered the European market and their works are being translated into many languages. Cela's *The Family of Pascual Duarte* boasts of being the Spanish novel most often translated after Cervantes's *Don Quixote;* it was even translated into Latin. Vázquez Montalbán's *Southern Seas* received the 1981 Paris International Detective Story Prize. Mendoza's *City of Marvels* was selected by *Lire,* France's popular literary journal, as the best book of the year for 1988. Some of the supporters of Ríos, quoted in the 1985 Book of the Year of the *Encyclopaedia Britannica,* have called *Midsummer Night's Babel,* the first of the projected five-volume set of his cycle *Larva,* "an instant postmodern classic, without doubt the most disturbingly original Spanish prose of the century." Padrón's poetry received the International Grand Prix of the Swedish Academy in 1972, the Brussels Gold Medal of French Culture in 1981, and the European Literature Prize from Yugoslavia in 1986. These examples, taken at random, and the recent award of the Nobel Prize for literature to Cela, clearly demonstrate the international attention that Spanish writers now enjoy. Cela himself said upon accepting that honor: "There are many other Spaniards and Latin Americans who deserved this distinction, and for this reason I believe that, through me, a prize has been given to Hispanic literature." Manuel Alvar, President of the Spanish Royal Academy, commented: "I have been studying Cela's novels for the past forty years and I have written about nearly all of them. For this reason, the award comes as no surprise. Cela is one of the great storytellers who writes in Spanish, and his style may well be unrivaled." Torrente Ballester, another giant of Spanish prose, expressed his happiness upon hearing the good news: "I must say that the awarding of the Nobel Prize to Cela seems to be quite just, and also that it is a few years overdue. As a friend, as a writer, as a Spaniard and as a Galician, I feel a deep sense of satisfaction."

Spain has caught the attention of foreign readers, who are discovering a literature they were unaware of. Critics talk about the renaissance of the Spanish narrative and discuss the new directions it is taking. What is really new, however, is that within Spain these writers are enjoying a long-awaited freedom, which makes everything permissible, and that outside of their country, people are aware of their existence. When their books come out, their authors go on tours and take part in symposia to promote their works around the world. Eduardo Mendoza confided: "To be a writer in Spain at this moment is an exciting experience." They also promote their new books by publishing them as serials in the leading newspapers. This is the case of Rafael Alberti, for instance, who likes—as he told me—to try out his writings on these readers before putting them in book form. His latest book of memoirs has appeared every other week in *El País.* Borrowing the words of Manuel

Vázquez Montalbán, "Rather than going through a cultural 'Boom,' I would say Spain has returned to a cultural life under a democratic government."

Writers may make us believe that they have laid aside traditional social realism to turn to new forms, when in fact what they have done is disguise it under new captions. Doesn't Pepe Carvalho, the main character of Vázquez Montalbán's cycle of detective stories, remind us in some way of the *pícaro?* The detective story and the historical novel, relatively new to Spain and espoused by such figures as Mendoza, Torrente Ballester, and Vázquez Montalbán, represent an interplay of genres. If we listen to what Mendoza has to say on the subject, we realize that these so-called new genres are a modern adaptation of the traditional picaresque novel: "I like detective stories. So I used their structure which has allowed me the freedom to move the way I wanted to. In a way, what I did was to write a picaresque novel and give it the body of a detective story." But playing with traditional set patterns is not something new to Spaniards. When, over twenty years ago, the secretary of a prominent publisher sent back to Juan Benet one of his manuscripts with a note saying his book could not be published with so few exchanges of dialogue, the author, out of spite, removed two of the three existing ones. The novel was *Return to Región,* which turned out to be one of his most famous works. He is also known for inventing a contraption, which he adapted to his typewriter, whereby the paper would enter the carriage and wind itself into another continuous roll of paper. This was his way of dealing with the flow of words and memory.

Experimenting with language is yet another way of exploring new spaces and defying established norms. Juan Goytisolo has been doing it for the past thirty years from his Paris home or his Marrakech hideaway. He has squeezed the Spanish language to the core, extracting its essence and giving it a new flexibility. It was his way of lashing out at an oppressive society. He refuses the term "avant-garde" given him, rejects the Renaissance period which set up literary canons, and finds his roots among the writers of the Middle Ages, when, to quote him, "writers were free to do as they pleased." Julián Ríos has taken up a similar game. Like Cela, Goytisolo, and other modern masters, he turns to Francisco Delicado and Francisco de Quevedo to rediscover that much-sought freedom. But, additionally, he is a polyglot and calls constantly on other tongues to give Castilian Spanish a multilingual dimension. The reader has become a "bricolecteur," a handyman who handles words and is as involved in the text as the author himself. The emergence of this new type of reader, whether of novels, poetry or plays, is perhaps the most important phenomenon that is taking place in today's literary scene.

The two strongholds of Spain's publishing world, Barcelona and Madrid, are booming. New books from the bastion of the old guard as well as the avant-garde constantly come out and many of them are awarded prizes. Yet, this is not a new occurrence. There has always been a trend in Spain to award prizes and encourage writers. As early as 1925, Rafael Alberti, who was then mostly known for his paintings, was awarded the National Literature Prize for *Marinero en tierra,* his first collection of poetry. Even during the dark years of the dictatorship, books were published and literary prizes created and awarded. In 1944, Carmen Laforet, a young, unknown author, was the first recipient of the newly created Nadal Prize—named after the writer Eugenio Nadal—for her novel *Nada.* Miguel Delibes was awarded the same prize in 1947 for his novel *La sombra del ciprés es alargada.* Ana María Matute won the Planeta Prize in 1954 for *Pequeño teatro,* a novel she wrote when she was seventeen. In 1952, she received the Café Gijón Prize for her novel *Fiesta al Noroeste.* In 1959, she was the recipient of the Nadal Prize for *Primera memoria,* and, in 1969, the Fastenrath Prize of the Spanish Royal Academy for *Los soldados lloran de noche.* In 1956 and 1958, Antonio Buero Vallejo received the National Drama Prize, among many others. Carmen Conde won the National Literature Prize in 1967 for her *Obra poética: 1922-1966.* José María Carrascal received the 1972 Nadal Prize for his novel *Groovy.* Francisco Umbral won the Nadal Prize in 1975 for *Las ninfas* and, that same year, Eduardo Mendoza was awarded the Crítica Prize for *La verdad sobre el caso Savolta.* These are only a few of the countless awards that were handed out during the years of postwar Spain.

A special tribute should be paid at this point to Carlos Barral, the poet and owner of the Seix Barral publishing house in Barcelona, who defied the machineries of censorship and published the works of young, unknown Spanish and Latin American writers. He is in great part responsible for promoting in the 1960s the literary explosion referred to as the "Boom." The Biblioteca Breve Prize brought overnight recognition to such Latin American writers as Mario Vargas Llosa, Guillermo Cabrera Infante and Carlos Fuentes. A land of paradox, the Spain of the Franco years opened the way to young Latin American writers who in their countries could not have published their works because of their own dictatorships. The now-legendary figure of Barral, the "old sea salt," as he was called, is dead. He passed away in December 1989 and asked that his ashes be scattered over the waters of Calafell, a seacoast town in the northeast of Spain. Juan Marsé, very saddened by his friend's death, recalled how as a young writer he brought his manuscript to Barral, who believed in his talent and accepted it for publication.

I would like at this time to keep a promise I made to the playwright Antonio Buero Vallejo and raise for the reader the curtains that were closed during the Franco regime, preventing foreigners from knowing that great literature had been written in Spain during those hidden years. Foreigners —I am not referring to Hispanists and I am echoing the words of Buero Vallejo, Delibes, Vázquez Montalbán, Mendoza, and many others—saw in Cervantes the beginning of Spanish literature and regarded Lorca's death as its end. Spain had become for the rest of the world synonymous with a romantic hideaway, sunbathing, and bullfights.

Buero Vallejo was greatly concerned that this misconception be clarified and corrected. As he explained: "If you are a good writer, you will write, no matter what stands in your way. Only those who had no real talent blamed dictatorship for their silence. With the onset of democracy, they still had nothing to say." But great books were written and censorship was helpless at silencing their authors. Writers found ways of evading the scrutinous eye of the censor, rewriting with different words entire sentences that had been crossed out. Umbral explains: "A Spanish author of that time whom I deeply admired, César Gonzalez-Ruano, once said that since the censors had forbidden the use of the word 'thigh,' writers were forced into discovering forty ways of saying it without actually using that word. When you have a rich vocabulary and you know how to say things, it is not necessary to use a particular term; you can find another word to suggest the same thing."

Writers have always enjoyed an enormous popularity in Spain. They are constantly in the public eye, they appear on television talk shows, their novels are made into television serials or into movies, chapters of their books are published in the most important newspapers. The following incident illustrates this point. Some ten years ago, when I took a cab to go from Madrid to Navacerrada, a small village about a hundred miles from the capital, to see Conde, the driver was so excited at the idea of meeting the newly elected academician that he offered to wait for me free of charge as long as I needed. Conde received him, gave him something to drink and told him to wait in the shade because the sun was very strong. Writers are public figures, but usually accessible ones. Delibes told me, for instance, that he took the time to read compositions that schoolchildren had written about his novel *The Path* and that he enjoyed meeting with them.

Just as actors have fans, writers have their own followers. People know the way they look, the way they talk, they identify with their sense of humor and the provocative remarks that are expected of them. Some writers—like Alberti, Arrabal, Cela, and Umbral—lend themselves to this game. Others —such as Buero Vallejo, Delibes, Goytisolo, Marsé, Torrente Ballester— prefer to keep more to themselves. Carmen Laforet has shunned all publicity for the past seventeen years; yet she agreed to break that silence to be interviewed for this book.

One of the aims of *Interviews with Spanish Writers* is to emphasize that it took more than forty years for Spain to come out of its isolation and be recognized as a nation with first-rate writers. Twenty-four of these writers graciously accepted to define for us their literary and personal worlds, revealing their inner traits and giving us insights into their works. In a blending of voices, some overpowering, others subdued, the authors express in their individual ways their views on politics, love, writing, and all the forms of art.

I was particularly impressed to meet these authors on their own territory, most of them in their own homes: in Barcelona and Madrid, as well as in Majorca, Salamanca, Valladolid, and Paris. There were some exceptions: I met José Luis Castillo Puche and Francisco Umbral at the Café Gijón in

Madrid, the one hundred-year-old gathering place for writers and artists, and Torrente Ballester at the Gran Hotel of Salamanca.

Today, as we are approaching the quincentennial of the European discovery of America, the world turns its attention toward Spain and Latin America. The writers I have interviewed for both this book and its predecessor, *Interviews with Latin American Writers* (1989), thought that it should not be a festive occasion, but a moment for reflection. Carlos Fuentes, referring to the cultural partnership between the Old and the New World, expressed it in a striking way when he said: "We have the caravels of Columbus coming back and forth over the ocean all the time. Sometimes they come from Spain to America, sometimes we send them back from America to Spain."

With the exception of that with José María Carrascal, all of the interviews were conducted in Spanish. Throughout this work, books that have been translated from Spanish into English are referred to by their English titles. Those that have not been translated are identified by their original titles. In the headnotes that precede each interview, however, both the Spanish and English titles of each book have been given in italics whenever a translation was available, together with the respective dates of publication. For the titles of those works for which no English version was available, I have provided my own translation in parentheses.

I would like to express my deep gratitude to each and every one of the writers who so willingly shared his or her time and thoughts with me. Almost all the interviews were conducted for the specific purpose of being included in this book. One of them, however, was part of a televised series I hosted, "The Hispanic Writers of Greater New York." I would, therefore, like to thank WABC-TV, as well as St. John's University Television Center, for co-producing this series, and the Center's former director, Winston L. Kirby, for his interest in promoting Spanish and Latin American literature. I am most grateful to the members of my family for their constant advice and encouragement, especially my mother and brothers. I would also like to acknowledge the strong support of my friends and colleagues. Special credit should be given to Enrique Camacho, director of the Casa de España, New York, and to Elizabeth Cuspinera, of the Consulate-General of Spain in New York, for their cooperation. Deep thanks are due to Anil Singh-Molares for his translations and valuable assistance throughout the preparation of this work. Special thanks are also due to the staff of St. John's Library, particularly Joan Collett, Lucy Heckman, Gloria Kelman, Maria Ptakowski, Drew Selvar, Arthur Sherman, my graduate assistant María Caamaño, and to my former student Mayra Pérez. I am also grateful to Richard Alan Francis for his suggestions regarding the translation of Julián Ríos's interview.

Interviews with Spanish Writers

Rafael Alberti

Rafael Alberti was born in 1902 in Puerto de Santa María, Cádiz, in the south of Spain. A poet, playwright and painter, he is one of the foremost survivors of the Generation of 1927. This generation gave birth to such poets and artists as García Lorca, Miguel Hernández, Vicente Aleixandre, Picasso, and Dali.

When Rafael Alberti first moved to Madrid in 1917, it was to study art. The Prado Museum became for him a second home: "My great home, especially in the summer, was the Prado, which I knew by heart."

First recognized as a painter, he did not turn to poetry until 1923. In 1925, he won the National Literature Prize for his first book, *Marinero en tierra* (Landlocked Sailor). Since then, he has blended the two forms to create an art which he calls *liricografía.* "I am like Góngora, I see the poem as a graphic art," Alberti tells us.

Rafael Alberti considers himself both a poet and a painter. He has carried into poetry the hues of painting, and into painting the musicality of poetry. For this reason, when he autographs a book, he simultaneously writes an inscription and draws a dove, a rooster, or a ship as part of his signature. When he was awarded the Miguel de Cervantes Prize in 1983, he felt impelled to sketch two self-portraits at the same time: one with words and another with lines.

Alberti lived through the years of the Republic and the horrors of the Civil War, which he recounts in his poems, in particular the moving poem about his dog, which fought the war alongside him. With his wife, María Teresa León, he also suffered the anguish of a thirty-eight-year-long exile that lasted until Franco's death. For nineteen of those years he experienced the trauma of a man who had been deprived of his passport. He and his wife first lived in Paris, from 1939 until 1940, then moved to Buenos Aires, where their daughter Aitana was born. During their twenty-four-year stay in Argentina, he painted, gave readings, put on plays, wrote nostalgic poems about the Andalusia of his childhood, and dreamed about a free Spain. In 1964, he moved to Rome with his family, to feel closer to his native land and to discover the culture of his Italian ancestors.

Since 1977, Rafael Alberti has joined the artistic and political scene of today's Spain: "I left with my fist clenched in a time of war, and I have returned with a hand reaching out in a gesture of fraternity."

He is the author of more than thirty books, among them *El alba del alhelí* (The Dawn of the Gilly-Flower), 1927; *Cal y canto* (Tightly Closed), 1929; *Sermones y moradas* (Homilies and Abodes), 1939; *Entre el clavel y la espada* (Between the Carnation and the Sword), 1941; *A la pintura* (To Painting), 1945; *Baladas y canciones del Paraná*, 1954 (*Ballads and Songs of the Paraná*, 1988); *Abierto a todas horas (1960-1963)* (Open All Hours), 1964; *El poeta en la calle: poesía civil 1931-1965* (A Poet in the Street), 1966; *Roma, peligro para caminantes* (Rome, a Danger for Pedestrians), 1968; *Los ocho nombres de Picasso* (The Eight Names of Picasso), 1970. The first part of his memoirs, *La arboleda perdida,* 1942 (*The Lost Grove,* 1976), covered the episodes of his life until 1931. In 1987, he published the second part. Three volumes of his complete works came out in Madrid in 1988. His play *La Pájara pinta* (The Spotted Bird), begun in 1925, finally premiered in August 1987 at the Centro Cultural Galileo of Madrid. The prologue to the play mimics the rhythm of the Spanish language through a series of invented sounds. Its main character, half bird, half human, is derived from Andalusian folklore.

In 1989, in a ceremony presided over by Queen Sofía, he was received into the Royal Academy of Fine Arts. In his acceptance speech, he spoke of the significant place that literature and painting occupied in his life and recalled that on the night of his father's death, when he wrote his first poem, poetry gained ground over painting. An avowed advocate of peace, Rafael Alberti is also the recipient of the 1965 Lenin Prize.

His private library has been moved from his house in Rome to Puerto de Santa María, where he was born, and his native house has become a museum.

I met Rafael Alberti for the first time in New York, and later in Madrid. I was struck by his incredible youth. He looked like a sea captain who had just stepped off his sailboat. He made me feel as if the Hudson River had merged with the Bay of Cádiz. During the week I drove him around Manhattan, he recited his poetry and talked about his friends Lorca and Picasso, visited museums where he was the best of guides, autographed books, and sketched ships and doves. One night, as we were returning from my university, he surprised me with three drawings he had made for me. But perhaps what touched me most was seeing him take out a small notebook and write a poem. We were sitting in the car, caught in the New York traffic, as Rafael Alberti broke loose from the chaos around us and absorbed himself completely in the writing of the poem. The Manhattan streets, the cars, and the noise had disappeared for him. When I saw him again in Madrid, this time in his home, in a modern building, I found him at his desk preparing his acceptance speech as an academician. He was sitting in a wheelchair because of a car accident, but as strong as ever. He was wearing a Hawaiian shirt in the bright colors he enjoys. His paintings and books surrounded him. A dove landed on the terrace as we were discussing the role of the dove in his poetry.

❖❖❖❖❖❖❖❖❖❖❖❖❖❖❖❖❖❖❖❖❖❖❖❖❖❖❖❖❖❖❖

Part 1

MLG: You were born with two callings: as a painter and a poet. Would I be wrong in saying that most of the images in your poetry are visual and that painting has had a strong influence on your work?

RA: As I have said many times, I am undoubtedly an optical poet, because I have a very acute visual sensibility. This underscores the fact that I have been a painter from the very beginning. I am like the seventeenth-century poet Góngora, who has influenced me at times and was one of the most visual poets ever. Seeing is very important for me. In fact, if I cannot visualize a poem, I am almost unable to write it.

MLG: You once said of the Prado Museum that it was the most fabulous home you ever had. What does painting mean for you?

RA: The Prado was indeed a fabulous thing for me, because I was born to be a painter, and when I traveled from the province of Cádiz to Madrid, I was absolutely dumbfounded by it. Because of the poor reproductions I had seen in magazines, I had a notion that classical art was something dark and obscure. When I first set foot in the Prado, I was dazzled by the Venetian school, by Titian, Veronese, Tintoretto, Rubens, and Velázquez. I realized that classical art consisted of paintings full of light, which moved me deeply. I cannot separate myself from painting, which is an integral part of my poetry. The two are fused to such an extent that nowadays I do not know if I am writing or painting. I am more than just a painter; above all, I am a graphic, linear person. I have held many exhibitions with words and signs, so that the two are the same for me now.

MLG: You once said, "I really never had the slightest notion that I would become a poet, because as a child I never had any special affinity for poetry or literature." When did you become aware of your calling as a poet?

RA: I realized that when I was over twenty years old. When I first arrived in Madrid, I spent all of my time painting, from 1917 until at least 1922. But I began to feel that there was something missing in my paintings, I was not satisfied, and what was missing were words. I had already begun to read such poets as Rubén Darío, Antonio Machado, Juan Ramón Jiménez. Little by little, almost unconsciously, words crept into my canvases, and then they took such a hold that they literally replaced the paintings, which disappeared, leaving only words.

MLG: In one of your poems, you say, "I no longer care about being new, old or outdated, what matters to me is the life that flees with every song." Why do you write?

RA: I write for the same reasons that I think all poets and writers do. It is something one is born with, it is like having black, brown, or blond hair. I cannot express myself in any other way. I speak with my own voice in a particular manner, I write because I have to; if I did not, poetry would not come spontaneously to me. Sometimes I provoke it, at other times it comes of itself, because I think that I would feel terrible and become crazy otherwise.

MLG: Do you believe in inspiration?

RA: Baudelaire said that inspiration is hard work, and I believe in work, because I work very hard as a poet from the onset of dawn. It is from this daily poetry that inspiration comes.

MLG: Do you consider poetry primarily as an artistic vehicle, or is it also a social vehicle?

RA: I think that poetry has its purpose; it is not just a sport or diversion. Poetry is something quite profound and serious; poets are bards, seers, diviners, almost prophets. Of old, the word *poet* meant seer, and although that sense is being lost, a poet is fundamentally a diviner, because he has feelings and sensations that can foretell many things. Poetry is much more than just a pastime or an aesthetic entertainment. Poets can direct many events, as has been shown in the past, but particularly lately.

MLG: Do you consider yourself independent from any literary movement, or do you feel linked to the Generation of 1927?

RA: Through friendships and literary beliefs, I feel very much linked with the Generation of 1927, because I am a part of it. Most of those writers died in exile, but in Spain, some of us still remain. I am very close to them, although I am a poet who has strayed to a certain extent from the tenets of my generation, because I was much more active and engaged in issues than my friends, whether in Spain or abroad. I believe poetry is a vital and factual tool, which can draw considerable attention.

MLG: You were a close friend of Federico García Lorca. Do you recall any anecdote you might want to share?

RA: I could recount so many things about Lorca, but I will tell you about the first time I met him. I had just given an art show in Madrid, which he attended. Although I was not well known for my poetry, I had already dedicated a poem to him, but he said: "Those poems are all very well, but you are a painter and must continue to be one. I want you to do a painting of me on the bank of a river or perhaps under an olive tree, above which would stand the Virgin of Blessed Love. And above the Virgin, you will put a caption which says, 'Apparition of Our Holy Mother of Blessed Love to the poet Federico García Lorca, while he lay asleep in the lowlands of Granada.' " It was a long title, but I did the painting nonetheless, and it was the last one I did until 1945. His family still has that work in Granada.

MLG: Do you want to say something about the Civil War, or is it a period you would rather forget?

RA: No, the Civil War is very interesting, and although it was beneath Spain's dignity, its effects are not completely over. The Civil War was an unforgettable event for all of us. I have always said that for some it was even a paradise in the shadow of swords. Poetically, we developed tremendously, we created the poetry of the battle, the streets, and the trenches. Along with Miguel Hernández, a young poet who died in jail two years after the end of the war, I was particularly active in the fight, and we could not forget the war. That conflict also produced some great works, because the best writers in the world—and let me just consider writers—supported the Spanish Republic. The great poet Neruda wrote an extraordinary book which is called *España en el corazón* (Spain in My Heart), while César Vallejo, a wonderful Peruvian poet, wrote *España, aparta de mí este cáliz* (Spain, Remove This Chalice from Me). In Spain, Miguel Hernández wrote *Viento del pueblo* (The Wind of the People) and I wrote *Capital de la gloria* (The Capital of Glory). So the war was a fruitful event in this respect, because we were so ardent and anxious that the Republic not suffer the fate that it did when it was eventually defeated.

MLG: You once wrote, "In the shoes of my childhood sleeps the burning sand of the dunes." Why does all your poetry have the fragrance of the sea?

RA: I am often asked that question. I come from a well-known European bay, the Bay of Cádiz, the oldest city in the west, older than Rome. It has three thousand years of written history, and I belong to those towns that are rich in lime and indigo, and where the sky sparkles. The sea there left an extraordinary and vivid impression on me. There is not one poem of mine that does not mention the word *sea*. In fact, that word is so prominent that even I sometimes don't know what it means. So the Bay of Cádiz has influenced me a great deal.

MLG: As a poet you surrender completely to the sea, eliminating your human characteristics. For instance, you say that "the sea rides on a bicycle" and that "the water rests on the beach." Why do you like to personify the sea and dehumanize yourself?

RA: I don't think I dehumanize myself, I blend with the sea. I have symbolized or personified the sea in my poetry as a male or female figure. As you know, in Spanish the sea can be both masculine and feminine, in contrast to other tongues. In Spain, we say "el mar" and "la mar." I began my book *Marinero en tierra,* which won the National Literature Prize, with the words "El mar, la mar, el mar, la mar, el mar solo, la mar / ¿Por qué padre me trajiste a la ciudad, por qué me desenterraste del mar?" ("Father/ mother sea, only you, sea / Father, why did you take me to the city? / Why did you tear me away from the sea?). The sea for me is everything, it is love, it is the family, it is the landscape, it is a character with which I have developed very close relations, almost in an elitist sense, as they would say today.

MLG: Another important image in your poetry is that of angels; in fact, you wrote a book called *Sobre los ángeles* (*Concerning the Angels*). Can you explain the meaning of the "fight" you started with the angels, so to speak?

RA: Angels were another emblem of my poetry. I did not address them as the plastic representations one finds in paintings, because for me they are spirits that symbolize psychic or spiritual states. I molded them to fit my changing circumstances. At a certain point, for instance, when I ceased to be a young poet, I went through a big crisis due to my physical and spiritual growth, and I conceived of angels as strange creatures that I could shape through all my moods. I wrote that poem in an almost haphazard manner at night, through a nebulous haze, and I think, in all modesty, that the book I wrote was truly of my generation.

MLG: You often speak of your childhood in your poetry. Sometimes it seems that your poems are a dialogue between Alberti, the grown man, and Alberti, the child you once were. In a nostalgic mood, you even said of your years as a child, "Take me by the hand, little Rafael Alberti, there below is the sea, the beach, the sand, from when there were no letters, no newspapers or radio, nor exhibition programs, nor so much death." What does childhood mean for you?

RA: I believe what Unamuno believed—that there can be no poet for whom childhood did not mean something essential, something which was even like a blueprint of one's life. I was very much formed by my Andalusian childhood and those landscapes that I have recently rediscovered in all their splendor, a splendor which I think other people also see. So I go back to my childhood in my poetry and in everything, without realizing it. I think I had a very rich childhood, plentiful in its revelations and other experiences. For me, it is like the sea, like the angels, and some of those early impressions are still with me.

MLG: Although you spent many years in exile, you were always dreaming of Spain, and your work is essentially Spanish in character. What does Spain mean to you?

RA: I left Spain because of the terrible things that happened there during the war. One million people died and five hundred thousand went into exile. Spain was a dream, like the one the Jews carried with them in 1492 when many of them had to leave. They took the keys to their houses and never forgot the country. Spanish emigration has really been full of achievements on the cultural level, because we took Spain with us and imbued everything we did with it. Great publishing firms developed in Mexico and Argentina, stupendous painters held showings all over the place, and there was a strong feeling of nostalgia that so many did not live to fulfill. Thirty-nine years is too long for an exile. So many people died, so many did not come back, because they didn't want to return, or if they did come back they stayed for only three or four days, because there was almost nothing left for them here. Those of us who did return found a Spain that had changed in many respects. But although we Spanish people have suffered many misfortunes and been trampled many times throughout our history, we are still a vital nation, and we will do great things again in the future.

MLG: Do you still paint?

RA: Not only do I continue to do so, but it is a fundamental thing in my life. I earn almost more from painting than from poetry, but it is not only important to me in economic terms. I have held many exhibitions . . .

MLG: Are there any similarities between poetry and painting?

RA: A great many; for instance, I paint many of my poems, and I call one facet of my painting "lyricography," because it combines the lyrical and the graphic. I have devised an alphabet with fifty-two engravings, twenty-six in color and twenty-six in black and white, with each letter representing a word. For example, *A* for *amor* (love), *B* for *botella* (bottle), *Z* for *zigzag,* et cetera. This was a huge exhibition I held in Rome, because fifty-two engravings occupied a big hall, and then I also had a lot of individual engravings. I engrave with lead, which is a very unusual technique. I have also published many portfolios of my poems and some books, like the one I dedicated to Picasso, *Los ocho nombres de Picasso,* or the one I did on Miró.

MLG: Of these two callings, which one gives you more joy?

RA: The two of them. I cannot do without either. I very much regret that, when I was younger, I did not have the necessary talent to combine them as I eventually did when I was over forty years old. I worry when I am only painting or when I am only writing, because I don't want one or the other to be left behind. I always fuse the two. Sometimes I even write short poems with the express purpose of drawing them, so that both may become one.

MLG: You were a close friend of Pablo Neruda.

RA: We were very close, like brothers.

MLG: Is there some anecdote about him you would like to share with us?

RA: There are so many I could tell, because we shared our lives and traveled together. Pablo used to like to collect many different things. For instance, he might spot an old shoe on the street, or some postcards, or a small organ, and take them all with him for his collection. He also used to buy a lot of those model boats that are inside bottles. When he left a bleak Paris, in the middle of the war, to go back to Chile, six or seven of us each carried one of those boats for him onto the train. The ticket collector was furious and must have wondered, "Who is that man who owns so many boats?" We had to ask passengers in other compartments if they would hold on to some of the boats, because the whole fleet didn't fit in one compartment. So Neruda returned to his beloved Chile with all his boats. I could tell so many childish and charming stories about Pablo because he was like a terrible and capricious child who delighted in these sorts of pranks.

MLG: Were you also a close friend of Picasso?

RA: Yes, for a long time. I put together Picasso's last books at his request. They were based on the final two great exhibits that he held at Avignon in the papal castle. He called me to see if I would write the introduction to the books, which were not fabulous works, just catalogs really. He put out two volumes because he held two exhibits in two consecutive years. I saw him a lot during the last years of his life, when he barely went out. Occasionally he would go to the beach. He had a thirst for eternity and a hunger for time; he was a man who felt each minute of his life. At ninety years of age, he would still work all night, go to bed for a few hours in the morning, and then go back to work. He would see people only in the early afternoon, and I was one of the few he would receive. I wrote *Los ocho nombres de Picasso* to amuse and cheer him because Pablo was a very funny Andalusian, a marvelous man from Málaga. When he died, I was in Rome, and I was shocked because I thought Picasso would never die, I thought he was immortal, as did everyone. He died at the age of ninety-two, and the news was proclaimed in the streets of Rome, which is rather unusual in that city. I was stunned by his death, because he had not been sick. It seems that he caught the flu, and since he was so old, he died. Those last five years that I was so close to Picasso are among my fondest memories.

MLG: Do you work at night like Picasso?

RA: I very often work at dawn. I am very uncomfortable in bed because I inevitably always wake up at six in the morning. No matter what I do, even if I go to bed at three, I am awake at six. So I work very early in the morning and to very good effect.

MLG: You have said of yourself, "I am Rafael Alberti, a Spanish poet, a fervent voice among the masses." Who is Rafael Alberti?

RA: I think I have been telling you that since you asked your first question. I am a poet who wants to live a long time. I used to say that I wanted to live to be 125, but that seemed too much, so I reduced it to 115, and perhaps I'll live . . .

MLG: You'll live forever!

Part 2

MLG: I remember that as I drove you from my university to your hotel, you took a small notebook out of your pocket and jotted down a poem in your very fine handwriting. I never asked you what became of that poem.

RA: Only God knows . . . I very often lose my notebooks or don't remember where I put them. I have no idea what I wrote that time, perhaps it is in my book *Versos sueltos de cada día,* a collection of my poems written between 1979 and 1982, and published in *Obras completas* in 1988.

MLG: Have you written a lot since I last saw you?

RA: I wrote the second volume of my memoirs, *La arboleda perdida.* It was published last year, sometime around my birthday, December 16. It is a huge book, and it has been very successful. Right now, I am writing the third volume, which is being serialized in *El País,* one chapter every other Sunday. It's going to take another year and a half to finish it.

MLG: How do memories spring up?

RA: Individual memories come up intertwined with others, somewhat hazily and disjointedly, so I write almost without order. Different things rush to my consciousness and I try to isolate them from each other and then reorder them more harmoniously.

MLG: Have you been writing poetry?

RA: I write loose poems, which I plan to gather in a still untitled book. It will be published as part of a seven-volume anthology of my complete works, three of which have already come out. So, I work hard, because even though one of my legs has failed me as the result of a car accident, I continue to be as lucid as ever. There's nothing wrong with me. I am eight-six years old and have a fabulous memory, so I don't feel my age in the least.

MLG: Have you been painting as well?

RA: I have been drawing a lot, many posters and engravings above all, like those over there on the wall. I work more than ever, because I don't go out very much and I have plenty of free time. What would I do otherwise?

MLG: You are a poet, a prose writer, and a painter. In what genre is the real Rafael Alberti most at home these days?

RA: I am a poet who is both elegiac and autobiographic. So I find that almost all I do comes from inside me, in relation to things I have lived. I am an old man who has lived a lot. Because of the Civil War I was forced into exile for thirty-nine years. I have experienced many things; I have traveled quite a bit and lived in many countries, and this has influenced me a great deal in writing my memoirs. I have many things to remember.

MLG: Could one say, therefore, that you are a narrative poet, a poet who tells his story and that of Spain?

RA: The poet always tells something, right? He either tells a story or sings a song, or as he sings the song he tells a story. However, it is one thing to tell a tale through narrative poetry, and quite another if the poetry is not narrative. In the latter case, it is the state of mind that influences everything, whether it be love, life, or disasters. Since I have lived and loved a lot, as well as suffered many calamities, I am in a position to talk about my life.

MLG: What has it been like for you to make the transition from living in exile to returning to a democratic Spain?

RA: Undoubtedly, the onset of a constitutional democracy with free elections has been a big and positive step for Spain. There are still some unresolved questions, such as promises that were made but not kept, but that is the case with any democracy. So it is really a new phase for Spain. If it weren't, I wouldn't be here, they wouldn't have let me in.

MLG: Do you agree that you represent a bridge between the time of the Republic and today's constitutional monarchy?

RA: People from my generation undoubtedly represent continuity, and we have been accepted by all the political parties because we fought the war against Franco. In turn, we accept all the political parties, including the communists, and our monarchs, Don Juan Carlos and Doña Sofía, who have done very well during the transition.

MLG: What obsessions do you bring to your work?

RA: Poets have to be concerned with everything that happens in their time, or at least try to understand it, because otherwise there is nothing to write about. A poet cannot isolate himself from the times in which he lives because that's where he draws sustenance for his poetry. So the poet has to be someone who is very much in tune with life and what is happening around him, whether it be expressions of anger, understanding, laughter, or sorrow.

MLG: Do you consider yourself a poet of contrasts?

RA: Yes, I draw on both the positive and negative aspects of life. Not everything can be laughter and song. This way, the poetry one writes can have some variety and richness.

MLG: If you had to define your work, what would you say?

RA: I don't know. I am a poet of my time and I try to express this in a lyrical form, as a poet would. I don't exactly have a definition.

MLG: What is poetry for you?

RA: Maybe poetry is the poet. Without the poet there is no poetry, so poetry is in everything, from a piece of trash you trample on the street to the stars in the sky. Poetry exists on all levels, as long as the poet knows how to track it and capture it, like a hawk hunting in the spring.

MLG: What is it like to be a poet?

RA: Very natural, because I believe I was born a poet, it is my language and my way of being at any time. I didn't set out to be a poet, and I think that if you are not born with that gift you may never become a true poet. Verse may be within your reach, but not poetry.

MLG: In other words, you write poetry when it strikes you.

RA: Whether the poem is good or bad, it is a moment one captures without knowing its origin. Poetry comes in different shapes, with or without embellishments, all depending on the temperament of the poet or what he feels compelled to say at that particular point.

MLG: Do you revise your poems a lot?

RA: Not really. When I write a poem I like to capture the spontaneous. So I don't take things out, because I consider them significant, whatever they are. However, I like my poetry to be well structured, although it may appear vague and mysterious.

MLG: Since you are talking about structure, do you ever feel the need to paint what you write or write about what you are painting?

RA: No, I am not a figurative painter who likes to express what might be considered poetic with concrete images. I call the sign the word, and the sign is poetry and it is painting. I have tried to draw many of my poems, although not figuratively, just the letters or the feelings expressed on the written line. Sometimes I convey the feelings in the poem by drawing what the accents mean to me, to see if the result is a sort of undoubtedly curious electro-cardiogram.

MLG: Do you recite your poems as you write them?

RA: There is no choice but to do that, otherwise you don't know what you are doing. Yes, I keep reciting until I know it is done.

MLG: What do you feel when you write?

RA: What am I going to feel? Nothing, what anybody who writes feels— the sensation of working hard and taking a certain amount of time to get things done.

MLG: What is your reaction when the book is finally published and people are reading it?

RA: I like it. Writers write to be read, don't you think? People read my works in Spain a lot nowadays, and my books have sold many copies, which is the best thing that can happen to an author.

MLG: Do you have a primary reader?

RA: I run individual chapters in *El País*, and after a year or so, when I feel I have enough material, I put it together in a book. My primary readers are those who have been reading my work all along in the newspaper, or those who later read the entire book once it has been published. So I have many readers.

MLG: How do you come up with the titles to your books?

RA: My friends send me many of the titles, they are not all mine. The title *Sobre los ángeles,* for instance, was given to me by Pedro Salinas, while Bergamín gave me *Cal y canto.* Titles are very difficult to come up with; I know, because I title many of my books, although not all of them.

MLG: What about the title to your memoirs?

RA: That was mine, it is named after "la arboleda perdida," a grove that still exists in Puerto de Santa María, where I was born. That grove is part of a lovely but decaying forest.

MLG: And the title, of course, refers to memories that drift in and out of consciousness.

RA: Yes, life is like a grove that is disappearing as the leaves of its trees fall. It is a title that has sold a lot of books because people like it very much.

MLG: Your book *Trece bandas y cuarenta y ocho estrellas* was published in 1936. Why that title?

RA: That's a very old book, dating back to the years before the Spanish Civil War, when I traveled to the United States, Cuba, and Mexico. The title refers to the American flag, which was used to intimidate all the Latin American countries. It is a very well-known and interesting book. It's good poetry, although very aggressive in outlook.

MLG: In our last interview, you spoke about your book *Concerning the Angels*. Do you want to add anything to that?

RA: It is a very famous and successful work of mine. It is a work of inner conflicts personified in angels. I use the angels as a means of transferring my own feelings, ideas, and poetic sensibilities so that they are more accessible. The image of the angel in flight appeals to me, but I am not referring to Christian angels or archangels.

MLG: Can you speak about *Yo era un tonto y lo que he visto me ha hecho dos tontos?*

RA: It is a book on the silent movies and the people who played in them. I think that phase of North American moviemaking, with people like Charlie Chaplin and Buster Keaton, was the most original the United States has produced. This is not to put down other types of movies, but Stan Laurel, Oliver Hardy, Charlie Chaplin, and Buster Keaton represent the highest peak of early moviemaking. People continue to be interested in these silent movies.

MLG: How do you tackle the blank page?

RA: That would depend on the book, the frame of mind in which it is being written and the meaning intended. Space can be filled with many different things: *Concerning the Angels* is one thing, *Marinero en tierra* another, and any of my other books yet another. I always write my books from a unified perspective, even though they may be different. I want them to be coherent, not disjointed. When the proper atmosphere has been achieved, I know the book is ready. If we are dealing with an anthology, that's another matter.

MLG: The visual aspect of things is very important for you. You often accompany your signature with some quick drawings. This is what I observed during our last encounter and I see you haven't changed.

RA: Yes, I do that, but not for everyone. I have signatures with stars, fish, and doves, but I use them only with friends or in those situations where a lot of people are asking me for one. I'll dash off a dove, which is something I do very often, although not all the time.

MLG: What does the dove symbolize?

RA: Without a doubt, it is the dove of peace.

MLG: Look, Rafael. What a coincidence; a dove has just landed on your balcony and it seems to be listening to our conversation.

RA: Those are my friends; I've got doves and other birds that I feed there.

They are not afraid, and they even come when I step out onto the balcony sometimes, although they do so with more caution. They come every day.

MLG: You love animals and nature. I remember that when you came to my university, St. John's, you read a poem about your dog Niebla, which died during the Civil War. We were all moved to tears.

RA: I am a poet of nature. Born next to the Bay of Cádiz in a house with a garden, among people who owned fields, I spent a lot of time there until I came to Madrid in 1915. I have always enjoyed the countryside. I am not a writer who likes to hold roundtable discussions or spend time in cafés, which has always been a popular activity in Spain. I am a poet of the open air.

MLG: You have received many prizes and accolades. What does all that mean to you?

RA: I don't seek them out. I have never pursued prizes or entered literary contests, except when a very important poetry award, the National Prize, was first established in Spain. That year, people like Antonio Machado were on the jury, and winning that prize for my first book meant a lot to me. It was a very high distinction for me to win and it heralded my appearance as a poet in Spain. Until then, I was known mainly for my paintings.

MLG: You are also a recipient of the Cervantes Prize.

RA: I have received the Cervantes Prize and the Lenin Prize as well. Those are the three most prestigious prizes I have won. But I have also garnered other awards.

MLG: Could you mention some of them?

RA: Most recently, I won the Mariano de Cavia Prize, which is awarded for the best article of the year. This year they gave it to me for a chapter I wrote and because my wife María Teresa died.

MLG: That must have been very difficult for you.

RA: It was particularly hard because she was such an intelligent, dynamic, active, and brave person. Unfortunately, she suffered from a disease that took away her senses one by one, until she didn't even remember who she was. She died on December 14 last year, two days before my birthday.

MLG: Do you have many friends?

RA: People know me, but I no longer lead the active life I used to. For instance, I gave over 350 recitals with the actress Nuria Espert, because I love to share poetry with others. When I was doing that, I would always be surrounded by people. I have some close friends, but I rarely see them now, because I don't go out a lot, although I occasionally catch a play.

MLG: You have had many famous friends in the past.

RA: It is enough for me to have been friends with Lorca and Picasso. I have been great friends with the writers of my time, those I was fortunate enough to meet. I speak about them a lot in my books.

MLG: If you could talk with someone from the past, whom would it be?

RA: With lots of people, I wouldn't be able to do anything with just one. I would like to speak with many anonymous Spanish poets, who wrote those wonderful ballads of long ago. I would also enjoy talking with Garcilaso de la Vega, Saint John of the Cross and Góngora. From the more recent past, I would have liked to converse with Rubén Darío, who died when I was a youth, but I never got to meet him.

MLG: Would you like to speak with Cervantes?

RA: Yes, a lot. I have great admiration for Cervantes, particularly his brief theater pieces, which I like very much.

MLG: What would you ask him?

RA: What a question! I don't know. I would invite him to the Bay of Cádiz and we could talk in the harbor by the boats.

MLG: In our last interview, you said that you had always thought you wanted to live to be 125, but that you had reduced it to 115. What do you think now?

RA: I still want to live to 115, but I prefer not to dwell on death. I have always said that people shouldn't die, they should disappear, which is different. If my time has come, I would like to disappear before your eyes. That would be a wonderful thing, don't you think? Wouldn't it be interesting to see a bull disappear moments before the bullfighter was to run him through? That would be an enriching event, full of poetry.

MLG: Do you believe in eternal life?

RA: Eternal life as it is described in the Old and New Testaments—all that talk about the Day of Judgment and the resurrection of the flesh—seems like a figurative way of speaking. Nevertheless, I would like to believe that one does not die completely and that life can be prolonged somehow. That would be more of a consolation than dying an absolute death, or being buried in a cemetery for centuries, until one terrifying afternoon when we shall rise from the dead. It's interesting that the notions of heaven, purgatory, and hell were invented, but I don't really like them.

MLG: What does life mean to you?

RA: Life is existence. We all have our own life, which is either the one that corresponds to us, or the one we create for ourselves with time and days and nights. Different people lead different lives. I have led a very dangerous life, but I believe in my destiny and my luck. I believe in my lucky star, because I have been on the brink of death forty times and it never happened. I think I have a long and complete destiny. I want to live a long time and express myself constantly.

MLG: In spite of all the sufferings you have had to endure, you have never lost the enthusiasm of your childhood.

RA: If I dwelt on all the terrible things that have happened to me, I would be in very sad shape, because so many awful things have occurred in this century; we haven't exactly been dancing sevillanas all along. Ours has been a cruel century, with the biggest wars in human history and the creation of the foulest instruments of death. We must save ourselves from all this. It all began in 1914 with the First World War. I was only twelve at the time but I felt it acutely. After the First World War, we had eighteen relatively peaceful years, and then the Spanish Civil War occurred, which was truly horrible. The Second World War followed, with the atomic bomb and all that. Let us hope that there will be no third world war, because we would all disappear.

MLG: I would like to end with the same question I asked you eight years ago: who is Rafael Alberti?

RA: A poet from Andalusia who was born next to the Bay of Cádiz, and who feels great nostalgia for the sea, which has been a constant theme in my life and my poetry. I am a poet who was happy to be born and raised there. I owe a lot to that place, which I have always carried inside me and expressed in many forms.

Fernando Arrabal

MIRIAM BERKLEY

Fernando Arrabal was born in 1932 in Melilla, the former Spanish Morocco. After enduring as a child the horrors of the Civil War and experiencing the hardships of the postwar years in Spain, he moved to Paris in 1955, where he has been living ever since. It is there that he acquired his reputation as the enfant terrible of the French theater. Some have also referred to him as "the anarchist."

A provocative figure of avant-garde theater, he is the creator of "Panic Theater" and his work has been compared to that of the beats. As a playwright, a novelist, a poet, a director and a movie producer, Arrabal has become an international figure. Among the films he directed are *Viva la muerte, I Will Go Like a Mad Stallion,* and *Odyssey of the Pacific,* starring Mickey Rooney.

Author of some sixteen volumes of plays, his drama, written either in Spanish or in French, has been performed in many countries. His play *Una doncella para una gorila (The Red Madonna or a Damsel for a Gorilla)* premiered under his direction at the Intar Theater, in New York, on 20 November 1986. Among his other plays are *Guernica,* 1961 (*Guernica and Other Plays,* 1967); *L'architecte et l'empereur d'Assyrie,* 1967 (*The Architect and the Emperor of Assyria,* 1969); *El extravagante triunfo de Jesucristo, Karl Marx y William Shakespeare,* 1982 (*The Extravagant Triumph of Jesus Christ, Karl Marx and William Shakespeare,* 1982); *La Inquisición,* 1982 (*The Inquisition,* 1983).

In 1983, Arrabal was awarded the Nadal Prize for his novel *La torre herida por el rayo,* 1983 (*The Tower Struck by Lightning,* 1988). Since then, he has published three other novels: *La piedra iluminada,* 1985 (*The Compass Stone,* 1987); *La vierge rouge,* 1986 (*The Red Madonna,* 1991), *La virgen roja,* 1987, his first novel written in French; and *La hija de King*

Kong (King Kong's Daughter), 1988. His poetic anthology *Mis humildes paraísos* (My Humble Paradises) appeared in 1985. An expert on chess, Arrabal also writes his own column on the subject for *L'Express,* a Paris weekly.

Arrabal is a man of contradictions. A true Spaniard, he lives in Paris; a thoroughly modern man, he sees the world through the perspective of Ciudad Rodrigo, the medieval town where he spent his childhood.

The first time I met Fernando Arrabal was in New York, where he was directing one of his plays. He was wrapped in a black cape his sister had made for him. The second time I saw him was in Paris. Getting to know Arrabal means entering into a game and playing along with him. This two-part interview is exactly that. As I walked into his apartment, I found myself drawn into that game, where the enfant terrible rules and awaits reactions. The first thing you see as you enter is a replica of the chair that centuries ago was used for torture. He made me sit in it and put a clasp around my hands and neck. On the walls of the living room, a series of portraits depicting him during his surrealistic period—more than sixteen of them—show him in every form or shape. The artists Arnaïz, Crespo, and Felez must have had a great time creating these works where Arrabal is always the protagonist and undergoes a constant mutation. He appears with the body of a child, or of a woman, but with his male face, or he is turned into Prometheus or into a giant. Arrabal is laughing at himself and at the world. Dressed in a black sweater and jeans, his feet resting on an old Spanish table, he offered me sherry and tried both to persuade and to dissuade me of his megalomania. He was enjoying himself. But underneath it all, he is a very shy and humble person. He made me promise not to mention the awards he had received. Our conversation ended on the following note: "My books are my medals."

❊❊❊❊❊❊❊❊❊❊❊❊❊❊❊❊❊❊❊❊❊❊❊❊❊❊❊❊❊❊❊❊

Part 1

MLG: Fernando, what do you feel when you see your work in a language that is not your own?

FA: It is a misfortune I have suffered since the beginning, because my works have always been published first in French. The same is true of all the openings as well—I know of no premiere that was done first in Spanish.

MLG: Do you write in French?

FA: No, I write in Spanish. I do the French versions with my wife, who is one of your colleagues from the Sorbonne.

MLG: What influence has France had in the development of your work?

FA: France has given me the setting, a free setting that has allowed my theater to be systematically edited, published, and performed. And along with other writers and artists we formed what could be called the "Paris school." I have also had the opportunity to make and direct movies in France. Even when I made movies in the United States—the last one I did in the United States was with the American actor Mickey Rooney—they were Franco-American productions.

MLG: What did winning the Nadal Prize for your novel *The Tower Struck by Lightning* mean to you?

FA: It was a big surprise, because of the kind of reception it received in the Spanish press. The response was excessive, as usual, because I do not think it was such a big deal. It was a surprise for another reason as well. While I traveled through the United States—where I gave forty lectures in thirty days, from Milwaukee to San Juan in Puerto Rico—my wife and my secretary decided to play a joke on me and sent the novel without my knowledge to the Nadal Prize committee. When I found out, I thought it was a very good idea, a brilliant idea, worthy of my wife. As you know, I am a very modern, very original, very avant-garde man; so in my house there are no Christmas trees or artifices of that sort, but rather a Nativity scene. And on Christmas we do not give presents, because in Spain Santa Claus does not exist; we exchange them on Twelfth Night, the night of Melchior, Gaspar, and Balthazar. On that night, as I was preparing presents for my children, the gift from Barcelona, the Nadal Prize, came.

MLG: Is there a close relationship between the novelist and the playwright?

FA: I have written fourteen volumes of theater or about one hundred plays. A play for me is a phenomenon, something rapid, urgent, nocturnal, and explanatory. In short, it is something that has happened to me, something that I want to demonstrate quickly. So in three or four weeks, the work is finished; it is like a lightning bolt. A novel, on the other hand, is something very long, like a marriage in which there are many troubled moments, to see if one is on the right or wrong path. It is like an odyssey.

MLG: Do you prefer writing novels or plays?

FA: What I like most is the theater. Some producers would like me to make more movies, but I have only directed five, because I prefer the theater.

MLG: What is the relationship between the playwright, the spectators, and the characters?

FA: Well, before I was short, dark, and ugly, but thanks to the theater, I am now tall, fair, and handsome. For me, the theater has meant what the Greeks called a catharsis; it has cured me. And I wish the spectators would see my plays the way I do, as therapy.

MLG: In reading your theater, I have the feeling that you are creating a modern mythology. Do you think that's true?

FA: Perhaps. Throughout my life I have always been in contact with avant-garde groups. In Spain, I was with the Postista Group; upon arriving in the United States in 1959, I spent a lot of time with the beats; in France, I had the well-deserved honor of having André Breton take me into his surrealist group. I have always been considered an avant-garde author, a modern author, an author of renewal. I think this is a misunderstanding; that is why I always speak about it with a bit of irony. I think I am a Spanish author, who was born in a small Spanish city and who has not stopped writing medieval-like works. What has always fascinated me is the world in which I lived in the small medieval town of Ciudad Rodrigo. I have reproduced the festivities, the rites, the sardine man, the processions, the stonings and all the endearing and barbaric elements with which I was confronted as a youth. This medieval world of Ciudad Rodrigo is far removed from the world of the Spanish establishment. Throughout my life, I have found this difference, this distance, this marginality in avant-garde groups. André Breton, who defended my theater, would have been very surprised if I had told him that, for me, surrealism was like Ciudad Rodrigo.

MLG: In reading your work it is immediately apparent that you cannot live without Spain, nor without God. Spain and God, nevertheless, appear as myths in your work.

FA: Especially God, because I am a religious writer. The themes that have most interested me are religious themes. That's why the day they gave me the Nadal Prize was a magic coincidence of destiny. On that day, it was great for me to have been invited to an anarchist convention in Barcelona. When I arrived at the convention, there were a lot of people there, not because of anarchism, but because of the prize. I told the anarchists that I wanted to speak about religion. I even asked them to pray so that Spain would remain what it had always been—the Spain of Quixote, Teresa de Avila, and Saint John of the Cross. In the midst of a convention where there were some anarchists who during the Civil War had burned churches and killed religious men, I thought it important to ask for support for the resumption of diplomatic relations between Spain and Israel, which has since been achieved.

MLG: In your play *The Inquisition,* the messages drop in parachutes. Why are some of them written on parchment?

FA: Don't forget that I am a medieval man. For me, the most interesting characters are those from the Middle Ages. It is the period when I would have liked to live and I dream of women like Eleanor of Aquitaine and Blanche of Castile. I dream most of all of a woman who was anachronic in her own age, the last woman of the Middle Ages, Teresa de Avila. In my apartment in France, I retain the Spain that I love. I would like to say, in all modesty, that I consider myself the humble ambassador of Spain, not of official Spain, but spiritual Spain. When some event occurs that affects the Spanish people, newspapers like *Le Monde* and the *New York Times* do not turn to a Spanish embassy; they have to come to people like me.

MLG: You use the theory of the double extensively. Do you see the theater as a game where characters put on and take off masks?

FA: As you know, I am a great fan of chess, although I am a bad chess player. I write the chess column for the French weekly *L'Express,* and it is a job that I love. For me, chess is life. When Spain was the most important country in the world, in the time of the conquerors, the chess world champion was a Spanish priest, López, and the most renowned version of the game was the Spanish one. In the Renaissance, the best player was Italian. When the French Revolution took place, the game was dominated by Philidor, a Frenchman who said the pawns are the heart of chess, not the king or the queen. So chess is life, and my theater, which you call a game, has the pawn as the captain. I think my theater can be debated in terms of what I say, but what cannot be disputed is how I say it . . . although perhaps everything can be debated.

MLG: The autobiographical aspect is therefore very important in your theater.

FA: I cannot write anything else. I have a main reader of my work, my wife. When I finish a play and she reads it, I always say to her, "Look, I have finally written something different, something new." She reads the work and says, "No, you always write about the same thing." I suspect I am always writing about the same themes. My autobiography, which includes the impact of the people around me, is very important.

MLG: Why do you like to juxtapose the lyric and the sacred with blasphemy?

FA: There are characters in my work who blaspheme, or who have blasphemed or may do so some day, but I am not one of them. What I really would like to say is that we, Ciudad Rodrigo, the beats, the surrealist movement, the Panic movement, have all tried to bring, to the world of the establishment, elements considered filthy or unconventional. We have also tried to undermine the foundations of established art. So, for that reason there is a mixture of heaven and crap in all our works.

MLG: You have taken the titles of some of the paintings of the great masters for your plays, like *The Garden of Delights, The Burial of the Sardine,* and *Concert for an Egg.* Could you talk about the influence of Goya, Bosch, and Brueghel on your works?

FA: As I have said, I think there are influences from Ciudad Rodrigo, with its festivities, and also from the plastic world of those painters you have mentioned. Perhaps also the work of some more recent surrealists, like Magritte.

MLG: Why do you attach so much importance to music, especially songs, in your theater?

FA: Only in some of my plays. Keep in mind that I have written over one hundred plays, so there are plays in which music is not important. I do not think that music is a bad noise, as André Breton used to say. I like music.

I included songs that we would call vulgar kitsch because of their nostalgic content. All of a sudden I feel like singing here . . .

MLG: Your son is named Samuel in honor of Beckett.

FA: Yes, his name is Samuel Gandhi.

MLG: What does Beckett mean to you?

FA: He was a great writer. I would like my son to be like him; not as a writer, because that requires a lot of suffering, although I would like him to feel the urge to write the way I do. I want my son to be like Beckett morally. When Franco's forces paid me the extraordinary tribute of putting me in jail, at the same time that they banned all my works, Beckett went to the Spanish judges and said, "Arrabal has to suffer greatly to write; do not add to his punishment." This shows the caliber of the man.

MLG: The image of the sheep and the flock is repeated in your works. What is its meaning?

FA: There is a professor who has done a study on the zoology of my theater, and there are many animals.

MLG: Even cockroaches.

FA: I am glad that when I stay in American hotels, which pretend to be luxury hotels, cockroaches come to visit, relieving my loneliness. So there are many animals in my works. And when I make a movie, there are always problems because of this. In every one of my plays there is an animal that is as important a character as a person. In the movie I did with Mickey Rooney, there are two characters more important than he: a duck and a train engine. In *Guernica,* it is not María-Angela Melato who is the central character, but a donkey. I have always liked to feel the earth through an animal.

MLG: If you had to explain in one phrase or one word what you propose to do in your theater, what would you say?

FA: I would say that I would like to be a poet. The poet is like the bird that knows very little of ornithology. If some American television reporter had stuck a microphone under the nose of Cervantes and had asked him, "What do you think of *Quixote?,*" he would probably have been unable to answer, as he was unaware of its magnitude. So I do not know if I am the best person to explain what I do. I have written some theoretical texts on the theater like "La vejez de viruelas" (The Pockmarks of Old Age). But as the founder of Panic Theater and the creator of a magazine called *Le Théâtre,* what I would really like to say is this: When I sit to write, I live the only adventures that I have, I laugh, I cry, I get excited, I truly enjoy myself. At those moments, I hope I will never apply theoretical formulas or dictums.

MLG: What does language mean for you?

FA: For a while, for ten years, we fought against words, we did a theater of gestures. I think that, thank God, the theater is returning to its roots, it is returning to words, because in the beginning there was the Word and that is the agent of all transformations.

Part 2

MLG: I would like to continue that long conversation I began with you two years ago. Can you tell me if you see an evolution in your work?

FA: Very little. I have written a great deal of theater in two years. I have written two novels and various plays—there is an evolution in terms of quantity. In terms of quality, it remains more or less the same.

MLG: On 20 November 1986, on the anniversary of Franco's death, your play *The Red Madonna or a Damsel for a Gorilla* opened in New York. How did you come to write this work?

FA: It came to me because I reread the case of Aurora Rodríguez and Hildegart. This is what inspired me to write the play in Spanish. I then wrote the novel in French.

MLG: Is it the first novel that you have written directly in French?

FA: I have written many plays directly in French, but this is the first novel. It was a lot of work.

MLG: Do you feel comfortable writing novels or do you prefer the theater?

FA: As I said before, a novel is like a voyage, it is like a wedding, one gets involved for a long time. It is not a *coup de foudre,* as the French would say, because it takes close to a year to write a novel. I prefer the theater because it is brief, urgent, quick, round, complete. The terrible thing would be if, halfway through a novel, an author all of a sudden began to have second thoughts. That would be horrible.

MLG: You are considered as much a French writer as a Spanish one. How do you see yourself?

FA: I am Moroccan. I was born in Morocco. I am Arrabal, the one and only.

MLG: Now that there is no longer a dictatorship in Spain, where are you going to find future themes, and which characters are going to people your works?

FA: In my work, Franco's dictatorship figures very minimally.

MLG: Yes, but indirectly, is it not present?

FA: It was present indirectly, but it will always be present ultimately. The dictatorship, the repression, the Inquisition, the intolerance were present indirectly. But out of one hundred plays, only very few were inspired by Franco or the Civil War—only *Carta a Franco* (Letter to Franco) and *Guernica . . .* two or three things. The life or death of Franco didn't change anything in my work. I kept on writing just the same. Franco and all of that is water under the bridge.

MLG: Your work has rhythm. Could you talk about *Red Madonna* from the director's point of view? How do you feel being both the author and the director?

FA: I don't like it. I have directed very few plays, perhaps a dozen or so.

MLG: Why don't you like it?

FA: It is not something I am enthusiastic about, because I prefer that others do the directing. But I don't mind doing it, however, because I have a very good rapport with the actors, as you have seen. We are part of a big family and we have always had an extraordinary relationship. In that sense, I have a lot of fun, although I regret that someone else could not improvise on my theater, because that would help; it is like a relay race.

MLG: So, in your view, the director should improvise?

FA: He should show me a side of my work of which I was unaware, although it many cases it is a bad one. Almost all of the directing I see is awful. But when it is good, then it is worth it.

MLG: What relationship exists between the director, the author, the actor, and the audience. Who influences whom? Do the actors have any input?

FA: I have always said that directing, at least the directing that I have done, has been the directing of the actors. I like to listen to the actors up close, and I make some choices—but the direction is theirs. I see a better show than any of the spectators because I am almost always a few feet away from the actors. When I can, I jump on stage and stand next to them, to watch them move their eyes, their retinas.

MLG: But you are also an actor?

FA: I was never an actor, I have only appeared a few times in plays. It is one of my nightmares to go on stage and have to perform a part from one of my plays that I don't remember.

MLG: In *The Red Madonna* all the actors wear a uniform with their own names on their backs. Why the names? And why did you wear a similar jacket on opening night?

FA: That was a joke; it was a present the actors gave me. So it doesn't enter into the notion I had for that direction. The concept for this direction and this play—indeed, of all my theater—is that of a new theater; a theater in crisis, a theater where there are economic problems and where one can rely only on talent and words. So I have no interest in an actor named Manero who dresses like a bull and now thinks he is a bull. It is important that it be obvious that there is an actor named Manero who plays the part of a bull. Elizabeth Ruiz, one of the actresses in this play, plays the role of Aurora Rodríguez, but there are constant reminders that she is Ruiz, not Rodríguez. In this way, we have the theater in the theater and we are faithful to the present. Four or five years from now, we'll be seeing many groups doing the very thing I did for the first time in theater history. Other groups will do it in different ways, perhaps not with the same emphasis, but it is going to be a method that will have to be used. It is Ruiz interpreting Aurora Rodríguez; we don't want to make believe that it is Aurora Rodríguez, as would be done in ordinary theater. Because of this, she can be more exciting than in normal avant-garde theater.

MLG: Are you saying that you don't want to break with reality?

FA: It is a realistic play, based on a real fact. It is the most important play of the rupture, the break with the theater of the past. A realistic theater is a theater with actors who perform, an economical theater where one can rely only on words and imagination. This is today's theater.

MLG: Why do you avail yourself so much of masks and mythology?

FA: I avail myself of fabulous animals, which is different. Mythology is a literary creation which corresponds to myth, which is to say a lie, the myth in the sense of a lie. What I wanted to do in the play was to present fabulous animals, which man has created throughout the ages, like the mermaid and the unicorn. So they are a part of man. That is why it is very important to know that the animal is not only a fabulous animal but also a human creation. For instance, the crocodile in the play is a girl who arrives on the stage and whom we clearly see putting on a crocodile mask.

MLG: But then is there no difference between human beings and animals?

FA: The fabulous animal exists only in the imagination. More specifically, it is an animal that lived in the imagination of the conquerors. All the conquerors saw fabulous animals: Hernando Cortés, Christopher Columbus, even the discoverers saw them. For instance, there is a text which indicates that on one of Christopher Columbus's trips, some Portuguese sailors saw a mermaid and fished her out. The mermaid started singing and wailing so sadly that the sailors returned her to the water. Another account tells of a priest from Cuzco who saw a tree, the leaves of which turned into fish if they fell into the river or into birds if the wind carried them.

MLG: Are you a conqueror of language?

FA: No, I am a freebooter more than a conqueror. We are really at a moment when society as seen through materialistic eyes is coming to an end. That is why *Red Madonna* is so important. With the decline of rational materialism we have the possibility, once again, of returning to the fabulous animal, although not to the mythological one.

MLG: Are you an optimist then? Because if we are coming to the end of materialism, aren't we coming to something better?

FA: Something different, I don't know if it will be better. In any case, my grandmother was right because she used to say that we are in a *valle de lágrimas* (vale of tears).

MLG: What about music? How do you relate to it?

FA: Music is the language of the Holy Spirit. The love between the Father and the Son creates the figure of the Holy Spirit. At a particular moment, during Pentecost, the Holy Spirit comes down and the apostles start speaking in tongues, which is what music is. It is the possibility of translating without needing today's materialistic devices, such as dictionaries and computers, but rather translating ineffably.

MLG: Have you ever written any music?

FA: No, I haven't. Unfortunately, music is in the hands of very few people, because as children we are taught very little music and very few people have access to it.

MLG: You are a playwright, theater director, moviemaker, novelist, poet, painter, music enthusiast. From all these things, which one best represents Arrabal?

FA: I don't know, painting perhaps, because I like to structure a painting like a mathematical formula. I like painting in its own right and I like to paint images in a play.

MLG: Rhythm is very important in your work.

FA: It is fundamental. Rhythm is a transition, a bridge between two scenes that must flow with ease, as in a symphony. This is what gave me the most work with the actors of *Red Madonna,* because they were unaccustomed to it. They had a traditional, causal concept of theater, whereas I think rhythm is the most important thing, the way two scenes intertwine. And the rhythm in this play has improved.

MLG: Do you feel humble before your work?

FA: Yes. Everything I may do or have done is like the shape of a nose or the size of the hands—these are things one is born with. I was born a writer, I had nothing to do with it.

MLG: Are you more a playwright than a novelist?

FA: Yes, I am. In Spain, however, I won the Nadal Prize for a novel, not for a play.

MLG: Do you see the theater as a game or as a reflection of life?

FA: I see it as both. That's why the theater, even in its primitive shape today, has the potential to be better than ever. The theater is like a mirror, the aura of the universe itself and society the way it is.

MLG: Do you like to live your life as a game?

FA: Yes, because I cannot live it any other way.

MLG: Why not?

FA: Because I didn't learn to fence, so I cannot be a conqueror.

MLG: Would you have liked to be a conqueror?

FA: Very much so! It would have been a great adventure. To conquer America as Ponce de León did would have been terrific. The New World is like Ciudad Rodrigo: the more I visit it, the less I know it, but it always amazes me. But, realistically speaking, I feel like a conqueror on a wooden horse with a mop for a sword.

MLG: Then there is no likeness with *Don Quixote?*

FA: No, except that, like Cervantes, I am in favor of the defeated. He used to advocate things that had become unfashionable. For instance, he defended the chivalric novel at a time when refined and intelligent Spanish people were condemning it.

MLG: Would you like to do the same thing?

FA: Yes, I am against this and that. I have had problems in Spain in this respect. When Franco died, for instance, people were hoping that I would draw up the bill, since I was the only Spanish writer to have written a *Carta contra Franco* and one of only six banned persons (the other five were politicians) during the Franco regime. But I didn't draw up the bill, because I am in favor of the defeated.

MLG: Is Arrabal the enfant terrible of whom we hear so much?

FA: No ... *terrible* I don't know, but *enfant* certainly not; I am fifty-four years old. These are the fabrications of some journalists. But as the French say, only the rich get loans.

MLG: What do you think of journalism?

FA: Although I am not a journalist, I write for newspapers very often. I am a constant contributor to *El País.* I also contribute on a regular basis to *L'Express.* I write only on topics of which I am quite knowledgeable.

MLG: For instance, on chess?

FA: In all modesty, I don't think there are many people in France who know more about chess than I do. In *El País,* I write about Cervantes and the chivalric novel, Ciudad Rodrigo, and New York. These are subjects that have interested me all my life, so I don't think anyone can reproach my handling of them in the least.

MLG: Do you ever bring these topics into the theater?

FA: No, I have never brought Cervantes into my theater, and he is my favorite subject. I wrote about him for *El País.* For instance, I wrote about a false novel by Borges on Cervantes. It is called *El espejo y el coito* (The Mirror and Intercourse). But my writings on Cervantes are not just fictions. Some people have come to me and said, "Fabulous, that stuff that you said about Cervantes at school. How imaginative!" But the things I said about Cardinal Acquaviva and all of that are true. The incident in which the king ordered his hand to be cut off is true. There are historical documents that support this.

MLG: Did you write some of them?

FA: No, it is known that there is a document about the sentencing of Cervantes. The thing is that biographers are afraid of Cervantes. They all want to show him as a formidable soldier, and they have created the worst possible image, that of an ex-fighter. There is nothing worse one can be. A close reading of the biographies reveals that the biographers really didn't believe this, but they thought Spain would reproach them if they said something else. So they depict him as a great novelist, a great fighter, and a tremendous patriot with a marvelous family. Recently, I had dinner with some professors of Spanish, and they all thought that Cervantes had studied at the University of Salamanca, an assertion that has often been repeated but that is false. In fact, Cervantes was held back at the very bad school of López de Hoyos in Madrid. He was nineteen when his fellow classmates were fourteen.

MLG: Who was Avellaneda?

FA: We have no idea. He was made a scapegoat for Spanish letters. But happily he existed, because Cervantes, being a lazy sort, would have never written the second part of *Quixote* otherwise. Some think Avellaneda might have been Lope de Vega, although I don't believe this. But the second part of *Quixote* was even better than the first, because Cervantes was angry.

MLG: And with that anger he created a masterpiece.

FA: Yes. If he hadn't finished the novel, Don Quixote would have been left alive, and it is fascinating that Cervantes should have killed him off.

MLG: If you could speak to Cervantes, what would you ask him?

FA: Why he wrote, because I believe he lived life very intensely, so he didn't need to write. Writing is an affirmation of failure. So why did he write?

MLG: What do you think he would answer?

FA: That he began writing when he was sixty years old, when he could no longer live intensely and enjoy himself in Seville, as he always had. From what I know of him, I believe he was a homosexual, by the way. In fact I would say he was homosexual just as surely as I think he never lost the use of an arm. I recently defended my view at a colloquium held in Alcalá de Henares, with a number of American professors in attendance. It is clear that he was not maimed; he made up that story.

MLG: Why?

FA: Because he had a complex resulting from the king's edict to cut off his arm when he was nineteen. So he wanted to be one-armed, and he made up that story.

MLG: Why are you so obsessed with Cervantes? I imagine that you would have liked to be friends with him.

FA: That's the subject of my latest novel, *La hija de King Kong* (King Kong's Daughter). The main character, like most of the women in my work, is extremely intelligent. She is a person who is attractive because of her intelligence, although she is completely amoral. She lives some amazing adventures in this world and she loves to travel. One day, she is being pursued by the police and she throws herself off a springboard and swims underwater for four centuries. When she surfaces, Cervantes is there and she talks to him.

MLG: Why did you choose a woman as your character?

FA: I identify with women, and this is strange, because I have never been a homosexual. I am a man, a woman, a Spaniard, an Englishman, I love bullfighting and despise it at the same time. I am all things. I identify with everything. I don't want to be pigeonholed.

MLG: I can't help but notice that we are surrounded by various androgynous and bisexual likenesses of you. Why?

FA: Androgyny is one of my inspirations, one of the facets of my personality.

MLG: So there is a feminine side to your personality.

FA: Yes, because the most interesting people I have met in my life have been women; my wife, for instance, and Nathalie Sarraute, Marguerite

Yourcenar and yourself. You are all extraordinary, classy women. I like to be surrounded by portraits of me because I enjoy the ceremony of megalomania.

MLG: Why is that?

FA: Because it represents something inaccessible. I like the contradiction that those paintings imply. You don't really believe I am a megalomaniac, do you? I was just joking. This megalomania shouldn't be taken seriously. If I were Paul Newman and a sex object, then this would be a different matter, but since the person behind those paintings is not, the whole thing is laughable.

MLG: Who is behind those paintings?

FA: He who stands before you.

MLG: Who is he?

FA: A no-good monster because he isn't even a monster. Those paintings were made in the sixties, when I was a member of the surrealist club. At that time, people used to gather for festive occasions in France almost every day. Nowadays, no one gets together in France. Those paintings are the off-spring of the dialogues we used to have.

MLG: I have noticed that you are very fond of ceremonies, but that when you have to attend one, you show up without a tie. Why?

FA: For a religious man, ceremonies represent the possibility of speaking with God, whatever his god may be. Religious people gather in temples, synagogues, and mosques to talk to God. Since they don't really know how God speaks, they resort to rituals. I used ceremonies for the same reason; I used them not to speak with God, but with the powers that were in Spain, because I too did not know their language. So my early theater is a cere-monial one.

MLG: What would you like most out of life?

FA: The newspaper *El País* used to ask people what their greatest desire was. Felipe González, for instance, replied that he would have liked to be Velázquez. Alfonso Guerra said he wanted to be a race-car driver . . .

MLG: What about you?

FA: What do you think I answered?

MLG: To be God.

FA: Of course. If you could choose, would you decide to be a race-car driver?

MLG: What do you think God is like?

FA: God is creation, love, and knowledge. What more could you possibly want?

MLG: Who is Arrabal?

FA: A unit of destiny in the universal sphere.

LAYLE SILBERT

Juan Benet

Juan Benet Goitia was born in 1928 in Madrid, where he studied engineering. In 1954, he became a public works engineer, an occupation he has held to this day. At the same time, he also dedicated himself to the craft of writing and has become one of the most important authors of the postwar era. Nevertheless, he insists that his true profession is that of civil engineer and that he writes only in his spare time: "I am a man of a single profession, I'm an engineer who writes on Sundays."

Benet is the author of numerous novels, short stories, essays, and plays. Among his books are *Nunca llegarás a nada* (You'll Never Amount to Anything), 1961; *La inspiración y el estilo* (Inspiration and Style), 1966; *Volverás a Región,* 1967 (*Return to Región,* 1985); *Una meditación,* winner of the 1969 Biblioteca Breve Prize (*A Meditation,* 1982); *Una tumba* (A Tomb), 1971; *Cinco narraciones y dos fábulas* (Five Stories and Two Fables), 1972; *Sub rosa,* winner of the 1973 Crítica Prize; *En el estado* (In the State), 1977; *Saúl ante Samuel,* 1980. With *Herrumbrosas lanzas* (Rusty Spears), a four-part series on the Spanish Civil War, Benet marks the end of his cycle on that conflict. His most recent book is *La construcción de la torre de Babel* (The Construction of the Tower of Babel), 1990.

The "region" he describes in many of his novels is inspired by the settings of León, in the northwest of Spain, where he worked as an engineer. Not only did he re-create its atmosphere, he even invented a fictional map for it. A master of his crafts, Benet builds with a firm hand a bridge or a novel, a road or an essay.

He has lectured extensively both in Europe and the Americas. In 1982, he was Visiting Tinker Professor at Columbia University.

This two-part interview was conducted at St. John's University and at the Gramercy Hotel in New York City. I had met Benet before and I could have recognized his aristocratic figure anywhere. Tall, handsome, a strand of hair falling over his forehead, the strong aquiline profile, no doubt it was Juan Benet. As usual, he played down his life as a writer and enjoyed talking about the exciting moments he had experienced as an engineer.

❖❖❖❖❖❖❖❖❖❖❖❖❖❖❖❖❖❖❖❖❖❖❖❖❖❖❖❖❖❖❖❖❖❖

Part 1

MLG: Juan, you are equally successful in two professions: as an engineer and as a writer. How can you function in both worlds and reconcile them?

JB: It's very easy, because I do not try to reconcile anything. I am really an engineer who writes on Sundays and during my free time, which is fairly extensive. For this very reason, you cannot say that I have two professions, one in which I am successful, and the other in which I am not, or in which I am successful to a different degree. I am really a man of one profession, the one that supports me.

MLG: You have given many lectures throughout the world: in Spain, Great Britain, West Germany, Puerto Rico, and the United States. I was fortunate to see you on two occasions, in Puerto Rico and in New York. Both times, I noticed that you prefer to talk about your life as an engineer far more than about your life as a writer. Why?

JB: Life as an engineer is undoubtedly the more interesting of the two because I get to travel the world and come face to face with more problems, people, and situations that are rather unique. Life as a writer consists of sitting at a desk with a pencil and paper, and the problems to be faced are purely of a technical nature, which I don't think merit the attention of the public, although perhaps they might be interesting to critics and professors. On the other hand, life as an engineer, as a "civil engineer" as it is called here, is undoubtedly far more interesting. I have to live in the countryside, and each project presents new problems and the opportunity to meet new people.

MLG: But isn't the same true of your writing? Each work is something new . . .

JB: Yes, but that is something new in my own world, it is not something objectively new. It is neither a new landscape nor new people.

MLG: New characters?

JB: They're not. Maybe my characters are always the same boring, tired, and taciturn individuals.

MLG: What are the factors that drive you to write?

JB: The main one is that I have a lot of free time. All engineers have free time. It is generally assumed that my profession is very tiring and exhausting.

But that is not the case with me. I am an engineer who likes the country more than the city and the office. Therefore, even though I live in Madrid, I return home at seven in the evening, and since I don't have many domestic responsibilities and I dislike television and hate the theater, I have a lot of free time. Along with the rivalry that reading the works of others incites, this is what eventually led me to write. Up to the present, I have not found any diversion more trustworthy than writing, or capable of competing with it.

MLG: So, for you, writing is a means to let off steam?

JB: To let off steam? No, no, because I am never steaming. To enjoy myself.

MLG: Jorge Luis Borges once said he felt more like a reader than a writer. Reading your work, one immediately recognizes your extensive knowledge of world literature. What does reading mean for you?

JB: I spend a lot of time reading. Not as much as Jorge Luis Borges used to, but, apart from writing, it is perhaps my favorite pastime, and the one which takes up the most time.

MLG: You have a very cosmopolitan vision of the world, but you nevertheless are thoroughly involved with Spain. How do you explain this?

JB: I don't really think I have a very cosmopolitan vision. I don't think I am a man of the world, in the sense in which that expression is understood. It is one thing for thorough involvement to have nonlocal connotations and perhaps, even if this sounds a bit presumptuous, universal implications. But I think that any individual who is truly involved with his surroundings, even though they may be in the most remote setting, can, should, and finally will achieve that universal understanding. There are many examples of this. For instance, writers who were closely constricted in terms of location, like Thomas Hardy in the nineteenth century, and Faulkner, García Márquez, and Rulfo in the twentieth. Because of their talents, they immediately achieved that universal understanding, using nothing more than the localisms in which they lived as a resource.

MLG: You have written novels, short stories, essays, and even plays. With which genre do you feel most comfortable?

JB: In the one that is most appropriate to the moment. That depends on inspiration or the first cause. Ultimately, I am not comfortable with the theater, and that's why I don't write any plays, because I have no ideas for it. Recently, a friend of mine, who is a film producer in Madrid, asked me something which he had never asked me before, and that was to write a script for a movie based on my novels. I don't know if it is the mere fact that he asked me to do this that has inhibited and prevented me from doing it. I can't seem to get started on that script, probably because he asked me to do it, although he didn't set a deadline. But the mere fact that someone requested something is sufficient cause for me not to do it.

MLG: So you are very independent?

JB: Let us say that my will is more independent than I am, because I would be very interested in doing that script. If I must be sincere, however, I don't feel I have enough drive to begin writing it.

MLG: Do you believe in inspiration?

JB: Yes, unfortunately I believe in inspiration. So I move along a shady path.

MLG: In what sort of inspiration do you believe? Divine inspiration? A muse? Enthusiasm? What is it for you?

JB: Not divine. Etymologically, enthusiasm means something like being transported or elated. And that elation is probably related to strength. Perhaps not a superhuman strength, but certainly a strength that is greater than the one individuals can muster under normal circumstances. But, irrespective of where it comes from, inspiration is a phenomenon that will not be denied. It moves the author, compelling him to write. In Latin etymology, inspiration is like infusing breath, it fulfills like an approaching wind, perhaps the Holy Spirit, so that one is transported. And since I don't have that inspiration for the script, I cannot be moved to write it. But we shouldn't try to explain. It has always seemed to me that looking for the causes of those phenomena and attempting to psychoanalyze them is somewhat superfluous. The phenomena occur nevertheless. Someday when you are walking down the street, for instance, or when you are reading something, or for any other reason . . .

MLG: Or at this very moment?

JB: Or at this very moment an idea springs forth that can lead to another, which the smallest experience can expand, and in this way an ensemble of ideas develops, a nebulous set that acquires a shape of its own, compelling one to write.

MLG: Reading your work, I notice how dedicated you are to polishing it. What does style mean to you?

JB: Let's distinguish. Polish is one thing and style is another. If I am dedicated to polishing, it must be because I am naturally uncouth, so I have to polish in order that the public will accept the product. It is quite possible that a writer who is more refined than I, and there are many, does not need as much polish. But style is something else. Style, for example, produces raw material, whether it is of good or bad quality. To go back to etymology, style is like a graving tool which Greek sculptors used in such a way that, even when two of them were making the same object at the quarry, one would be distinguishable from the other. It was a tool used to collect, so that one sculptor would not get paid for an object his colleague had graved. And that "style," which Buffon would later qualify as the most secret and intimate part of an individual, is what makes an object unique and distinguishable from the competition. That polish which you speak of might not even be necessary, because another tool could come along that would give a work its finish.

MLG: Do you believe in a plurality of styles, or in just one?

JB: I believe in just one style. If a man had a plurality of styles, perhaps his personality would be less focused. Above all, I believe it is style that solidifies an individual, even if his personality is dispersed among various occupations.

MLG: Do your characters speak as Juan Benet?

JB: I try to let my characters speak as little as possible, maybe because I am a bit of a charlatan. But . . .

MLG: Then you don't believe in the power of dialogue?

JB: Yes, how can I not believe in the power of dialogue? But, we ought to make some distinctions between written dialogue and the conversation we are having, for instance. Of course, it was very hard for me to write the first novel I published, *Return to Región.* It is very hard for me to do anything. For many years, I tried sending it to a series of publishers who replied with silence, as was customary in those days. After scouting for publishers in Spain, Europe, and America, my manuscript was sent to a literary agent, who in turn passed it on to the secretary of a publisher. And the secretary gave me a lesson: not only did she tell me that my novel did not fit the requirements of that publishing firm, but she also made some literary suggestions. She said that the novel had too little dialogue, and that the public usually did not buy works like that. She gave me a lesson, because I then opened my draft, which had only three pieces of dialogue in three hundred pages, and crossed two out. I did not think her reasons were sufficient to stop me from doing what I wanted.

MLG: Do you give priority to style, emotion, or imagination?

JB: I don't think that there is any question of priorities here. Style is a tool. Style is what one has handy to sculpt a block of stone, which can sometimes be marble, sometimes granite, and sometimes clay. Style treats feelings, circumstances, and the description of nature in the same way. It is the most important tool. Giving priority to one thing or another depends on the paragraph, on that mysterious equilibrium that we are never sure is going to turn out well. At those moments, a writer may stop and say: "I need a little more description of the landscape here," or "I have to say something about the character there, he is badly drawn," or "I must make some philosophical observations." This is the way it goes. There are no priorities.

MLG: You have an analytical mind that makes you a very demanding and original critic. Do you approach your own work with the same criterion?

JB: For better or for worse, I have a mind rooted in the study of mathematics. I don't know if that gives me analytical powers, probably not. And if it does, what it usually does not give is the ability to observe, which is a much more useful tool for a writer. Coming to your second point, I think that an accumulation of criteria in exaggerated proportions and with maximum intensity should be applied to one's work. And for this reason, it is my work that is the only worthwhile thing about me. I shouldn't have to be looming behind it, and I have nothing to add to it. I think self-criticism is implicit in every book. And if a book is written with that awareness, there is nothing to add to it afterward. I have never understood those writers who complement their books with a preface, an introduction, or critical notes. Even a writer as complex as Henry James, in his last novels, when he was at his most creative, devoted himself to writing prologues expounding on the implications of his characters. He took advantage of these prologues to comment on the literature of his day, even on the novels of George Eliot. But I have always thought of this as "superfetation," or overexplaining, which indicates in some way the author's discontent with what he has done. Another facet of this is that there are many authors who like to go around the world explaining their work. I recall an anecdote about a famous dancer from the first quarter of this century, Pavlova, who was once asked, "How do you explain your art?," to which she replied, "If I could explain my art, I wouldn't dance." This is the same thing. I must emphasize that self-criticism should be implicit in every page of the book.

MLG: You began to be published in the sixties. Do you see some resemblance between your work and that of the Latin American authors of the Boom, like Mario Vargas Llosa, for instance?

JB: No, I don't think there is much of a likeness between Vargas Llosa's work and what I do. In fact, I began to be published eight to ten years after Mario Vargas Llosa, even though he is much younger than I am. So there is not even a chronological relation, if we are going to speak in terms of precise figures. Mario Vargas Llosa began writing and was published when he was in his twenties. I was first published in my forties, although I had been writing since the time of Luis Martín Santos. To tell you the truth, that famous Boom caught us when we were already over the hill. So there isn't any parallel between my work and the Boom, whether it be on stylistic or thematic grounds. My novels are European or Spanish; they don't have much in common with Latin American works. Of course, the language is the same, but within that language there is room for anything. And yet, even the Boom is not a unified literary experience. It is a coincidence in time. Look at the difference there is between Rulfo and Borges.

MLG: Flaubert wrote a moral chronicle of his age. Your work also has moral ramifications, since it is an account of postwar Spain. Do you feel that there is a moral or social obligation in a work of art?

JB: I don't know, but, irrespective of whether there is or not, I wash my hands of it because I do not believe in categorizing conscience. When a critic says that Flaubert wrote the moral chronicle of his age, what he is doing is applying a label to evade the far vaster problem of what is a generalized conscience. When people bring up concepts like "historical conscience," what are they really saying? That there is a part of their conscience that is historic in contrast to another part that is not? Or that an individual can separate his historic conceptions of the world from the non-historic ones? I believe that conscience is one, and that not only morality, but history, society, and the world of values in which we live, are all indissolubly tied to this conscience. In this world of values, an individual has an awareness of the society and the history of his time, of the moment in which he was destined to live, of his friends, of his country, of his landscape, of what the human soul is—which all correspond to what he experienced. It cannot be any other way. And with regard to that very pretentious phrase that says that he was the writer or the artist of his age—who is not? Who is anachronistic? It would be very nice if we could free ourselves from our moral, social, and historical conditioning, so that we could travel to another time and another place. But we can't.

MLG: Why do you attach so much importance to the return of your characters?

JB: I don't give it any more importance than if they did not return. There are some characters who return, and others who stay. Perhaps what I give importance to is the contrast between those who stayed and those who came back. In the words of a brilliant, contemporary, young Spanish writer, "Returning is the greatest of infidelities." Perhaps you are referring to the circumstances in which I have depicted some of the characters of my novels as returning from a somewhat hypocritical exile to face the basically sordid reality of postwar Spain. In that case, it is in a way the history of an infidelity that, as always, is justified by the limitations, the incompetence, and the dissatisfaction of a character who left behind those to whom he wanted to be faithful.

MLG: You have said, "The man of letters who writes only about what he knows is a false scientist." Since you are also a man of science who likes to differentiate between one point and another, what is the proper mix of reality and fantasy with which you craft your works?

JB: That is a question which is very hard for me to answer quantitatively. In the first place, I am not really a man of science, I'm a technician, which is something lesser, or perhaps greater. Nowadays, science is a by-product of technology, because the latter controls money. But I do not have that scientific mentality that attempts to observe nature to the smallest detail that the scientific apparatus will allow. Of course, when I adopt the posture of a naturalist, I like to be as precise as possible. I don't know if this is due to my professional training, or because to be able to earn my living, my occupation demands a certain degree of precision. In that sense, it is not very hard for me to apply the same principles to various narrative elements. Of course, these elements would amount to nothing or would not entertain me unless they were compensated in good measure by some outings in the realm of fantasy. But which one dominates? The reader should really be able to tell, more so than the author. I must emphasize that I do not think the writer is in a position of speaking about his own work, or analyzing it, nor should he be expected to have set guidelines and some very learned answers about his work readily available.

MLG: Región is a mythical area that you invented and where three novels of your unfinished cycle take place. How did you come up with Región, that distant town which symbolizes postwar Spain?

JB: It is a region of my own making, but it is not mythical. Ricardo Guyón is the one who said it was mythical, in an article that he wrote. Other critics continued with that designation, and since then it has been labeled as such. I came to that area when I finished my engineering degree, and I began working on some hydroelectric projects in the northwest of Spain, which is a very backward place and very picturesque. It was very enticing for a youth who up to then had only known the city, although I had occasionally spent my summer and Christmas vacations in the country. That area was very isolated, very striking, and I was quite knowledgeable about it, since I had to study many books on its geology and biology. I later gave it a fictitious name, so I could move within it at my own discretion, without having to explain anything to anyone. I could then be the absolute and arbitrary owner, and determine where I wanted to put a country estate or a river, or how high a mountain would be. I could even set up a battle of the Civil War there and describe it, develop it, and finish it as I liked.

MLG: Do you think censorship caused you to create symbols?

JB: Symbols are created by critics and professors.

MLG: Why did you call that world "Región" when it is really Spain, then?

JB: But I didn't call it that! I emphasize that it was a professor who said that Región symbolized Spain. I have never symbolized anything. I described a place and gave it a name. I could be reproached for taking over the role of the parish priest in christening a whole area, something that is never mentioned in university departments. But God saved me from creating a symbolic region. Moreover, with each passing day I have less tolerance for symbolic writing and for that modern craze of finding symbolism or a reference in every line, in every concept, in every phrase and every insinuation. As if what is hidden is always more important than what the reader has in front of his eyes, as if literature were only there to uphold insinuation or an obscure legend. I think this craze is somewhat pernicious. It is little less than surrendering literature into the hands of critics.

MLG: It has been said that *A Meditation* is one of the most important novels of the postwar era and one of the most lyrical works of the last thirty years. What does poetry mean for you?

JB: I am probably partially responsible for that label, because I told the publisher that I was planning to write three novels: one with an ethical bent, another with a lyrical focus, and a third with an exclusively narrative approach. But it was only a plan so that we could understand each other. I have to confess that I do not read much poetry because I don't know how.

MLG: Have you written poetry?

JB: I'm not going to reveal that. I don't know how to read it, I have no background for it. I cannot read poetry for more than half an hour at a stretch. I will never succeed in spending a whole afternoon reading poetry. In the space of one year, if I read one hundred volumes of prose, I may manage to read three of poetry. So my lyrical education is very deficient. But that has nothing to do with the designation I gave to that novel, which was a general definition. When I said that I wanted to give the first novel an ethical bent, I merely meant that I wanted to describe certain events that, although not supernatural, are uncommon, singular, and outside the normal course of things. The epic is always the narration of extraordinary events with words that are very normal. Leaving aside the shape this description can take, the lyrical can in some way be described as the narration of normal events with very cautiously chosen words. But there are no great conflicts or catastrophes. Narration is the conjunction between both things in a neutral zone.

MLG: In *A Meditation* there is not just one plot, but rather a series of arguments that help sustain the structure of the novel. You give readers a puzzle, and leave it to them to put the pieces together. Do you see the work of art as an exercise in hieroglyphics? Why do you force your reader to do mental gymnastics?

JB: It is possible that readers may see *A Meditation* as a challenge to which they have to respond by deciphering and unthreading a tangled ball. But that's not the point at all. Moreover, that jumbled web is not sufficiently thought out, so it can't be unraveled. And anyone who tries to is wasting his time. That book is like a tangled web because that is its aesthetic, but it is meant to be read or enjoyed line by line and phrase by phrase, without any further ado. And if the general flow of the novel is broken at some point, well, it is broken, and it is not necessary to know the relationship between some characters and others, or the temporal sequence of events that are described, or the chronology, or the geographical setting. Everything is as is, no more. If the reader accustomed to analyzing, conditioned by logical puzzles, and steeped in mystery novels, wants to untangle the ball, then fine. But I can warn him right now that he will reap no rewards, because that is not the main objective of this novel.

MLG: You wrote that novel without paragraphs. Is it true that you used a continuous roll of paper with your typewriter?

JB: Yes.

MLG: Why? To convey that continuity?

JB: No, I didn't want to write on a continuous roll of paper like toilet paper. What I did, with the help of a carpenter friend of mine, was to build a device, which we placed behind the typewriter, so that the paper would enter the carriage and then wind itself into another roll. I did this on purpose so that as I wrote the text, what I was writing would get rolled up and out of view. I wanted to trust in my memory alone, even when it might introduce contradictions, breaks, and falsehoods into the text. So, this is what I did, even if it meant creating a mess. When I finished the roll, and the publisher asked me to give it a somewhat more accessible form before printing it, I wrote it in folios with the same device. And then, of course, I corrected certain structural brutalities, and in a way I amended the text fairly extensively. But I stuck to the basic system I had developed of not depending on anything more than what I remembered from the previous day. I won a prize for that book, by the way.

MLG: What did you think when you read the English version of that work?

JB: It is much better in English than in Spanish.

MLG: Why?

JB: Because Mr. Rabassa did an excellent translation, and I think the book is more interesting and readable in English than in Spanish. The Spanish version was well received but little read. I don't know if it will be equally well received in English, but I'm sure that, thanks to Rabassa, it will probably be more extensively read. He has accomplished the remarkable feat of making me read my own novel twice. It was very interesting, because I had practically forgotten the work, and many of the pages written with an English phrasing sounded quite new. I liked it.

MLG: What does destiny mean for you?

JB: In a way, destiny is a conjunction of circumstances.

MLG: And what about time? Do you like to play with it?

JB: No, time likes to play with me. I don't play with time. Time plays with me the way a master plays with his disciple, or the way a boxer spars. It is time that teaches us, and I am just one more person. I understand that I am a bad student, and that time, that old teacher, sometimes gets impatient with me and throws me out of the classroom. But all I try to do is follow that whimsical and irreducible master, and take advantage of "his" complex and never-ending lessons.

Part 2

MLG: Do you still work as an engineer?

JB: Yes, and I will never stop working as long as they put up with me. I will never stop working because, first of all, that's how I make my living. Secondly, even if I could earn a livelihood writing, I would prefer to write in my spare time. To be a writer, you really only need to be at home between eight and ten every evening.

MLG: Which do you prefer?

JB: I can't say. But, in any case, I don't want to give up being an engineer until I have to retire.

MLG: Your experiences as an engineer have undoubtedly influenced you.

JB: Yes, because, as I told you, my first experience was living in a very unusual place, the mountains of León, where I spent ten years. The view from my window became the basis for the world I called Región. But I have few anecdotes to tell. Life as an engineer is like any other. There were some encounters that were interesting, like meeting some old miners, or an aged guerrilla. In the world of public works, there are always very varied people.

MLG: And where do your characters spring from?

JB: From the imagination, although sometimes the characters have certain traits of people I have known. But generally I don't draw exact likenesses.

MLG: You recently said something very interesting about style. You said that structure was the most important thing for you. Do you think the reason for this is that you are an engineer, so that structure is fundamental?

JB: I've been told that before, but the structures that an engineer thinks of are definitely very different from those that a writer imagines. Perhaps I cannot avoid the need to have some sort of structure. But it is as if you said to me, "You are an engineer, so your house has to be arranged in a set fashion." Well, you can be an engineer and have a very chaotic house.

MLG: And is your house chaotic?

JB: No, it isn't. I have to admit it isn't. My life is very simple and peaceful. I have little to boast about.

MLG: Do you feel humble before your work?

JB: I don't care to be like those mothers who speak about their children as if they were the most handsome, intelligent, and outstanding in their class.

MLG: Do you see yourself as an intellectual writer?

JB: I have never understood what is meant by "intellectual." What does it mean? In contrast to the United States, in Europe an intellectual is understood to be someone who delves in politics and embodies certain political ideals, be they of the Right or the Left, although they are usually more leftist. Those are the European intellectuals. In the United States, an intellectual is usually believed to be an elite writer who does not devote himself to writing best-sellers for the masses. A man like Mailer, for instance, is the American idea of an intellectual.

MLG: Or like Borges in Latin America?

JB: Or like Borges, of course. But in Spain, an intellectual is someone whose name comes out in the press and who speaks in public with political overtones, usually leftist ones. In that sense, I am not an intellectual. I don't like the term, because it is too often abused, as if it were the sole province of people who use the pen or who have a name in the art world. But doctors or lawyers are not considered intellectuals because they don't have public renown. Yet, they could be, and they may in fact reflect better on public affairs than the man who writes stories and who does not always have a very organized mind. And let's not even begin speaking of poets. I don't like to be considered an intellectual.

MLG: Do you have any new projects in the works?

JB: No, this last one will take me a long time, perhaps two or three years. And once it is done, I will have covered the Civil War definitively, I hope. I cannot imagine or see beyond this.

MLG: So you think that after two years you will finally be done with the Civil War?

JB: Yes, personally, I will be. Although I don't discount the possibility that I may write a book of essays on the war someday, from the point of view of its military operations. But that would no longer be fiction. And until I finish this novel, I don't plan to devote myself to anything else.

MLG: It's incredible the impact the Civil War continues to have, even after all these years.

JB: Yes, but it is nothing to marvel about. Keep in mind that Tolstoy wrote *War and Peace* eighty years after the invasion of Napoleon, and Faulkner wrote his saga eighty years after the Civil War in the United States. Neither Tolstoy nor Faulkner, however, saw either of those wars, while I did witness the Spanish Civil War. I lived through it when I was very little, at an age when it leaves indelible marks.

MLG: You have produced a remarkable work, for which you even invented a map. What willpower!

JB: That is more a product of free time and a willingness to have fun than willpower. It's a lot of fun to draw a map. The places on the map, by the way, are almost all named after my friends.

MLG: Do they know it?

JB: Yes, they do.

Antonio
Buero Vallejo

MARIE-LISE GAZARIAN GAUTIER

Antonio Buero Vallejo was born in 1916 in Guadalajara. In 1934, after receiving his bachelor's degree, he moved to Madrid and for two years studied painting at the School of Fine Arts. In 1939, he was arrested for "his support of the rebellious cause" (he was a Republican) and received a death sentence that was then commuted to six and a half years of imprisonment. As he recounts in the following interview, his life as a painter was drastically interrupted by those traumatic years. When he was set free, he slowly made the transition from art to literature, in particular to the drama.

In 1949, the virtually unknown playwright received two prestigious awards, the Lope de Vega Drama Prize for his play *Historia de una escalera* (Story of a Staircase), and the Friends of the Quintero Brothers Prize for his play *Las palabras en la arena* (Words on the Sand). Since then, he has turned in an average of one play a year and is the recipient of countless honors and awards. To mention but a few, the 1956, 1957, 1958, and 1980 National Drama Prize; the 1962 Larra Prize; the 1967, 1970, 1972, 1974, and 1976 Leopoldo Cano prize; the 1987 Golden Medal from Guadalajara, and the 1988 Golden Medal from Castilla-La Mancha. In 1986, he received the Miguel de Cervantes Prize, one of Spain's most coveted awards. In 1971, he became a member of the Spanish Royal Academy.

Buero Vallejo has had to contend with censorship, but he managed to overcome many obstacles and present some of the most important theatrical productions, proving that if you have something to say you can never be silenced. His plays have been performed both in Spain and in over fifteen other countries, bringing him international acclaim. His work is mainly concerned with man's inner conflicts in a stifling society. His approach to the theater is based on both ethics and aesthetics, and is one of the most innovative, reaching out for new techniques.

43

In 1959, he married the actress Victoria Rodríguez, with whom he had two sons, Carlos and Enrique. The younger died in an accident; this personal tragedy comes up in the course of our conversation.

Among his productive output are the following plays: *En la ardiente oscuridad,* 1951 (*In the Burning Darkness,* 1985); *La tejedora de sueños* (The Weaver of Dreams), 1952; *Las cartas boca abajo* (Letters Face Down), 1957; *Un soñador para un pueblo* (A Dreamer for a People), 1959; *Las Meninas,* 1961 (*Las Meninas: A Fantasia in Two Parts,* 1987); *El concierto de San Ovidio,* 1962 (*The Concert at St. Ovide,* 1967); *El tragaluz* (The Skylight), 1968; *El sueño de la razón,* 1970 (*The Sleep of Reason,* 1985); *La Fundación,* 1974 (*The Foundation,* 1985); *Caimán,* 1981; *Diálogo secreto* (The Secret Dialogue), 1985.

Although he left painting for the theater, he has brought into his plays many of the techniques of an artist. He contrasts light and darkness, and has dealt with such figures as Goya and Velázquez.

I was lucky to stay in Madrid three houses away from the building where Antonio Buero Vallejo lives. The many writers I had seen prior to our meeting held him in great esteem. When we met, I was struck by his deep sense of commitment to the theater and his concern that the right image of Spain during the Franco years be given to the rest of the world. He wanted to make sure people knew that, in spite of censorship, great literature had been written. After taking me through a long narrow corridor, he invited me into his study where we were surrounded by books and sketches. There was a self-portrait drawn in pastel shortly after his release from prison as well as one of the poet Miguel Hernández during his political imprisonment. A photograph of Unamuno was hanging on the wall. Wearing a long-sleeve beige cardigan over a blue shirt and matching pants, Buero Vallejo spoke about his life and work, and also spoke about the tragic death of his son.

❖❖❖❖❖❖❖❖❖❖❖❖❖❖❖❖❖❖❖❖❖❖❖❖❖❖❖❖❖❖❖❖❖

MLG: You are one of Spain's most important playwrights. How would you define your work?

ABV: Like any author, I believe that the fundamental definition of my work is that it is an attempt to understand the problems of my own personality as well as the difficulties of this world. If you want a more literary definition, I would say that my theater tries to provide a tragic perspective of human existence, as long as you understand that what I mean by "tragic" is not something ominous or hopeless, but rather a riddle that can be solved. This could be described as the fundamental intent of my theater. It is expressed in concrete terms through specific subjects that are usually related to a critical vision of social problems in this world and our own personal reality. I achieve this through a modest examination of dramatic forms I feel to be in touch with current sensibilities. But enough of this!

MLG: Do you acknowledge Unamuno's influence in speaking of the word *tragic?*

ABV: Of course, and this is something I have pointed out before to other people, and that those who study my works have commented on. Unamuno is one of my more obvious sources, of course.

MLG: Is that a painting of Unamuno on your wall?

ABV: It's not exactly a painting, it is a photograph of Victorio Macho's sculpture of Unamuno, which is at the University of Salamanca. I have it here because Unamuno influenced me greatly, although he is not my only influence. There have been many other authors who have made an impact on me.

MLG: Can you say something about some of these authors?

ABV: This may seem pretentious to you, but I have to point to the Greek tragedies as direct influences. They have been very enriching and valuable for me, although regrettably my Greek isn't good enough to allow me to savor the originals. Although it may seem trite for a Spanish writer to say, Cervantes has been a great influence. Scholars of my theater have pointed out—as I have on occasion—that there is a hidden Quixotic theme that is recurrent in my work. But Cervantes's influence is not limited to that; it is also apparent in his literary conception of reality. By this I mean the totality of the immediate aspects of daily life occasionally in subtle connection to other more fantastic or magical elements.

MLG: It is interesting that you should mention Cervantes, because when I spoke of you to several writers, they referred to you as *bueno* (kind).

ABV: It's very nice of them to say that about me.

MLG: That's how Don Quixote wanted to be remembered.

ABV: That might be, but this would immediately take us from the creative or stylistic realms to the ethical one. Ethics is a constant concern for me, not in terms of fixed codes, but as a recurrent problem in all of my works. Nevertheless, in spite of the fact that ethics has its literary import, I don't think it is the most significant aspect of my theater.

MLG: To borrow the title of one of your plays, *Un soñador para un pueblo,* might I call you "a dreamer for a people"?

ABV: It wouldn't be wrong, but perhaps insufficient. Titles usually reflect us to some extent, in the same way that our books do. That title, therefore, does reflect me a little, although it is not the only one nor the most adequate. Some of my other titles could also represent me. For instance, let us take the second play I wrote, *In the Burning Darkness.* Although I am not blind like the characters of that work, it should be obvious that to live "in burning darkness" is also a way for me to come to terms with my own life. Another one of my titles, *The Sleep of Reason,* also comes close to describing one of my fundamental experiences. Many of my titles are personally significant.

MLG: How do you come up with them?

ABV: That is sometimes a very trying and difficult task, for which there are no rules. Sometimes the title comes right away, and when it does it might even be said that the work proceeds from it. This is not totally true, but to some extent. On other occasions, the opposite can happen: the work has been completed and given its best possible form and I still can't find an adequate title. I struggle with several of them, and sometimes I am not even satisfied with the one I eventually choose, so I couldn't give you a set rule. If I could, I would have no problems with my titles, but that isn't the case. While it is true that what happens in a play largely determines its title, it is still difficult to find it sometimes.

MLG: The words *dreamer* and *dream* have special meaning for you, don't they?

ABV: Of course, they have always had meaning for me, even before I started writing theater, because of those influences we have already discussed. Perhaps the greatest work in Spanish drama is *Life Is a Dream* by Calderón de la Barca. Certain aspects of my theater owe a lot to him, particularly those dealing with life: life as a dream, and dreams as reality at the same time. These elements are all in my theater. Sometimes I stage dreams overtly in my plays, at other times they are part of the narration, and on occasion I try to create what we might call a waking dream, which is the way some characters view reality. To make this clearer, let me mention my play *The Foundation,* where dreaming in the precise sense of the word does not occur, although the main character has a prolonged dream in a state of vigil from which he wakes little by little.

MLG: When did you first feel the need to write?

ABV: There are two answers to that question, although there should be only one. If I answer in a normal fashion, I would have to say that I began to feel a strong urge to write in 1946, following a somewhat dangerous and difficult life. These years of hardship led me to the certainty that I needed to write, and, more specifically, to write plays. This answer, nevertheless, is not completely correct, because I have been writing since I was a child, although I then thought I was going to be a painter. Even so, during my childhood and adolescence, I would occasionally draft a short poem or some prose for fun. I can remember attempting a poem as early as the age of nine; it was fortunately left unfinished. As I grew up, I continued my flirtation with literature; I even won the first prize of an insignificant student literary competition in my hometown of Guadalajara. All of this means that my connection with literature dates back to my childhood, when I was accidentally creative, if the word fits, and when my father would encourage us to read literature and take us to the theater. My call as a writer remained dormant until 1946, when I came out of jail and decided that I would have to write even if I continued painting. Following my release, I resolved to write creatively and I got involved with the theater.

MLG: Were you a political prisoner during the dictatorship?

ABV: Yes, two or three months after the war ended, they arrested me for an attempt to organize an illegal political group, which in those days was a severely punished activity. A short while later, someone turned us in, as might have been expected. Some of us were sentenced to death (I spent eight months on death row myself), and eventually the sentence was commuted and I ended up spending six and a half years in jail.

MLG: Did you write while you were in jail?

ABV: I wrote many things, but they weren't yet creative. During my first years in jail, I still thought that my call in life was painting, so I would try to draw and paint what I could. I filled many pages with thoughts on possible projects, such as a book related to painting that I never got around to doing. So this is what I mainly wrote about while in prison, although on occasion some of my friends, who were putting together a scrapbook for their families, would ask me to jot something down, and I would rhyme something quickly for them. What I did mostly, however, was to draw pictures of my fellow prisoners, as well as some watercolor sketches. I didn't do any oil paintings, although there were painters in captivity who made deals with the prison authorities to receive oils and an adequate place to paint. In return, they would paint the Virgin Mary for the nuns or a portrait of the prison director. Since I was never willing to compromise, I had no choice but to work without an easel. So I limited my pictorial interests to whatever I could draw on my lap, like the heads of my friends or perhaps a more elaborate watercolor but still requiring little material. What this means is that when I was set free I returned to oil painting as a beginner. I started writing, but I hadn't yet decided to give up painting.

MLG: Do you still paint?

ABV: No, not anymore.

MLG: When did you start writing for the theater?

ABV: I started writing plays soon after my release in 1946.

MLG: Why did you choose the theater over novels or poetry?

ABV: I did try some narratives and some poetry, but I think I focused on the theater because I have always been a theater enthusiast ever since I was a child. My father was a great theater fan and he cultivated the same passion in us, so we read and saw many plays. I think this accounts for my special attraction to the theater, although I read many other forms of literature as well. This is a way to rationalize my fondness for the theater, although ultimately there is probably no logical explanation for these things. Perhaps the most accurate way I can answer your question is that I devoted myself to the theater because inside me there was a playwright, God knows why.

MLG: What difference is there for you between reading and seeing a play? And also, what difference is there between writing and seeing a play?

ABV: The differences are very great, but this does not mean that writing or reading a play is any less than staging it. Nowadays, it is commonly believed that a play, although useful from a certain perspective, is not really theater until it has been staged. Of course, this is not completely untrue, but it does not in any way mean that reading plays is an incomplete activity, or that the written text is nothing but the precursor to real theater. I believe that writing plays is (and has been for centuries) a very important part of literature. It is very difficult to write a good play, and just as hard to please a director who insists on making changes in your play to present a so-called more theatrical production. This would be acceptable in the case of mediocre plays or with good plays where the author has indicated in the text, or even during rehearsals, that changes may be in order. But once a play has achieved its textual excellence, I deem it petulant on the part of directors to go in there and rewrite it. I am not saying that some small changes may not be necessary, but to modify the play in the way that is common today can sometimes be a very grave error. I say this in reference to the text itself. On the issue of reading theater (and excluding those plays that are either so bad or difficult to stage), I believe that plays that are relatively easy and effective to stage should also be read by the usual reader of literature. The common belief that only poetry, essays, or other narrative works should be read, but not plays, can be detected at book fairs or in book reviews, where they are rarely mentioned or reviewed. This is because it has become a truism that plays are only meant to be watched, not read. I think this is very far off the mark. I'll put it even more bluntly: a people or a society cannot be said to be truly enthusiastic about staged theater unless they also read plays continuously. In the heyday of Spain's theater, the public went to the theater in far greater numbers proportionally than today, and they also read plays quite extensively. People enjoyed the theater so much that they wanted to read it as well as see it, so they might devise their own internal, intimate stagings. I believe that reading plays also allows us to see qualities and flaws in them that may not be obvious on stage, no matter how good the production is. Our present disinterest in reading plays seems to me one of the worst symptoms for the life of the theater, because although theater is meant to be seen, it is also meant to be read.

MLG: What relationship do you have with directors, actors, and the public?

ABV: In the best of cases it is harmonious, and in the worst it is antagonistic. Since I am a man of the theater and knowledgeable about my craft, I try to be at the director's side for almost all the rehearsals. If the director is reasonable and recognizes that not only did I write the play but I understand what should happen on stage, then a harmonious relationship usually develops. We may not agree on everything, but he will allow me to make suggestions, sometimes to him and on occasion to the actors. I think this approach is positive and fruitful. There are directors, however, who despise any intervention on the part of the playwright, because they think that the author is only good for the written script. To put it more crudely, one can say that there are directors who think that playwrights are poor devils who understand nothing about the theater. This is not true, of course. It may be so in the case of some second-rate writer who seeks to be an author but can't make it. A good playwright often knows more about the theater than a director, because there are many mediocre directors. The megalomania of many current directors sometimes reaches paranoid extremes. The same is true with actors; occasionally, there may be some arrogant actor who believes that the playwright knows nothing about acting, which can lead to clashes. But I don't think this is true of any real playwright. If it were so, he would have devoted himself to other things, not to the theater. A real playwright knows a lot about acting, although he may not be an actor himself, or do as good a job acting as a professional actor would. Nevertheless, there is an instinctive actor in every playwright. The proof of this lies in the fact that a majority of playwrights, including myself, append notes to their plays in which they state how various characters are supposed to react: what the tone of their voices should be and what gestures they should adopt, for instance. So we also know about acting. When the actors understand this fact, as most of them do, they accept our suggestions without problems. And not only do they do this, but they often ask for our advice and tell us to hold their hands throughout rehearsals, because they are very unsure of themselves.

As far as the public is concerned, there can be playwrights who try to meet all of the audience's requirements, and produce a type of theater that is very commercial and has wide appeal. Although they can be quite successful, they cannot be considered good playwrights. A good and ambitious playwright is one who does not try to satisfy the whims and fancies of the public, but who would rather create his own captive audience, which is different. Sometimes he succeeds, while at other times he does not, although he may be a very good playwright. On still other occasions, success comes only after death; there are many instances of this in literary history. However, the norm tends to be that after some years a good playwright will gain a following, whether it be large or small, but usually sufficient to feed him. A good playwright will not only attempt to create his own public, but also to shape it (which is really the same thing). In so doing, he may contradict the expectations of the audience in an attempt to create his own mores, sometimes succeeding and sometimes failing. So the relationship with the public is one that is always more or less antagonistic. Another consideration is that the audience is always the unforeseeable factor; no one has the formula on how to make the public happy, especially when you are trying to contradict its expectations. Nobody has this formula, not even those who want to please the public. In fact, they sometimes fail spectacularly with plays they thought the audience would enjoy a lot. All of this means that the public is unpredictable, which is a good thing, because only a playwright can tell you the number of times a producer has turned down a play saying that, although it was a good work, the public wouldn't like it. Years later, another producer may stage the play—perhaps to fill some gap in his schedule—and it turns out to be the surprise hit of the season!

MLG: Did this ever happen to you?

ABV: Yes, on more than one occasion.

MLG: What is your relationship with your characters?

ABV: It's not easy to answer that. In the first place, one can say that there are two types of characters: those that come from within us, and those that are necessary to the action. The first kind are characters that are central to the main dramatic conflict of the play. They are characters we carry inside of us and that reflect us to some degree. Then there are those characters that are necessary to the action but don't have that inner resonance with the playwright. They are more reflexively crafted to the needs of the action, although once this has been done, they may also acquire a life of their own and be internalized by the playwright.

MLG: So they become people.

ABV: Yes.

MLG: Who is the strongest: you or your creations?

ABV: Many people have remarked that the characters sometimes impose their will on their creator. Although I believe this is true to some extent, I think it is no more than a metaphorical way of talking. It is accurate to say that when the characters are constructed, there comes a time when we start seeing things in them we had not before. But I would be loath to describe this phenomenon as the characters imposing their will on the author. I don't believe this is true; what happens is that the playwright imagines that his characters are alive, which in turn leads him to believe that the characters are speaking on their own. All of this, however, is in the mind of the playwright.

MLG: Is the playwright inside or outside his work when he writes?

ABV: Both. Generally speaking, and although there are exceptions, one cannot achieve any artistic output if those two elements aren't combined. On the one hand, the author has to allow himself to be tugged and pulled by the experiences that have led him to begin a particular play; on the other hand, he has to have a second self that is constantly critical and observant, remaining outside to correct and modify.

MLG: What do you feel when you write?

ABV: To put it succinctly, great torment. Writing for me is a very, very laborious task.

MLG: So it must be a great relief for you to finish a play?

ABV: I wouldn't say that. All I know is that it is finished, I have drawn the final curtain, and no further modifications are possible. But this does not mean that what I have written is impeccable or definitive. I usually feel a sense of discontent when confronted with that final product. When I confess this to people, they ask me why I don't continue revising and correcting, but I reply that I wouldn't know what to change. So I've done all I could, but I am still unhappy with the final result. This is how I usually feel when I complete a work. It is true that I don't trust myself, so I give my dissatisfaction the benefit of the doubt, because as time passes, the play may receive good reviews and eventually I may reread it and tell myself that it isn't as bad as I thought it was when I finished it. Generally speaking, nevertheless, I am dissatisfied with the finished product.

MLG: Are you the primary reader of your work or does someone else look at your plays as soon as you finish them?

ABV: I am always the primary reader in the sense that I read the work as I write it.

MLG: Do you read it out loud sometimes?

ABV: When I read it occasionally to my wife or my friends, then of course I am reading out loud, and I try to read the parts of the characters as I think they should be spoken. As has been the custom in the Spanish theater for a long time (although it is gradually being lost), theater producers designate a particular day when a playwright does a reading of his play for the theater company, before they start rehearsals. After this, parts are assigned.

MLG: Do you read all the parts?

ABV: Yes, I read the whole play.

MLG: I believe you have brought painting into your theater. How did you achieve this?

ABV: I have done this in many ways, because of my background as a painter and its relevance to staging. Of course, there are many playwrights who have a painter's eye although they are not painters. I believe that my way of understanding staging and of describing scenes owes something to my former profession as a painter. Additionally, both real and fictional painters have made appearances as characters in many of my plays.

MLG: Like Velázquez, for instance.

ABV: Yes, Velázquez appeared in one, Goya in another, and there are fictional painters as well. So painting has had an effect on the staging of my plays, as well as being related to the substance of the play, especially with the play that was dedicated to Goya, because many of his paintings appeared on stage.

MLG: You have also brought poetry into your theater.

ABV: When I first started writing plays, many critics said that one of the limitations or defects of my theater was that it lacked poetry. They said I was a playwright without poetic flair.

MLG: But the opposite is true!

ABV: At least, I believe the charge to be untrue, although I don't know. Poetry is more difficult to rationalize than anything else, because it comes from inside. It is an intuitive and authentic manner of expressing ourselves, but we wouldn't be able to explain how this happens. My early critics also accused me, among a thousand other things, of being pessimistic and destructive. Of course, there was also praise; otherwise I wouldn't be here.

MLG: Music also plays an important part in your work.

ABV: In addition to my early fascination with painting and literature, I have always been a great enthusiast of good music, although I have no technical knowledge of it. When I started writing theater, of course, many musical facets had to be incorporated into my plays, just as with the creators of Greek tragedies, who always used music for their theater. My theater, therefore, could not be done without music, and I don't just mean background music of the kind we find so often in movies, but music as a dramatic entity pivotal to the play and its characters. In some of my plays, music is dramatically connected to the essential conflict. That's why in *The Concert at Saint Ovide,* the character closes the action by saying something like "Perhaps music is the only possible reply to some questions." This might be connected to that famous saying of Walter Pater that all art aspires to music. I believe this too. Despite the importance of discursive, rational language in literature, I think there are some things that cannot be expressed with words which are nonetheless vital. Sometimes they can be said with painting, which is apparently silent but speaks its own language. Other times they can be communicated with music, even though music has no words. I have always tried to keep in mind these expressive and dramatic qualities of music.

MLG: Is your work autobiographical?

ABV: As with any author, it contains constant autobiographical elements, but I very much doubt that any of my plays can be considered predominantly autobiographical.

MLG: What are some of the obsessions you bring to your theater?

ABV: As I pointed out at the beginning, I am concerned with writing plays with a tragic bent, and I mean tragic in the sense of a struggle between freedom and necessity. Consequently, both the personal and social problems associated with this struggle between freedom and necessity are obsessive ones for me. I have other more concrete obsessions as well, such as my frustration with man's limitations, again both in the personal and social realms. This is related to what I have just said about the struggle between necessity and freedom, where necessity sometimes brings with it physical or psychic defects, which are very personal obsessions. Sometimes, these things point up the reach of necessity, which curtails potential freedom, but it is something that must be fought nonetheless. Another theme that obsesses me is the horror of torture, which appears in two or three of my plays. We could go on looking for things.

MLG: What about symbols?

ABV: Almost everything acquires a symbolic significance in my work. From the time that I started writing, my own aesthetic sense has been grounded not only in reality as such, but in the symbolic reach of that reality.

So there is ample symbolism throughout my works, although it is not allegory, as the two are quite different. I am very much a partisan of symbolism, not only in the theater but in literature generally, because I believe that symbolism has many meanings and is alive. This is important to me, so I use it. By contrast, allegory has but one meaning, and as such it is dead.

MLG: How did you come up with the symbol of the blind man, for instance, and what led you to write that powerful play *In the Burning Darkness?*

ABV: That was the first play I wrote, although not the first one that was staged. Since it was my first play, it represents my vomit, so to speak, the first thing that came out when I seriously decided to be a writer. Consequently, it was the most authentic reflection of what I was carrying inside me. Quite possibly, it was my own intense personal awareness of how human limitations can either destroy or become our destiny, which is pretty much the same thing. This awareness was a learning experience for me, both on the personal and general levels. How can this be translated through the symbol of blindness? I don't really know, but I am obviously not the only writer who has used blindness more or less symbolically: this has been around since ancient times when Oedipus became one of the most powerful symbols of humanity. More exactly, blindness is a symbol of our own limitations and inability to see, and there are only two possible responses to this: resignation or struggle.

MLG: What about the symbolism in *Caimán?*

ABV: That play turned into a symbol little by little. When I first conceived it, I wasn't thinking of it as a symbol. Rather, I focused on the notion of a play in which a father and a mother in some Caribbean country would suffer the loss of a child to the jaws of an alligator. These parents would be so affected by the death of their child that they would go and seek out the alligator so that it might devour them too. They would do this to meet the same fate as their child, and perhaps also to be reunited with him, although they knew full well that he was not in the belly of the alligator. This was the initial idea. But as I thought about this notion and strove to find an adequate dramatic form for it, I modified it to such an extent that it became a legend. Logically, of course, an alligator cannot devour a man and maintain him alive inside his belly. But this is possible in ancient legends, so I elaborated one, and as I did this, the alligator became a symbolic foil for that poor mother.

MLG: Did you write the play after the tragic death of your own son?

ABV: No, I wrote it prior to that. When my son died, I thought to myself, "What a strange thing. Did I foresee this without knowing it? Human beings are very mysterious. Did I unwittingly set the stage for my son's death?"

MLG: Or foresee it.

ABV: Perhaps, I don't know. I have thought about this, but when I wrote

Caimán my son was alive and well. It is very strange that you should ask me that, because no one else ever has. But his death really has nothing to do with my writing that play. When my son died, I thought I was going through something like the agony experienced by the characters in *Caimán.* Imagine the pain that my wife and I have had to endure. When you lose a son, you are initially obsessed with being able to bring him back any way you can, maybe through dreams. Later on this feeling subsides, but at first my wife would look for signs of our son Enrique—"Quique," as we called him—in things surrounding us, like a light spontaneously turning on. Being more cautious than she, I would bracket the incident and discount it as I discovered natural causes to explain it. But both my wife and I experienced these things.

MLG: Are you religious?

ABV: That's a difficult question to answer, because in the general sense of that word, I am not.

MLG: What about in the deeper sense of the term?

ABV: Perhaps yes, but this doesn't lead me to faith in a creator god. This problem is ineffable in some sense, and I prefer to meet it with silence.

MLG: In spite of your personal suffering and obsessions, could I call you a playwright of hope?

ABV: Many people have said that my theater is tragic, but with an open window of hope. This is probably true, but I always stress that I believe all writers with tragic bents have windows that are open to hope, although it may not be noticeable. In many of my plays, this so-called window is more or less apparent. In others, it isn't, and those plays appear closed, desperate, and without issue. I would hold, nevertheless, that even in those closed plays there is a window of hope. It doesn't matter that this does not seem to be the case: the play must call up that window in the audience. I think that the great tragedies were written to strengthen the hope of the public, not to weaken it, even though the text may seem to hold out no hope.

MLG: In your work, we can see the duality between life and death. What can you say about this?

ABV: Life and death are the two faces of the mystery of our existence, and as such they are intimately linked. In dramatic plays, therefore, the two usually appear as connected and interrelated. I could say a thousand things about life and death for hours and hours, but I don't know if this would be appropriate.

MLG: You have spoken about your years in jail under Franco's dictatorship. Has your theater changed since the advent of democracy?

ABV: Fundamentally, no. There may be a little more expressive clarity, but my theater has basically not changed, for many reasons. First of all, I think that art generally speaking and theater specifically are indirect in orientation; even the most direct and realistic protest play has many ambiguities and multiple meanings. This approach was used under Franco by many playwrights so that their works would be approved by the censors, whether grudgingly or not. The onset of democracy and the demise of censorship do not mean that this indirect, ambiguous angle has to be abandoned. Although this approach was sometimes used as a trick under Franco, more often than not it was employed as a legitimate artistic tool, which is valid regardless of whether there is censorship or not. So my theater continued and continues to have these ambiguous elements despite the advent of democracy, because I consider them assets, not drawbacks. The justified distaste for Franco's regime throughout the world, however, hurts us greatly, because we were always blamed for defects in our works that in many instances were not of our own making. It must be mentioned in passing that this has also led many people to think that Spanish culture under Franco, particularly Spanish literature, could not possibly be good, because the censorship prevented it from being so. This has been said in good faith for many years, and it is still claimed quite often. If this were true, it would mean that some outstanding authors such as Dostoyevsky, Tolstoy, Chekhov, and Gogol—who all had to work under conditions of censorship sometimes far worse than those we experienced—were really bad writers. So one has to make this point repeatedly to foreigners, because they cling obstinately to the belief that everything that was done under Franco was false, deformed, and mediocre. This is quite simply not true, and it must be emphasized repeatedly or they will continue doing us an injustice. It was very difficult to write under Franco, but the results were often outstanding in all fields, not just the theater. When democracy came, there were authors who said that they would now write what they couldn't before. But this was an illusion. Those who were genuine writers made their mark felt under Franco despite the obstacles, while those who could not write never made an impact, either before or after. Aesthetics is not completely dependent on social events, although they are significantly related. Art is such a great and magnificent thing that it finds ways to get around even the worst of situations.

MLG: Although I feel that I know you now, who is Antonio Buero Vallejo?

ABV: I am a quiet and concerned person who feels serious problems deeply. I also try to see things from the most balanced perspective possible. I think this defines me, more or less.

MLG: So you are a very genuine, ethical, good person.

ABV: I try to be, although I am not free from flaws. Though I have already mentioned that I am not a believer, the Bible says that even the just man sins seventy-seven times a day. If we can use the word sin, I must say that I sin and have sinned. It is likely, however, that I am not the worst of sinners.

MLG: If you could speak with some writer from the past, who would it be?

ABV: I would like to speak with all those authors I have liked or who have influenced me; they would be ideal interlocutors. I would love to talk with Sophocles, Cervantes, Kafka, and Herbert George Wells, whose science fiction has also influenced my theater, although this may not be immediately obvious.

MLG: What about Chekhov?

ABV: Yes, a lot.

MLG: And Pirandello?

ABV: Let's not broach the subject; I could spend hours talking with him.

MLG: What would you ask these authors?

ABV: I am not certain, but if I were speaking with a playwright, I would ask him how he resolved some purely technical problems in his theater, which are difficulties that we all encounter from time to time.

José María Carrascal

José María Carrascal was born in 1930 in El Vellón, a small town near Madrid. After studying seamanship, he went to Berlin where he began his journalistic career writing for the *Diario de Barcelona* and Madrid's newspaper *Pueblo*.

In 1966, he moved to New York, using the United Nations headquarters as his base of operation. He continued working for Madrid's *Pueblo*, but also became correspondent for the newspaper *ABC*, also from Madrid, reporting from New York about the United Nations and the United States. He wrote as many as three daily columns, and also found time to write fiction as well as essays. Some of his novels are based on the research he did as a journalist. In 1985, he received the prestigious Mariano de Cavia Prize for his journalistic achievement. Some of his articles have been gathered in book form.

His novel *Groovy* (1973) won the Nadal Prize for that year. Some of his other works include *El capitán que nunca mandó un barco* (The Sea Captain Who Never Took Charge), 1972; *USA superstar,* 1973; *La muerte no existe* (Death Does Not Exist), 1974; *Mientras tenga mis piernas* (As Long as I Can Run), 1975; *Cuatrocientos años triunfales* (Four Hundred Triumphant Years), 1982; *La aventura americana* (The American Adventure), 1982; *La revolución del PSOE* (The Revolution of the Spanish Socialist Workers Party), 1985.

Carrascal now lives in Madrid, where he has been asked to work as anchorman for the new privately owned Spanish television channel, Antena 3.

José María Carrascal has a very dedicated attitude toward his profession as a writer and journalist. My first impression of him dates back to the time I interviewed him for a television program I was hosting. Before we went on the air, anticipating the future anchorman he would become, he wanted to see all the questions I was about to ask in order to study them and organize them in his mind. I didn't know that I was about to experience something very interesting. When we did go on the air, and the program was halfway through, the whole show had to start over again because of technical problems. This time, Carrascal answered with variations on the same theme. It was no longer the journalist speaking, but the writer who improvised answers to the same questions, taken from a different angle. This experience clearly illustrated the two facets of Carrascal's talent.

❊❊❊❊❊❊❊❊❊❊❊❊❊❊❊❊❊❊❊❊❊❊❊❊❊❊❊❊❊❊❊❊

MLG: It has been said of you that you are one of the best present-day Spanish journalists. Do you feel more at home when you work on a novel or a newspaper article?

JMC: That depends on the day, on the story, on many things. Many people ask me if I am more of a journalist than a novelist. That is a question I can't answer. Perhaps I am a better journalist, though I would prefer to be a better novelist.

MLG: As a journalist you observe reality and report on it, but as a novelist you abstract from that reality and create fiction. Are these professions compatible?

JMC: Yes, they are compatible but they are also interrelated. The biggest difference between journalism and the novel is in the language. The first commandment of the journalist is not to interfere in what is being told to the readers. He must put his thoughts in a language that is as plain, as easy, and as accessible as possible. To write a novel, on the other hand, one should destroy normal language in order to create a new one. That's the task of the novelist: to destroy the usual language, the day-to-day expressions we use, and create new ones that make up the atmosphere of the new novel. Before writing a novel I always ask myself, "Which kind of language will I use? Will I use long sentences, short ones, many verbs, many adjectives?" This is so important that, without it, one can't write. Journalism is a transmission of facts from one point to another without interference. But writing a novel is a completely different thing. One has to create something, one has to will up some theme. The novelist always tampers with things and persons, so even the most realistic novel is an interference with reality.

MLG: Your novels deal with experiences that are foreign to Spain, for the most part. Have you thought of writing something about your country?

JMC: Yes, as a matter of fact I have written *Cuatrocientos años triunfales,* my first novel about Spanish life, not today's life, but life in the 1940s and the 1950s when I was there. It is a novel about three friends who conquer a little village in Spain. One is a judge, another is a physician, and the third one is the secretary of the local mayor. They found a "Platonic" republic in that mountain village. It is a very funny novel and a very tragic one.

MLG: So there is a lot of reality and fantasy.

JMC: In a novel, usually you don't differentiate between reality and fantasy.

MLG: Writers in exile or self-imposed exile keep writing about their native countries. You have also lived outside of Spain since 1957, not as a writer in exile but as a correspondent for Spanish newspapers. Your novels are about the countries in which you have lived. For instance, the United States has had considerable influence on your writing. Why did you write *Groovy?*

JMC: The simple answer is because as a journalist for my paper I had to write about the revolution of the 1960s, the cultural explosion among youth in California and in the East Village in New York. But I also wanted to put together in a creative way all the things I had written about in the paper. At that time, Spain was still a very closed country; the influence of the outside world was very limited. In my daily articles I had to write about Vietnam, about the Manson family, about all these things, but always in very fractional ways, a column each day about a certain aspect of the whole. In the novel I had the opportunity to put all these pieces together.

MLG: You have said about *Groovy,* "It is a pessimistic book perhaps because it was written at a time of disenchantment when hippies were disappearing." Why did you write about the hippie life when it was coming to an end?

JMC: When I began to write, it was not disappearing. But you are right, by the time I finished the novel, that movement was coming to an end. I think you can't write about a thing at its peak, you don't have perspective on it.

MLG: When did you start writing it?

JMC: At the end of 1969. Immediately after the Manson family crime, I was struck that these flower children could commit this monstrous crime, and I thought, "The party is over, something went wrong here." I went to San Francisco to see Haight-Ashbury. I found drugs, crime, and many other aspects of the hippie life that I hadn't suspected. I envisioned the novel immediately. I didn't need to consider several generations to put together the story. All I had to do was to place a young girl in the East Village in 1969, and perhaps a week later the story would be over. Today we are witnessing a very interesting aspect of history: its acceleration. One movement such as the counterculture movement of the 1960s in another century might have taken fifty or seventy years to develop in full. Today, with mass media, television, telex and so on, we have acceleration of every process. In five years you can have a whole chapter of history that you can summarize in a book.

MLG: So it's a chronicle of the hippie life through the biography of a girl named Pat who leaves her home in New Hampshire and drifts into a hippie commune.

JMC: It is not a whole biography, just a small slice of life—the most important and also the most destructive part of it.

MLG: How did you penetrate the world of the hippies and capture their jargon, their behavior, their alienated and rebellious spirit? Was it through journalism as an observer, or as the novelist you are, or was it as Carrascal the man who was attracted to the hippie life and wanted to participate in it?

JMC: I was struck by the hippies, as I think everybody else was at that time. But I approached the East Village as a journalist, to write a story about it. I remember going to the Fillmore East and to the Electric Circus, and I wrote about these places for my paper. Thereafter I began to put together not only life in the East Village but life in America at that special moment—how parents of runaway children, and society in general, reacted to the new cultural scene (such as *Hair* and all those other shows that suddenly appeared off Broadway). I put these things together and began to write a completely fictitious story.

MLG: Do you think the influence of the hippies is still felt today?

JMC: Yes, in some ways. They disappeared, but many of their ideas are still alive—their love of nature, their belief that life is not competitive. And I think these things will stay for a long while, if not forever.

MLG: You have created in your novel the same thing the hippies created in real life—a new language. You have taken hippie expressions and transposed them into the Spanish language. How did you manage to do that?

JMC: I began putting together a new vocabulary, a dictionary, not only of words but of expressions. Consider, for instance, the use of repetitions. You know that in Spanish, when you are writing literature, you should avoid repeating a word in the same sentence or even in the same paragraph. But the hippies were always repeating the same words. I had to break the usual Spanish language to create, not just new words, but a new syntax for Spanish.

MLG: Wouldn't it have been easier to have written about this American experience in English?

JMC: Of course, if I could have! Yes, it would have been easier, but not for me.

MLG: Have you ever tried writing in English?

JMC: Yes, I have tried many times, almost daily. It is an interesting experience, a very productive one, but an almost impossible task. It is a "mission impossible" to write in another language, because, as I said, if you write a novel you have to destroy the usual language and create the one that you want. You can do it in your own language, in your mother tongue, and nobody will say anything. I remember that after *Groovy* some of the critics told me, "You don't respect the *consecutio temporum,* all the verbs in the paragraph are not in the same tense." I said, "So what? I can do it, it's my language." But I can't do that in English. The first thing that they will tell me is, "You don't speak English well," which is true, but irrelevant.

MLG: Do you consider your novels to be experimental because of your introduction of new terms into the Spanish language?

JMC: Everything we do is experimental, but experimenting is necessary because otherwise we would always stay where we are, we would be immobilized. I hope I experiment in each novel, to break new ground, especially in language, and to try a new approach to reality with a new kind of literature.

MLG: Each of your novels is an exploration into an unknown world for you. What is the significance of your novel *Mientras tenga mis piernas?*

JMC: I don't know the significance. You, the literary critics, the readers, should say what it is. I was struck by the riot in Brownsville in 1967. I went there to write about it for my paper. I loved that area. It was one of the most interesting neighborhoods in New York—Danny Kaye was born there, as were many other artists and writers. And I saw it in flames. What could account for this violence all of a sudden? I began to study the story of Brownsville and its special culture. And I learned that after World War II it was completely destroyed by the conflict between the residents and the newcomers. Most of the Jewish families left for Manhattan and Queens, and the blacks and the Puerto Ricans moved in. It was a tremendous change, which ended in a riot. I told myself this could be the basis for a very tragic and interesting novel. I told the story of a family, three generations with a small child, who was the last one to live through this inferno. There was enough material there for a novel.

MLG: What was the reaction of the Spanish reader to your descriptions of the United States?

JMC: Today everybody in the world is interested in the United States and everyone is an expert on the subject. But it's difficult to write about this country, because there is none other like it. I would say that there are more similarities between Spain and Thailand than between Spain and the U.S. The United States is different because it was born with a constitution. Spaniards think that they know the U.S. because they watch American TV shows. I tried to put in my novels a different view of this country, and the reaction was, "This is not the United States we know." And it was impossible to convince them that there are many different facets to it.

MLG: You also probed a new world, that of science fiction, which had not been explored much in Spanish literature. Why did you write *La muerte no existe?*

JMC: At that time, I was fascinated by science fiction, perhaps because I had to write about the moon and the Apollo mission in my paper. I have always been interested in science. As you know, I studied to be an officer in the Spanish Merchant Marine. I think science is one of the most marvelous things we have today, because we not only can imagine but actually see the results of most of our theories.

MLG: You create a new dimension by looking at the earth as a point suspended in space. Why is the element of perspective so important?

JMC: I wanted to have another perspective on the whole solar system in the next eight thousand years. What will we do? What will we be like? I tried to say that even if we were on another planet in a spaceship, man and woman would still be the same. Our problems, dreams, and passions would be absolutely identical to the ones we have today.

MLG: In 1985, you were the recipient of the Mariano de Cavia Prize, the most prestigious journalistic award in Spain, for an article you wrote on your impressions while vacationing in Spain. Why do you think you received that award?

JMC: I think because of the freshness of my approach.

MLG: What made you write *La revolución del PSOE?* Did it begin as an article and slowly turn into a long essay?

JMC: As a matter of fact, this book is about the lack of real revolution in Spain, a country that was medieval until a short time ago and still is in many respects. Only in the last chapter of the book do I study the intent of the present socialist government to enact both its own socialistic cultural revolution and a bourgeois revolution. Of course, there are problems in the attempt because these revolutions are incompatible.

MLG: What is your novel *La llave* about?

JMC: It is about a Sephardic Jew from New York who goes to a village in Spain looking for the house of his ancestors and at the same time searching for himself.

MLG: Can you speak about the publishing house Seix Barral and its role in bringing about the literary explosion of the 1960s and the awarding of literary prizes to many Latin American writers?

JMC: Seix Barral introduced to Spain not only the new Spanish-American literature, but also the French *nouveau roman,* and the German *Neue Welle,* Günther Grass, Heinrich Böll, all the new literature of the last twenty or thirty years. Seix Barral published all the books that the other firms did not.

MLG: Why do you think the Biblioteca Breve Prize was awarded mostly to Latin American writers, to be exact five times out of seven from 1962 to 1968?

JMC: Because they were better than the others. At that time, Latin American writers were really good and very creative in many ways. Also, as I said, Seix Barral was most interested in the new kind of literature— more experimental, more aware of the language problem—than the traditional Spanish publishing houses were.

MLG: Do you think the purpose of awarding these prizes to Spanish-American writers was to erase the boundaries between Spain and Spanish America and create a literary partnership based on a common language?

JMC: I don't know what was intended, but the most important thing was that Latin American writers taught Spanish authors a new conception, a new way to write novels.

MLG: What is your definition of the Boom?

JMC: The Boom was really an explosion. All of a sudden we began to discover new writers all over Latin America. At that time, Latin America was the richest and most interesting part of the world from the literary point of view. Small countries had big writers, who not only wrote about the problems of their particular countries but about universal concerns. Spain discovered many of them, and many of them went to live and work there. Some people said at the time, and still say, that it was just a commercial boom. I don't think so. It was really a literary boom.

MLG: What was the influence of the Boom on Spanish writers?

JMC: We were in shock at the beginning. Ever since Cervantes, we in Spain had been thinking of literature as *arma arrojadiza* (a throwing weapon). You can do many things with literature. With *Don Quixote,* Cervantes destroyed the novels of chivalry and many political things. Our best novelist of the last century, Pérez Galdós, used his books in order to attack the Catholic church. Almost always, when someone in Spain writes a book it is against something or somebody. What Latin American writers showed us is that you can write a book just for the pleasure of it, for litera- ture's sake. We have to remember that during the 1950s the Spanish novel was dominated by what we now call *realismo,* social realism. All the novelists of that era thought they could promote social justice by showing the social failure of the Franco regime. This was a political objective that sometimes worked and sometimes didn't. But it had very little to do with literature.

MLG: In 1962, the Peruvian author Mario Vargas Llosa, then twenty- six years old, won the Biblioteca Breve Prize for his novel *The Time of the Hero.* Can you say something about the impact of that book?

JMC: The impact was enormous. The book showed us a new way of writing, even though Vargas Llosa is the most classical of these new Latin American authors. Everybody was surprised and confused. Many of the typical Spanish writers began to change their styles from one day to the next. Others attacked him. When novels like *One Hundred Years of Solitude* appeared, we realized that we had to change our approach to literature. I think the most important result was that today in Spain we write much better books than we did before the Boom.

MLG: Could we say that the Boom was as beneficial for Latin Americans as for Spaniards because there was a constant give-and-take between the two?

JMC: I think we took more than we gave. Latin Americans are more free to write the way people speak. They are more in touch with the earth, with their old legends and traditions. The most interesting writer for us was García Márquez, with his magic touch and his overwhelming imagination. We Spaniards are perhaps too attached to realism.

MLG: Could you compare *One Hundred Years of Solitude* to *La saga/fuga de J. B.,* by Gonzalo Torrente Ballester? Do they share the same magic?

JMC: Torrente Ballester is Galician, from the northwest part of Spain. The *Gallegos* are Celtic, they are very imaginative people like all Celts. The Irish are too, as are the Bretons in France—they love legends and old mysteries. Torrente Ballester wrote his book at the end of the 1960s and the beginning of the 1970s. I wonder if he would have written *La saga-fuga de J. B.* if he hadn't been preceded by García Márquez.

MLG: García Márquez has Remedios ascend into the air and Torrente Ballester has a whole town rise up.

JMC: But before García Márquez, a twentieth-century Spanish writer would not have dared to write such a scene, it would have seemed childish. We thought we should write about injustice, the transcendental, the philosophical questions.

MLG: The Cuban novelist Guillermo Cabrera Infante received the 1964 Biblioteca Breve Prize for *Three Trapped Tigers.* Did his experiments with the Spanish language influence Spanish writers?

JMC: Yes, even if we hadn't read his book. There was something in the air after the first breakthrough. Everybody wanted to write just like Latin Americans. A friend of mine who was a member of several literary juries said, "Oh God, we have fifty novels like *One Hundred Years of Solitude.*" Cabrera Infante's novel is a charming one, but I don't see that his influence was as strong as that of García Márquez.

MLG: Carlos Fuentes, who also received the Biblioteca Breve Prize, was the central figure of the Boom. Would you like to say something about him?

JMC: Of all the Latin American writers, Carlos Fuentes is most like a Spanish writer, because he is always attacking or defending something. His first novel, *The Death of Artemio Cruz,* was very Mexican and his most direct comment on society. His other works are more international, but he is still concerned with society, as we are in Spain.

MLG: In 1979, the Miguel de Cervantes Prize, one of the most prestigious literary prizes in the Spanish-speaking world, was awarded to the Cuban Alejo Carpentier. Can you speak about his influence in Spain?

JMC: Carpentier was a novelist with a tremendous sense of fantasy. Every Spanish writer read his book *The Lost Steps.* The Miguel de Cervantes Prize is one of the best ideas we have had in a long, long time. First, it is a very substantial prize (ten million pesetas) and, second, both Spanish and Latin American writers can win it. Such distinguished authors as Borges, Vargas Llosa, and Onetti have received this prize, which is wonderful.

MLG: Can you say something about Juan Rulfo and his works of the fantastic?

JMC: Rulfo was one of the most marvelous writers I have ever read. He was so natural, so authentic. *Pedro Páramo* is a masterpiece, so concise, so intense, so genuine. Rulfo was one of the great artists of our time and of all times.

MLG: What is the common bond between Spanish and Latin American literature?

JMC: Language. It is the salt of the earth. We have the same language, they learned it from us and we learned from them how to put together new syntactic constructions, new words. Now there is a relationship, a partnership between writers in Spain and Latin America. The connection is very profound, very deep. I think we should remember Valle Inclán, the Spanish writer who went to Mexico and wrote *Tirano Banderas,* a novel that could have been written by a Mexican. In fact, it can be considered one of the best Latin American novels ever written.

José Luis Castillo Puche

José Luis Castillo Puche was born in 1919 in Yecla, Murcia, the region of Spain that was so minutely described by Azorín in *The Confessions of a Little Philosopher*. As a child, Castillo Puche attended the Colegio de los Escolapios in Yecla, the same school as Azorín. At the age of nine, he studied at the San José Parochial School in Murcia and later received a scholarship to study at the Seminary of San Fulgencio. At the age of fourteen, he received first prize in a short-story contest.

Castillo Puche studied philosophy at the Universities of Murcia and Madrid, and philosophy at the Madrid Official School of Journalism. His countless articles have led him to travel around the world (Europe, Africa, North and South America), meeting figures such as Lumumba, Mobutu, and Batista. From 1967 to 1971, he lived in New York and worked as a correspondent for the daily *Informaciones* of Madrid. Since 1974, he has been Professor of Writing and Style in the Department of Information Sciences at the Universidad Complutense of Madrid. From 1976 to 1978, he served as director of the literary review *Mundo Hispánico*.

A friend of Ernest Hemingway, Castillo Puche wrote a valuable study on the novelist titled *Hemingway: Entre la vida y la muerte,* 1968 (*Hemingway in Spain: A Personal Reminiscence of Hemingway's Years in Spain by His Friend,* 1974). In June 1984, he was made an honorary member of the Hemingway Society of the United States.

Castillo Puche is the author of numerous works, including *Con la muerte al hombro* (With Death at My Shoulder), Bellas Artes Cultura Hispánica Prize, 1954; *El vengador* (The Avenger), 1956; *Hicieron partes* (The Split), winner of the Laurel del Libro Prize, 1957, the Novela Católica Prize, 1958, the National Literature Prize, 1958; *Paralelo 40* (The 40th Parallel), 1963; *El perro loco* (The Mad Dog), 1965; *El cíngulo: Como*

ovejas al matadero (The Priest's Girdle: Like Sheep to the Slaughterhouse),
1971; *Jeremías, el anarquista* (Jeremiah the Anarchist), 1975; *El libro de
las visiones y de las apariciones* (The Book of Visions and Apparitions),
1977; *El amargo sabor de la retama* (The Bitter Taste of the Broom Field),
1979; *Conocerás el poso de la nada* (You'll Know the Lees of Emptiness),
1982, winner of the National Literature Prize, 1982; *Ramón J. Sender, el
distanciamiento del exilio* (Ramón J. Sender, The Isolation of Exile),
1985; *Los murciélagos no son pájaros* (Bats Are Not Birds), 1986.

In 1956, the Minister of Education of Spain granted Castillo Puche the
Encomienda de la Orden de Alfonso X el Sabio (Knighthood of the Order
of Alfonso X the Learned). In 1981, the government of Ecuador awarded
him the Medalla de Mérito Civil de Primera Clase (Medal of Civil Merit,
First Class).

The last time I saw José Luis Castillo Puche was over a dinner at the Café
Gijón, one of the most famous gathering places for writers and artists in
Madrid. He was dressed in a plaid jacket and shirt and a light blue vest,
without a tie, and gray pants, and wore glasses that made him look somewhat like Benjamin Franklin. He walked into the place as if he were in his
own home. He knew everyone and everyone knew him: the people who
work there and all the writers, journalists, and artists who are regulars in
that establishment. He asked for a quiet table and we went downstairs
where he talked about his work, his daughter's poetry and painting, and the
role of literature in present-day Spain. He was in a very talkative mood and
told me many anecdotes.

❖❖❖❖❖❖❖❖❖❖❖❖❖❖❖❖❖❖❖❖❖❖❖❖❖❖❖❖❖❖❖❖❖❖

MLG: José Luis, your work is a constant reliving of the Spanish Civil War,
and your characters move in a stifling, oppressive society, unable to achieve
freedom. Could your work be called "liberation literature," both in the
personal and collective senses?

JCP: Of course. My intention was not solely to engage in a search and
exploration of myself to find spiritual or moral well-being, because I think
that a sincere novelist is under an obligation to portray others, his neighbors,
the people close to him. In that sense, to liberate oneself is also to liberate
others.

MLG: Your book *El perro loco* recounts the horrors of the Civil War
from the perspective of Lili, the little dog. How did you manage to write
such a moving book?

JCP: That book was a random occurrence. I wrote it for my son, to teach
him what the Civil War was all about. I wanted to show it to him in a natural,
lively manner, without eliciting the circumstances of opposing factions or
brutal deaths. I wanted to stress that the real monstrosity was the separation

and discord between brothers. Above all, the Civil War was a schism or tragedy within the same family, within the same nation. So I used the dog as a symbol. We had a very affectionate dog in our family, and I think the war disturbed it a great deal, as it was accustomed to a comfortable, peaceful, even capricious domestic life. When the dog had to be put into hiding, because it might give us away, it entered into a kind of pronounced schizophrenia, more than neurasthenia, and it tried to become aggressive. So, from the points of view of the child, the author and the father, who is teaching his boy that barbaric lesson, I decided that I would establish the dog as a dumb witness, with a completely silent sort of intelligence, to the cruelty that civil wars imply. And the dog almost became an element of justice—it was kinder than people.

MLG: In many of your novels the characters are captive, whether in a cell or a monastery. Is this because you lived your childhood and youth in an atmosphere of oppression and religious fanaticism?

JCP: Yes, in Spain the education was at times very sordid, conflictive, menacing, and punishing. It made an impact on me when I was a boy, and this is reflected in the case of the child in *El libro de las visiones y de las apariciones,* who has great anxieties, fears, and nightmares. I made him go through a bitter adolescence and then finally freed him completely when his mother died. She was the greatest link in his life and she is the strongest and most redemptive symbol in the book, in her love for her child. When the boy falls prey to a childhood disease that leaves him trancelike and weakened, the mother has a strong intuition to take him to the seaside, where they had never been, to save him. When he sees the seashore, he discovers the infinite, immense aspects of life. At the same time, he realizes the smallness and frailness of his own mother when he sees her lying vulnerable on the beach with her legs exposed, as he foresees that she is mortal. It is a discovery made through the infinity of the sea—the discovery of something as contingent and threatening as death itself, and the death of the mother specifically. The water of the village well, with its bitter taste, also becomes a symbol. There is a shortage of water and the neighbors will go there and stand in line to receive even a drop of water. Their thirst is an allegory for the thirst for justice and liberty. A parable that critics have been discussing lately is that of the youth as he arrives at the front, having seen blood, cruelty, infamy, and injustice on the part of both factions. On his first night of guard duty, he enters the river with his gun, slowly advancing in the water, and he dares not go to either bank, he refuses to give himself to either side. Instead, he devotes himself to self-discovery, to the pilgrimage toward innocence, because he throws away his gun and continues his journey on a long, infinite night toward the sort of purity that does not distinguish sides.

MLG: Why do you juxtapose true religion with religious hypocrisy?

JCP: I think a man's life should be concerned with asking questions, and novels often contain answers. They are not complete or absolute, but they do attempt to give some response. Man is full of queries and we have been brought into this life in a state close to blindness; we are in emptiness and solitude, very forsaken. I think the novelist has to ask why we are here, what we are doing, and where we are going. It is in this sense that I speak, not with a catechist or apologist bent, because I don't involve myself with doctrine. I do think that the religious approach is one of the most essential and fundamental of the human experience, especially as it is intrinsically tied to the notion of death. Because death is always close and not to think about it is to be ignorant about ourselves.

MLG: Your novels have some of the characteristics of a confession. Do you think this is a result of your years as a seminarian?

JCP: Yes, in the sense of words half-spoken, but only if the confession is testimonial. Many times, confessions are very voluble and hypocritical. People confess to ease their conscience and they don't tell the whole truth. If a confession is made from the perspective of a testimonial—this is what I am, this is what I amount to, this is what I want to be, this is what I wished for, this I was unable to do—then the testimonial has true value and human dimension. So my novel is confessional, but it is not ascribed to any creed, just to man, his roots, and his destiny.

MLG: You write many of your novels in the first person, as if they were autobiographical.

JCP: I mix the "I" and the "you," and sometimes even the "we." I think I am one of the writers who has put a great deal of dialogue in a novel, and monologues above all. I think my novels are essentially an interchange of identity, because I am you and you are I and in that sense the identities become fused. What can never be confused are words, the destiny of words, because the reader understands them as the consciousness of the character and the silent and absent wisdom of the author. This wisdom is sometimes very limited, but the reader enlarges and illuminates it, which is what always happens. The reader perfects and complements a novel, because he takes it as far as it can go. The reader, more than the critic, is the true participant in creating a novel.

MLG: Is your work autobiographical then?

JCP: People always ask me that. I have disguised myself and I speak through many different characters. For instance, in *El vengador,* which is the story of an official on Franco's side who enters the village where all his family was killed, the whole town unites as a tragic chorus in inciting him to avenge his relatives. But the avenger does not avenge, because he is morally disarmed when he finds out that in his own family there were also weaknesses and serious sins. He then achieves great moral stature and some critics, like Sobejano, have suggested that he is a modern Hamlet. But some people say that since Castillo Puche depicts one of Franco's officials, he must have been on the nationalist side. I never was. In fact, I was an official in the "red" zone. For a novelist to be even more authentic, sometimes he has to put himself in the shoes of others, because confessing one's own reality is often not enough to write a novel. If a writer did only that, it would make for a short and uninteresting novel. Other realities besides one's own have to be experienced.

MLG: What is the relationship between the novelist and the characters?

JCP: The author spreads, diversifies, re-creates, screens, punishes, and purges himself through his characters.

MLG: Who dominates whom?

JCP: Many times it is the characters that dominate. When a character acquires great stature and imposes himself, then the author only follows along, not in a passive manner but with a type of somnambulistic docility dictated solely by the characters.

MLG: In your prologue to *Parelelo 40,* you say, "I confess that many times I devote myself to listening to conversations in the street. I am not embarrassed to do it." Is your work realistic then?

JCP: As you know, one hears many things in the street: good, bad, and average. The problem is one of listening and being capable of hearing and distinguishing things of interest, so they can be sublimated and even transformed later on. I was referring more to being faithful to the words and language of the people. In this sense, I am one of the most interesting writers in Spain today. Not long ago, a book was published by the Gredos publishing firm, the most important publisher of lexicographic manuals. It is called *El español de Castillo Puche* (The Spanish of Castillo Puche) and written by a Canadian professor. In that book, there are something like three hundred phrases and sayings made of very pure, very alive, very spontaneous colloquialisms, which even the Royal Academy has not incorporated into its dictionary. Some of these words were popular in the sixteenth century in villages, inns, farms, and among the shepherds in the mountains. In this respect, I am very much a man of my region, a man of the people. I have incorporated many beautiful words from Murcia, as the poet Miguel Hernández did in his time. I have a special gift for hearing. That is why the most important works being done about me refer precisely to the value of language. Not in the sense that I created language, but rather because the language that I picked up is completely decanted, at its purest, and full of life's experiences.

MLG: You once said: "Literature has abused words, it has combined them, it has polished them, it has repeated them, it has perverted them, it has betrayed them and it has sold them to such an extent that a thorough purification is in order." How can that purification be achieved?

JCP: If you were a coin collector or an avaricious usurer and you saw many coins circulating, and among them were some made of pure silver or dating back to the time of Christ, you would separate these from the others and make a little pile. Overused words are like coins that have lost their markings. When that happens, we have to turn to words that are still rich in meaning. The greatest enemy of words is rhetoric, which is an artifice created by playing on words. To play so elaborately with words is not to take them seriously. Words have their properties and their appropriate moment and instance. Playing with words can be a very amusing and recreational literary game. But I am very loath to play those games. I really like to grab a word by its horns. It is like bullfighting—you have to fight the bull from its difficult side. Words have to be taken seriously. And when a word is weighty and substantial, one has to enjoy it and maybe feel a little satisfied with it.

MLG: And do you like to revise?

JCP: That is a sin. Revising is a sin for me. When the publisher sends me the proofs to a novel that I have already finished, I read them and think the novel is awful and then I begin to rewrite it. So, we have agreed that once he receives a manuscript from me, he doesn't return it to me. Occasionally, I add or subtract so much that the final result is a completely different novel. Yes, I have a conception and an ideal of perfection. What happens is that in life one goes so fast, running madly to and fro, that one is forced to surrender one's work on the street to cries of "Give it over, give it over, it is finished, leave it alone." This does not really agree with the ideals of a writer, who up to the very last minute has to sacrifice them all to the opportunisms of the moment, including considerations of commercial success and publicity prospects. We writers betray our profession to some extent on a daily basis.

MLG: In your novel *Conocerás el poso de la nada,* you have achieved an inner musicality, where several pages can form a single phrase. Can you speak about rhythm, which is so important for you?

JCP: The pulse is internal. As you have ably pointed out, it is like inner, unforced music. I employ a technique that in Spain has been labeled *del berbiquí* (with a drill), because it is akin to that tool craftsmen use to bore delicate, perfect holes, drawing out wood from the opening without spoiling it. I think I have been very consistent in my search in not clinging to the first solution that comes to mind. I search deep within me for a fundamental, almost substantial identity, which is similar in all people. So I try to delve into my soul, to discover ineffable secrets. That is what art consists of: breaking through the outer shell of a thing, through its periphery, to enter into a deeper, quieter, and more serious area. There is music and vibration in this zone, everything is interconnected—it is like a fantastic remembering, because things attract each other. This is where the seeds of beauty and poetry lie. But to achieve this, one has to suffer greatly and be patient; you cannot find what you seek in a hurry.

MLG: Your prose can be harsh but also magnificently poetic. For example: "It must be lovely to fly, it must be like going beneath the water in a river, above the clouds, under the water, swimming, floating, swimming, swimming."

JCP: If you are saying this in context, it does not appear as commonplace or ridiculous as if I began to say "floating, swimming" out of the blue. In this case, the story requires that poetic passage. It is necessary because it reflects a need for an inner escape on the part of this man, who longs for a spiritual flight as a fish. There is a saying by a Chinese poet that is truly astounding: "The world walks on the loins of fish." This is one of the most beautiful, poetic phrases ever written, and truly, poetry and spirituality do float and travel on the loins of fish, on the backs of birds. This may seem a little infantile or puerile, but it is really very serious and profound. The poetry in my work, in all its liberating aspects, is forced upon me, I don't seek it out.

MLG: In one of your novels you said, "Nevertheless, I floundered in a whirlpool of unreality, my will paralyzed." In that work, it is the mother who has the will to live. Do you see the influence of Pío Baroja on your work?

JCP: As you know, Pío Baroja was the sort of man who said, "I am a traveler who took to the road singing and humming. I journey the world with a jacket on my shoulder." Baroja was carefree and a vagabond. Because I have more problems, I suffer more than Baroja; I am a more agonizing pilgrim than he ever was. Fortunate are those without problems! But because of my pathology, my biology, or my spirit, my path is more internal than Don Pío's. His life and his writing techniques have always interested me and he has been a good guide, although I have never been his disciple.

MLG: What about Unamuno?

JCP: I like Unamuno, although he can be very tedious. He belabors and overanalyzes things, and his egocentrism is deleterious. At some point Unamuno is giving a show and he knows it. I think the show is dialectic, speculative, and even a little threatening at times. It can also be blasphemous and yet almost pious, and at the same time virtually ignorant. This is all to Unamuno's credit. His system is logical, while mine is more unconscious. I am a less intelligent breed than Unamuno.

MLG: Your work is a spiritual song to the mother. Do you refer to your mother in particular, or to mothers in general?

JCP: Always to "the mother," in everything I have done. I arrived late into the "real world," because I was studying theology and philosophy, and I was not going to devote myself to mothers or girlfriends or anything of that sort. But when I left the seminary of Comillas, my friends were already university students, and as we walked in the streets or in the gardens, I would say, "Look, that one carries herself like a mother." And they would ask, "What do you mean?" I think I was searching for an ideal of the mother, which I later found. I discovered it in my wife to such an extent that she has become indistinguishable from my own mother. My wife is everything I idealized a mother to be, and this is what I always see in a young girl who is going to be a mother or is someone's girlfriend or wife. There are some women who are very attractive and yet you can immediately tell that they were not born to be mothers. One can be tempted by them, but at a given moment, a man can start seeing and appreciating another type of beauty or gift in these women.

MLG: Has journalism influenced your work?

JCP: Journalism gave me the opportunity to travel the world. You said before that I spent a lot of time behind bars, either at the university or the seminary. But I have also spent some time in jail. When I went to the Congo, I didn't know what I was doing and I got myself into a huge mess. When I first got there, I interviewed Lumumba, who got killed very shortly afterward. I am not a sophisticated man of the world, fluent in many languages—although I did write a good book about the Congo as it became independent. Being slightly confused, I was dashing from one side to the other; first the Soviets were fashionable, they were the liberators of the Congo, then they all left in a hurry. The new authorities, such childish barbarians, then got hold of me and said, "You are Russian. Your eyes look Russian." And I said to myself, "Why would I have Russian eyes?" But they put me in jail, and if the Italian ambassador hadn't found out I was there, I would be raising mallows in the Congo right now.

MLG: You worked for several years at the United Nations. In your novels, you compare its building to a luxury cruiser beached near some rocks. Can you tell us something about that international body?

JCP: I think all experiences are good. I have told you about the Congo and I think my experiences at the United Nations have also taught me a lot. One of the good novels I have written, which people do not read, perhaps because its print is so small and the book is so thick, is *Jeremías el anarquista*. There is a theme of escape in the book, stemming from the ruinous, roughshod desertion of priests, in favor of marriage. These characters are based on the priests and other Spanish exiles whom I met at the United Nations. I remember that I compared that great transparent building that is the United Nations to a fishbowl, a huge fishbowl, because there are a lot of fish there.

MLG: You were a very close friend of Hemingway. What was your reaction when you discovered that Mario Vargas Llosa had won the Hemingway Prize?

JCP: Vargas Llosa deserves every award, but the Hemingway Prize was not decided by great critics or writers. If an Arab wants to give a lot of money in Hemingway's name to laud the Hotel Ritz, that's fine. The Ritz was very attractive for Hemingway. At the end of World War II, he went into Paris before the troops did. That was just a show because he brought some commanders and Spanish madmen with him and went straight to the Hotel Ritz, to the basement, where he proceeded to take all the champagne available, which they sold to him. Later, they brought a lawsuit against him, so the current owner of the Ritz did not really want the prize to carry Hemingway's name, but rather the name of the hotel. Vargas Llosa deserves every praise, he has many virtues as a writer, but he really did not need that prize, particularly since there are writers who have been influenced by Hemingway to a greater extent, not only among Spaniards, but also among Latin Americans, which is important.

MLG: How much has Hemingway influenced your own work?

JCP: In my own work there is nothing more than a great stimulus, certain experiences which I lived with the man and which always heartened me, because he believed in my work from the beginning. In Paris, he spoke with praise about a work of mine, *Con la muerte al hombro,* and this put me on a platform, almost in orbit—it established me. Besides the great empathy, admiration, and devotion I felt for Hemingway, regardless of the fact that I consider *The Old Man and the Sea* an extraordinary legend, constructed like a Homeric poem, despite the incredible power I feel from *For Whom the Bell Tolls* and some of his short stories, which were discussed more thoroughly in Spain, what most impressed me about this man was his inner tragedy. I think he realized that I was not just curious about him, but that I felt an intimate solidarity with him. From the very first, our encounters were friendly. When he was in a bad mood, I preferred not to see him. He cursed a lot, as I did, and we would both become very angry. But there were some very tender, affectionate moments with him. I will never forget that when I was bored in Spain, he came to me and said, "You have to go to Cuba and spend some time with me, and then you will go and watch the shepherds." I wrote a novel on those shepherds because Hemingway gave me a grant to travel through Cuba. So I am very grateful, enormously grateful, but I am also very sad because he was a very good friend who was very unhappy. I knew he led a very dramatic existence, and I foresaw he was going to kill himself. Although he could have done it in any number of ways, he chose what he thought would be the quietest, but, of course, he made a great deal of noise. An explosion of that sort in one's head always makes a great deal of noise.

MLG: Are you writing another novel?

JCP: Yes, one cannot live in the desert. Whenever I am writing, I always wait for the rain or whatever to come, so I can begin to write a novel. I am writing a novel, but it is very different from all the others I have written.

MLG: In what way?

JCP: I don't speak about the Civil War, priests, or prostitutes—I don't even mention childhood or the mother.

MLG: Then what is it about?

JCP: That is a problem. I can't tell you because it is a kind of macabre fantasy that occurred to me. It is related to the night, it is a definitive study of the night. Not one night, but all nights. From the time that nights were born, I want to tell what happened in them, what they mean for human beings. So there is a lot one can do with that, and I explore many angles, from the medieval facet, with its terrible people, to certain areas of the night when

dawn begins and when there is a light, a transparency, an ineffable something. So I try to bring myself closer to the elemental forces, to the divine
nature. We were speaking before about fish and birds. One has to be close to
fire, air, wind, clouds, storms, and snow. This can give new meaning to
many dark, hermetic, and almost indescribable areas of the soul.

MLG: How is a novel born?

JCP: In the silliest way; I don't think about the sort of novel I am going to
write. A novel is born from an encounter, from a phrase, a character, or a
place one visited. And then one thing leads to another. When I begin a
novel, I don't have a theme prepared: this is going to begin this way and end
that way. It starts one way and it finishes as God wills, because the good
novel writes itself.

MLG: Why do you like to write trilogies? You don't believe in the novel
as a separate entity?

JCP: I don't like to think of novels as isolated occurrences, written at
random. I feel that one's commitment to a novel must reflect a long process.
I conceive it as a cycle that encompasses a global view of the world, in
which characters journey through life. I am interested in giving a full picture
of my characters, their inner thoughts, emotions, struggles, their relationship to the world that surrounds them, and their sense of adventure as they
tackle that world. I am not concerned with a peripheral vision of things; I
would rather approach my characters from within. My intention is to give
my writings the shape of a vertical line that slowly finds its place at the core
of things. I feel no urge to follow the easy flow of a horizontal line. I consider
the total scope of my work, whether it is one or more novels, as fragments
and pieces of the same obsessions and restlessness. For that reason, each of
my novels is part of a whole. I have followed in the footsteps of Galdós, the
French, the Italians, and the Russians who designed their novels in an all-
encompassing architectural structure. For me, it's not a necessity to follow
the pattern of a trilogy, but yes, I find it fundamental to have a flow and continuity that run throughout my novels and that reflect the human condition.
An isolated novel may have the magic of a winning number at the lottery,
but it does not represent a heroic determination, persistence, and fore-
sightedness.

MLG: Turning to another form of art, is painting important to you?

JCP: Yes, I have said that Hemingway wrote through Goya, and under
the influence of Cézanne also, but particularly of Goya. I would have liked
to have been a painter. From time to time I draw some things. But I do the
same thing with them that I do with my poems: I rip them up, because they
are only an outlet. I am very friendly with painters, because they say I
understand a lot about painting. If I ever run out of ideas for novels, I will
probably be a great art critic, because I have written a book on a very good
Mediterranean painter from Spain, Paco Lozano. I've been friendly with
many painters, including Miró. I have always been close to painting, and in

my home there is an atmosphere imbued with art, because I have a daughter who is both a poet and a painter, although she would kill me if she heard me describing her as a painter. She is an important poet in Spain, but she paints as well. Except that she hides her paintings instead of destroying them, and maybe someday she'll sell them.

MLG: How do you feel about music?

JCP: With respect to music, I have one ear in front of the other. Music may be very beautiful, but personally I find it very alienating. I probably don't know how to appreciate music, although I cannot write without it. People who come to visit me always leave a little crazed, because my taste for music doesn't fall outside certain parameters. I like Sephardic music, Gregorian chants, and Bach, but I don't go beyond the sixteenth century in my musical taste. So when I walk along the streets of New York and see a youth with a screw loose, blasting loud and barbaric music, I look at him with such eyes that he feels compelled to turn the volume down.

MLG: You are very good friends with Carmen Conde. What can you say about her?

JCP: What I said earlier about my concept of the mother also applies to Carmen; she is like a mother image to me. She was one of the people who supported my candidacy to the Royal Academy of the Spanish Language. I cannot forget this. But I have always been closely linked with her. Before the Civil War (I was sixteen years old), there was a contest at the Universidad Popular of Cartagena, which both Carmen and her husband founded, and I sent a work of mine that won a prize. They gave me a watch with the inscription "Gift of the Universidad Popular de Cartagena," and a cash prize of five thousand pesetas. That was quite a bit of money in those days, and thanks to it I was able to bring a cake home several Sundays in a row. So I am very grateful to her. During the war, I helped her get a safe-conduct to go to Madrid, as I had some influence in these matters. We have seen a lot of each other since. Recently I wrote to her, because I found an article by her dating from around 1942 amidst some of my own papers. I am very fond of Carmen Conde, and not only because she backed me with the Academy. Murcia belongs to an autonomous region, which includes both the city of Murcia and the city of Cartagena, which have a long-standing rivalry. We have broken through all this; she has come to Murcia and I went to Cartagena. We created friendship and affection between the two. She took me to the windmills of Cartagena and I took her to the orchards of Murcia, where they have started raising silkworms once again. I think it is very important to say that Carmen Conde is not only a vibrant, powerful, and substantive poet of pain and pleasure, but also that she has written some very good stories.

Camilo
José Cela

GENE LUTTENBERG

Camilo José Cela Trulock was born in 1916 in Iria Flavia, in the province of La Coruña, in Galicia. His father was Galician, his mother English, and his grandmother Italian. As he says, "I was born within the boundaries of a definite culture, with one foot in another. No one is Galician, Chinese, Serbian, or even part British as I am, by choice, and you have to live with it." Cela studied law, medicine, and philosophy and, among many other things, worked as a journalist and an actor.

One of the most outstanding masters of contemporary prose, although little known in the United States, he received from the hands of King Carl Gustaf of Sweden the Gold Medal of the Nobel Prize for 1989, the highest recognition for his literary achievement. In his presentation speech for the stately ceremony, Knut Ahnlund said of him, "Cela has revitalized the language as few people have done in these times. He has joined the ranks of such masters of the Spanish language as Cervantes, Góngora, Quevedo, Valle Inclán and García Lorca." In his acceptance speech, he declared, "I am going to tell you exactly what I set out to say, without leaving the slightest chance to inspiration and improvisation, two notions which I despise." And he read a twelve-page speech in which he said that Quevedo, Cervantes, Baroja, and Valle Inclán would have also deserved the Nobel Prize. He stressed that it was important that the government take action to protect the Castilian language from foreign influences, the way France had done with French.

Cela has been called "the father of *tremendismo*," a title he has categorically rejected because, in his own words, "*tremendismo* is as old as literature." He finds his roots in Spanish tradition and his sense of realism is reminiscent of the picaresque novel of Quevedo or the paintings of Goya. As a person, he is known for his nonconformism; he likes to shock people

77

and entertain them, although he insists that he should not be confused with his characters.

His first novel, *La familia de Pascual Duarte,* 1942 (*The Family of Pascual Duarte,* 1946), brought about the revival of the postwar Spanish novel. This particular work is the most widely read Spanish novel after Cervantes's *Don Quixote,* yet all the publishers he saw when he was a young man tried to dissuade him from writing. With *La colmena,* 1951 (*The Hive,* 1953), he braved the censorship of the Franco regime, and with the use of the three hundred characters or so that appear in that novel he described the bleak life of Madrileños during those postwar years.

From 1956 to 1979, Cela directed *Papeles de Son Armadans,* a magazine he had created, which became one of Spain's most important literary outlets during the years of repression. In 1957, he was elected to the Spanish Royal Academy. After the death of Franco, he was appointed by King Juan Carlos to serve as senator in the parliament in 1977 and 1978, and he played an important part in the drafting of the Spanish constitution.

Just as the three initials C.J.C. represent a perfect symmetry in his name, there exists a perfect balance in his work. It embraces all the literary genres, from poetry, with which he started, to essays, travelogues, memoirs, plays, short stories, and novels. He is the author of more than one hundred books, including *Pabellón de reposo,* 1943 (*Rest Home,* 1961); *Esas nubes que pasan* (The Clouds That Pass By), 1945; *Viaje a la Alcarria,* 1948 (*Journey to the Alcarria,* 1964); *Mrs. Caldwell habla con su hijo,* 1953 (*Mrs. Caldwell Speaks to Her Son,* 1968); *Gavilla de fábulas sin amor* (A Batch of Loveless Tales), 1962, with illustrations by Picasso; *San Camilo, 1936,* 1969; *María Sabina,* a play set to music by Leonardo Balada that premiered at Carnegie Hall on 17 April 1970; *Diccionario secreto* (Dictionary of Forbidden Words), 1968, 1971; *Oficio de tinieblas 5* (Service of Darkness, no. 5), 1973; *Rol de cornudos* (Catalogue of Cuckolds), 1976; *Mazurca para dos muertos* (Mazurka for Two Dead People), 1983, for which he received the 1984 National Prize for Literature; *El asno de Buridán* (Buridan's Donkey), 1986; *Nuevo viaje a la Alcarria* (New Journey to the Alcarria), 1986; *Cristo versus Arizona* (Christ versus Arizona), 1988.

Cela possesses an incredible capacity for work. He reads and writes more than ten hours a day, and still finds time to give lectures that are vivid portrayals of his wit.

He has received many honors both at home and abroad. In 1981, for instance, during a trip to the United States, he was made an honorary citizen of Texas as well as of Tucson, Arizona. Many streets and town squares bear his name, and he holds an impressive list of honorary degrees from many universities, among them the University of Syracuse (which he refers to as his Alma Mater), the University of Birmingham, the University of John F. Kennedy (Buenos Aires), the University of Palma de Mallorca, the University of Santiago de Compostela, the Universidad Interamericana (Puerto Rico), and the Hebrew University of Jerusalem.

Cela has enjoyed the friendship of many writers and artists, including Baroja, Hemingway, Picasso, and Miró. From 1954 to 1989 he lived in Palma de Mallorca; he now resides in Guadalajara. His son, whose name is also Camilo José Cela, recently published a book about his father, *Cela mi padre.*

It was in Puerto Rico that I met Cela for the first time. Since then, I have seen him in New York, Madrid, and Majorca. He took me around his two homes, overlooking the sea. The walls were covered with a wide range of paintings from Zabaleta to Miró. In the house next door, which Cela bought to accommodate his very large private library, there was a huge portrait of him by John Ulbricht, the American artist who lives in Majorca. The walls around the patio were covered with street signs all named after him. On a separate wall, Picasso had painted a huge mural especially for him. He showed me his dogs (a Persian greyhound and three Airedale terriers) and the parrots that live in semiliberty in the back of the garden. Cela welcomed me warmly. He had just come back from a fitting at his tailor. Although he commented on his having lost sixty pounds, he still had the same imposing figure. Holding his latest book in his big, forceful hands, he autographed it for me in his delicate handwriting. He also addressed an envelope for me with the seal of "cartero honorario," which grants him the special privilege of not having to use stamps on his personal mail. He told me anecdotes in a jovial tone and punctuated the last word of many sentences with laughter.

❖❖❖❖❖❖❖❖❖❖❖❖❖❖❖❖❖❖❖❖❖❖❖❖❖❖❖❖❖❖❖

MLG: I guess congratulations are in order. How does it feel to be a Nobel Prize-winner?

CJC: I was astonished and delighted. I had been nominated for many years, so I expected it and didn't expect it. I thought to myself, if I get it, I get it, and if not, what can I do about it?

MLG: Has the prize changed your life?

CJC: It's very important not to change your way of life: one should remain consistent and not lose perspective. Don't forget that I am part British, and that the British practice self-control and don't show their emotions. Right now, I am overwhelmed with phone calls, telegrams, letters, and the like, but I think it will soon pass, and I'll be able to work the way I always have. I'm very happy to have won the Nobel Prize, of course.

MLG: Is this a personal triumph?

CJC: Anyone could have won. I accept it on behalf of all Spanish-speaking writers. I only wish that some of my good friends like Picasso and Pío Baroja could be here to enjoy this moment with me.

MLG: What are your plans for the future?

CJC: I am going to keep writing, which is what really matters to me. Winning the prize was an important step for me, but not an end in itself: the only end is death.

MLG: You have been called a nonconformist, the enfant terrible of twentieth-century Spanish letters; nevertheless, you adhere to tradition. Can one be a nonconformist and a traditionalist at the same time?

CJC: Yes, naturally, apart from the fact that nonconformism is also a form of tradition. In Spain, the best thinkers have always been nonconformists. A line can be traced from the archpriests of Hita and Talavera down through our times. Of all the writers in that line, Quevedo is the leader who has raised the flag high for nonconformity.

MLG: Your maternal great-grandfather was called Camilo Bertorini, your father's name is Camilo, your mother's is Camila, you are Camilo José, so is your son, and now your first granddaughter is also called Camila. The tradition of Camilos and Camilas apparently goes on.

CJC: My granddaughter is a very strong, healthy baby, which is the most that anyone can want. She is a Taurus, like her grandmother and myself. She was born on May 8, I was born on May 11, and Charo, her grandmother, on May 13.

MLG: What does the name Camilo represent in your family?

CJC: It means a lot, and it happened by chance. My mother was British, although the name Camila can neither be written nor pronounced in English. It came from the Italian side of her family. My great-grandfather, whose name was Camilo, was an Italian who came to Spain. It just happened that my parents were called Camilo and Camila. In my father's family, the oldest son has always been named Camilo. I believe it is not tradition but a habit.

MLG: Why is it so important for you to play with the names of your characters and to give them nicknames? You even play with your own, adding David and Levi to your already long list of baptismal names.

CJC: I do not play with names. I use nicknames a lot because in Spain almost everybody has one. I took most of these names from books such as *Santoral cristiano* (Lives of the Saints) and *Martirologio romano* (Roman Martyrology), where the names are absolutely foolish. In Spain they are even more so, for there are truly dramatic names dedicated to the Blessed Virgin, such as Dolores, Angustias, Consolación, Visitación, and there is also Circuncisión, which is worse.

MLG: Why is it so fundamental for you to write new introductions to the numerous editions of each of your books?

CJC: Because my impressions change with the passage of time—what I think today is not necessarily what I will think tomorrow. But recently I haven't been writing as many as before. I used the introductions to speak about aesthetics. Occasionally, the publishers insist that I write a prologue, and I eventually give in to their demands.

MLG: You have said, "Literature is a test tube handled by an ignorant chemist who mixes products and temperatures, and one does not know if the end product will be a colorless ointment that cures itches, or a green, orange or black-colored explosive that kills one's fellowmen." Have your two volumes of the *Diccionario secreto* and *Rol de cornudos* been explosive?

CJC: No, I think my books are very constructive. The two volumes of the *Diccionario secreto* are derived from classical Latin, *col colius,* which in colloquial Latin is *colio colionis;* and from the Roman onomatopeia *pis,* which served to teach people how to speak in Spanish. And the *Rol de cornudos* can be truly useful in classifying the world around us. There are many types of *cornudos* (cuckolds), according to Charles Fourier, the French socialist who also classified them in his day, and to whom I dedicated this book. I found many more. There was only one type that I missed, which was the anarchist cuckold. Of course that is an unacceptable concept, for to be a cuckold one has to allow for institutions.

MLG: How many other "explosions" have you devised, and how many have detonated?

CJC: None, I never set booby traps. Sometimes people are scandalized by a book or a page of mine, as they may also be with the works of other authors. What we don't know is whether there are a greater number of scandalous or scandalized people in Spain. Often people are shocked simply because someone says hello in the street. We should not overlook this. On the other hand, to be shocking is nothing new in Spanish literature. The two archpriests and Quevedo, in his satirical poems, say things that would make people blush were it not for the beauty and nobility of the language.

MLG: Have you cured any itches with the colorless ointment I mentioned before?

CJC: I guess so. In any case, I wrote a work extensive enough so that it might remedy at least some evils, if not all.

MLG: You have been a reporter, a poet, a bullfighter, a movie actor, a painter and a vagabond (these are the words with which you are described in *Who's Who in Spanish Letters*). Why did you become a writer?

CJC: It is not true that I have been all these things, although I have tried my luck at all of them. I never wanted to be a bullfighter or a soccer player. I enjoyed seeing bullfights and soccer games, as well as acting in several very poor movies. But to draw the conclusion that I have been a bullfighter, a soccer player, or an actor is highly inaccurate. To say that I was a journalist is a different story, because I did write. I contributed short stories and essays to newspapers and magazines. In that sense, I was a journalist but not a news reporter.

MLG: Do you still write articles?

CJC: Yes, I write long articles for *El Independiente,* which takes me three days every week. If I go on a trip or have some other commitment to fulfill, then I don't have the time for that. I call my column "Desde el palomar de Hita" (From the Pigeon-House in Hita), after the name of the town where the great medieval poet, the Archpriest Juan Ruiz, lived. It's a generic heading, but everything fits under it. The articles are more literary pieces than critical essays, so there is a lot of narration with some thought also thrown in, of course. I try to express my views on some issue or another, I cover many topics.

MLG: You have said, "The writer is a man whose soul needs every kind of nourishment." Do you find themes for your books in your own experience or from the world that surrounds you?

CJC: I find my material everywhere. I observe some aspect of reality, which my mind transforms, forcing me to move the pen upon the paper, which in turn produces the phenomenon we call literature. Of course, I do not think that initial reality can be recognized in my books. First of all, it would be unfair merely to imitate a passerby. Secondly, it would be dangerous artistically. Finally, that reality has become remote, because the work has been fictionalized through the imagination. Someone took an inventory of the real and fictitious characters in *The Hive,* and the real characters outweigh the fictitious ones by a margin of 3 percent.

MLG: What is realism for you?

CJC: Realism for me is everything that can be perceived with the senses or intuited. It can be assumed that realism encompasses surrealism and subrealism. Not just what man is aware of, but what came before and what will come after. Whether we are able to reflect this is another question. The subconscious is also a form of reality, even though we may not be able to articulate or interpret it.

MLG: How would you define the worlds contained in a book then?

CJC: I think they reflect particular aspects of reality, from one end of the spectrum to the other. These reflections are what make up the novels, which very often have little anecdotes as the vessels that link the action, although this is not necessary. I have written some novels with no plots, such as *Oficio de tinieblas 5,* where I locked myself in a dark room to elicit the necessary feelings of anxiety.

MLG: You have compared literature to a ship, saying, "It is a pirate vessel, without a flag and without lifeboats. . . . It is a ship that sails because God so wishes." But you also write, "It is a boat without destination . . . in which each man rows as he is so inclined." Are you religious? Do you see literature as a divine inspiration or as a profession in which one never rests?

CJC: As neither. I do not believe that God makes us write. I think that there are very few people, perhaps none, who write under divine inspiration. To write, one must work hard, be patient and persistent. But writing should not be considered strictly a profession, because the writer would turn into a caricature of himself if he decided to do nothing more than put out a certain number of pages a day. That would be unfortunate, particularly if it led to his demise. There have been many writers throughout the history of litera- ture who have written their own epitaphs because they do nothing but plagiarize themselves. Because of this, I try to use a different technique in each of the novels that I write, so as not to fall into a regular pattern or become sterile. But to get back to your question, the only profession I would want as a man is precisely to be a man, a human being. Everything else would be secondary.

MLG: Your books are all different in terms of techniques.

CJC: I think the technique of a book is like the scaffolding used to build a cathedral, something necessary which later disappears. When the cathedral stands, it is time to take the scaffold down. In a book, the technique is absorbed, otherwise it would remain a mere experiment.

MLG: So the technique is there, but it cannot be seen . . .

CJC: Or it shouldn't be seen, or not too much, but of course it does exist.

MLG: You are both a lyrical and a comic troubadour, and seem almost embarrassed to express your tender feelings. Why do you cover them up with irony and caricatures?

CJC: I don't know. It may be a defense mechanism that prevents me from exposing myself, but I am not sure. I would have to study myself objectively. In any case, it seems to be a constant in my work that many critics have pointed out, but which I did not think I should redress. Something similar happened to Cervantes with *Don Quixote.* Each time he used an elegant adjective, he followed it with a colloquial synonym, thinking that the reader would perhaps understand it better.

MLG: Picasso once said, "When one is truly young, one is young for one's whole life."

CJC: Picasso told me this when he celebrated his ninetieth birthday. I said to him, "I find you very young, Pablo," and he replied, "You are wrong, Camilo José; when a man is young at heart then he is young for his whole life." This is beautiful because he died at a very old age and still he was young at heart.

MLG: How did you manage to recapture the freshness of your childhood years in *La rosa,* where you recount the first six years of your life with great sensitivity and grace?

CJC: It is a biography of my early childhood and my wonderfully foolish family. I hold that memory dear because I was a very happy little boy who lived a golden childhood. I remember those years fondly and nostalgically. My aunts used to ask me, "What would you like to be when you grow up?" and I would cry because I did not want anything—I did not want to grow up. I was very content just being a little boy. I would have been happy to remain five or six years old forever in beautiful, pastoral, rustic Galicia.

MLG: What does Galicia mean for you?

CJC: A lot, of course. A person is never born in a vacuum. One is not just Galician, Greek, or Chinese by birth; we carry that heritage with us all our lives, for better or for worse. In my case, I trust that it was all for the good, of course. Since we are all products of the family we were born into, and my mother was British, my father was Galician, and my grandmother Italian, all those elements have influenced my development.

MLG: How do you feel being a mixture of those three elements?

CJC: Very comfortable, very comfortable.

MLG: Do you feel more Galician or Spanish?

CJC: Both, they are two different spheres. Although one remains the same, the diameter of the sphere increases, from Iria Flavia to Padrón, Galicia, the Kingdom of Spain, Europe, and finally the world.

MLG: The Galicia West Railway was designed by your great-grandfather Camilo Bertorini, and your grandfather John Trulock was its manager. Since the train played such an important role in your family, have you ever thought of writing a story, novel, or poem in which it would be the main character?

CJC: I don't know if I have not already used it somewhere. The train was my great-grandfather's property. It was the line that ran from Pontevedra to Santiago, an eighty-kilometer run. The railway sustained the family. Later, a young engineer was brought over from England. His name was John Trulock, my grandfather-to-be, and he married the owner's daughter, which was the normal, sensible thing to do, because everything remained in the family that way. This is a great idea, and I think that young engineers should always marry the daughter of the owners.

MLG: You have said that before you learned how to write, you were already dictating verses to others. If poetry was your first love, why did you abandon it, even though not completely, to write in prose?

CJC: As a matter of principle. One is never faithful to one's first love. Very often we prose writers begin by writing poetry, although there have been many who have not written a single verse in their lives. I started out writing in verse, and I enjoyed it, until some of my friends who ran the literary section of a magazine in Madrid heard me tell some anecdotes in a café. They asked me, "Why don't you write some stories?" This was at the end of the Spanish Civil War. "I don't know," I replied, "I think that I am a better poet," to which they said, "We insist that you write at least one story." I then wrote "Don Anselmo." They liked it, and asked me for more. That's how I began to develop a liking for prose. These first stories prior to *The Family of Pascual Duarte* are collected in a book entitled *Esas nubes que pasan.* They are included in my complete works. I have never rejected a single page I have written because I do not like the attitude of writers who have complete works that are not really complete.

MLG: You see poetry and prose as two branches of the same tree. Could you talk about that relationship?

CJC: The novel encompasses poetry and, in some way, all poetry also encompasses the novel. *El cantar de Mío Cid,* for instance, is a very long poem, but it is also a chronicle or a novel because it gives an account of many events. The same thing is true of Jorge Manrique's "Coplas a la muerte de su padre" (Eulogy at the Death of His Father). Medieval poets were extraordinary. They have greatly influenced me and everyone else. Let's not forget that, contrary to what is claimed by literary historians, Boccaccio's *Decameron* was not the first novel to be published; it was *El Conde Lucanor,* by Prince Don Juan Manuel. I have never believed in literary genres, and I do even less as time goes on. These genres are very comfortable for professors and critics; they are a sort of literary etymology, a way of pinning a little tag on us with a Latin name on it, if at all possible. But that is a lie.

MLG: Is that the reason why rhythm is so important in your novels?

CJC: Of course, as it should be in any work. I have always said that to be a prose writer one has to have a far better ear than a poet or a musician, because the rhythm of prose is considerably more mysterious than that of music, which usually follows a set pattern.

MLG: Do you speak out loud what you write?

CJC: I write by hand and usually read my text aloud as I put it together, because that way I can catch many stylistic imperfections, repetitions, and discordant sounds. These things are more discernible through the ear than through the eye.

MLG: How can you explain the affinities between your work and the picaresque novel?

CJC: I think it was Virginia Woolf who said that all later novels are derived from the Spanish picaresque novel. I think literature is culture, not just the spontaneous product of a generation. Every generation carries the torch as far as it can, and then it hands it over to the next one. Technically speaking, writers today know far more than authors of the seventeenth, eighteenth, and nineteenth centuries. Whether they are as good now as they were back then depends on the talents of a particular writer. But any high school student knows about the circulatory system, which Hippocrates and his great school of doctors in Greece were unaware of. Culture is transmitted, and the picaresque novel has its place for various causes and reasons. The picaresque novel is astonishing, from *Lazarillo de Tormes* (although some people argue it is not a picaresque novel) to a more erudite work like Quevedo's *El Buscón.* However, I don't believe in labels very much.

MLG: Do you think Cervantes handed you his torch?

CJC: Yes, but all the writers in between us also carried it. The torch was around even before Cervantes, of course. It has been passed from generation to generation, and I will probably hand it to someone, whoever he is. It's like a relay race.

MLG: Do you identify with Cervantes in any way?

CJC: *Don Quixote* is a perfect work, a true wonder. I never tire of admiring it; so yes, I do identify with its author. If I could speak to him, I would congratulate him and tell him of my healthy envy at his having produced such a masterpiece.

MLG: If you could speak to another great writer from the past, whom would you choose?

CJC: Quevedo. I think he is the most astonishing writer the Spanish language has ever had. I would undoubtedly ask him how he was able to achieve this and master all the things he knew.

MLG: Do you have followers?

CJC: I don't know. When people ask me the opposite question of who my influences were, I always reply that they were all the authors who wrote before me, not just in Spanish but even in languages I don't know. All writers have undoubtedly influenced me, and we will all probably influence those who come after us.

MLG: Who are some of the people who helped you when you started out as a writer?

CJC: The three people who helped me the most were Pablo Neruda, María Zambrano, and Pedro Salinas. María Zambrano paid particular attention to me, encouraging me to keep writing. She is still alive, although the others have died.

MLG: Your first works were published in Argentina, for political reasons. Do you think that sometimes censorship can have a positive effect on the development of imagination because it causes mental exercises worthy of a tightrope walker?

CJC: My first poems were published in Argentina by pure chance. This was before the Spanish Civil War. They were poems written when I was eighteen or nineteen years old (in 1935), and they were first published in *Argentino,* a newspaper of Río de la Plata, and then in a literary magazine called *Fábula.* They had been sent to Luis Enrique Délano, director of those publications. But *The Family of Pascual Duarte* was published in Buenos Aires in 1944 for political reasons, because the second edition, published in Spain in 1943, was not allowed to circulate. Later, *The Hive* was also published there, when it was censored in Spain. Each time I lost a fight with a censor, I considered it a personal failure. When words and sentences were crossed out from my manuscripts, I felt I was being persecuted. I can't forget how the chief censor in Spain boasted that as long as he held his post, "Mr. Cela would never publish a single book."

MLG: Wasn't Luis Enrique Délano a friend of Gabriela Mistral?

CJC: He was the Secretary of the Chilean Consulate, first under Gabriela Mistral and later under Pablo Neruda. He was a fellow student in the Universidad Central of Madrid. The last time I saw him he was living in exile in Mexico because he had been the Chilean ambassador to Sweden during the time of Allende. Naturally, when the Allende regime fell he did not return to Chile.

MLG: You have said that the writer has two rules: to write and to wait. His best accomplice is time. Upon publishing *The Family of Pascual Duarte* in 1942, did you think it would bring about the revival of the Spanish novel and that you would become the most illustrious of prose writers?

CJC: No, not at all. I did not even write this novel with the intent of having it published. Actually, I was writing a chapter a day because a sister of my wife, who was my girlfriend then, was sick and I used to read her the novel. Each time she would grow worse, poor thing. It was not a soothing balm but the complete opposite. I did not think it would be published because at first all the editors refused it. Publishing is the profession that produces the most jackasses in the entire world. I can now say with pride that *The Family of Pascual Duarte* is the most translated Spanish work after *Don Quixote*. It has even been translated into Latin. I carried my manuscript under my arm for two years, and publishers told me the same old nonsense they always tell young writers: "You are young, you can still change professions. Thank you very much. You must understand that this is a business enterprise and that your book could barely sell ten or twelve copies. I am sorry." And so it was for two years, until it was published thanks to Rafael Aldecoa, who was the son of General Ibañez de Aldecoa, the owner of a very conservative and conventional publishing house. Rafael lived in Madrid and that month his father had not sent him any money because they had quarreled, and he told me, "Since my father is never aware of what is published in his firm, let's pull this one on him to teach him." And that's how the novel was published by Aldecoa. Its success came later and I was the first one to be pleased by it, of course.

MLG: You do not like the title of "father of *tremendismo*" that has been applied to you. Would you be against being called a chronicler of your time and your people?

CJC: No, this is what I would aspire to be. *Tremendismo* is a sexton's term that was created to be used against me by one of the so-called very proper critics in my country, with the purpose of picking a quarrel with me. Later on, people in foreign countries used that term affectionately when they spoke of me, so it has now turned against him and in my favor. But I think the term does not mean anything. This attitude attributed to me is a constant in all Spanish literature, even as far back as the sixteenth and seventeenth centuries. There is such a thing as chronological order which should be respected.

MLG: What do you think of critics?

CJC: As with everything in the vineyard of the Lord, there are intelligent critics and there are critics who just want to look good, and they are very confusing. On occasion, I have read a review of one of my books where the critic spoke very highly of me, and lavishly heaped adjectives on my work. And at the end I had to say, I am very grateful, but how much more grateful I would have been if he had actually read the book! This is very dangerous.

Frequently, university professors and doctoral students write theses on my work that are more coherent than those penned by newspaper reviewers. The opposite can also be true, however, so I do not think we can draw any general conclusions.

MLG: Do you believe authors always write autobiographical works?

CJC: Yes, in some sense they always do, undoubtedly. An author always writes the same work, with variations and degrees of maturity. Although he may not identify completely with his characters, there is something in common between them. A true novelist is capable of unfolding himself in ways that a chronicler cannot. The chronicler limits himself to reflecting what he sees from moment to moment, while the novelist creates his characters as needed and gives them the freedom to act. But with these qualifications, I would say that an author's work is always the same.

MLG: Do you ever conceive your works geometrically?

CJC: I suppose they would be polyhedrons with multiple vertices. I think you would have to work hard to find the exact geometric representation for each of my books. I have always believed in the geometric aspect of everything, not only in biology, where we clearly see that the molecules of any body adopt distinctive geometric shapes (snowflakes, for instance, and let's not speak about the wonder of flowers or insects), but even in fate. What happens is that we are probably still far from discovering this formula. Just because we haven't arrived at it does not mean it doesn't exist—the earth was round long before man realized it.

MLG: As an author, where do you situate yourself in your works?

CJC: Probably in all places and in none, probably underlying each word.

MLG: So you are inside the book . . .

CJC: I suppose, I suppose so.

MLG: Not outside . . .

CJC: No, not outside, inside. I think this happens with all sincere, genuine authors.

MLG: As a good father of your novels, do you have a favorite child?

CJC: I would like to answer you truthfully, but I don't know. It is the same as asking a father or mother of several children who is their favorite— they would be unable to answer. Furthermore, it would not be strange for the father or mother of several children to prefer not the best, nor the brightest, nor the strongest or most handsome of their children, but instead the weakest, the one who would need their help the most. What I can say is that I don't regret any of the pages that I have published. I have a fondness for *The Family of Pascual Duarte* because it was the book that broke the ice for me. I think that *The Hive* is better constructed, that *San Camilo* is better written, and perhaps that *Oficio de tinieblas* has achieved a level of perfection that I did not have before. This is a logical progression, because as time passes, a writer gains in wisdom what he loses in freshness or vigor. But I should not complain. It is the law of life. One must know how to take advantage of every situation and every moment. I also have a liking for *Journey to the Alcarria,* because it is about the first trip I made on foot through Spain.

MLG: You have written over one hundred books. Do you have a favorite character?

CJC: I would have to reiterate that a question such as this is like asking the father of many children which one he likes best. For one reason or another, I have many favorite characters. I am very grateful to Pascual Duarte, as I just said, and also to Martín Marco, an indispensable character of *The Hive.* But I shouldn't forget to mention Mrs. Caldwell, Catira, or any of the multiple characters of *San Camilo, 1936.* No, I could not pick a favorite character.

MLG: You speak about them as if they were real people.

CJC: Yes, of course, as if they had been alive. I make them concrete. A book really starts to exist for me when I place the last period and the work gets published. My characters have become objectified. I consider them my friends, although I could also see them as my enemies (which I don't). In any case, they are far removed from me personally, which I think is a healthy thing.

MLG: Do you continue talking with your characters once the books have been published?

CJC: Naturally. I have a book entitled *Los viejos amigos* (The Old Friends), in which I continue the lives and actions of several of my characters from previous novels. I could talk to them forever.

MLG: Do they talk to you too?

CJC: Perhaps, it would depend on which ones. I am not in their shoes. I don't know, I suppose they do.

MLG: You speak of the free will of your characters and you treat them as old friends. However, sometimes you refer to them as if they were puppets. Which ones have become independent of you, having rebelled and won their freedom?

CJC: All of them. The first one I realized had done it was Pascual Duarte. I wrote an outline with all the development, chapter by chapter, of *The Family of Pascual Duarte,* saying what had to take place in each chapter, the anecdotes and even some situations. I can assure you that, before I finished the first chapter, Pascual Duarte had rebelled and gone off on his own. As a result, I carefully threw my notes into the wastepaper basket, for I realized that they were absolutely useless. I believe that when a character is created well, the task of the novelist is to follow him and report on what he does as his chronicler, open the door for him and let him loose. That is the best way of writing a novel. There remains the possibility of controlling characters in subliterary genres such as adventure novels, detective stories, sentimental novels, cowboy stories, and science fiction.

MLG: Why is Pascual Duarte such a violent character?

CJC: The world made him crazy. There were many young men like him at the end of the Spanish Civil War.

MLG: What do you think about all the violence in the world today?

CJC: It is the result of living in large cities. I now espouse the theory that big cities are responsible for the downfall of humanity. That's because people don't know each other in large cities, so they are more prone to be violent.

MLG: I remember that in 1981 you went to Arizona. Was that the basis for your book *Cristo versus Arizona?*

CJC: Yes, I was very taken with that state. Arizona has always been, and continues to be, the state with the most native Americans. There are many reservations, which you can see from the streets of Tucson. And let's not forget that the chief of the Chiricahua Apache tribe, Cochise, kept the men of the Seventh Cavalry Regiment (who were not charitable monks) at bay for five years in Arizona.

MLG: Are you writing a novel now?

CJC: To speak about works in progress is very dangerous. I am not superstitious, but there are some writers who have a fear of such things. In 1916, the year of my birth, Ortega y Gasset mentioned the title of his next book in a footnote to one volume of *El Expectador*—the book never came out. It would be pedantic or naive to play the game of publishers, to make statements to the press about books in order to make a few more pesetas. I have always said novels don't really exist until they have been published and placed in the hands of the readers. Until that happens, any piece of writing is but a futile project.

MLG: But you have talked about your forthcoming book, *Madera de boj.*

CJC: In the same way that *Mazurca para dos muertos* was my homage to landlocked Galicia, *Madera de boj* will be my tribute to Galicia on the seaboard. But we shouldn't talk about a work until it is finished, because we don't know how it may turn out. There is an anecdote about two people waiting at the door of a church to watch a procession and they wonder what religious figure will come out first. As the old Spanish saying goes, "If it comes out with a beard, it's Saint Anton, and if not, the Immaculate Conception." The same is true of my writings. If I haven't finished writing a book, it does not exist. Although I work hard and write a lot, something is always bound to be left behind.

MLG: An edition of *The Hive,* with illustrations by Lorenzo Goñi, came out on your birthday. Do you like it?

CJC: It's very beautiful. Nowadays, books are published with great care. Lorenzo Goñi is an excellent artist, very closely linked with my work. He has illustrated many of my books. We became friends shortly after the Civil War ended. It is difficult to communicate with him because he is a deaf-mute. He has learned to speak, but the pitch of his voice is very shrill, making it a bit hard to understand him.

MLG: Your son just wrote a book about you.

CJC: He is a professor and dean of the Department of Philosophy at the University of Palma de Mallorca. He is more of an essayist than a novelist. His book is called *Cela mi padre* and I like it very much. He wrote it from memory, although he occasionally asked me to clarify some things.

MLG: How do you come up with the titles for your books?

CJC: They come to me all of a sudden, and usually before I write the book. I start with the title and then proceed. If I didn't already have a title, it would be more difficult to write a book, although not impossible. Sometimes I modify my initial title as the book unfolds.

MLG: Why did you call your first book *The Family of Pascual Duarte,* when in fact there is only the semblance of a family?

CJC: I made a mistake there. I came up with the title before I started the book, and then I didn't bother to change it. I should have called it "Pascual Duarte," or in any event, "Pascual Duarte and His Family."

MLG: When Pascual kills his mother, we do not feel any compassion; yet we are moved when his dog dies. How can you explain this?

CJC: That's because the dog was an innocent victim, while the mother was hateful. Since I am part Anglo-Saxon, I feel more sympathy for dogs than for the human race.

MLG: *Pascual Duarte, The Hive,* and *Journey to the Alcarria* have been adapted for the screen.

CJC: They did a very good production of part of *Journey to the Alcarria* on television. They are now adapting *Del Miño al Bidasoa,* although I have yet to see it. It's a travelogue.

MLG: What's your reaction upon viewing your works on the screen?

CJC: It's another language, of course. The language of films is very different from that of literature. I am happy with the adaptations as long as they don't betray my work. And I haven't been betrayed. I am very happy with the film that was made of *The Hive.* I think it is a great movie, and I say this in complete honesty, because I didn't work on that adaptation. I gave them the rights to the book, and they adapted it from beginning to end.

MLG: You have just finished a television series on *Don Quixote.*

CJC: It is a very respectful adaptation of Cervantes's text, which I have divided into parts, each several chapters long. The first and second parts have eight chapters, and each runs for one hour, so there was a lot of leeway to work with. I did away with the many stories Cervantes interjected into his narrative, because I thought they would make the adaptation too long and distract the viewer from the main plot. So, I have tried to stick to the events in which Don Quixote and Sancho Panza are directly involved. I have high hopes for this television series.

MLG: Did you adapt the language of Cervantes?

CJC: I tried to respect it as much as possible. Of course, I couldn't render the text in terms of twentieth-century colloquialisms, because that would have been false, but neither could I leave many of Cervantes's archaic usages, because the viewers wouldn't have understood them. I hope I have achieved a good balance, but it will be up to the viewers to decide.

MLG: How do you think Cervantes would have reacted to the television adaptation of his masterpiece?

CJC: It's very hard to imagine what a man who died at the beginning of the seventeenth century would think about an invention created three hundred or so years after his death. I would like to think that he would be pleased with it.

MLG: During the premiere of *María Sabina* at Carnegie Hall, what was your reaction upon hearing your text set to music?

CJC: I enjoyed it very, very much. It was a great success at Carnegie Hall. There were also two performances in Madrid. The first one resulted in a horrid stamping of feet. Women, especially, stamped their feet with vehemence. I recorded it on tape. The audience insulted me, but did so very respectfully, using the polite form of *usted* (you), and in Spanish, of course, when people insult they use the familiar *tú*. So it was a surrealistic experience. On the following day, the people who really wanted to see the performance came. The success was enormous, and I very much enjoyed watching those large choruses led by Leonardo Balada, who is a great composer.

MLG: You have written poetry, short stories, novels, travelogues, memoirs, even plays. In what genre do you feel most at ease?

CJC: Whichever genre I happen to be writing in at the moment. I am perhaps most at ease with narrative fiction. But I have also written essays when I wanted to say something. With essays, there is the need for intellectual rigor, which is not necessary with purely narrative works where you can do anything you like with your characters, if they let you.

MLG: When you sit down to write, do you know whether you are going to work on a short story or a novel?

CJC: I know more or less that it's not going to be an essay, but nothing is concrete in any way. For instance, I started writing very enthusiastically what I thought would be a novel, and then I realized that I didn't have enough material for it. What one cannot do in a situation like this is to inflate the story. You cannot put the body of an elephant on the frame of a canary, everything would topple. So one has to be courageous enough to face up to the facts.

MLG: What does writing mean to you?

CJC: Writing is a very arduous task for me. I have an obligation to do the best job I can, don't you think? I will tell you one thing: a book of mine may be good or bad, but it is as good as I could have made it, because I applied my five senses to it. If it didn't come out better, it must have been because I lacked talent. That's too bad, but I always write as well as I can. Writing is writing, period. To be able to write, all you need is to have something to say. All I know is that it is an absolute necessity for me. I cannot conceive of doing anything else with my life. Perhaps I would have been a great or mediocre criminal, I'm not sure which! I write because I enjoy it, I have no intention of changing the world with my writing.

MLG: The written word is very important to you, obviously.

CJC: Yes, that's all literature is. Words are the raw material of literature. They are the only things that separate man from the animal kingdom. The day that the first man uttered a word designating something, humanity took a step forward far greater than the discovery of America or the landing on the moon.

MLG: Some writers say they always wear masks. Do you?

CJC: I don't know. I don't think it is a good thing, in any case. I attach great value to authenticity and sincerity, and to the genuine expression of the truth we all carry inside us. I am not at all sure that wearing masks is a good thing, because writers run the risk of becoming caricatures of themselves if they do. This would be a very unfortunate result, not to mention the far worse fate of wearing a death mask.

MLG: Is there a particular time of day when you like to write?

CJC: I usually write all morning long, sleep the siesta, and then I keep writing a little bit. I write constantly.

MLG: What do you feel when you write a novel?

CJC: Great satisfaction while I am writing it, and a great sense of peace when I finish it. At my age, the only thing I care about in literature is the process of pure creation. I am not as concerned with the final product. If a good edition of one of my books comes out, I am very happy; if the critics like it, I am grateful to them; and if it sells well, so much the better, because that's what I live on. But I don't consider these factors when I am writing. The mere act of writing is what comforts me the most at this point in my life.

MLG: When do you know that a book is done?

CJC: At some point I just stop writing, because otherwise I would spend my entire life changing commas, and I would become hysterical. This happened to some extent to Juan Ramón Jiménez, who would publish a poem anew every time he changed a comma in it. Once one of my works has been published, I never change it. I don't even correct the proofs for the book; my secretaries do.

MLG: What do you think about authors who don't use periods?

CJC: I have written some books without periods. There's nothing wrong with it; the reader places the periods himself. However, if you are going to put periods, you have to put them in the right place, that's for sure.

MLG: Do you think of the reader when you write?

CJC: No. Fortunately, later on there are many thousands of readers who think the way I do, and who are anxiously awaiting my new book. But I never think of them. That would be a mistake, if not a sellout.

MLG: Do you expect your readers to play an active role?

CJC: Absolutely. Nowadays, novels require effort on the part of the reader, whereas in the nineteenth century everything was provided pre-digested.

MLG: You have said, "Everything that is not humility, and blatant humility, is superfluous in the baggage of the writer." Do you have other rules that you would like to share with young writers?

CJC: One has to write with absolute humility, without believing that one is going to revolutionize world literature. The writer who thinks he is the center of the world is nothing but a hopeless fool. Some writers believe that because they have had a novel published in Barcelona with some commercial success, they have become geniuses. They are just vain young fellows fishing in muddy waters and they don't go beyond that. Consider this fact: if Cervantes, Dante, and Shakespeare had never existed, it wouldn't have been the end of the world. But they did exist and I am thankful for it.

MLG: Do you see some similarity between your works and those of Latin American authors?

CJC: Language is a common tool, and not by chance. I think there has always been a great novel in Spanish America. The works of Rómulo Gallegos, Ricardo Güiraldes, Benito Lynch, and Miguel Angel Asturias are more important than those of current writers. There have always been great Latin American authors.

MLG: What do you think of the upcoming quincentennial celebrations?

CJC: It's a touchy issue, at best. I don't know if those celebrations will be seen positively. I think Spain should proceed with caution, without adopting a paternalistic, not to mention imperialistic, attitude. Unfortunately, intellectuals have been left out of this project, and it has fallen into the hands of politicians.

MLG: Can you speak about your role in drafting the new Spanish constitution and your experiences as a senator?

CJC: We all worked more or less successfully in drafting the constitution. I was an independent senator appointed by King Juan Carlos, and not a member of any political party. I belonged to a minority group called Agrupación Independiente. There were thirteen of us, each one appointed by the king. To give you an idea of his influence, he also appointed Justino de Azcárate to head our minority, even though he had been a Republican minister and lived in exile in Venezuela during the entire Franco era. In the constitutional commission, all my proposals were approved, but when they reached the joint sessions, the Socialists and the Centrists formed a consensus and then I would lose, of course, since I stood alone. Actually, I didn't lose on all my proposals, because what I wanted was that my points of view be set down in the official records of the sessions. Everything I said is there, except for one thing they begged me to take out and which I am not going to repeat here; otherwise your book won't get published. I felt it was my duty to be in Madrid at that time and to fulfill the duties the king had appointed me to carry out.

MLG: You have said: "I studied in Madrid and Salamanca. I studied medicine and nothing happened; I studied philosophy and nothing happened; I studied law and nothing happened. It's strange, I do not have a university degree in anything, but I have many honorary doctorates." What is your reaction to the numerous honorary degrees you have received both in Europe and in America?

CJC: My reaction to the first honorary doctorate was one of amazement and gratitude. It was from Syracuse University, my North American alma mater. I have received so many honorary degrees since then that now, when I get another one, it seems the most natural thing in the world. It's the same thing with the streets that have been named after me. When four or five months pass without a street being named in my honor, I think things must be going poorly. You get accustomed to this, as to anything else. But of course you should take it casually and not let it go to your head. If you believe that you are important because you have a doctorate or seven doctorates, you are nothing more than foolish and conceited, because man is exactly the same after receiving honors as he was before, or he should be.

MLG: I notice that your house is filled with mementos and that you are surrounded by paintings. Do you paint?

CJC: I used to, and I would like to paint again, but I haven't had the time. I love all painting, but I am especially fond of Spanish painters, people like Picasso, Miró, Solana, Zuloaga, Tàpies, and Zabaleta, whose works you see all around you.

MLG: John Ulbricht's portrait of you is particularly striking.

CJC: He is a North American artist who lives on the island of Majorca.

MLG: Living in the country is very important to you.

CJC: Don't forget that I was born in Galicia, so I am very fond of nature and wide-open spaces. I couldn't live in a small apartment, it would take a lot out of me. The sea, the mountains, all of nature is important.

MLG: I hear some birds in the background . . .

CJC: I have a very large cage over there where I keep turtledoves and parrots in relative freedom. They reproduce in captivity, so it can't be that bad. I also have a Persian greyhound and three Airedale terriers. They are in the house next door, which I bought because I needed more room for my books. We built this house ourselves.

MLG: You have written some philosophical reflections on what having a house means to you.

CJC: A house is born from man's love of the earth, with walls that serve as shelter, and give him a sense of structure and order. But that order has to be earned, sometimes at the expense of health and sanity. If a man cannot exercise self-control, it is very difficult to imagine that he owns anything.

MLG: You must have been interviewed over one thousand times, and I guess every interview sounds pretty much the same to you.

CJC: I have always said that the success of an interview depends on the interviewer, not the interviewee. If the interviewer asks intelligent questions, it elicits intelligent responses. Of course, there are some authors who are not fond of talking, like Azorín or Gerardo Diego, but I am not one of them. I hope that our long conversation will continue for many years to come.

Camilo José Cela receiving the Nobel Prize for Literature from King Gustaf of Sweden during presentation ceremony, 10 December 1989 (*photo credit:* Reuters/Bettman)

GENE LUTTENBERG

Carmen Conde

Carmen Conde Abellán was born in 1907 in Cartagena, Murcia, and spent her childhood in Melilla. She studied education at the Escuela Normal de Murcia (a teacher's college) and philosophy and letters at the University of Valencia. This well-known Spanish poet and novelist received the National Prize for Literature in 1967 for her *Obra poética 1922-1966*. In 1979, she became the first woman elected to the Spanish Royal Academy. Five years later, another woman, Elena Quiroga, joined her in the prestigious institution.

Carmen Conde's work is the story of her life and the story of twentieth-century Spain: the years of the Republic, the Civil War, and the social struggles of postwar Spain. When she married the poet Antonio Oliver Belmás in 1931, their gift to one another was the creation of the Universidad Popular de Cartagena (the People's University of Cartagena), which enabled working people to acquire an education.

Conde is a self-made woman who began working at the age of sixteen. She once told me: "I am not a feminist, but I believe that women have the same rights as men. Women must express themselves not as men see them, but with an authentic voice that reflects their own reality." For many years she taught poetry and the contemporary Spanish novel at the Instituto de Estudios Europeos, a branch of the University of Chicago, and at the Cátedra Mediterránea of the University of Valencia, in Alicante.

She is the author of more than fifty books, including *Pasión del verbo* (Passion for the Word), 1944; *Honda memoria de mí* (Deep Memory of Me), 1944; *Ansia de la Gracia* (Longing for Grace), 1945; *Sea la luz* (Let There Be Light), 1947; *En manos del silencio* (In the Hands of Silence), 1950; *Las oscuras raíces* (Dark Roots), for which she won the Elisenda Montcada Prize, 1953; *Cita con la vida* (A Date with Life), 1976; *La rambla* (The Ramble), 1978; *El tiempo es un río lentísimo de fuego* (Time Is a Very Slow River of Fire), 1979; *Creció espesa la yerba* (The Grass Grew Thick), 1979; *Soy la madre* (I Am the Mother), winner of the 1979 Ateneo de Sevilla Prize, 1980; *La noche oscura del cuerpo* (The Dark Night of the Body), 1980; *Desde nunca* (Never), 1982; *La calle de los balcones azules* (The Street of Blue Balconies), 1986; *Por el camino, viendo sus orillas* (On the Road, Observing Its Edges), a three-volume memoir, 1986; *Memoria puesta en olvido (antología personal)* (Memory Recalled, a Personal Anthology), 1987; *Una palabra tuya* (One Word from You), 1988. She has also written many books for children: *Cuentos del romancero* (Stories from the Romancero), 1978; *Belén* (Bethlehem), 1979; *Doña Centenito, gata salvaje* (Doña Centenito, a Wildcat), 1943; *Un conejo soñador rompe con la tradición* (A Dreamy Rabbit Breaks with Tradition), 1979; *El monje y el pajarillo* (The Monk and the Little Bird), 1980; *El lago y la corza* (The Lake and the Fallow Deer), 1980; *Canciones de nana y desvelos* (Lullabies), the 1987 National Prize for Children Literature, 1985.

Carmen Conde is a friend I see on each of my visits to Spain, whether in her apartment in Madrid or in a country house in Navacerrada that her long-time friend Eulalia Ruiz de Clavijo named after her first book, *Brocal*. Carmen is a strong, passionate woman who loves being with people and yet is fiercely independent. The first two parts of the interview were held in the Television Center of St. John's University in New York. The third part was held in Madrid on a spring day. It was raining heavily. I rang the bell and Carmen herself opened the door. We sat around a coffee table in the small living room that also serves as a library. In her old apartment in the building next door, where she used to live until her husband's death, she keeps the rest of her enormous library. Her cat Doña Centenito made a quick appearance to greet me and then slipped away from my arms. Eulalia walked in and, with the warm hospitality of the people from Andalusia, brought a big box of chocolates. As usual, each of my visits with Carmen Conde ended on the same note: "Call me when you get home!" And it doesn't matter whether home is Madrid, Alicante, Paris, or New York. I know that if I don't call she will worry.

❖❖❖❖❖❖❖❖❖❖❖❖❖❖❖❖❖❖❖❖❖❖❖❖❖❖❖❖

Part 1

MLG: What are some of the most characteristic traits of your works?

   CC: Authors know themselves very little and I can't pick out objectively which are the most fundamental traits of my works. I think that you have been a good reader of my books and you are better equipped to say what their characteristics are.

MLG: What is the importance of the sea for you?

CC: It is decisive because I was born in Spain, next to the Mediterranean Sea. I spent my childhood in Melilla, on the coast of North Africa. I had always lived near the sea, but in 1939 I moved to Castile. Sometimes I live in Madrid or in the surrounding area, so I miss the sea very much.

MLG: In your poetry and prose one can see the importance of childhood.

CC: Childhood is a vital thing in which one can program like a computer all the answers of the future. It also depends a lot on education. That's why I am so concerned with education. It's not the same as culture or instruction. Education means bringing out what an individual has inside, not imposing someone else's views on that person. Childhood is the perfect moment to mold a creature into a marvelous man or woman or into a stupid being.

MLG: One can hardly distinguish between your poetry and you because your work is so personal.

CC: I have always thought that to separate the work from the person is not to understand either of them. The work is the result of the person and the person has to be loyal to his or her work.

MLG: Do you identify with the characters in your novels?

CC: To a certain extent, although sometimes my characters have episodes in their lives that are unrelated to me. Narrative is something that does not only come from the author, it also feeds on everything that is in the world, that world which transcends the writer's knowledge. I can get into the shoes of a woman that I have never been, precisely because I am a woman.

MLG: Do your characters lead you or do you lead them?

CC: At first I invent them; afterward they choose their own way. After I have created them, they have lives of their own.

MLG: Almost all your characters are passionate people.

CC: Yes, because I think life without passion, without enthusiasm, is not life but a routine.

MLG: In poetry or prose, the word that best describes you and your work is "light."

CC: If it weren't for the things in the world, light would not exist. Light has to have a reason to illuminate things. Without trees, or rivers, or sky, one cannot find light.

MLG: You have said that poetry is written in a state of grace.

CC: Yes, I believe that. Juan Ramón Jiménez said that poets are driven. They don't sit down, place themselves in front of a sheet of paper and think, "What am I going to say now?"

MLG: How do you arrive at poetry?

CC: I arrive at poetry when I have no other choice. I feel it deeply; it lives inside of me. There are times when I am very depressed and I don't know what is the matter with me, and what I really want is to write poetry. It's a command. I don't believe in intellectual poetry. Intelligence should have some kind of control over poetry, but intuitive, spontaneous thoughts must be free. To me, poetry is like a small river that you follow until you arrive at the sea. You have to find the right word, you have to transform it into a tunic that fits the form and the contents of your thoughts. If the word is not like a tunic, you are dead.

MLG: Could you mention a contemporary poet who is very important to you?

CC: I can mention many, but Dámaso Alonso is truly the great poet who has interpreted Spain from the distress of the 1930s to the present. We are no longer in distress. Dámaso Alonso, for me, is the representative poet of our times.

MLG: How did the Spanish Civil War change your life?

CC: It changed my life and the lives of all of us who were young then. We lived with a feeling that we were going to be torn apart. There was nothing left but ashes after the war. In fact, the postwar era was perhaps worse than the war itself. The war changed me from a young and idealistic adolescent into a mature woman because of the pain I endured, but it did not embitter me.

MLG: Did you remain in Spain?

CC: Oh yes! My husband and I stayed in Spain. We did not want the victor to get the spoils.

MLG: In what way has your life changed now that you are a member of the Spanish Royal Academy?

CC: I was a woman with a quiet inner life. I wouldn't go anywhere and now I go everywhere because of this obligation to give a good impression as the first woman accepted into the Academy. I also want the Academy to admit other women while I am still living.

MLG: What does the role of women mean to you?

CC: It is immense, just like the role of men but in a different way. We have the same rights, but we have never been allowed to enjoy them. Now is the time to start enjoying these privileges. In fact, we have already begun.

MLG: Details are very important in your novels. There is never a superfluous word in your work.

CC: I acquired this discipline unconsciously. I started out being very baroque. If you accumulate words upon words, the reader is bored and he leaves; one has to find the substance. I don't look for it, it comes to me naturally.

MLG: What do you do as an Academician?

CC: The same as other members. The Academy tries to clean and preserve the splendor of the Spanish language. We take care of the language —that's all we do.

MLG: What is your impression of the United States?

CC: I was here before, but this is my first trip as an Academician. I like this country very much. It has a very beautiful countryside, and I accept its beauty with all my heart, but I would like to live and die in Spain.

MLG: What does Spain represent to you?

CC: Spain is my mother. Everything in the world is very well made but it is made even better in Spain.

Part 2

MLG: I know that you do not like to reread your works. How do you feel when you hear your poems set to music?

CC: I like them a lot more sung than read, because the voice and the music make them more beautiful. For instance, Antoñita Moreno recorded many songs of my poems. She has one of the best voices in Spain to sing my poetry, and I have written many poems with her in mind.

MLG: Our mutual friendship with Gabriela Mistral brought us together. How do you remember her?

CC: Gabriela? She is eternally alive in my memory and my heart. She was a wonderful human being. I remember that, because she was so tall, and truly I am not, when we parted she would take my head in her hands to kiss my brow, and my husband, Antonio, would say, "Dear Lord, it is like the Heavenly Father kissing his daughter!" That is what it looked like: the Heavenly Father bending over the humble human daughter that I was. She was a precious human being, and I loved her very much.

MLG: She once said that you rediscovered the long lost fountain of childhood dreams. Do you think one can be a poet without maintaining the spirit of childhood within?

CC: I think it is necessary to sustain our memories of childhood not only to be a poet, but to be a fully accomplished human being. Childhood has to be intrinsic to every aspect of our lives, whether in our daily experience or in our memory. Because as children we are embryos of the future that we will become, undeniably. By the age of seven or eight, at the most, one can tell what a boy or a girl will turn out to be. I knew what I would become, at least. I knew I had to invent things, and of course I had a horrible reputation as a liar, since I made up everything. Later in life I continued to invent things, although not in the same way.

MLG: Children can speak with invisible friends, whereas adults are not allowed that privilege. Poets, however, are.

CC: No, adults can as well. People speak to themselves all the time, perhaps not aloud, so as not to be mistaken for being crazy, but they do speak to themselves.

MLG: Don't you think that the poet is a privileged being?

CC: Humanity might think so, but the poet himself with his experiences is never private or privileged.

MLG: Never?

CC: No, neither materially nor morally.

MLG: As a child you used to sit in the cemetery and read the Bible . . .

CC: Let me explain . . . it sounds as if I went to the cemetery to see all the dead people, and that is not what it was about. At the end of the street where I lived in Melilla there was—and continues to be—a beautiful cemetery that faced the sea. Since I had traveled by sea to Melilla, an experience which I have always cherished as one of the most beautiful in my life, I used to go to the cemetery with my book under my arm to sit along the walls by the sea, so as to be able to look at it. The dead people really didn't matter much to me; I read the Bible unperturbed.

MLG: Weren't you scared?

CC: No, I have never been scared of anything.

MLG: Would you sit today in that cemetery and read the Bible?

CC: I think it would be a needless repetition. One cannot do as an adult what one did as a child. I would need a more comfortable seat, first of all, because I used to sit on the ground.

MLG: Do you still converse with the child you once were?

CC: When I write stories for children I am most definitely in contact with the girl I once was. I very much enjoy children's stories. Of course, on occasion I believe they are not really stories for children but for adults. But I can seek out the child in the adult, and that is enough.

MLG: Your stories for children are very beautiful.

CC: I am very glad you said so, because I like them very much.

MLG: Upon reading them aloud one can almost hear you speak.

CC: Yes, that is true, I never adopted a different language than the one I use on a daily basis to communicate with my peers. I believe that anything that reeks of pedantry and ostentation is quite simply ridiculous, and I try not to get too close to the ridiculous because we Spaniards are very aware of it.

MLG: After corresponding for a long time with you, I finally met you at the small village of La Unión in Cartagena.

CC: Yes, because I love flamenco singing very much. This village of La Unión, in the mining region of Cartagena, is ten kilometers outside the city. For many years I have been going there every August to hear the *cantejondo* and mining songs that I like very much. You came with a friend and her children and we met personally. It's been quite a few years now . . .

MLG: Yes, quite a while. I know that you cannot live without music. Why do you identify so much with Mahler's music, for instance?

CC: I don't know. In fact, I don't like to speak about Mahler anymore, because the vice president of Spain, whose name is Guerra, Alfonso Guerra, likes Mahler, and people keep throwing that preference in his face. So now I am very shy and I will say nothing about Mahler. Guerra can have him.

MLG: Painting is also very important for you.

CC: Yes, but what I like most are guitars and singing and dancing. And I seriously mean dancing, like *sevillanas*. I am very much a woman of the people in this respect. I like these things very much.

MLG: Upon reading your novels one can see the great influence, if I may say so, of light and shadow on your work.

CC: I love painting and particularly sculpture, but I don't place restrictions on either of those things. I can't paint, and I wouldn't try to because it would be going against God. If God did not give me the talent, I am not going to go in search of it.

MLG: Then creation is only possible through divine grace?

CC: Without a doubt. I always have great respect for the opinions of others, but sometimes I feel pity upon hearing certain things. I don't know who they think created the world, unless it was built by some robots before God appeared on the scene. For me, everything I have I have received from God.

MLG: And when you write you already know . . .

CC: I know nothing, absolutely and definitely not. It is not as if there were a lined paper underneath on which was written, "Now he gets up and looks out the window. Now a cloud appears." No, it is not like that. I believe in inspiration although many intelligent people don't—of course, I am not intelligent. I write what I feel, what I desire, what I have no alternative but to say. I don't set out by saying, "Now I am going to write." I never do that. However, when I have felt harried for a number of days because I don't know what is wrong with me, then I know I have to write.

MLG: And what are you writing now?

CC: Right now nothing. But I have had a long, unedited novel in the works for many years, as well as many poems. Sometimes I get an undeniable urge to write short prose pieces, as happened with "Los perdidos pasos" (Lost Steps). I felt very pressured to write that, although later I didn't publish it. Maybe it will get published on the hundredth anniversary of my birth, as is customary.

MLG: What is "Los perdidos pasos" about?

CC: It is about life, human beings, cities, and the search within oneself, because we carry many lost steps there. It is a recreational exercise for me, an amusement.

MLG: Is it poetic prose?

CC: I don't know what others will think when they read it. I have tried to be simple and straightforward. I don't like that label "poetic prose," though. Prose either has poetry or it doesn't, but "poetic prose" . . .

MLG: Let's say a poem in prose then.

CC: No, they are not poems, they are experiences remembered.

MLG: Your critical eye always zooms in on a physical aspect of a person, be it a smile (the other day you were speaking about Gabriela's smile, for instance), a look, hands, feet, or bearing. Why?

CC: It must be for aesthetic reasons. I could not choose the way I look. I was born looking a particular way. I love beauty, although not stupid beauty, but inner beauty, which also informs the spirit and transforms another person's body into a brief miracle that lasts only as long as our eyes meet. I was once walking in Venice looking for one of those artisans who blow glass into little figures. I walked over a small bridge and found myself in a lovely little Venetian street. And there on the opposite side of the street, I saw an old, ordinary peasant woman carrying a small basket. She looked miserable. And all of a sudden a beautiful young girl appeared, like something out of Botticelli, a vision of spring. And the old lady stopped in her tracks and exclaimed, "My Lord, what a beauty!" You couldn't have witnessed a scene like that anywhere but in Italy. Upon seeing such beauty she had no choice but to sigh, and that is truly wonderful. That is what I most love in life, the beauty of another. I never look at myself in the mirror because I don't like the way I look. In that respect, I am not unintelligent.

MLG: So you focus on a specific part?

CC: Yes, I do. Whenever I am giving a lecture, I always seek out someone's eyes from among the crowd, for instance. I don't see everyone, I search for some place to rest my eyes, and this encourages me to read and speak about my inner world. Smiles are very enticing; I won't mention *La Gioconda* because it is such a cliché, but Gabriela Mistral's smile was marvelous. She was a very serious, solemn person, and then all of a sudden she would break out laughing and become a little girl running through a garden. Some people have very expressive hands, while others don't know what to do with them. That is when I feel sorry for them.

MLG: And what are you focusing on right now?

CC: Well, you'll want me to say I am looking at you! I can do nothing else! You are right in front of me!

MLG: You need to write poetry. How do you feel talking about it?

CC: It is very difficult. One has to be inspired even to be able to talk about it. I have been a professor of literature and poetry at the Instituto de Estudios Europeos in Madrid (although it is based in Chicago) for fifteen years, as you know. I could speak about poetry to the students because I didn't know them. They had new eyes, new mouths, and they listened with enthusiasm to what I had to say, so I told them about Spanish poetry, although never about mine. And every one of the students left my class with a love for Spanish poetry, and many of them still write to me. One cannot speak about poetry just like that. Someone has to give you the right impetus, and those attentive, beautiful youths did allow me that opportunity.

MLG: The other day I attended one of your lectures, and it was wonderful to see the expressions on the faces of the students . . .

CC: I couldn't tell, because there were bright lights in front of me.

MLG: Do you get along with other poets? Do you have many poets as friends?

CC: I deal with them from a distance, because we are all part of the same flock. In Spain we are all friends and colleagues and either I like them or I don't. I have always helped others. If something I was doing could benefit someone else, I would try to help that person, whether a poet or a carpenter.

MLG: Do you seek out friends?

CC: Never. But friends come to me. I like things to come to me, like the Holy Spirit and friendships, love and happiness. Let them come. But I have never forced a door to get what I want, irrespective of what some crazy people claim. I like doors to open in front of me.

MLG: You have suffered much in your life . . .

CC: Let's not talk about that!

MLG: In spite of all that pain, or perhaps because of it, you are a hopeful woman. From where do you draw that vital strength?

CC: Physically speaking, I think my vital strength comes from my mother. Spiritually speaking, I think my strength comes from my devout faith in God. It cannot come from anywhere else.

MLG: Would I be mistaken in saying that your work is a song to life?

CC: No, you wouldn't be, because you can sing with happiness or with sorrow, as in flamenco singing. Sometimes I felt hopeful and happy, while at other times there was no choice but to render unto sorrow what I feel is its proper due.

MLG: You have lived for over forty years in Madrid, but nevertheless, your work is always permeated by a Levantine spirit.

CC: We Mediterraneans are marked people. We always feel the sea above all else. In Madrid, of course, you can't see it, but you can dream about it.

MLG: Do you think that the place of one's birth has an impact on personality?

CC: Both your place of birth and where you spend your childhood are important. My first childhood was in Cartagena, and my second one was in Melilla. Both have been useful to me, they are like two little girls that I always carry within me. And I distinguish between them and remember them.

MLG: Do you plan to write a poem about Melilla?

CC: I already did in a book called *Empezando la vida.* I cannot be completely sure, because I never remember my books, but I think so.

MLG: You do not know any of your poems by heart, and yet you know those of others.

CC: Yes, that is true. I know poems by Juan Ramón Jiménez, Machado, and many others. But once I have written my own poems, they are of little consequence for me.

MLG: You just came from Madrid from a session with the Royal Academy, which King Juan Carlos attended.

CC: Yes, he attended a regular working session of the Academy. He is not an Academician, but he came and presided over the session, which is logical, given his stature, and he participated in the discussions and had his say like anyone else. It was a very nice meeting, and very pleasant for all of us and him.

MLG: Several years have passed since I asked you, "What does your work as an Academician consist of?" What would your answer be today?

CC: The same thing I answered last time. The job entails nothing more than the study of vocabulary, its innovations, its regressions, and its aging. When a word is so old that it is not used anymore, it must be preserved as a relic. We have to try by all means possible to purify a language that has been invaded by many harmful expressions.

MLG: How does a new word become incorporated?

CC: Ten years ago, before I was a member of the Academy, I wrote a poem on that subject, but unfortunately I think I have lost it. I speculated on how the Academy analyzed words. But now I have been shamed into way-laying that poem, for fear that other Academicians might read it, because it was a horrendous dissection. I truly don't know how a poor word has the energy necessary to make it into the dictionary.

MLG: The word is almost an obsession for you.

CC: No, it is not an obsession, it is a search. The accurate word, as Juan Ramón Jiménez used to say, does not depend on its being better or worse, more or less beautiful or appropriate, but rather on its interpreting the feeling or the cause it evokes perfectly. If that word is to be eliminated, then in every instance in which it was used it must also be removed. If, however, an example can be found where that word is not replaceable, then it must be kept.

MLG: When you write a poem do you go through feelings of anxiety?

CC: No, I am never anxious, I always do it with a great deal of happiness. Nowadays I do what Juan Ramón Jiménez recommended: I submit spontaneity to consciousness. I write a poem, I leave it and let it sit for a while. If I don't like it, I tear it up, and if I do like it and it requires some correction, I do that. Generally speaking, I write a poem with all my love, it never has any defects in my eyes. What others might think of it is another matter.

MLG: What do you feel now that Elena Quiroga has been admitted to the Royal Academy?

CC: I didn't want to be the only one. I fought so that another woman might be found. But once she got in, I washed my hands of the whole affair; she can do what she wants. She is a good novelist with an excellent command of the language, and besides a very brave woman.

MLG: One has to be brave to get in?

CC: Undoubtedly. Do you know of any other enterprise more unpleasant than having to convince others that what you wrote is interesting and that they should read it? But I didn't do anything to get in. I am proud to say that they sought me out, I didn't ask for it. Others may have lobbied and I helped them as much as was necessary. But Carmen Conde didn't ask to become a member of the Academy, Carmen Conde was chosen, and I like that.

MLG: You have cultivated every genre. In which one do you feel most comfortable?

CC: In whichever one I am using at a particular moment.

MLG: But poetry is . . .

CC: That is the Carmen Conde I have inside me. But whenever I do something I do it willingly, with pleasure—otherwise I wouldn't do it. Why would I write something I don't enjoy? Like any of us, I write for myself, because I want to. A professor or a critic may then speak about it . . .

MLG: Do you ever think of the reader?

CC: No, only as a by-product. I don't care whether he is going to like or dislike my work; he can do as he wills.

MLG: Not even when you write stories for children?

CC: Not even then. I am not saying that I write them for myself, but I do write about what I like, for instance that book you mentioned, *Un conejo soñador rompe con la tradición* (A Dreamy Rabbit Breaks with Tradition). It is about how children are named, an idea I have been playing with for a long time. How will this boy or that girl be named? Like his grandfather or her grandmother. Poor child! He will be named Saturnino or something strange like that, and he will wander through life with his grandfather's name as a relic. I wanted to do away with this—why should all the children throughout the centuries be named Juan because their fathers were Juan? So that rabbit did my bidding: he did away with the names of grandparents.

MLG: What about *Doña Centenito?*

CC: That was about a cat who actually lived. She was a wildcat, and I found her in the mountains of El Escorial. She later died, because wildcats cannot be domesticated. We loved each other so much that she agreed to live with me, but the veterinarian warned me that when she reached the age of eight or nine months she would die. And this is indeed what happened, because she had no freedom. Later I found another cat at my doorstep, similar to the other one, and I named her Centenito II.

MLG: And she lives like a queen!

CC: She is beautiful. She gets extremely upset whenever she sees my bags. When she sees a suitcase she becomes incensed, as if saying, "There she goes again!" And since I am always leaving . . . But you know her, and you know how beautiful she is!

MLG: A great serenity forms an intrinsic part of your personality.

CC: I don't know about that, because I am a very nervous person.

MLG: But you never give that impression.

CC: No one should have to suffer from my nerves. If something good or bad has happened to me, there is no reason why I should say, "Look here, I am very happy today!" That would be horrible, wouldn't it? One has to be moderate and contain oneself. Especially if it is something bad. I am very modest about my feelings.

MLG: How do you achieve that inner peace?

CC: Through the passing of time. How can I be like a woman of twenty, or thirty, or forty, if I am older than that?

MLG: Nevertheless, you have a great inner vitality.

CC: That is true. I am not afraid of anything, and I don't care what the consequences may be. I do whatever I want, especially if it is on someone else's behalf. But it is quite another thing for me to share my happiness, and stifle others, or my sorrow, and sadden them. That would be indecent, and I would never do anything like that.

MLG: You have said, "I am a hopeful woman."

CC: Do you think if I were not a hopeful woman I would be here today? Madrid is very far away, very far. I am an old person, but I don't care. Why should I deny myself something? I even went to China, where I traveled forty thousand kilometers, many of them on foot, which was a terrible experience.

MLG: What do you think of New York after having been absent for a while?

CC: I like New York very much. But I do think it would be a horrendous city for someone living alone. A person who no longer has to work and who has no family or friends nearby would probably go crazy here. I advise my friends who are professors and who are not North Americans that when they retire they should leave this city and go to Madrid, or Málaga, or Murcia. In Spain everyone speaks to everyone else. I wouldn't say there is a great deal of personal egoism in New York, but there is a lot of coldness and indifference. Our friend has a neighbor who lives alone, and the poor man is crazy. Do you know how he passes the time? By opening and closing the door. It is horrible, every time he opens the door he makes a lot of noise, and likewise when he closes it. He is crazy, of course, but maybe he wants someone to listen to him. I have told our friend that she should talk to him, but she is afraid. If I lived here longer, I would make friends with that poor man because he is so lonely.

MLG: Since you like dispensing advice, is there anything you would say to future writers?

CC: Not to worry about the effect that what they have written may have on others. They must acquire their own self-criticism. They should break with tradition and never be content with what they have written. The person who says, "My poem is excellent," is a fool. The true poet who demands a great deal from himself should never be satisfied. He should always want something more, and aspire to infinity, because no one can be stopped there.

Part 3

MLG: You published three volumes of your memoirs in 1986. What impelled you to write them?

CC: They are a collection of things that I had already written about my life.

MLG: In 1987, you published a personal anthology, *Memoria puesta en olvido*. How did you come up with that lovely title?

CC: Those words come from the Bible.

MLG: Are you presently writing a book?

CC: No, the doctors have told me to give reading and writing a rest.

MLG: In the last year, nevertheless, several of your children's stories were published.

CC: Yes, but I had written them before. They are very nice. *Canciones de nana y desvelos* won the National Prize for children's stories.

MLG: If you had to define yourself in one word, what would it be?

CC: Nobody can do that. It's all right to speak in terms of love, death, happiness, all of those things. But to define oneself in just one word would be a lie.

MLG: You are very sincere, this is perhaps your most striking characteristic.

CC: Yes, I am that. But I don't go around saying so. That's for others to say!

MLG: If you could speak with a writer from the past, whom would you choose?

CC: I would speak to Gabriel Miró, Gabriela Mistral, and the prince of our century, Juan Ramón Jiménez.

MLG: What would you say to Gabriela if you could speak with her right now?

CC: The last time we were supposed to meet, I fell ill and couldn't visit her in Italy. So the final words were left unsaid.

MLG: What would you say to Juan Ramón Jiménez?

CC: His poetry has always been a bible to me. I would just like to hear him.

MLG: What about Gabriel Miró?

CC: The same thing. I loved him dearly. In Spain, in this century, I sincerely believe that the prince of poetry was Juan Ramón, while Gabriel Miró excelled in prose.

MLG: What's your opinion of Gabriela Mistral?

CC: She was a frustrated mother, like me.

MLG: What do you think about when you are not writing?

CC: I don't know, thinking travels its own roads. More than thinking, I dream a lot. Many times, I write my dreams down, because they are very rich.

MLG: Do you remember some?

CC: Look, when I was sick, not too long ago, my doctors prescribed sleeping pills for my insomnia. They were very strong, but I had to take them. One night, I told a friend of mine, who was staying with me, that I wasn't going to take any more pills. I wanted to be myself and not under the effect of drugs. That night, I dreamed about my mother. As I drew close to her to kiss her, she smiled at me and I felt her warmth. And I thought to myself, "My mother told me I did the right thing." From that moment on, I started to feel better and the doctors told me that if I was strong enough to do without the medicine, it was a sign that my condition was improving. When I die, I want to be lucid, not drugged.

MLG: You have great inner strength.

CC: Yes, you are right. I have had to overcome many obstacles. It is one thing to write, and quite another to live.

MLG: The death of your friend Amanda Junquera has been quite a blow to you.

CC: Yes, Amanda was an extraordinarily sensitive and refined person. We were best friends for over fifty years. She always respected my privacy, and never asked me what I was writing or where I was going. It was always I who volunteered the information.

MLG: Do you feel the need to write?

CC: I have written so much. I have tons and tons of unpublished material.

MLG: If you had to give your books a geometric shape, what would it be?

CC: They would each have their own shape. All books are different, although they may have things in common. One thing I have never liked in my life has been a monotonous, repetitious inner rhythm. When on occasion I have written something like that, I have ripped it and thrown it out.

MLG: You never reread your works.

CC: I never do, although I may glance at them occasionally if I am asked to give a sample of my work.

MLG: So what's your reaction when you glance at your works?

CC: They look very strange.

MLG: As if they had been written by another person?

CC: Yes, and I will pay more attention to that person than to myself.

MLG: If you could change something in your past, what would it be?

CC: Nothing, I have lived a full life, nothing has escaped me. I have lived enough, and I have lost a lot. I don't want to lose anything more. I have no more room in this apartment, nor in the one next door where I keep all my books. There are some precious things I wanted that I couldn't get, but God's will be done. Our human environment is filthy, there is so much hunger, people are so greedy and all they think about is money, money, money. Everyone is so concerned with power and material possessions; but it all comes to nothing, because people die. Juan Ramón Jiménez has a wonderful line that goes, "I'm taking with me what I've left behind," and that's what I'm doing too. One of the things I sometimes wonder about, although I shouldn't, is where all my books will go. I have read them and admired them, but I have nobody to leave them to. And what about all my pictures? Let me tell you something that happened to me last year at a book fair. A woman came to my table and said, "Don't you remember me? I'm Clota, your friend from Melilla." She showed me a picture of the two of us as children, which was taken before I left Melilla. She told me she always carried it with her. We started to cry. She now lives in Venezuela with her two children, and she is very rich. She invited me to spend some time with her, but I told her I could no longer travel. I asked her if I could borrow the photograph to make a copy, and she made me swear that I would return it. I said, "Do you think I'm going to take this away from you after you've had it for so many years?"

CIRCULO DE LECTORES

Miguel Delibes

Miguel Delibes was born in 1920 in Valladolid. As a young man he studied commercial law and later turned to journalism when he realized that what he most enjoyed was writing. He served as editor in chief and director of *El Norte de Castilla* until 1963 when, for political reasons, he was forced to resign. He also taught law and journalism.

In 1946, Miguel Delibes married Angeles de Castro, with whom he had seven children. His wife was an avid reader and took a great interest in his work. Since 1974, he has been a widower.

Being awarded the Nadal Prize in 1948 for his first novel, *La sombra del ciprés es alargada* (The Shadow of the Cypress Is Long), marked a turning point in his career as a novelist. Since then, he has been writing an average of one book a year. He is the recipient of many other awards, although he does not like to talk about them. Some of these awards are the National Prize of Literature and the Cervantes Prize, 1955; the Fastenrath Prize of the Royal Academy, 1957; the Crítica Prize, 1962; the Prince of Asturias Literary Prize, 1982; the Literary Prize of Castile and León, 1985. In 1974, he became a member of the Spanish Royal Academy.

Delibes is the author of countless books, among them *Aún es de día* (Still by Day), 1949; *El camino,* 1950 (*The Path,* 1961); *Mi idolatrado hijo Sisí* (My Adored Son Sisí), 1953; *La partida* (The Band), 1954; *Diario de un cazador* (Diary of a Hunter), 1955; *Un novelista descubre América* (A Novelist Discovers America), 1956; *Siestas con viento sur* (Siestas with Southern Wind), 1957; *La hoja roja* (The Red Leaf), 1959; *Viejas historias de Castilla la Vieja* (Old Stories from Old Castile), 1964; *Cinco horas con Mario,* 1966 (*Five Hours with Mario,* 1988); *La primavera de Praga* (Spring in Prague), 1968; *La mortaja* (The Shroud), 1970; *Con la escopeta al hombro* (The Rifle on the Shoulder), 1970; *Un año de mi vida*

(A Year of My Life), 1972; *Parábola del náufrago,* 1969 (*The Hedge,* 1983); *El príncipe destronado* (The Deposed Prince), 1974; *El disputado voto del señor Cayo* (The Challenged Vote of Mr. Cayo), 1978; *Los santos inocentes* (The Innocent Saints), 1981; *377A, Madera de héroe,* 1987 (*The Stuff of Heroes,* 1990); *Pegar la hebra* (To Start a Conversation), 1990. Of these novels, five have been made into movies and three were adapted by the author himself for the theater: *Five Hours with Mario, La hoja roja,* and *Las guerras de nuestros antepasados.*

Delibes writes in the mornings in a studio where he cannot be reached by telephone and spends his afternoons at home, where he corrects his writings and receives visitors. He particularly enjoys chatting with children because they take very seriously the characters he writes about, and to him characters are essential to a novel. He is a sharp observer of Castilian life and his works are a reflection of it.

Delibes also excels in several sports, such as cycling, hiking, and hunting.

I had corresponded with Miguel Delibes for over a year before I met him in his home in Valladolid. Everyone had told me that he was a friendly, very considerate person. So when I actually saw him I felt I already knew him. A tall man, somewhat like a gentleman farmer, he spoke about his work with great sensitivity and humility. We sat across a small table near the window. It was a cold spring day, and he was wearing a windbreaker over a sweater. The living room was large, with a high ceiling, and the walls were covered with books neatly placed on the shelves. At the other end of the room there was a huge portrait of the author in his youth by Ulbricht, the American artist. In a conversational tone, Delibes talked about rural life and how he depicted it in his work and about his concern over pollution. What impressed me most was how accessible he was to people. Even though he is a prolific and well-known writer, he makes a point of receiving all those who want to see him, especially if they are children. He enjoys reading the compositions that children write on his works.

❖❖❖❖❖❖❖❖❖❖❖❖❖❖❖❖❖❖❖❖❖❖❖❖❖❖❖❖❖❖❖❖

MLG: You studied law, began teaching commercial law at the University of Valladolid, turned to journalism, and became editor in chief of *El Norte de Castilla.* When did you first realize that you would become a writer?

MD: Later, and by accident. I was involved in the study and teaching of commercial law for nine years and didn't like it. Then a book fell into my hands, *Derecho mercantil* (Commercial Law), by Joaquín Garrigues, and I was taken by its literary style, which, by the way, led me to Ortega. Around that time, I decided to take a quick course in journalism in Madrid, and I started to work as an editor for the newspaper *El Norte de Castilla.* That paper was known for its long liberal tradition, which explains why four of its editors in chief were fired by the Franco government. So between my enthusiasm for Garrigues and my work as an editor, the writer in me was born. My girlfriend Angeles de Castro, who later became my wife, also encouraged me to write. She was an avid reader, and she turned me into one too. By 1945, these three factors had solidified into a firm conviction that I wanted to write. I then wrote my first novel in 1946, and in 1947 I won the Nadal Prize.

MLG: Since then, you've received many prizes.

MD: Too many!

MLG: The National Prize of Literature, the Fastenrath Prize of the Spanish Royal Academy, the Crítica Prize, the Príncipe de Asturias Prize, and many more . . .

MD: All of them.

MLG: What does all this mean to you?

MD: The Nadal Prize meant everything to me. That prize made it possible for me to continue writing. If I hadn't won, I probably would have stopped writing. The other prizes are quite different. In some way, they are like trophies given posthumously. I am not dead yet, but they give off a scent of incense, as if praising a work that's mostly done. I consider the Nadal Prize the most important one of my career, and I cannot help but see the others as tributes to my age.

MLG: The Civil War, the postwar era, and the dictatorship have all had a great impact on your work.

MD: Yes, and their effect on me was directed by a terrible institution that thrived under the dictatorship, namely censorship. I had to fight censorship in the press, because I was the director of a newspaper, and in my novels, as a novelist. My motto was to mock the censors every day and to try to push their limits, so that my room to maneuver would keep increasing. This didn't work for me in the case of the newspaper, because Mr. Fraga framed me by appointing one of my colleagues to supervise my actions. At that point, I decided to leave, so that strategy against censorship didn't work very well for me there. In the case of my novels, however, it did. If you study my books, you will see that from *La sombra del ciprés es alargada* to *The Path, La hoja roja, Las ratas,* and *Five Hours with Mario,* there was increasing room for me to move. On this front, I struggled with censorship continuously and this fight bore its fruits. I think the majority of Spanish writers also did this, and that's why today, with forty years of censorship behind us, we can be proud of our work. We wrote more or less good literature, but we never rolled over and played dead for those in power.

MLG: Could you be called a chronicler of your time?

MD: In a way yes, but more than that I would say that my novels accurately describe people as they expressed themselves in the postwar years of rural Spain. I realize now that many of the novels I have written belong to a time of transition, and that quite a few of my characters are representative of that period, but not of present-day Spain. For instance, I could mention the retired man in *La hoja roja,* who is almost finished with life, whereas nowadays a sixty-five-year-old is almost beginning life. In the same way, the illiterate maid who works for him is also a relic of times gone by. There are hardly any illiterate servants around today; you address them differently, and they speak with far more propriety than my characters. I also think that the petite bourgeoisie, like the narrow-minded reactionary character Menchu in *Five Hours with Mario,* is on its way out. Fewer young men and women today speak and think that way; a whole behavior prevalent in Spain for centuries is being done away with. Sometimes I cannot help but wonder how some characters, who were perfectly alive and integrated into the society I knew when I wrote the novels, are left behind thirty years later. For instance, all the books in which I refer to a pre-industrial Castile have little to do with today's rural life. Nowadays, they don't sow the way they used to, scattering the seeds by hand, nor do they collect honey from beehives manually. The machines virtually do everything for them, and the end product seems so far removed from their place of origin.

MLG: Do you think your characters should adapt to today's reality?

MD: No, one has to faithfully recreate life at a given historic time, as Galdós did. If you have been faithful to your time, it is there for all to see. A character from 1930 may or may not be similar to one from 2030. The world keeps on changing, although I don't know if it is for the better.

MLG: Why do you think children relate so well to your book *The Path?*

MD: This book has become required reading in schools. Children write to me asking me what happened to the various characters; sometimes they even send me a one-page composition they have written about the child who goes to the city. They take the story very seriously and identify completely with the characters. I think I was lucky to create in that book an atmosphere that appeals to both children and grown-ups. The children because they are children, and the adults because they recognize themselves in those children in the book. The same thing happened when the book was translated. So I have to say its appeal is universal. In Spain alone, it has sold over two million copies. They sell a hundred thousand each year.

MLG: How does an author feel when he is so popular?

MD: It is rewarding to receive spontaneous letters from people you do not know. Some identify so deeply with my characters that they tell me, for instance, that they want to avoid Menchu's mistakes so they can salvage their own marriage. The greatest satisfaction for an author comes from those unexpected reactions to his writings. Or, when I go to a book fair, and I see a line of people who want my unworthy autograph, or when a lot of people attend one of my lectures. I sometimes wonder whether I haven't deceived them all and made them think that I am far better than I am.

MLG: Do you want to remake history through your work?

MD: I have to disagree whenever I hear my colleagues say that literature has no bearing on history. I think books greatly influence history; I always give two examples for this: the works of the Age of Enlightenment were a direct cause for the French Revolution, and the Bolshevik writings were an immediate precursor to the Russian Revolution. It seems to me that to consider those two major historical events without making reference to the writers who triggered them is to give an incomplete account.

MLG: Why do you write?

MD: I write to communicate with others, so perhaps there is an ethical element to my work, which I don't think is a good or necessary thing. But it does exist in me.

MLG: Do you believe in inspiration?

MD: No, I believe in work. Some people call this inspiration, but I call it hard work. I suppose inspiration could be when you come up with a theme for a book, but then you have to spend weeks and weeks working on it. On occasion, you are troubled by children or grandchildren, or whatever, so you can't concentrate that day.

MLG: So in order to write you must isolate yourself?

MD: Absolutely. If you are worried or disturbed it is very difficult to write. Writing is a most solitary journey. I have breakfast at home, and then I go to my studio where there is no telephone. I work there from 10 A.M. to 1 P.M. and then I take a one-hour walk and come home for lunch. In the afternoon, I see friends like you, journalists, and as many schoolchildren as possible who want to meet me; but I have to put some limit, otherwise I could go crazy. I like to feel accessible to people. I also write letters, go over the corrected copy of what I have written in the morning. I must confess to you that as I get older, I write less, and at sixty-eight I am also feeling a creative drought. Perhaps this is happening to me because I realize I can go no further. I could write another five novels, but I don't think they would be any better than the twenty I have written. I've lost the desire to improve my work.

MLG: Do you revise your books?

MD: I used to revise what I had written by hand a little, and then I would hand it over to a typist. But then people like you started analyzing my work closely, questioning why some things were expressed in one way and not in another. So it seemed to me that I had to take my writing more seriously. Consequently, I started doing two and sometimes three drafts in deference to the scholars. However, while it may be true that the third draft has gained something in terms of quality, it may also have lost the spontaneity and directness of the first draft.

MLG: Which version do you give to the publisher then?

MD: I always turn in the final one, because I think it is the best, but I am conscious that it may have lost some of the freshness of the initial draft.

Nevertheless, I must admit that I don't modify my novels all that much, although I will make alterations if I decide to do without a particular scene or chapter.

MLG: Do you have a first reader?

MD: My wife, when she was alive, was my first reader and censor. Not censor as in censorship, but more of a literary critic. She would suggest that I say some things another way, or that I restructure a chapter, and I followed her suggestions. She had more of a literary background than I did when I started out. At first, I didn't like her making comments, but after I thought about them, I would agree with her and make the changes. Nowadays, two of my children and two very good friends of mine are my primary readers. I usually pay heed to what they say because they are intelligent and well-read. When they agree on something, I say to myself, "They must be right."

MLG: Do you consider your novels experimental?

MD: No, but neither do I believe that they follow the routine pattern displayed by nineteenth-century writers. My novels are modern in terms of language, narration, the absence of an omniscient narrator. However, I don't consider my works avant-garde or surrealistic. I believe that what gives credibility to a novel and makes it interesting is the fact that it relies on human emotions.

MLG: How is a novel born?

MD: I think that all novelists use the same tricks. I don't sit around thinking about what I am going to write. The plot comes to me unexpectedly when I witness some incident, such as seeing a guy trapping rats with a small dog and a prod by the stream, or observing a romantic encounter or a public display of jealousy. So the theme of the novel takes you by surprise. Then you play around with that seed in your head until you arrive at an indefinite mixture of increasing complexity that eventually takes the form of characters and situations. That's when you are ready to give birth to the novel. This is how it happens with me, and I think with 90 percent of all writers.

MLG: Do you speak out loud what you write, as Camilo José Cela says he does in order to be able to hear the cadence of the phrases?

MD: No, I find this smacks of rhetorical narcissism. I don't go to those lengths. I am very concerned with the form, but not as much with the sound. What I do insist on is writing by hand, because I think the artist's pulse cannot be replaced by a computer. To feel the warmth of your hand and the touch of the pen, and to be able to transmit your feelings and your interpretation of beauty through the tip of that pen, is far different from doing it with a typewriter, because then there is a machine that stands in the way. I don't want anything to do with those machines, so I write by hand on really poor-quality paper, something I got used to doing when I worked for the newspaper *El Norte de Castilla.* That type of paper absorbs a lot of ink and lends itself to very thick calligraphy. After using it, in fact, I found that I could no longer write on better-quality paper with a good pen.

MLG: What do you feel when you finish a novel?

MD: On the one hand great peace, and on the other dissatisfaction, because what one has achieved is never close to the original conception. In my case, the finished product is always beneath my expectations. Some authors say they are fulfilled because they have reached their goal, but not I. I never believe I have achieved the peak of my potential. But nevertheless, some novels give me great happiness.

MLG: How would you explain the space between the first and last pages of a work, and does it vary from novel to novel?

MD: Yes, it does. In *Mi idolatrado hijo Sisí*, for instance, the action takes place over a twenty-year span, while in *El príncipe destronado* everything happens in nine hours. So I don't think that it is necessary for the plot of a novel to respond to a time frame. The story could go on for centuries, as in *One Hundred Years of Solitude,* or last one day, as in *El príncipe destronado.*

MLG: If you had to give shapes to your books, what would they be?

MD: Each one would be different. Yes, because once you have the theme, you have to stop thinking in literary terms and consider structural problems, such as whether to use a monologue or not, and other technical considerations. These technical matters are the second most important concern for a novelist.

MLG: Do you stand inside or outside your book when you write?

MD: Completely inside. This is a great problem for a writer, because if he spends his whole life writing about the life of his characters, he won't have lived his own, but unlived it. That is to say, he won't have felt or thought for himself, but rather for his characters. This is what's wrong with immersing oneself in the novel, because when it is being conceived and written, the author doesn't live his own life. He eats and walks in his sleep, because he is immersed in the life of his creation, not his own.

MLG: Do the characters dominate you then?

MD: No, absolutely not, I am with them but I am always the boss. I don't understand these stories writers tell about their secondary characters turning into the protagonists of their works. When I begin writing, I have already selected my materials and my characters, and everything fits in its place. When I write, no character exceeds his or her importance; if the character has a value quotient of ten, then he remains at ten, if twenty, then twenty, and so on. What I don't understand is how a character to which you have given a value of ten ends up having a value of seventy. I will never understand that, because I don't allow my characters to rebel. I am the boss, and not on account of a whim, but because I have already planned out the entire novel in my head before I start writing it.

MLG: What's more important to you: the book, the characters, or the ideas?

MD: In my opinion, what gives a book power and credibility are the characters. If you create lively characters, then whatever they do is believable, whereas, if you devise characters made of straw, the readers will not accept anything they do. So characters are the most important thing for me, and consequently, dialogue is essential in my novels.

MLG: What is language for you, and how do you adapt it to your various characters?

MD: It is a means for rational beings to communicate with one another, although everyone uses it in a different fashion. In the same way that there are several classes in society, there are various languages as well. There is an upper-crust language, a bourgeois language, a street language, a rural language, a female language, a male language . . . I like to listen to all these types so I can reflect them accurately.

MLG: How do you manage to convey all these voices?

MD: I think this is somewhat akin to a musician's ear for music. I have a bad ear for music, but a good one for expressions. When I go to a village, I already know the colloquial expressions they are going to use. For instance, in Castile they have a very peculiar form of greeting that is very distinctive and unlike that of other parts of Spain. So I have a good ear that allows me to pick up and re-create dialogue, as I did in the novel *Las guerras de nuestros antepasados.* The plot is about a doctor talking to one of his patients who is in jail. The patient speaks like a villager, while the doctor speaks like a man of his profession. I think that mixing these two modes of expression creates an interesting, entertaining effect in the novel.

MLG: Do you agree with the statement "Delibes and the absent interlocutor"?

MD: In some cases yes, in some no. In *Five Hours with Mario,* for instance, the interlocutor is a dead person. The technique of that novel allows for dialogue even with a dead man. Specifically, Menchu is responding to criticisms she imagines her dead husband to be leveling at her. So in that case, there is a dialogue even though the dead don't speak.

MLG: People have also wondered whether Mario dies of natural causes or kills himself in that novel. Can you clarify this?

MD: It was not a suicide. What I say in the book is what Mario's friends say: that he was a man who was killed by power and he ended up suffering a heart attack. The circumstances killed him, but he did not commit suicide.

MLG: Why does the child Gervasio García de la Lastra ask his grandfather, in *The Stuff of Heroes:* "Can I be a hero without dying?"

MD: The child is fascinated with stories about heroes, but what he doesn't like is that to be a hero you have to die. What he would love is to keep on living as a hero, respected by the townspeople. So that's why this six-year-old child asks his grandfather that question.

MLG: Is the character from *Cartas de amor de un sexagenario voluptuoso* derived from a real person?

MD: Yes, it is a literary joke I played on a person I really knew, but who never found out about it because he had passed away. He was a small, pretentious man who believed himself to be a great writer. I stuck him in this light novel—a collection of letters barely a hundred and fifty pages long. That work ends with a cruel and somewhat bloody mockery of that man who believes he has conquered a ravishing young beauty through his letters, when in fact he has been played for a fool by a cunning old woman. This book was my small revenge . . .

MLG: How do you come up with the titles for your books?

MD: Sometimes they come to me before starting the novel, because I already know what I want to say in it. Other times the opposite is true, and it is a great struggle to arrive at the title after the novel has been completed, as was the case with *Mi idolatrado hijo Sisí. The Stuff of Heroes,* on the other hand, is a novel that I had in my head since 1939, title and all.

MLG: Why did you choose the title *Mi idolatrado hijo Sisí?*

MD: It has nothing to do with my own children. It refers to the son of the main character of the book, Cecilio Rubes. My titles are usually more objective, but not in this case. As I told you, I really struggled to come up with that title.

MLG: What was involved in writing *Five Hours with Mario?*

MD: That was a long process. *Five Hours with Mario* was my way of seeing the dictatorship through the eyes of a young intellectual. So there are many autobiographical references, because I worked for a newspaper, taught at a university, and had many friendships with young people, and I knew what they thought. So my own experience was central to that novel. In the book, Mario is attacked by a *guardia civil* as he returns from his job at the newspaper; there is also an incident in which he uncorks champagne bottles and fires the tops at lampposts; and in an attempt to get his son a better grade, the butcher tries to bribe Mario with a rack of lamb. These incidents actually happened to me. I believe that *Five Hours with Mario* is more representative of the second period of the dictatorship than any other novel of that time. The references to Menchu and Mario in newspapers and in conversations nowadays are constant, perhaps because I did an adaptation of the novel for the stage. It has toured Spain three times in ten years, always to full houses. Many young people between the ages of seventeen and twenty-five go to see it, and although they didn't live through the dictatorship, they identify with the conflicts in the play. I think this is because they can relate to the sociological references of the play (particularly those dealing with relations between the sexes), more than with its political tenor. Relationships are a universal and eternal theme, so young people today see the play with the same enthusiasm as those who lived in Spain in the 1960s.

MLG: How did you conceive *The Stuff of Heroes?*

MD: I came up with the idea for that novel in the late 1930s.

MLG: But the book was published in 1987.

MD: Of course, because it couldn't be done before. I needed to write about the war I lived through with complete independence and objectivity. I don't know if objectivity is the right word—or whether such a thing is possible for any Spaniard who lived through that historic moment—but that was my aim. Naturally, that book could never have been published during the time of Franco. I accumulated data in my head, until I was finally able to write the novel two years ago. There are many autobiographical elements in the story of Gervasio, such as volunteering for the navy during the last year of the war, because I was afraid they would send me to the army otherwise. All of my novels have autobiographical elements, but some more than others.

MLG: In your works you pay a great deal of attention to detail. Is it to make fantasy and reality one and the same?

MD: There is fantasy, reality, and observation. In my work, there is more observation than autobiography or invention. By this I don't mean things that have happened to me, but rather observations that I have made in the streets or the countryside. Reality is only real because of details, and this is perhaps the reason I pay more attention to details than to things that might seem more important. Yes, your observation is relevant: I am more concerned with detail than with the sum of reality. In *Five Hours with Mario,* for instance, I am more interested in how Menchu utters her phrases than in what she says in them. I already know their content, which can be described in terms of the small-minded, cheap, bourgeois philosophy she espouses. This is made obvious by the turn of the phrases and the words, as well as the manner of placing adjectives. All of this is the verbal detail, so to speak, and it concerns me more than the content of the phrases, properly speaking.

MLG: How do you combine poetry and realism, gentleness and harshness?

MD: Intuitively. When I am elaborating a scene in a book, I don't think about what doses of gentleness, dramatism, and poetry I have to put in. I think this is implicit. If the writer is a sensitive man with some degree of humor or poetic flair, he will give a particular scene a sense of humor or a poetic touch. When you sit down to write, all these things are already assumed, they spring forth out of you, as if you were giving birth.

MLG: I have noticed that rhythm is very important to you, and that sometimes there are no periods in your work.

MD: Yes, *Los santos inocentes,* for instance, is a rhythmic novel, quite simply. It is a work with a cadence, and that's why I didn't put any periods in it. I wanted to give this cruel work a poetic form where rhythms and cadences—I would even add meter, because the syllables in the phrases are almost measured—are present. So you are right, rhythm is a great concern for me, and not only in that novel, but also in *Viejas historias de Castilla la Vieja, The Path, Las ratas,* and many other works.

MLG: Have any of your novels been made into movies?

MD: Yes, five of them: *The Path, El príncipe destronado, Los santos inocentes, El disputado voto del señor Cayo,* and *Mi idolatrado hijo Sisí.*

MLG: What do you feel when you see your works on the screen?

MD: Usually, one feels disappointment, because the characters one conceives in the book are very different from the way they appear in the movie. Nevertheless, I must say that I have been lucky with the movies, and I have liked most of the film adaptations of my work, except for *The Path,* because it was made at a time when Spanish moviemaking was still at a primitive stage.

MLG: Are you writing anything presently?

MD: Yes, I recently finished a work I had a lot of fun with called *Mi vida al aire libre.* Unlike most men of letters, I love sports and the great outdoors, and I have spent my life riding bicycles, playing tennis, mountain climbing, fishing, and hunting. So I decided to write a book about this part of my life most people don't know about. I decided to show them that I am not just a writer, I am also a sportsman, one who enjoys open skies and broad spaces. I love to practice sports, although I am not very good at it and don't take it too seriously. So the book is lighthearted and pleasant.

MLG: When you don't write, is the call of the great outdoors the only form of relaxation?

MD: I read, but less and less. I'm beginning to act like an old man. If I'm not interested in the book I am reading, I fall asleep; if I don't like what I see on television, I fall asleep; I'm always falling asleep, except when I go to bed at night. I love going to the movies, but they are not making too many good pictures these days. As I just mentioned, I also ride my bicycle, play tennis, hunt, fish, go for a swim or on hikes with my children or my friends. I'm always doing something.

MLG: What does nature mean to you?

MD: Everything. Nature is the one great cause nowadays, and one that brings me into conflict with political parties of various stripes, because in Spain all the ecological groups have a political ideology. I would like to see a movement concerned purely with defending nature. Who cares whether it has to be nationalized or turned over to private industry. The important thing is that we defend nature, because we are nature. We depend on it, and if it dies, man will die with it. So we have to defend it, even if only for selfish reasons. Ecological fears are numberless, don't you think? Aren't you afraid of the greenhouse effect? This is terrible, and what is worse is the indifference of governments around the world in the face of this problem. Wise men are concerned, but they never run the world, which is why it is in such terrible shape. If governments gave power to these wise men, you would see how quickly they would put an end to the problems of the ozone layer and the pollution of our seas and rivers. We would resolve all those difficulties. The problem is that wise men are not warriors, while politicians are to some extent, so they always prevail over the wise. We are governed by politicians and not wise men, and as a result we are profoundly uncomfortable and afraid.

MLG: Nevertheless, you like to hunt!

MD: Yes, because I don't believe I'm harming nature in any way, nor killing it. The only animals I hunt are those whose population increases in Spain every year. Why is this so? Because we take care of their nests when they are nesting and we give them water in the summer when it doesn't rain. For instance, if there are one hundred partridges at the end of the hunting season, there are five hundred at the beginning of the next one, so they are in no danger of extinction.

MLG: What do you hunt?

MD: Only small game: partridges, rabbits, and hares. I cannot bring myself to hunt larger game, such as deer or gazelles, because they have eyes that are almost human.

MLG: So you couldn't hunt them.

MD: I couldn't extinguish those eyes. I find those animals too close to us. I'll tell you the formula I use: for me, two dead partridges mean food for the storehouse, while one dead deer is a corpse. That's the difference. Most people don't understand this. I don't suffer pangs of conscience from killing and eating a partridge, because it is the same thing as with a chicken. It is quite another matter, however, to point a shotgun at a deer with its beautiful horns and expressive eyes; I have never been able to do that, because I consider it monstrous.

MLG: I'm very glad to hear that you would not kill a deer. You mentioned ecological fears. Would you care to comment on the role fear does play in your work?

MD: Not only in my work, also in my life. I am a man of great fears. When a grandchild is born, I am always beset by fears that he will be deformed or suffer from some terrible condition. I am also physically afraid of war. I didn't have the stuff that heroes are made of, like Gervasio García de la Lastra. War made me genuinely scared, fear would eat at me, leave my stomach dry and my heart paralyzed. I could withstand those fears, however. Fear is a great concern in my life: I am afraid of a nuclear conflict, the spread of Islamic fundamentalism, fanaticism in general, and Nazism, that horrible system that used people's fat to make bars of soap. I think that there are plenty of reasons to be scared because of our history, and he who doesn't feel afraid is a completely callous person.

MLG: Do you view the future of our children with a certain amount of apprehension?

MD: I feel very close to my own childhood, because death seemed thousands of centuries away and there was no ambition, egoism, or greed to reckon with. I think it is the most wonderful period of our life. I love children for the simple reason that they represent the potential to do or be anything— that unknown factor which makes us wonder what the child is going to become. Adults have already chosen their path, so for me they have lost that mystery. I am the father of seven children and I have twelve grandchildren.

If each of my children had as many offspring as I did, I would have forty-nine grandchildren, although I realize now is not the time to have so many. This is another cause for fear. In Sweden only .5 children per couple are born, which means that in a few years there will be only one new Swede for every four that will die. The Turks and the Spaniards will have to fill the empty spaces. But the same thing is true of Spaniards today. Each couple now has 1.5 children, instead of two as they used to, so they have also learned the lesson. This is another problem. Of course the alternative is also unacceptable. When I said in *Mi idolatrado hijo Sisí,* "Grow, multiply and swell the earth," I was thinking of a planet with two to three billion inhabitants. Since then, the earth's population has more than doubled, so I think Malthus was right when he said that while man's reproductive capabilities are limitless, his capacity to produce food is limited. So I have many fears.

MLG: You are very sincere in admitting to those fears, while many people try to ignore them, although they feel them too. What is your attitude toward death?

MD: Any thinking, feeling man has to find death unsettling. I suppose if we were all as egocentric as Don Miguel de Unamuno, we would turn death itself into the Gordian knot of our work! I believe that we have to try to overcome our fears and doubts about death, and not be so concerned that it affects us directly. Otherwise, all books would be dedicated to death and have the same tone as the works of Unamuno. They would be infused with a tremendous survival of the self in a search of immortality which—to borrow one of Unamuno's outlandish statements—"preferred hell to nothingness." In some sense or other, nonetheless, we all feel these doubts the way Unamuno did.

MLG: Are you a religious person?

MD: I am a thoughtful religious man, and as such I have many doubts, although I wish I still had the simple faith of my childhood years. So I would like to have a blind faith, although I do not. I do meet certain religious requirements of my faith: I go to church, I pray, and, in general, I try to perform acts that have something to do with the spiritual life. Nevertheless, I must emphasize that my religious sentiments right now are dominated by doubt and concern.

MLG: Your work *La sombra del ciprés es alargada* certainly displays a religious inclination.

MD: My faith was stronger then.

MLG: What other obsessions do you bring to your work?

MD: I don't know, I think they are all mixed in with these fears, although I am obsessed with the destructive potential of absolute power, a subject I tackled in my novel *The Hedge.* I am referring to people who, because of their faith, are progressively degraded until they become sheep or dogs. That happens because those who rule don't want complete, whole human beings. This was the case with the Nazis in Germany, and we also witnessed it in the Soviet Union and in Argentina, as well as in other parts of the world.

MLG: Now that Spain has become a democratic country, do you think you have fewer things to say?

MD: There are always things to fight against. I just mentioned some of them to you in a moment of inspiration: all those fears have to be attacked.

MLG: If you could speak with a writer from the past, with whom would you share these thoughts?

MD: I'd be interested in speaking with Proust, and especially with Kafka. Mental conflicts, depressions, and hallucinations would give me plenty of material to talk over with Kafka.

MLG: Do you see some resemblance between your work and that of Latin American writers?

MD: I think that my work, like theirs, has a personality: it is ethical, melancholic, humanistic. I believe that each writer creates his own world, and it is easy to define it with simple words. Elaborate descriptions are superfluous.

MLG: Who is Miguel Delibes?

MD: An unsophisticated country fellow who decided to scribble one day, and to whom excessive importance has been ascribed by journalists, scholars, and critics. I am always in a quandary because you expect so much from me. I am unable to say more, because I think you have attached more importance to me than I deserve. I say this from the bottom of my heart. Some people may put up a mask when they are interviewed. But I don't have anything to hide.

Lidia
Falcón

CABRERU

Born in 1935 in Madrid, where she now lives, Lidia Falcón O'Neill spent most of her life in Barcelona. Her parents were journalists. Her mother, Enriqueta O'Neill, wrote under the name of Regina Flavio; her father, César Falcón, was a Peruvian who settled in Spain prior to the Civil War and disappeared at its outset. Her childhood was spent among five women: her mother, her aunt, her grandmother, and her two cousins.

In 1954, at the age of eighteen, she started writing short stories for women's magazines. In 1956, she began to study law at the Barcelona Law School. She also studied dramatic arts at the Barcelona Theater Institute. She then entered the Barcelona Official School of Journalism and, in 1959, graduated from the Madrid School of Journalism.

Falcón is a writer, journalist, lawyer, and founder of the First Feminist Party in Spain. Since 1960, she has been working as a lawyer in her own law firm, specializing in labor, constitutional, and marital law. In 1979, she founded the feminist magazine *Poder y libertad,* where she serves as editor in chief.

Falcón has written countless articles that have appeared in many leading newspapers in both Madrid and Barcelona. She is also known for her many books, which include documentary essays about the status of women and fictional works. Among them are *Mujer y sociedad: Análisis de un fenómeno reaccionario* (Women and Society: Analysis of a Reactionary Phenomenon), 1969; *Cartas a una idiota española* (Letters to a Spanish Idiot), 1974; *Es largo esperar callado* (The Long Silent Wait), 1975; *Los hijos de los vencidos* (The Children of the Vanquished), 1979; *La razón feminista, I: La mujer como clase social* (The Feminist Reason, I: Women as a Social Class), 1981; *La razón feminista, II: La reproducción humana* (The Feminist Reason, II: Human Reproduction), 1982; *El juego de la piel*

(The Skin Game), 1983; *El alboroto español* (The Spanish Uproar), 1984.

Imprisoned on several occasions for political reasons, she first spent five months at the Trinidad women's prison of Barcelona for having printed in 1972 the clandestine pamphlet *La verdad*. In 1974, she spent nine months in the Yeserías women's penitentiary in Madrid, falsely implicated in a trial against a Basque terrorist group.

While in prison, she became a chronicler of the nightmare women underwent in jail. In a tiny handwriting on onionskin paper, she managed to write about that hell and pass the manuscript on bit by bit to her family and friends who came to visit her. This material makes up the following two books: *En el infierno: Ser mujer en las cárceles de España* (In Hell: To Be a Woman in Spain's Prisons), 1977, and *Viernes y 13 en la Calle del Correo* (Friday the Thirteenth on Correo Street), 1981.

Lidia Falcón is a very committed author who said, "If it is true that the male writer is the conscience of the world, the female writer must be the conscience of womankind."

Part of this interview with Lidia Falcón took place in my home, during one of her trips to New York. A tall, attractive woman, she is articulate, very much in love with life and most passionate, especially when defending the cause of battered women. While I interviewed her, both of us seated around the dining-room table, she did a sketch of me. The rest of the interview took place in her Madrid home in the spring of 1989. She lives in a tiny top-floor apartment in an old section of town, which she has turned into a cozy abode. Books and paintings, including some of her own sketches, cover the walls. An inside staircase leads to an upper-level floor where there is just enough room for her desk and bookshelves.

❖❖❖❖❖❖❖❖❖❖❖❖❖❖❖❖❖❖❖❖❖❖❖❖❖

MLG: As a novelist, playwright, poet, and journalist, you always approach your work from a feminist point of view. As a lawyer and founder of the First Feminist Party in Spain, you write articles, take polls, conduct seminars, and participate in conferences dealing with the condition of women all over the world. Do you think that we could now discuss your work from a literary point of view?

LF: I believe we can. I have never really abandoned the idea of giving my writings a literary form. As a matter of principle, when I develop an idea for a newspaper article because I am defending a cause, I keep in mind that it must be to the point and precise, but at the same time never turn into just another pamphlet. I endeavor to stay away from a purely informative and militant writing and make sure to attract the attention of my readers through the beauty of the language and the structure of the article itself. To me, the aesthetics of form is imperative.

MLG: So you do not see the written word just as a combat weapon?

LF: Of course not! It is, however, the only weapon that I do accept, but it is also a means of communication between people and an expression of beauty.

MLG: How does one write a novel?

LF: Your question brings to mind something that Unamuno once said. He would classify writers into two separate groups, those that were viviparous and those that were oviparous. The oviparous ones constantly take notes, jotting down in their pads ideas from books they have been reading or thoughts that occur to them and, after a period of time, they organize these notes and use them in the making of the novel. The viviparous ones establish a mental filing system without putting down on paper the novel that is slowly taking shape in their minds and, one day, all of a sudden they sit in front of the typewriter and go to work. I must tell you I partake a little bit of both, but perhaps more of the latter; I am more viviparous than oviparous. I slowly elaborate the plot and the structure of the novel in my mind. First of all, I must find the crux of the novel. I believe that for a narrative to be attractive to the reader it is essential to sustain the interest in the plot. My subjects for a novel may arise from almost anything, an event on the street, something I have just read, memories of things gone by that I personally experienced. I describe my main characters in the light of the particular plot and I add on others, setting them in the appropriate surroundings, as Simenon used to say. The rest is easy. I sit at my typewriter and I write the novel in one go.

MLG: Where do you find those characters?

LF: In everyday life. The moment I sit down in my office, my clients come to me with thousands of stories. I would love to have the time and energy to write about them. It would make for a very interesting gallery of characters. I sometimes wish I could live two parallel lives, one in which I would continue what I am doing now, and the other where I would play only author. That other Lidia would be sitting at her typewriter, writing about all the women that come to see me at my law office. They are all very rich in emotions and as you can see I am not lacking in ideas for characters.

MLG: Since we are on the topic of characters, who dominates whom?

LF: I suppose that all authors have told you that at a given moment characters begin to live their own lives. At first, I shape them after people in real life, taking from them some distinguishing marks, the look in their eyes, the way they walk, the way they react. And then all of a sudden I realize that the characters don't follow the patterns I set for them; they begin to do things I did not expect them to do. Often, when I have reached the midpoint of the novel, I must go back to the beginning and make changes so that the characters will not behave in a contradictory fashion. At the onset of the novel, some characters are sober and then they begin to drink; others are intelligent and they become fools, and still others do strange things. As a result, I must sometimes make drastic changes, eliminate characters and circumstances, and let them alter the world I had created for them.

MLG: Are there more women characters than men?

LF: Not exactly, not in numbers anyway. It is not the number that counts! Women are always surrounded by men, they have fathers, husbands, brothers, sons, bosses ... The important thing is to describe these women in depth in relation to themselves, with other women and with men, in their personal tragedy and everyday drama. I never consider men and women with indifference as some authors do, because this would be a terrible injustice.

MLG: You lend your voice to the silent cry of oppressed and battered women to tell their untold stories.

LF: What you say is beautiful; this is what I would like to do!

MLG: When you tackle a novel or a play, do you do it from the point of view of a chronicler?

LF: Yes indeed, this is the way I want to transmit through the spoken word the tragedy of oppressed women.

MLG: Your works then are based on reality?

LF: Of course. I am often indignant when I read a critic of my works who claims that I make up unreal situations or that I exaggerate or dramatize events. On the contrary, I'll never be able to describe accurately enough the everyday reality of women. Real life always surpasses literature.

MLG: Fantasy holds no place in your literary creation?

LF: I would say that imagination claims its own space in my literary creation. Fantasy, on the other hand, transports you to an unreal world that does not interest me. This does not mean, of course, that there are not great writers of fantastic adventures in which magic plays a crucial part. It seems to me that to take refuge in a magical world is like running away from your own reality and that of others. Fantasy plays no part in exposing or resolving one's problems and those of others, nor does it serve as a diversion, at least not for me. Fairy tales began to bore me at the age of twelve. But going back to the part imagination plays in writing, I think it is imperative. Without it, no literature would be produced, one would then be a lawyer writing a brief, and a bad one at that. It would be like holding a tape recorder before a character and having him tell his own story. Not even Truman Capote, who claimed to do just that, stopped seasoning his works with his imagination or creativity, if you prefer to call it that. I do not write a detailed chronicle of real people; I create characters that are symbolic and universal, based on my own experience and that of others. Each character is a composite of traits that pertain to many people in real life. And, of course, as I have said before, it is imperative to find a plot that holds everything together. Even to include some mystery, so that the reader will be kept in suspense until the end.

MLG: Do you think about your reader when you write and who is that reader?

LF: There are some authors who say they write for themselves. Of course, they are entitled to their own opinion. For my part, I think it would be egotistic and narcissistic to see literature as just a form of personal enjoyment. It would turn literature into a catharsis or psychoanalysis rather than a channel for transmitting a work of art. Basically I write for women, although personally I would like my works to have a universal appeal and be read by all. I always feel very fulfilled when a male reader becomes better acquainted with the feminine condition through my books and expresses awe or surprise. Recently, a college professor, who is a philosopher and not a writer, read *En el infierno* and told me how much he had been moved by it. This was very gratifying for me. He had been totally unaware of the sufferings endured by women in prison.

MLG: Do you believe that women write differently from men?

LF: Yes and no. Yes, from the point of view that we experience things we do not share with men—for instance, maternity. They do not know what it is like to be pregnant or give birth or breast-feed. In addition, we have been educated differently, we are more in tune with everyday activities, more in touch with reality. We have a better perception of minor details, we are better prepared to take care of others and to preserve life. Not only do we transmit life, but we also conserve it, even those of us who never had any children. We are far better prepared to take care of children, of the elderly, and to make life easier for everyone. This is what constitutes the feminine experience, and therefore it produces a very different kind of literature. This is not to say that men do not have the necessary sensitivity and humanity to get involved in the daily life of their family. But some men do not choose to; they do not take care of their family or watch after their sick ones, they are not concerned with minor problems and do not raise their children. On the other hand, there are men who are capable of caring; and, as a result, works like Ibsen's *A Doll's House* are produced. When writers, regardless of whether they are men or women, possess that capacity for sensitivity, they produce works that are equally powerful. As for my own style of writing, it cannot be classified as traditional feminine literature; I hope it is stronger and universal.

MLG: You have written works of fiction as well as research works. What is more appealing to you?

LF: Perhaps at this stage in my life it is more interesting for me to write fiction. I would like to write a book about love. It would be an essay reflecting some of the different aspects that love elicits in human beings, and how men and women relate to it. This is another viviparous book that I have in mind. On the whole, I feel more and more the need to write fiction.

MLG: *Cartas a una idiota española* has brought you great success. What made you want to adapt this book for the theater?

LF: Strictly speaking, the success achieved by that book. When I meet strangers in any part of Spain, the first thing I am asked is how I came up with the characters for that ironic essay. So last year, when I organized the

First Women's International Theater Show in Madrid, I was persuaded to bring to the stage three of the twenty women prototypes taken from that book. The actress Conchita Velasco told me that she always had wanted to do a film or play in which she could portray some of my "idiotas," and she gave me the idea for it. So, I sat down and chose the following: the frustrated middle-aged woman, frustrated because she was taught only to look for a good husband and get married, a typical old-fashioned Spanish girl with almost no schooling. The second is the clerk/typist, the young girl who wants to work and prosper, but cannot succeed since the large companies are run by men who belittle women and claim that the only place for them is in the typing pool. The third is the kind of woman who chooses a free, sort of hippie lifestyle, has had children from different men, and then realizes that, with two or three children around her, there are not too many things open to her in life and she cannot fulfill herself. The actress who played them, and identified with each of them, was Gemma Cuervo. She was fantastic. You would love that play, it is quite beautiful. I think a video will soon be released.

MLG: What impact has censorship had on your works?

LF: Some things were censored. I had to wait for over a year before *Mujer y sociedad,* for example, could be published. Lines in red ink were drawn through many parts of the manuscript, but in most instances I managed to overcome censorship by rewriting basically the same thing over what had been crossed out. Since the censors were not using a magnifying glass to scan through the corrections, they seemed satisfied. The truth is that I have never succumbed to censorship. I would never have agreed to mutilate my texts. Of course, it was impossible for *Es largo esperar callado* to be published in those days and I had to wait a long time for the book to come out.

MLG: Do you feel that censorship may have had a positive effect on literary creation, because it forced authors into inventing devices to evade its restrictive control?

LF: No, no, censorship stifles the imagination and enslaves the mind. And the worst thing that can happen to a writer is to write under the yoke of fear. It can never be a positive sign. One may have to develop a defense mechanism to be able to carry on, but the creative mind needs to be as free as possible. It would be like saying that to be in jail is a positive experience because the outside world stimulates in the prisoner a sense of survival. All restrictions reduce an author and his work to nothing.

MLG: What are you writing at present?

LF: I am finishing a novel and I have another one about to be published. The one I am working on now is about two hundred pages long, it has a different structure from my previous novels. There are many characters, both men and women. I don't make value judgments, I just describe them as they act in concrete situations. If the publisher agrees, I would like to call that novel "Postmodernos." It sums up the misery, lack of enthusiasm and ambition, and the pettiness of a broad sector of today's Spanish society.

MLG: Do you feel most comfortable writing novels, short stories, or plays?

LF: It has been many years since I have written a short story. I did write hundreds of them that were published in Spanish newspapers when I was younger and starting out. I believe that they were of the oviparous kind since I took many notes. These notes amount to a collection of tales that someday I may structure into a book about women living in New York, Puerto Rico, and different parts of Spain. For the time being, I am more interested in the novel and the theater.

MLG: Do you always take notes?

LF: Sometimes I take mental notes, sometimes I jot them down on paper, especially when I am traveling. In that way, I do not feel so much the endless waiting time at airports, or in flight, or in hotel rooms, after conferences I have attended or lectures I have given. I always bring back notebooks from every country I go to and I keep them on file. I like to read these notes later on, and I may make use of them in some of my works. They may relate to an experience I have gone through, people I observed while sitting at a café.

MLG: Do you have a favorite work of yours?

LF: It is perhaps *Es largo esperar callado.* Why? Probably because it is very autobiographical. In it I describe my first emotions, I speak about the resistance movement against Franco, the suffering of my companions and of people that were exiled. It is also a description of my relationship with Eliseo. All these things make the book very dear to me; it is a continuous series of flashbacks.

MLG: Do you believe that if you had not lived in such a critical moment in Spanish history, if you had not gone through the postwar experience and the oppression of dictatorship, your life would have been different?

LF: Definitely! All these things had a profound impact on all Spaniards, those that escaped and those that remained behind. My life would not have been so hard. My family was made up of intellectuals, involved with writers and journalists. I would have lived in a more stable economic position, I could have studied in peace. But I don't believe, however, that those years affected me as far as my views on women's problems are concerned. The feminist movement now encompasses the entire world.

MLG: Recently you visited Peru for the first time, the land of your father. Would your life have been different had he not disappeared from your home during the Spanish Civil War?

LF: Of course, life would have been somewhat different. Although I don't believe that war was the factor that severed his relationship with us. I think my father would not have stayed at home had there been no war, nor would he have shared special moments with me. Had he done so, of course my life would have been enriched by his presence. Apart from his irresponsibility as a family man, he was a very intelligent person, very progressive in his way of thinking and a fighter. In order to become a member of the Communist Party in the twenties, he abandoned a very good professional and economic position (he was the London correspondent for *El Sol* and his articles were coveted by the major Spanish newspapers and magazines). He left all this to devote his time to social battles in the defense of the poor and the oppressed. And I believe I have followed in his footsteps.

MLG: Your father's family in Peru had no knowledge of your existence?

LF: My life is like a soap opera. Imagine, he never spoke about my mother nor myself to his brothers. I recently met one of his fellow comrades, an elderly journalist who has now returned to Spain. He had worked with my father before the war and even during the war, and had seen him in Paris, in the forties, while in exile. He told me that my father had never once mentioned us to him. From Paris my father moved to Mexico, but chose to go back to Peru to die. When he died in 1971, my uncle Jorge wrote a book in his honor. Jorge Falcón is a great writer, very well known. He published a biography of my father which also includes an anthology of his works. Using my father's address book, he sent this volume to a series of people in Spain, France, and Mexico who must have known my father. This is how my mother received the book and found out about her husband's death. You can imagine what a shock it was to her! Jorge Falcón had no idea that he was writing to his late brother's wife and his letter to her, although friendly enough, was addressed as he would have to any other member of the profession, telling of the death of César Falcón. A few months later, I received a letter from Jorge Falcón, explaining that he had found my book *Mujer y sociedad* in Lima and that he was wondering whether I was using a pseudonym or whether I might be a niece, born in Spain during the Civil War. This is the way I established contact with my father's family, when I was more than thirty years old!

MLG: You spent your childhood among five women: your mother, your grandmother, your aunt, and your two cousins. Do you believe that this has had a special impact on your life?

LF: Yes, this has been a determining factor. I am a feminist because both my mother and my grandmother were feminists. I owe everything to them. I was educated to keep my eyes open and my other senses sharp. In the postwar years it was difficult for five women to survive. These were intellectuals who had not been brought up to do menial tasks. My mother took employment at an office as a secretary and had to learn shorthand and filing. My father was in exile, my aunt Carlota's husband had been executed, but both my mother and my aunt were able to bring up their daughters without ever having to resort to the indignities that were very common in those days. They never lost that inborn dignity and taught us how to defend it as well.

MLG: What are some of the works that have influenced you?

LF: I have read many books. When I was younger, I studied the works of Cela and, through them, especially *The Hive,* he was like a mentor to me. Later on, I found Céline's style very interesting. Today's American novel and feminist works such as Alice Walker's book *The Color Purple* represent what I am searching for: a concise style and penetrating emotions. I could add that Mercè Rodoreda, although she writes in Catalan, could be taken as a guide to follow in any language.

MLG: What do you think of literary prizes?

LF: It could be a way to open new avenues for young writers, but it is not always so. The winner is often decided beforehand and it becomes public knowledge. The literary critic goes by these awards and, therefore, it is very difficult to join the ranks of the most important writers in the country if you have never been the recipient of one of these prizes.

MLG: Do you think you could write a short story, novel, or play without ever including the feminist point of view?

LF: I don't always include the feminist theme. In my last novel, I let my characters interact and I never show my point of view, I just describe the facts. It so happens that the facts denounce women's rights. These women face problems that are peculiar to them. Not to write about these problems would be the same as tracing empty words that do not relate the truth, describing women's lives as they are not.

MLG: A few years ago you said, "If it is true that the writer is the conscience of the world, the female writer must be the conscience of womankind." Do you still believe this?

LF: Of course, I do. I have not changed my way of thinking.

MLG: You also said, "I believe that a woman writer cannot abdicate her responsibility to report the reality that surrounds her."

LF: It hurts me to see that there are great women writers who are capable of describing a world devoid of women as they truly are. In Spain, since there are many prejudices, women writers are afraid to admit to their feminism, for fear that publishers might not print their works. If they write about women, they describe them as men see them, not from the women's point of view. Writing as feminists would belittle them. Yet there are great feminist authors in other countries, who are not afraid to declare themselves as such: Nadine Gordimer, Doris Lessing, Alice Walker, for instance.

MLG: I have often wondered why the nineteenth-century novelist Fernán Caballero, being a woman, would give in *La Gaviota* the good character to the male and the bad one to the female.

LF: This is precisely what I was saying. She had to adopt the ideology of the male culture, the machista ideology that portrays women as wicked and corrupt. She had to wear the mask of a man to become successful and position herself in a world where male values were predominant. But Fernán Caballero is not the only woman guilty of that. Other women have had to adopt a male pseudonym to be accepted: Víctor Català, George Eliot, George Sand. Some of them, of course, were able to denounce the conditions that oppressed women and write important feminist works. Note that, when Ibsen wrote *A Doll's House,* he could defend women because he was a man. A year ago, I wrote an article entitled "If I Were a Man." If I had been a man, I would have had more opportunities to defend women. If I had written as a man in favor of women, I would have received many literary prizes and medals for my social activities. I would have been among the ranks of important writers. A man can do anything without being criticized; at worst they would say he is a bit of an eccentric. Whites can defend blacks, men can defend women, from an altruistic point of view. But when the oppressed stands up and speaks out loud, people who hold the power consider them crazy and say that they exaggerate and they don't know what they are doing.

MLG: Why do you think that Emilia Pardo Bazán portrays a weak woman in *Los pazos de Ulloa?*

LF: I believe that it is a feminist novel. She merely describes a woman of her time who, unfortunately, still exists today. These are sweet, submissive women who want to live a tranquil life and that's why they are beaten. The nicer and more tender a woman is, the more she is put down. In addition to this, the social conditions in Emilia's time were terrible. This is what she denounces in her work. It is in no way an allegory of a Joan of Arc, there are not too many of them. And we lift our voices in protest because they cannot do it themselves.

MLG: The young priest in *Los pazos de Ulloa* is so good and gentle, but he cannot change the order of things.

LF: The good are crushed by the villains who thrive on violence. I find this novel to be a capital work in describing the plight of the good who are murdered or belittled.

MLG: Are there other writers like you in Spain today?

LF: We are all different. When the feminist movement became important in Spain in the seventies and many women came out to protest their living conditions, I published several feminist magazines. It was prestigious to be called a feminist. The truth is that they have backtracked quite a bit. Now these women have ideological doubts. In a man's world they have to be respected by a male boss, a male director of personnel, a male lover, a husband, and in the end it is very difficult to resist. If you follow this line of thought, if you don't give in, you will miss out on many opportunities. You take the risk of remaining marginal, much like the black writer, the proletarian writer, or the man or woman who is defending the cause of the oppressed.

MLG: You have been in the United States on several occasions. What is your impression of that country?

LF: It has been an extraordinary experience to know and live in a country where all is possible. Of course, not everything is perfect. But in Europe, and in Spain in particular, you are limited by social classes, by family names, by traditions. Work is not always rewarded. In the United States it seems that opportunities are given to those who wish to fight for them.

MLG: Who is Lidia Falcón?

LF: Heavens! All that you have heard and a bit more. You know her very well!

LAYLE SILBERT

Juan Goytisolo

Juan Goytisolo was born in 1931 in Barcelona into a bourgeois family. His father was the main shareholder of the Barcelona Gum and Fertilizer Company and was a rather austere man. His mother was an avid reader who valued culture. She was killed by a "nationalist" bomb in 1938, during an air raid. Goytisolo recounts in a very moving fashion in *Coto vedado,* 1985 (*Forbidden Territory,* 1989), how the mother had gone shopping and never returned home. In her bag were the books and toys she had bought for her four children. In his memoirs, he tells of the hardships brought about by the Civil War and the intolerance and hypocrisy that prevailed in postwar Spain and in his own home. All this led him to abhor that society and made him feel an outsider.

Goytisolo was educated in a Jesuit school and later studied law. But, like his two brothers, José Agustín and Luis, his call was writing. In 1952, when he was in his twenties, he won the Janés Young Literature Prize for a short story, "El mundo de los espejos" (The World of Mirrors).

After spending a few months in Paris, he decided to make it his home. Since 1957, he has been living in Paris and in Marrakech. These two settings have given him the room to breathe and expand, which he so much yearned for when he was a young boy. The return of Spain to democracy could have put an end to his self-imposed exile, but he chose not to move back.

Goytisolo is one of the Spanish writers who has been most translated into English and who enjoys the same kind of popularity as Latin Americans. Carlos Fuentes has called him "the greatest living Spanish novelist." Like the writers of the Boom—although he does not like that term—he tackles provocative, taboo topics and makes constant attacks on the Spanish language to give it a new dimension and vitality. He chastises the Spain that oppressed him and discovers the Spain that he loves in writers like the Archpriest of Hita, Francisco Delicado, and Francisco de Quevedo. On more than one occasion he has been referred to as the Spanish Joyce.

Among his books are *Juegos de manos,* 1954 (*The Young Assassins,* 1959); *Duelo en el paraíso,* 1955 (*Children of Chaos,* 1958); *Fiestas,* 1958 (English translation, 1960); *Campos de Níjar,* 1959, *La Chanca,* 1962 (*The Countryside of Níjar and La Chanca,* 1987); *Señas de identidad,* 1966 (*Marks of Identity,* 1969); *Reivindicación del Conde don Julián,* 1970 (*Count Julian,* 1974); *Juan sin tierra,* 1975 (*Juan the Landless,* 1977); *Makbara,* 1980 (English translation, 1981); *Paisajes después de la batalla,* 1982 (*Landscapes after the Battle,* 1987); *Coto vedado,* 1985 (*Forbidden Territory,* 1989); *Las virtudes del pájaro solitario,* 1988 (*The Virtues of the Lonely Bird,* 1991).

Goytisolo is a modern man who finds his roots in the Middle Ages and rejects the Renaissance.

I saw Juan Goytisolo in Paris. He received me in a study, separated from his apartment by a narrow corridor. It had a private entrance. I rang the bell at the wrong door and his wife Monique Lange showed me the way. Goytisolo looked like a medieval monk, sitting in a very austere room, with a bed, two chairs, a bookcase, and a small desk. He showed me some of his manuscripts and explained that he always wrote by hand. I could feel that objects did not have a hold on him. A rather shy and withdrawn person, he spoke in a soft voice and for a moment I was concerned that the tape recorder would lose some of his words. I had just flown from New York, it was May Day, a national holiday in France, and it was very warm. Goytisolo went across the hall to bring two glasses of Perrier. As the interview progressed, he began to open up. He talked about his isolation from twentieth-century Spain and his strong ties with pre-Renaissance Spain.

❖❖❖❖❖❖❖❖❖❖❖❖❖❖❖❖❖❖❖❖❖❖❖❖❖❖❖❖

MLG: In your memoirs *Forbidden Territory* you explain why you left Spain in 1957 and settled in Paris. Would you like to say something about this?

JG: I wanted to escape from a closed cultural environment and oppressive censorship, so that I might join a society that was more open, where I could really come into contact with all the strands of modern culture. So my reasons for leaving Spain were both political and cultural. I was against Franco's regime and the stifling cultural isolation Spain had to endure at the time.

MLG: Haven't you thought of going back to Spain now that there is a democracy?

JG: For the past fifteen years, I have spent most of my time in Paris and Morocco. You get accustomed to certain things as well as to people.

MLG: Why did you choose Morocco?

JG: Because of my interest and affinity with that culture. When I write in Paris, I have to lock myself in my house and sacrifice my entire social life, whereas in Marrakech I can both work and live. There is something about that great city that allows me to write and stimulates my personal life.

MLG: Would I be wrong in saying that you represent a bridge between the European and North African civilizations?

JG: I wouldn't put it that way. In Spain, they usually speak about me as the representative of the modern literary avant-garde. I have always said that I am more a writer who brings up the rear, because I have learned the most from medieval authors. You mustn't forget that Spain was once a country that stood at the crossroads and was home to three different cultures. The monks of Cluny came through Santiago and brought us the emerging culture of Europe. Meanwhile, the Jewish translators of Toledo transmitted all the literature the Arabs had written and compiled. In those times, Spain was a cultural center. I am very interested in other traditions, and I don't believe in cultural nationalism—there can be no such thing as a French, Spanish, English, German, Italian, or even European culture. What Spain's history teaches us is that, when a society is open, it produces some true literary masterpieces, but as soon as it shuts itself off, it crumbles, with some exceptions.

MLG: Do you believe that you stand as a link between the Americas and Spain because of your ties to the writers of the so-called Boom?

JG: I don't like the word *Boom*. I would say that there are affinities between some Latin American writers and myself, which are stronger than with my compatriots, even though I was born in Spain. For instance, I feel closer to Cabrera Infante, Severo Sarduy, or Carlos Fuentes than to the majority of my colleagues in Spain. In the same breath, I should also say that my connection with Spanish writers from the past, such as the Archpriest of Hita, Francisco Delicado, Fernando de Rojas, or Saint John of the Cross, is far stronger than the one with my Spanish contemporaries. So I am a little uncertain about the concept: after all, what possible reason can there be for my belief that a sixteenth-century writer, such as Delicado, is my contemporary while I don't consider that many of the writers you have interviewed for this book are? With the exception of Julián Ríos, I am on a different wavelength from them. I am splendidly isolated.

MLG: When I interviewed Carlos Fuentes, he told me that the Boom came to an end at a party given in your house.

JG: Yes, there was a gathering at my house, attended by Vargas Llosa, Cortázar, Donoso, Carlos Fuentes, etc., when we started a literary magazine. When its publication stopped, the friendship among some of us disappeared. It was the Padilla case and the Cuban Revolution that split us up. In the sixties, I supported the Revolution while I thought it needed support, and I stopped backing it when I felt this became appropriate.

MLG: In *Forbidden Territory,* you recount that your great-grandfather made a fortune in Cuba and that your grandfather was born there.

JG: Yes, there is a great Cuban tradition in my family. I have always felt very close to that country.

MLG: In 1984, they made you an honorary son of the Spanish town of Níjar in Almería. Can you explain what's behind this?

JG: Shortly before leaving Spain in 1955, I discovered a landscape in Almería that I liked very much. In fact, for the first time in my life, I felt close to something Spanish. Strangely enough, Almería is the most isolated province in Spain. Anyway, I wrote two books, *Campos de Níjar* and *La Chanca,* about Níjar and a slum there, respectively. Because of these two works, the local authorities declared me persona non grata and I could not return there while Franco was in power. When Franco died, however, some people from Almería—who had read the book and became aware of a cultural and social reality through it—had risen to positions of power. When they offered me this honor, I accepted, not as an honor, but as a reality. I have never accepted any honors and awards; when the French offered me the medal of the Legion of Honor, I declined, partly because I didn't want to be associated with French officials who had distinguished themselves by killing innocent Algerians and Vietnamese some years ago.

MLG: How do you reconcile the contradictions between living outside Spain and yet devoting your life to writing in Spanish?

JG: I think this is very common in our century; there are many authors who live outside their countries because of political or other reasons. To be an exile can be difficult in that it cuts you off from a familiar landscape and certain emotional ties, but it can be beneficial in that it provides you with distance and perspective. Seeing your own culture in the light of other cultures can be especially rewarding. If you are immersed in Spanish culture, for instance, you may not realize that what you consider original isn't, and what you deem commonplace is in fact unique to your society. So your scale of values changes when you encounter other cultures. My values, for example, have long ago ceased to be in tune with traditional Spanish values. As I distanced myself from Spain and the values it holds true, I gained my own truth and my own way of looking at the world.

MLG: Living abroad hasn't hindered your ability to write in Spanish?

JG: When language is a working tool, it is far more powerful than when it is a mere form of communication. Since I live my life surrounded by people who speak English, French, Arabic, or Turkish, Spanish is simply a tool for me. As such, it has a special quality that it wouldn't under more normal circumstances.

MLG: Are you saying that the language you speak and write has nothing to do with the language as it is spoken in Spain? Would you agree with Cabrera Infante when he says that his language is his creation and is not really Cuban?

JG: An author has the right to create his own language to some extent. I have always said that a writer's only moral obligation is to produce an original language from the language he started with. If I have done this, then I am satisfied. If I have transformed the language and claimed some new space for it—in the same way that the Dutch reclaim land from the sea by building dams—then that is literature for me. Those writers who haven't modified the language could disappear from the literary world, and no one would know the difference.

MLG: What does the written word mean to you?

JG: One of the things that has struck me the most about twentieth-century writers is the little interest they have shown in what Jakobson called "poetics" and what we could term "linguistics." I am one of the few who were truly fascinated by this subject ten years ago, and I read everything that was published about it, from Ferdinand de Saussure to Chomsky. These books helped me to see more clearly, although they didn't directly influence my writings.

MLG: Why don't you use capital letters or periods in your work?

JG: Because the rhythm of my writing requires it; it wouldn't work with periods, commas, and breaks. It would have been impossible for me to write *El pájaro solitario* any other way, for instance. It is the text which demands this type of writing. It wasn't my conscious choice. At first, people were not particularly fond of my lack of punctuation. It suggests that one read somewhat differently. This is why I have always been in favor of reading out loud. When I taught courses in the United States and Spain, I would give public lectures to teach people how to read my work. Anyone can verify that it has rhythm this way.

MLG: Reading your work is like a breathing experience. Don't you think everybody should read it out loud?

JG: I don't ask that everyone read it out loud, but I think it can help. We should not forget that, before the invention of the printing press, oral tradition played a fundamental role. Rojas's *La Celestina,* for instance, is fabulous when read out loud, because of the rhythm it suggests. In this respect, I have gone back to the openness and originality of our literature before the onset of the Renaissance, which I think impoverished our language a great deal. The Renaissance tried to set up literary canons and models that would be immutable, whereas authors before that were free to do as they pleased. With the exception of *Forbidden Territory,* none of my books since *Count Julian* has started with a plan, but rather with concrete images. I have let the texts grow on their own, uncertain where they were leading me. Those works grew organically.

MLG: Perhaps that's why there are no final periods in your work, because we could continue with the text.

JG: Or you could start all over again.

MLG: It takes on a circular shape. Your literary influences include the

Archpriest of Hita and Saint John of the Cross.

JG: They are my mentors, of course. Some of my books are conceived as dialogues with the works of others. *Makbara,* for instance, is derived from Hita's *Libro de buen amor; Count Julian* borrows from Góngora; and *Las virtudes del pájaro solitario* relates to the *Spiritual Canticle* of Saint John of the Cross.

MLG: Are you religious?

JG: I am not religious by nature, but in the last few years I have discovered and been fascinated with the literary expression of the religious experience. I have read the works of Saint John of the Cross and those of the Sufis extensively. What has surprised me about them is their boldness in naming the unnamable and the ineffable. They managed to create a language so modern that it wasn't matched until Rimbaud. Some of their verses would seem to have been written by a surrealist poet, someone who came after Rimbaud, because of the way they use the language to hint at the religious experience.

MLG: It has been said that you draw and quarter language. Was this your way of attacking Franco's Spain?

JG: Franco belongs to the past now; you have to put him into historical perspective. Since *Count Julian* I have tried to maintain a dynamic relationship with that aspect of Spanish culture that I would call the tree of literature. I am not in touch with current fads and tendencies, or with what is valued in Spain today, although Madrid is somewhat different from the rest of the country. So, while I maintain a relationship with the tree of literature, I am completely isolated from Spain's political sphere, whether that of Franco or the socialists. Although I don't have the same animosity toward the socialists that I did toward Franco, I feel just as alienated. I don't have any relationship with power structures or their representatives—I may be the only person who has never seen the king or the prime minister. I live totally isolated from the system. I am not a valuable commodity on the stock market.

MLG: Spain has remained a central concern in your work, nevertheless.

JG: Of course, but Spain in its totality, from its beginning in the Middle Ages to the present. Many people consider me a Spaniard, and I don't know of any contemporary author who has pondered Spain's cultural roots as constantly and profoundly as I.

MLG: So you struggle to go back to the roots.

JG: No, it's just that I think every author has to acknowledge his literary genealogy. In modern times, all writers want to be renowned and have disciples, but this has never interested me. What I did want was to forge a lineage that would reclaim my great literary ancestors like the Archpriest of Hita, Cervantes, and Saint John of the Cross.

MLG: Who else would you include in your lineage?

JG: Fernando de Rojas, Góngora, and Francisco Delicado, without mentioning people from other cultures.

MLG: Would you include Jean-Paul Sartre in the list of authors from other cultures?

JG: He is more of an affinity. We are contemporaries. I have things in common with authors like Carlos Fuentes, Octavio Paz, Severo Sarduy, Cabrera Infante, and sometimes Roa Bastos. But when I speak of lineage, I am not only talking about Spain, but also of people like the Sufis, whom I mentioned. In terms of twentieth-century authors from other cultures whom I feel close to, I would mention Joyce and Céline, who wrote *Journey to the End of Night.*

MLG: You have been compared to Joyce. Do you agree that there is a similarity?

JG: I think the author who is most like Joyce—in terms of doing with the Spanish language what the Irish author did with English—is Julián Ríos. I consider Joyce in the same breath as Arno Schmidt and Carlo Emilio Gadda; they have all done revolutionary things with the language.

MLG: You also like to play with words, or is it more than just play?

JG: Cabrera Infante and Julián Ríos play with words better than I. My forte is modifying syntax and putting phrases together. Spanish allows great flexibility for playing with syntax.

MLG: What do you enjoy most about experimenting with syntax?

JG: It became a creative need after the normal run-of-the-mill phrases ceased to interest me. I cannot read twentieth-century novels as a rule, because they are written according to the literary canons of the nineteenth century. This is not to say that I don't like nineteenth-century novels, which I do, but I simply cannot read many contemporary works because they follow the literary dictums of the nineteenth century.

MLG: Do you enjoy reshaping history?

JG: Yes. To go back to what I said earlier, my interest in pre-Renaissance texts lies in their not following any norms. My works are both literary and nonliterary; you can read them as poems, novels, or literary criticism, however you like.

MLG: You have never written poetry?

JG: Everything I have written since *Count Julian* I consider poetry.

MLG: What's more important for you: the rhythm of the language, the characters, or the book as a whole?

JG: The book is always the most important thing. As for characters, I haven't used any since *Count Julian.* Until Cervantes came along, there were no characters, and authors used them as mere plot devices. My characters, likewise, are purely linguistic creations: they are constantly transformed, they die, they are reborn, and they change age and sex according to the rhythm of the narration. I admit that it must be difficult for someone accustomed to a fixed conception of the novel—with characters, situations, and all that—to be interested in my works.

MLG: Who are your narrators? They vary from the "I" to the "you" to the "we."

JG: It is a polyphonic system, so to speak. It is obvious who the narrator is in *Count Julian,* because the basic reference in that book is to Góngora. I should have added Lezama Lima to my list of great authors of this century. Lezama Lima very clearly saw that, while Góngora is a difficult poet, he is not obscure like Saint John of the Cross. So, when Linda Levine wrote a critical study of *Count Julian,* she had no trouble identifying almost all the references I made, page to page. When I wrote *Las virtudes del pájaro solitario,* on the other hand, I tried to create a text similar to Saint John of the Cross's *Spiritual Canticle,* and as such, I wouldn't even be able to tell you what some of the references are. The *Canticle* is the most obscure work in the Spanish literary corpus.

MLG: Your work therefore seeks to return to the past.

JG: Yes, as I just said, I learned a lot from writers like Rojas and Delicado. I remember that a critic once said that a reference I made in *Landscapes after the Battle* made him think that I had been infected with the structuralist fads of Paris. I didn't bother to answer him, but I should point out that *Libro de buen amor* by the Archpriest of Hita is written in the first person and that the book itself talks. So what they consider to be at the forefront of the avant-garde had already been written in the fifteenth century.

MLG: Your book *Las virtudes del pájaro solitario* elicits many different reactions from people.

JG: They are now planning a colloquium on that book, and there will undoubtedly be differing interpretations, none of which I will be able to validate, because it is up to the readers to decide. The text doesn't lend itself to clarifications over and beyond what it says.

MLG: Do you think the reader, who sometimes is also a critic, can see more in a work than the author himself?

JG: There may be things in a book that the writer did not see. If the reader uncovers other interpretations without distorting the text, then I think it is valid even though I might not have seen them. Of course, there are interpretations that are clearly off the mark, but when a personal reading is based on the text, then I think it is valid.

MLG: How do you feel about critics?

JG: I have always defended the critical imagination because I deem it important. I have myself written many critical works, and on occasion I have used authors such as Fernando de Rojas for my own literary ends.

MLG: Do you think of the reader when you write?

JG: I do in general terms, but never with a special, privileged reader in mind. The ideal reader would be one who understands the context of the author. Nowadays, we have to make critical remarks about Cervantes precisely because we are not his contemporaries and do not comprehend his world. People in Cervantes's time understood perfectly well the irony of Dulcinea coming from El Toboso, because that was a Moorish town.

Cervantes was criticizing the caste system, of course, but today we need critical notes to put this into context for us. So the ideal reader is one who shares all the knowledge of the author and understands his references. In my case, many people have asked me about an event, described in the first few pages of *Count Julian,* that took place while I was living in Tangiers, working on the book. In that work, I make a reference to a weather forecaster who promised to shave off his mustache if it didn't turn out to be a sunny day for an important soccer game. When it did rain, he shaved his mustache and became a local hero because of his integrity. People who were in Tangiers at the time understood the reference, but if I didn't explain it to other readers, they would have no clue what I was talking about. So, historical criticism is inevitable to give context to a particular work.

MLG: Writing is a mixture of fantasy and reality for you.

JG: I can't really distinguish one from the other.

MLG: So you can't fault people for mistaking reality for fantasy in your work.

JG: I don't know . . . In this case, I didn't mind explaining that reference to reality. The text in itself does not change for me. These explanations are for those readers who want the most accurate reading and who need to know all these details.

MLG: What do you feel when you write?

JG: That's very difficult to explain. It is a strong and pleasurable experience, although it also causes me anxiety not to have said everything I wanted to.

MLG: Why do you write?

JG: Because I can do nothing else.

MLG: When did you first become aware of this need?

JG: Since the age of seven or eight, I haven't been able to conceive of doing anything but writing.

MLG: You end *Las virtudes del pájaro solitario* with the following phrase: "He lived alone / and alone he made his nest / Solitude was his guide and his life / and also the place he reposited his wounded love." Is writing a lonely activity?

JG: Those verses are by Saint John of the Cross, and I included them as a way of summarizing my work. You mustn't forget that *Pájaro solitario* is a tribute to the author of *Spiritual Canticle.* Some people may know that Saint John of the Cross wrote a treatise on the virtues of a solitary bird, and that he was forced to eat it when they came to arrest him. What was in that work? The only thing we can say is that it ran counter to the religious tenor of his day, which is why he ate it. My tribute consisted in giving back the work he was forced to eat to Spanish literature.

MLG: What is there about the symbol of the bird that you like?

JG: Its ambiguity. In Sufi poetry, the bird is an important symbol of the soul. But in my book, "bird" also has homosexual connotations.

MLG: Do you need to be alone when you write?

JG: I need to be very focused when I write. I am obsessed by my work, and it is very difficult for me to communicate with others when I am writing, because any conversation seems to rob me of the energy I need as an author. I must thank my wife, Monique Lange, for her understanding of me under those conditions.

MLG: It must make you happy to finish a work then.

JG: If I think I have achieved what I set out to do, then I am relieved when I finish.

MLG: Before you write a work, do you know if it is going to be a novel, a story, or a biography?

JG: I don't know. Since I never do outlines, use characters, or develop projects, it is the thrust of the writing itself that moves me. It is all contingent on whether I have something to say that I need to express. When I wrote *Las virtudes del pájaro solitario* I knew two things very clearly: it had to be related to *Spiritual Canticle,* and it had to dwell on the issue of death. These were the only two factors in my head; I didn't know what was going to turn out.

MLG: Do you see an evolution in your work?

JG: I suppose there is one.

MLG: In *Juan the Landless,* one of your characters says in French: "I don't seek credibility. I paint what I see, then I invent. I impose situations. What are the reasons for your success? Not boring the public. This is the only law of the novel. You must have a well-constructed story for a novel, something has to be happening all the time. The European novels of today are dying from anemia. We must return to the source, like the Americans." Are you being ironic when you say that?

JG: That is a parodic paragraph that pretty well sums up the current state of the novel. It reflects the thinking of those average writers who often appear on television, for whom the most important thing is that a book be properly structured. One of the problems we face with literature today is precisely the inability to distinguish a literary form from its content. There are writers who construct their works very well, but I wouldn't call what they produce literature. Nevertheless, it is these writers who are usually favored by critics and the public. Their works are normally well received because they already have an audience, whereas other books have to create their own public. Lautréamont's *Songs of Maldoror,* for instance, had no public when it first came out; it had to attract readers on its own.

MLG: What happened in your case?

JG: In all modesty, I think that my works create their own public. The proof of this is that when my books first come out, they are panned by critics whose thoroughness is very suspect. Whenever they come across a page they do not understand, they tend to dismiss a work out of hand.

MLG: How do you come up with the titles for your works?

JG: Sometimes I have the title before I start, while in other instances I don't come up with it until the end, and there are times when I don't find it at all.

MLG: What about *Juan the Landless?*

JG: "Juan sin Tierra" was the pseudonym that Blanco White used following his exile to London. His chronicles were published in Spain under that pen name, which I liked immediately, so I borrowed it.

MLG: Did you also like it because it is your first name?

JG: Yes. That was a coincidence, but it did enter into it.

MLG: Can you say something about the autobiographical element in your books?

JG: When life enters literature, it becomes literature and I like to show it for what it is. When an author writes an autobiography, however, he has to speak about what really happened and not what might have occurred. I have written two autobiographical works. It was quite an experience. I tried to limit myself to my memories and to any written documents from the time that might contrast with my recollection. So I attempted to give my subjective view, keeping in mind the larger picture. When you are dealing with your childhood, you are limited by your own memories, of course. This can be frustrating for an author like me who is used to a thousand possibilities or options in works like *Juan the Landless* or *Pájaro solitario.* With those books, I had enormous freedom, whereas with the autobiographical texts I had to move within very prescribed limits and give up my omnipotent role as a creator and a god to become a concrete incarnation (to borrow the Christian metaphor) limited by what was.

MLG: Since you are using religious terminology, do you consider an autobiography a form of confession?

JG: No, I have nothing to confess. I would term it a free examination of your conscience. This is what they call it in Protestant countries, where it has been a tradition since the sixteenth century. This did not exist in Catholic nations, where people were limited to confession. This is why there are so many autobiographical texts in English literature, whereas I know of none in its Spanish counterpart. I wrote *Forbidden Territory* for the simple and even moral reason that there was no such work in Spanish literature.

MLG: Why did you choose that title?

JG: Precisely because in Spain, traditionally, there has been great reluctance to speak about intimate matters. The Spanish authors of memoirs tend to engage in small talk about others, while remaining very quiet about themselves. They don't want their self-image destroyed. That's why in Spain they have always been either hypocritical, more commonly, or exhibitionistic, and I can't bear either. I have said the things I needed to say with a great deal of modesty and in a very unpretentious way.

MLG: What terms would you use to describe your work?

JG: It is impossible to define one's work with a few words, but perhaps I would mention the concept of a search. It could be seen, among other things, as a cultural, moral, and personal search.

MLG: Do you find some similarities between your notion of searching and that of the Generation of 1898?

JG: No, because they started with completely different premises. I think of Machado and Unamuno in particular when I speak of that generation, and how they were always looking for their roots within a very narrow framework of Spain and Castile. I was very much against that generation, and *Count Julian* is a frontal assault on it. When we speak of roots, we shouldn't forget that men are not trees and that we have feet so we can walk. So the concept of movement is also important in one's search. We cannot be tied to one spot—our vision of the world should be global.

MLG: So your sense of culture is not enclosed by national boundaries, but encompasses the world.

JG: Yes, it is impossible to reduce a culture to something limited and call it purity. I don't believe in racial, national, or literary purity. If we analyze a type of literature well, we can see that it is the sum total of influences it has received. If you cut off those influences, literature ceases to exist. As long as Spanish culture assimilated all of its influences, it was great, but as soon as it shut itself off and tried to follow certain political and religious dogmas, it died. Exactly the same thing happened to Arabic culture, and the parallel is really quite striking. While Arabic culture was open, it devoured all influences for three hundred and fifty years. But as soon as it tried to reject these influences in favor of Islamic dogmas, it collapsed on itself.

MLG: Your work seems to be both a liberating rejection of Hispanic culture and an obsession with it. How can you reconcile these two opposite emotions?

JG: All our relationships, whether with culture, life, or other people, are always ambiguous. Ambiguity is precisely the domain of literature. Politicians have to propose clear solutions, whereas writers do not. Literature does not seek votes or attempt to win elections. It is directed to certain readers who are as ambiguous as the author they read, and who should see themselves reflected in a particular work that will explain their ambiguity.

MLG: What do books represent for you, physically speaking?

JG: I like nice editions of my works, but I am not a fetishist, I'm not a book collector or bibliophile. The proof of this is that whenever I need a book for my work, I find that I have given it away. Books as objects don't concern me; what does interest me is knowing that they have enriched me.

MLG: If you had to give your work a geometric form, what would it be?

JG: Every work has its own shape.

MLG: Do you consider that no matter how many books you write, you are basically elaborating on the same work?

JG: No, I don't. For instance, *Count Julian* would be a circle, because it starts where it finishes. *Juan the Landless* was written in a zigzag fashion.

MLG: Do you correct or revise your work a lot?

JG: Chapter by chapter; I never move on until what I have just written is completely polished.

MLG: What do you feel when you read your books in translation?

JG: I read the English and French translations, because the translators consult me. I sometimes help them come up with equivalent terms. For instance, at the end of *Count Julian,* there is a parody of the death of Julian and I mention two verses that were very well known to people of my generation; it's the hymn of the Spanish Legion and in its original it goes like this: "Derramaste tu sangre preciosa, legionario de brava legión" (You shed your precious blood, brave legionnaire). If you translate this into English or French, it doesn't mean a thing. Finally, my French translator, Aline Schulman, had the idea of mixing a verse of "La Marseillaise" with a verse of the song "Mon légionnnaire" by Edith Piaf, which everybody knows. With that, the parodic effect remained . . .

MLG: It's very difficult to achieve, isn't it?

JG: Yes, it is, but I can manage with languages that I know more or less. It is also interesting to see the translating process from one language to another. For instance, my work is translated more easily into English, because the English language is flexible and can be stretched without breaking. This is not the case with French, which is a far more rigid language that snaps more easily. Spanish has that flexibility as well. Góngora can be translated into English beautifully, but none of the French translations work. Sterne's *Tristram Shandy* can be translated into Spanish far better than into French. Before reading that work in English, I was acquainted with the novel through a French translation. It was nice enough, but it had little to do with Sterne's work. That's why to be a great French poet is far more admirable than to be a good English or Spanish one.

MLG: What relationship do you have with your brothers, who are both writers as well?

JG: I don't see them very much, because we live apart. We used to be close thirty years ago, but not so much anymore. But, of course, I read their books.

MLG: Do you see some similarity between their work and yours?

JG: No. My work has its own personality.

MLG: If you had to give advice to some young writer, what would it be?

JG: It is impossible to give advice, because the experiences of every author are different from those of others. I could share with them practical knowledge I have acquired over the years.

MLG: Would you have liked to live in the Middle Ages?

JG: No, because I like many twentieth-century things.

MLG: So you are a twentieth-century man with many elements of the Middle Ages. Maybe you are even a man of the twenty-first century.

JG: Why not? It could be, that's what modernism is for me. I have written a lot about this subject, explaining in detail why the Archpriest of Hita is modern, and why I consider him my contemporary.

MLG: Is there another writer or artist who shares your perspective on the arts?

JG: I have researched the work of Gaudí, the architect, and I discovered that he also rejected the canons of the Renaissance and the neoclassical era. He wanted to return to the origin of architecture in Spain, which is the Gothic. Originality for him meant precisely returning to the origin. I admire this in Gaudí and, for me, it is the paradigm of what a creative person should be in our times.

MLG: In *El pájaro solitario* you say, "Who was I and what was I like?" I'd like to ask you, who is Juan Goytisolo?

JG: I am the worst person in the world to give you an answer to that question. Ask somebody who knows me, or better yet, ask somebody who doesn't know me, because the less they know about me, the better their answer will be.

Carmen Laforet

MARIE-LISE GAZARIAN GAUTIER

The family name of Carmen Laforet is French. Her great-grandfather, as Carmen enjoys saying, was in his twenties when he married a rich fifty-year-old woman from Seville. They had a son, her grandfather, who, although he had been engaged for many years, wasn't allowed by his mother to marry until after her death.

Carmen Laforet Díaz was born in 1921 in Barcelona, but when she was still a baby her parents moved to Las Palmas, in the Canary Islands. Her father was an architect who, like his own father, was fond of painting. He had met his future wife while he taught drawing and studied architecture in Toledo. She was studying to become a teacher. The mother was eighteen when she married and never took up teaching, although she put it to good practice in the upbringing of her children.

Her parents educated her and her brothers in a very liberal way. They were brought up reading the classics, encouraged in a love for the arts and an active participation in sports. The death of her mother in 1934, when she was only thirteen, was a traumatic experience and put an end to a carefree existence. Her father remarried and none of the children liked their stepmother.

In 1939, Laforet moved to Barcelona to study at the university. In the Canary Islands the effect of the Civil War had almost passed unnoticed. Her experiences in postwar Barcelona are described in her novel *Nada*. When it was published in 1945, it brought about immediate attention and was awarded two outstanding prizes, the Nadal and the Fastenrath prizes. That book contributed to the rebirth of the Spanish novel.

Laforet abandoned her studies (she was in her second year of law school in Madrid) and turned to literature as a way of life. In 1946, she married Manuel Cerezales, a journalist and critic, from whom she is now separated.

They have five children. Laforet is the grandmother of twelve grandchildren, and one of them is named after Andrea, the main character of her first novel.

She is the author of several important works, among them *La isla y los demonios* (The Island and the Devils), 1952; *La mujer nueva* (The New Woman), 1955; *La insolación* (Sunstroke), 1963; and *Paralelo 35* (The Thirty-fifth Parallel), 1967, an account of her first trip to the United States.

Since the seventies, Laforet has systematically refused to write anything, although the second volume of the trilogy *La insolación* has been in galleys for the past twenty years. One hopes she will at least write for her children and grandchildren the many colorful stories about her family.

Laforet claims that she does not even answer her correspondence and that, when the pile gets to be too high, she just tears the letters without opening them. She shuns all publicity and has a fierce terror of critics. She does not care about fame, and what she values most is the love of her family and friends.

This interview with Carmen Laforet, held in 1989, is the first one she has allowed in the past seventeen years. It took place in her youngest son's home in Madrid. Two beautiful salukis, dogs that the Moslems once held as sacred, greeted me. Carmen and her son Agustín Cerezales were waiting for me. I don't think she really wanted to be interviewed. I felt as if she had agreed to break a seventeen-year silence because she was so excited about her son's book that had just come out. This interview has all the spontaneity of a genuine conversation, including several interruptions. A grandchild wanted to take part in our dialogue and play with the tape recorder, the telephone rang perhaps ten times, her son and daughter-in-law also got into the game. Carmen skipped from one subject to another, making me feel totally at home with her family. So much so that she invited me to spend the next day at her daughter's home where she lives. She smoked one cigarette after another and talked to me as if I were an old friend. "Let's make a deal," she said to me, "if you want to know about my life, tell me about yours." She didn't have a single copy of her books around; neither did her son, not even a copy of the book he wrote about her. Like a gypsy, she wants all her belongings to fit in an overnight bag so that she is not tied down by anything she owns.

MLG: Carmen, why did you want me to meet you at the home of your son Agustín?

CL: I wanted you to meet him. Agustín has just published a book of stories called *Perros verdes* (Green Dogs) which, in my opinion, is an extraordinary work. I think that he has developed a new form of narration.

MLG: Do you see some relation between his work and yours?

CL: No, it is completely different. I would be glad if you could read his book, or even just the first story in it, because Agustín is very good and has an excellent sense of humor. After reading my son's book, a critic whom I knew from my days at the Ateneo in Madrid, Adolfo Prego, told me I had given birth to a genius. I thought that was silly, because I hadn't read the book yet, but I thanked Prego. I told him I had known my son was a poet since he was a child because when he was five he wrote me a poem on Mother's Day that said, "You are sweetness and light, I can see myself in your eyes." This is not the sort of thing that was copied from a greeting card. I knew then that he had a knack for poetry, but I didn't know how good he really was.

MLG: Your own prose is very poetic; have you ever written poetry?

CL: Never, but I have always loved it. Poetry is the impetus behind everything else, it is the most important thing.

MLG: Didn't Agustín also write a book about you?

CL: Yes, it is a short biography that was very much needed. It was commissioned by the Ministry of Culture and he volunteered to write it. I thought he would be the perfect person to do it, because he knows me well and he is one of the only people whom I would allow to look through the suitcases where I store all my mementos. I never open them, because I am afraid of finding things there that I would rather not remember. When Agustín opened them, he even found letters from Gerald Brenan and Juan Ramón Jiménez, which I thought I had lost.

MLG: Juan Ramón Jiménez?

CL: Yes, it was the first letter he sent to Spain from exile. It was published by *Insula,* and since it praised my first book, *Nada,* I was given the original. It was very moving that exiled writers would take such an interest in my work.

MLG: You took the title of your book from one of Juan Ramón's poems.

CL: I always kept notebooks in which I would place bits and pieces of things that had struck me. When I opened one of them and saw the poem "Nada," I said, this is it. No other titles ever came to me as explosively as that one.

MLG: Your book provided a new perspective for many people, particularly women.

CL: Perhaps this was because after the Civil War everybody was writing symbolically, while I wrote an ordinary book about life in Barcelona in the 1940s. The other writers spoke about angels and devils and many stereotypes like that, but not about the truth. They glorified the moment out of fear that they would be labeled "reds" and suffer terrible repression. I wasn't afraid of anything. I just wanted to show what Barcelona was like soon after the end of the war: people were very hungry, although not as hungry as in Madrid, because Barcelona had always been a rich city, with lots of fruits and the like. When I went to Madrid, the situation was a lot worse, although thanks to my aunt, who knew how to bake bread, we got along well. But there were a lot of people starving, which tended to make them frantic.

MLG: What was your reaction to the movie version of *Nada?*

CL: I disliked it violently, because they made a mockery of the novel by not accurately portraying the hunger in Barcelona after the war. The film director, Edgar Neville, wanted to do something like Buñuel without being Buñuel. It was very interesting that, when the movie premiered in a town in Catalonia, people broke chairs. They were as upset as I was, because they knew the movie didn't reflect the novel.

MLG: *Nada* has a very vivid quality, as you strongly rely on the senses of sight and smell. I can't forget the scene when Andrea first arrives at the house.

CL: If I had known the novel was going to be so successful and everyone would want to know where I lived in Barcelona, I wouldn't have used the name Arribau Street in the book, because that's where I really lived. I used it because I knew its smell, and I loved the way it looked in the fall. I come from the Canary Islands, where there is no fall or winter, only an extended spring. Anyway, I loved to watch the seasons, so the name of the street is the only really personal detail I put in the book.

MLG: Did the characters who lived in the house that you describe in your book exist in real life?

CL: Yes and no, they are partially based on people I had seen here and there telling their stories, and partly on my own imagination. So I created a family.

MLG: Is the family a mixture of fantasy and reality then?

CL: It is fantasy, but it is the reality of what those times were like. I borrowed real-life people from that era for my stories. For instance, there was the case of the chauffeur who went crazy because there were no cars left, so they took him to the hospital, fed him, and cured him. Then there was no way that he wanted to go home cured.

MLG: Is Andrea based on a real person?

CL: Andrea is a fictional character, and I am very different from her. I didn't want to include a character like me in the story, but all of a sudden I saw that I had no choice but to create one that was my age. An older character would not have understood my perspective on life and what I saw in people. My curiosity about people is reflected in the novel.

MLG: Who was stronger: you or Andrea?

CL: Perhaps Andrea led me along somewhat, but I was a lot happier than she. I pictured her always in confinement, whereas I had my freedom. I would go wherever I liked in Barcelona: I was fascinated by the red-light district, which had cabarets and prostitutes by night and looked very different by day.

MLG: That scene appears in your novel.

CL: Yes, that's why it's there. During the day the red-light district turned into a black market. I once went to eat at a food kitchen, which cost only a few pennies then, when a peseta could still buy you a bag of peanuts. I went there but I couldn't eat because I was so disgusted, not by the food, which looked better than in some places I had been, but by the people who would grab the saltshakers with their filthy hands. I went there out of curiosity, to see how the other half lived.

MLG: Andrea's friend is called Ena. You are a mixture of both characters, aren't you?

CL: No, I am like no one. The character, however, draws on me and Linka Babecka, who has been my best friend since university days. We had a lot of fun running around Barcelona and playing tricks on people to see how they would react to our fanciful stories. I dedicated that book to her and her husband. Linka is completely unlike Ena.

MLG: Are Ena's parents based on Linka's parents?

CL: No, they are totally fictional, but derived from what I would hear about the wealthy Catalonian families. Linka's father was Polish, her mother came from a well-to-do Catalonian family, and they lived on Montcada Street in the old section of town. I was very fond of them and they became like a family for me.

MLG: When you wrote *Nada* did you expect it would have the tremendous impact it did?

CL: No, absolutely not. How could I have known such a thing? I let some people read my book and they liked it a lot. That's how I met my husband, because he was a friend of Linka's. Manuel Cerezales was a journalist and a good critic, and Linka decided to give him my book to read. He then said it was very good and suggested I submit it to a literary contest that had been created that year in Barcelona. Since I didn't read the newspapers very much, I was not aware of it. He was sure they would publish the book even if I didn't win the contest, because he found my work magnificent. So I sent it, and I won the Nadal Prize.

MLG: You didn't think Andrea was going to be friends with so many people, and that her language and her world would command so much attention.

CL: One cannot know something like this. Even though I wrote my first book with all the energy I could muster, how could I have known it was going to be so successful? I had just wanted to write an entertaining novel. The strangest thing is that *Nada* is currently popular in Reykjavík, Iceland. In the space of two years, they have done two readings of *Nada* on the radio, and now they have requested the rights to the book and its translation, because it has been so popular.

MLG: If you hadn't undergone the hardships of postwar experience, do you think that such a book would have existed?

CL: Another novel would have been written about my first encounter with life, apart from my family and the Canary Islands. When I first arrived in Barcelona, I was an eighteen-year-old girl full of energy and enthusiasm. Everything interested me despite the pangs of hunger.

MLG: You are especially fond of minor characters.

CL: Yes, I disguised people whom I thought were funny and I put them in my books. I enjoyed doing it a lot. Humor is the only thing that can save us. Let me briefly explain how I came up with my minor characters. When I was living in Rome, my daughter Silvia, who also happened to be there, told me that she liked my book *La isla y los demonios.* So I leafed through it and said, "What is Mr. X doing in here?" to which she replied, "What do you mean, Mr. X? That's Marta Camino's uncle." That character was based on a real person who had a very funny sounding name, which I won't repeat. I had noticed him while I was at the Ateneo, a cultural place where I would gather with my friends. My minor characters came directly from people I thought were funny. I was not concerned about giving a complete account of them, just the parts that I found peculiar.

MLG: You create an impression of reality through details.

CL: Yes, the details are real. That's why I placed the house on Arribau Street, because when I went to the university, I would step out onto that street, and I knew there was a pharmacy and I loved the leaves on the trees in autumn and spring, and I thought all this was wonderful.

MLG: Is the grandmother a fictional character?

CL: Yes, she is, but my grandparents did live in that house on Arribau Street, as well as other grandparents. That character is based on all of them.

MLG: I can almost smell the living room where Andrea slept, and feel the tension around the dinner table because food was scarce and people didn't want to share it, except for the grandmother.

CL: I am very moved that you are telling me this.

MLG: Did you also invent the other characters?

CL: I also invented them, but they are based on real people who lived upstairs or downstairs from me, or even in other houses. They would tell me their stories. I now realize that I never found out what made them so strange. Of course, it was the war.

MLG: The two brothers in your story were painters, right?

CL: Yes. By the way, all of my children are also painters, except for Agustín and Silvia.

MLG: How many children do you have?

CL: Five. Agustín is the youngest.

MLG: Why are Agustín's children named Miguel and Marcela?

CL: Because Agustín loves Cervantes, whose first name is Miguel, and one of the characters in *Don Quixote* is named Marcela.

MLG: If you could speak with a writer from the past, whom would you pick?

CL: No one, because I have their works. I believe that writers are their books, although once in a while you may meet someone wonderful who is both a writer and your friend.

MLG: Do you equate yourself with your work?

CL: Yes, that's why I don't like to talk about myself.

MLG: Who are the narrators?

CL: All of my characters are part of me. I only did first-person narration with *Nada;* all the other works are in the third person. That's why I made Andrea completely unlike me.

MLG: What can you say about *La mujer nueva?*

CL: It grew out of something that happened to me while I was passing by a fountain at El Retiro Park in Madrid. All of a sudden, I felt a tremendous surge of happiness and a certainty that humanity was moving toward something wonderful, namely God. I spent three days saying I discovered the world, I discovered life, I discovered religion. I was so happy when I woke up each morning that I would wander in awe in the streets and think that all the horrible, ugly people I saw were actually wonderful because we were all moving toward God. The third day I woke up as I was before, without understanding anything, but knowing that this had happened to me. I started doing many things then that have led me to be a much better person.

MLG: Are you deeply religious?

CL: No, I tried to be dogmatically religious during one year or two within the Catholic church, which is where I, and almost all Spaniards, have been baptized. But the things that I felt I had to do—like not dealing with some sinful people because I was a religious person—started making me sick. I began to feel very acute stomach pains, and one day I said, "This is because I have given the religious thing a wrong focus. I am not going to do it anymore." And as soon as I said that my pains went away and I went back to treating people the same way I did before. I haven't stopped believing in God, or believing that human beings are moving toward God. I still go to church, but without being subject to a series of prejudices. My experience was so overwhelming that I wrote a novel about it. I haven't wanted to reread it, however, so I don't know if it is good or bad . . .

MLG: I like it a lot.

CL: The main character of that novel, Paulina, tried to become a better person following her religious experience. I was very anxious to explain this in the novel, but it can't be explained.

MLG: When did you first start writing?

CL: I had always told stories to my brothers. It was what I did well; I always wrote little things and I read a lot because I loved literature. I was in Madrid when I wrote my first novel, which is a recollection of my initial impressions of Barcelona.

MLG: What did you feel when you wrote it?

CL: I really wanted to do it and have fun with the characters. I was fascinated by them and cared about them. I read my book to my brothers who, like me, were living in the house of our aunt. We all were studying at the university. I changed majors when I came to Madrid. I have no university degree, but I studied literature for two years and law for two years. I was studying law in Madrid when I wrote the book, and when I won prizes for it, I decided to dedicate myself to writing.

MLG: You won the Nadal Prize and the Fastenrath Prize. When did you win the Cervantes Prize?

CL: That was much later. I also won a prize for *La mujer nueva,* but I forget what it was called.

MLG: Not only one, but two of the most prestigious ones: the Menorca Prize and the National Prize for Literature. So I know more about your work than you do, and I am going to become your biographer along with your son!

CL: Yes, you know a lot more, because I forget about things like this.

MLG: What did you feel when you finished a novel?

CL: Whenever I finished a novel, I was always exhausted, but the work was still alive . . .

MLG: If you had to give your books a geometric shape, what would it be?

CL: Like a closed or open circle. Perhaps *La mujer nueva* would be closed, but everything else would be open so that life may continue and the characters be set free.

MLG: When you used to write, did you stand inside or outside your novels?

CL: Inside. To write I had to isolate myself totally from everything and everyone. When I wrote *La mujer nueva,* for instance, I spent three months completely by myself, even though I already had several children. A girl from the town would bring me food, and she would wonder out loud how I could possibly be writing, because all she could see were loads of torn paper in the fireplace! I would write by hand first, then dictate, correct, and dictate or correct again.

MLG: Did you have a plan in mind?

CL: I would draw up the plan first, then the book would come out.

MLG: Did you think you would be able to make a living as a writer?

CL: I had heard that writers faced very trying circumstances financially, but I knew I would be all right. I wanted to find a cheap attic to live in, as in the times of Galdós. Nowadays they are very hard to find and very expensive.

MLG: What's your novel *La isla y los demonios* about?

CL: It is the story of a young girl who lived in the Canary Islands at the same time I did, during the Civil War, which incidentally was never felt much there. My father hindered that book a little, because he asked me not to write anything that might resemble our family. That was terrible for me, although I probably wouldn't have written about our family anyway. I just didn't like having limits imposed on me. I haven't reread that book either, nor any of my other novels.

MLG: Can you say something about *El viaje divertido?*

CL: It is about a girlfriend of mine who as a child lived in a village and always thought it would be so much fun to travel on the train or eat at the station. So I invented a character who took the fantastic trip she had dreamed about.

MLG: What can you say about *Paralelo 35?*

CL: That was the idiotic name the publisher gave to the book about my first travels in the United States. I wanted to call it "Mi primer viaje a America." Another publisher is now printing the book with my original title. The State Department invited me to visit North America, I don't know why. I spent two months traveling there, seeing things that fascinated me. It was in 1963, the year they shot Kennedy. The magazine *La actualidad española* (Spain Today) gave me a blank check and asked me to write my impressions. I protested at first, saying I wasn't a journalist, but they insisted that I send articles as I wrote them and that they would publish them. And that's what I did. They paid me extremely well for those brief accounts, which were later made into that book.

MLG: Can you say something about *La niña y otros relatos?*

CL: It's a collection of short stories.

MLG: What difference is there between writing a novel and a short story? Which do you prefer?

CL: I prefer novels, although it is much easier and quicker to write a short story. A novel demands a tremendous commitment, whereas I could sometimes write a story, even a long one at that, in a night or two if a character or something sprang to mind. Most of my stories were written between 1940 and 1960, and many of them are recollections from the time of *Nada.*

MLG: What about the last novel you wrote, *La insolación?*

CL: I like that book, although I regret giving it that title. I just couldn't find anything else that would convey what it was like to be young and spend time on the Mediterranean coast under a steaming sun. It has nothing to do with the novel *Insolación* written by Countess Emilia Pardo Bazán, but I liked that title and borrowed it. It's the first part of a trilogy I wanted to write. It is like the prelude to an entire life. I wrote the second part but I didn't allow its publication. It has remained in galley proofs for the past seventeen years. I wrote it too hastily and wasn't happy with it. It was about the same young people as in *La insolación,* but set in Madrid in the 1950s, when love was uppermost in their minds. In the third part, these same characters would meet again as adults. They make up a family, always centered around Martín, who is an artist. If I ever write again, this is the first thing I will do.

MLG: Why did you stop writing?

CL: I think that initially it started as a reaction to things journalists wrote about me. They put words into my mouth and made me say things I had never said. For example, many years ago, there was a famous critic named del Arco and everyone wanted to be interviewed by him. He was a friend of my husband's, so I had no choice but to put up with him. He once asked me what I would do if I had to choose between the loss of one of my children or the failure of one of my books. And I replied, "What sort of question is that?" The next day he wrote an article about me with a headline that went something like this: "Carmen Laforet Prefers Being a Housewife." Another instance happened during one of my trips to the United States, when I accidentally ran into a journalist who knew me. I mentioned in passing that the noise in New York didn't bother me because Madrid was the loudest city in the world. But the headline the next day was, "Carmen Laforet Is Delighted to be Back in Madrid after All the Noise in New York." Recently I was told that during a television show people were discussing whether *Don Quixote* should be read in school. Someone claimed that I had said that I had never read that work. I should have complained but I decided it wasn't worth the trouble. Of course, I read the condensed version of *Don Quixote* when I was a child and I certainly think it should be read in schools. This is why I don't like journalists, because they always twist things around. It is also the reason why I haven't given an interview in Spain for seventeen years. Cervantes has always been deeply loved in my home. As I said before, my son Agustín even named his children after Cervantes and one of his characters.

MLG: Is there a chance you will ever write again? I wish I could convince you.

CL: I have stopped writing completely, and I think it has become something of a sickness or phobia for me now. I feel very lazy about writing. Not only have I stopped writing articles, which was very easy for me to do, but I don't even write letters to my friends anymore.

MLG: Yet, you are interested in people and want to hear their stories. Doesn't that mean that deep down you are still a storyteller?

CL: Yes, that is true! I want you to tell me your story, whenever we meet again.

MLG: You have twelve grandchildren. Why don't you write twelve stories about the Laforet family for them?

CL: What I have promised to the family and to myself is to tell them stories, things like how great-grandfather Laforet came to Spain, and what my great-grandmother was like . . .

MLG: Where did your great-grandfather come from?

CL: From France, it is a French name. He was a twenty-year-old young man who married a fifty-year-old woman from Seville. She came from a Basque family who had settled in Andalusia. Doña Encarnación Rodríguez de Alfaro was very aristocratic. After a year they had a child, and he couldn't stand it because he thought the child would be spoiled by the mother's family, so he looked upon it as an enemy within the house. My great-grandfather loved this woman all his life.

MLG: Was she beautiful?

CL: No, my grandmother Carmen, who didn't like her mother-in-law very much, showed me a medallion with a picture of her. She had a very bossy face. She made her son swear that he would not get married while she was alive, although she allowed him to have as many girlfriends as he liked. She was ninety when she died suddenly while they were combing her hair. My grandfather didn't marry until he was in his forties. Like most Andalusian women, my grandmother spent most of her time at home, although she enjoyed traveling. My grandfather, on the other hand, liked to go out every day but he disliked traveling. So whenever there was a need to travel to Seville to take care of the estate, it was my grandmother who went.

MLG: What were your parents like?

CL: My parents? My father was a very special person who was an avid sportsman. He won sailing as well as bicycle races and shooting contests; he was Spain's national champion at pistol-shooting. He was a very good shot, but he didn't like to hunt. When he was a student, he chased after women a lot, which upset my grandparents. They asked him if he couldn't find one decent woman to marry among the thousands of girlfriends he had. They didn't care whether she was tall or short, rich or poor, as long as she was decent. My father replied that he had met a girl of very humble background who was very nice. She was studying education in Toledo while he learned architecture. She was eighteen when they got married. My grandparents decided that the young couple should move to Barcelona and live with them while my father worked for his degree. That's how I came to be born in Barcelona. When he received his degree in architecture, we moved to the Canary Islands, where he began teaching at the Industrial School of Las Palmas. My father emphasized sports and music in our education and never treated me any differently than my brothers. I enjoyed as much freedom as they did, a legacy perhaps we inherited from our grandfather. My mother, on the other hand, taught us the true meaning of friendship and a sense of duty. She died when she was thirty-three and I was thirteen. My father immediately remarried, which was a very trying thing for me because my stepmother was very nasty.

MLG: You were determined to leave home and study in Barcelona?

CL: My father and stepmother didn't want me to take that trip. So I had to blackmail my father with something I don't want to talk about. I actually turned eighteen on the boat on my way over to the mainland.

MLG: Did fantasy play a big part in your childhood years?

CL: Yes. Fantasy is something wonderful. I loved to be able to invent, create other worlds, and give shape to my dreams. I can't recall a time when, as a child, I didn't make up lots of things and say whatever came to my mind. One day, for instance, when I was only four, I dreamed up an incredible story about dunce caps and punishment. I was attending at the time a kindergarten run by some very nice nuns. I went home after school and told my mother that my friend Carmencita and I had been the only ones in school to pass all our exams. As a special treat, the Mother Superior and another nun had taken us in their arms to what was referred to as the Natural History Room, where stuffed storks and other things I thought wonderful were kept. From there, we saw that all the other girls had been punished and were standing in the yard with dunce caps placed upon their heads. My mother, who knew that such punishments never existed in my school, was amused and laughed, but to teach me a lesson said, "Let's go see Mother Superior. I want to thank her for the reward, but we must ask her forgiveness for the other little girls. I find it strange that they should be punished. I know that some of them are more intelligent than you!" Since Las Palmas was a very small place, we could walk to school. As we turned the corner, I cried out, "Mama, don't say anything, it's all been a lie, I made the whole thing up!" So that clipped my wings for a time. When I was a bit older, I remember telling my little brother, who was two years younger and shared the same room with me, "Look, grandmother is flying down the stairs." But when I heard my mother's footsteps I stopped talking. Before I turned ten, I started inventing dreams and I would tell my brothers stories. Whenever they got mad at me or I at them, they would come running into my room and say, "Carmencita, tell us a story, tell us a story." My brothers still remember the stories I made up about captains who had to be three years old because if they were older they were not worth mentioning. I was a very imaginative child, and I was in my glory telling my brothers about these dreams. I wanted to be a great painter like Andrea del Sarto, until I found out in one of my father's books that Andrea in Italian is a man's name.

MLG: Do you still play with reality and fantasy? Can you keep them apart?

CL: It is one and the same thing. Reality is made up of dreams, impulses, friendships. Sometimes I think there is no reality at all. But I don't like to philosophize, you know . . .

MLG: We have talked about the Laforet family and your recollections of them. Can you speak about your children?

CL: There are people whom you feel good to be with and whom you love, whether they are your children or not. I have many clans. I live with one of my daughters, Cristina, a wonderful girl who is a very good painter, and her husband, who is a fabulous human being. They live in a chalet outside of Madrid, in Majadahonda. I have another daughter, Marta, who lives in Santander, where she teaches at the French Institute. She is also a painter. Silvia, my third daughter, does some writing. Manuel has a tremendous talent as a painter and is married to another artist, who is from Colombia, where they now live. Agustín is a writer and a translator. My children have all turned out to be great animal lovers. Have you seen the lovely dogs Agustín has? They are the kind of dogs used by Arabs in the desert.

MLG: What do you do now that you don't write?

CL: Many pleasant things: I take walks with the dogs, spend time with my beautiful grandchildren, see my friends, come and go as I please, and read, which I love. I also have a pile of letters that I need to answer, even though I don't. When they have been there a long time I rip them up.

MLG: Haven't you given a similar fate to some of your manuscripts?

CL: Yes. I either ripped or burned them. Once they were typed out, I never felt the need to keep them. I have always had the notion that everything I own should be able to fit in two suitcases, should I have the urge to leave all of a sudden. Even when I was settled in a particular place, that still bothered me. I like to feel free and not be forced to remain in one spot. So I don't like to keep many things, or be in a situation where I have to choose what to take. For instance, I have never had animals of my own, although I adore them, because if I had to go on a trip I would have to take them along or leave them behind.

MLG: You lived in Rome for a while, didn't you?

CL: Yes, I ran from Madrid and for two years I lived in Rome, which I loved very much and where I have a lot of friends. Let me tell you a story about Roberta Johnson, a woman who had been doing research on my work. She wrote me a letter asking if she could visit me. I just happened to see it, because I usually don't open my mail, but I told her it would be all right for her to come for three days. Then I met her, she was a delightful young woman, and she told me that she wanted to ask me a few questions about my life. So I said, "Let's make a deal, I will tell you about my life if you tell me about yours first." And then we became very good friends. She wrote a book about *Nada,* which was published in Boston. She persuaded me to travel to the United States and give some lectures. I don't like to speak a lot about myself, but I decided to go. I would speak for about a quarter of an hour and then ask for questions. I loved being on university campuses and enjoyed the company of the students.

MLG: Do you remember some of their questions?

CL: Well, for instance, a student asked me if *Nada* was basically optimistic or pessimistic. I replied that I thought it was optimistic because I am an optimist.

MLG: What was your impression of the United States?

CL: What impressed me most was to discover that many of the cities on the West Coast had very small urban areas. They seemed like an enormous, endless garden. In New York, I was struck by the square pattern of the streets, as I looked down from my hotel room. I loved Manhattan with its skyscrapers lit by night. It's a big country where one can move about unnoticed.

MLG: Some authors say they wear a mask. Could running away from literary fame and from writing be a sort of mask?

CL: I don't wear any masks. I don't like to hide either, but what I don't appreciate is the personal popularity and publicity surrounding my name. My private life is very important to me. It's not that it is more important than a book though. When I was writing a book, it was at that moment the most important thing in the world for me, but once it was finished, that was it, while I went on.

MLG: You don't like to talk about yourself or your work. You don't even keep copies of your books and, if you do, they are hidden somewhere in a suitcase, where no one can find them.

CL: I lead a very quiet and peaceful life, I am always available to help out someone in need, and I value my freedom, so I don't like to be surrounded by many things. In fact, I throw many things away. The other day, I came across a blouse a friend of mine gave me when I lost my suitcase during one of my trips. She thought it was a tragedy, but I didn't see it that way. I didn't mind going to the lecture not wearing a pretty dress and nice shoes. I like to think that I own very little, and that it can all fit in those two suitcases I never open. The next time I go on a trip I will take only hand baggage.

MLG: Who is Carmen Laforet?

CL: Who is she? I don't know.

MLG: But you have known her all your life! Who is she?

CL: Nobody, nobody.

MLG: What do you mean by nobody?

CL: An average person, for whom at any given moment friendship is what matters most. What I cannot bear is that false publicity given about me.

MLG: Thank you, Carmen, for breaking seventeen years of silence. I didn't want this book to be published without including you.

SIGFRID CASALS

Juan
Marsé

Juan Marsé was born in 1933 in Barcelona. In 1946, when he was only thirteen, he began working in a jewelry shop where he stayed until 1959. In that same year, he started writing short stories and publishing them in *Insula* and received the Sésamo Short Story Prize. He is also known as a journalist and has written for the magazine *Por Favor* and the newspaper *El País*.

His first novel, *Encerrados con un solo juguete* (Shut in with a Single Toy), was published in 1960. Two years later, *Esta cara de la luna* (This Side of the Moon) came out. His third novel, *Ultimas tardes con Teresa* (Last Afternoons with Teresa), won him the Biblioteca Breve Prize. In 1970, he published *La oscura historia de la prima Montse* (The Dark Story of Cousin Montse) and in 1973, he was awarded the First México International Novel Prize for *Si te dicen que caí*, 1973 (*The Fallen*, 1979). For *La muchacha de las bragas de oro*, 1978 (*Golden Girl*, 1981), he won the Planeta Prize. Four of his novels have been made into movies.

The works of Juan Marsé infused new blood in the novels of his time. His sense of realism is based on the way people act and talk, especially those who live on the fringe of society. Although he is concerned with style, his main interest lies in telling a story, in describing the world in which his characters move. Many of the characters are related to his own childhood memories and his youth. His novels and articles have been a constant attack against dictatorship and a struggle for freedom. The critic Rafael Conte has described *Si te dicen que caí* as one of the best Spanish novels of the 1970s.

Some of his other works are *Señoras y señores* (Ladies and Gentlemen), 1975; *Confidencias de un chorizo* (A Thief's Secrets), 1977; *Un día volveré* (Someday I'll Return), 1982; *El fantasma del cine Roxy* (The Ghost of the Roxy Theater), 1985; *Teniente bravo* (Lieutenant Bravo), 1987.

I met Juan Marsé in his Barcelona home, overlooking the city. The spacious, bright living room opened on a wide terrace with many flowers in bloom. A strong-looking, handsome man with a youthful face, crowned by thick, grayish curly hair, Marsé was very relaxed while his dog Boris, a beautiful pointer, sat comfortably in the best armchair, watching every move I made. During the interview, the novelist got up several times to answer the phone, refusing to be interviewed, saying he had no time for that. By then Boris decided she could trust me and left her armchair to put her head on my lap. As we were about to finish our talk, Marsé's wife came in and we stepped onto the terrace.

❖❖❖❖❖❖❖❖❖❖❖❖❖❖❖❖❖❖❖❖❖❖❖❖❖❖❖❖❖

MLG: I can't help but notice that your dog Boris wants to take part in this interview. Why did you call her that?

JM: My daughter wanted to call her Vodka, but I thought this was a bit extreme, so we settled on Boris.

MLG: So she's very Russian.

JM: Yes, and she has a dog friend called Natasha. She is a great companion when I work. She sleeps in an armchair and watches me.

MLG: You started working at a jeweler's.

JM: I started working at a jeweler's when I was thirteen. We made jewels, medals, bracelets, earrings, necklaces. We designed the jewels and made them with very delicate machinery. It was very time-consuming. We worked with gold, silver, and platinum.

MLG: I'm sure that the patience and precision you learned at the jeweler's served you well as a writer. When did you first feel the need to write?

JM: I took up writing out of curiosity, to see if I could do it, as with any other activity at a young age. I had always liked to read adventure novels, from Salgari to Stevenson, so I moved between two poles: cheap novels and literature, strictly speaking, such as some of the excellent books of Dickens. But my reading was very haphazard, as I had no one to guide me. I thought I too would be able to write a story. Anyway, I would say that I began writing out of curiosity, not out of some vital need. When I started writing, I imitated what I was reading, not the life that was going on around me.

MLG: Is that when you realized that writing was what you wanted to do?

JM: I wrote a few stories, but I did nothing with them, and they got lost. And then I didn't write for a long time, until I did my military service, when I started jotting down the personal impressions that became my first novel.

MLG: Do you still take notes before you write?

JM: I used to, but I don't as much anymore, I don't know why. More often, I rely on my memory. In any event, my experience with taking notes tells me that they are relatively useless. If an image is forceful enough, it will stick; and if it is not, it won't fly, no matter how many notes you take.

MLG: What does a book mean to you?

JM: It is always intriguing to discover what a book contains, what it discusses and suggests, and what entertainment value it has, that is very important. The books that I most dislike are intellectual novels, novels of ideas. I will always value a novel that conveys feelings more than one that deals with ideas. For instance, I will always place Dickens before Joyce. *Ulysses* has considerable poetic value, but it is not a great book. On the other hand, Dickens's *Great Expectations* and Stendhal's *The Red and the Black* are great novels.

MLG: If you could speak to some great writers of the past, who would they be?

JM: I would love to speak with many, but I would probably choose to speak with Stendhal first, followed by Flaubert. I'd like to talk with Stevenson and Conrad as well.

MLG: What would you say to them?

JM: I don't know, maybe we'd speak about literature, but I'd like to talk about the sea and traveling with Conrad. I would want Flaubert to tell me about his private life and to explain how he constructed his work, laboring over it with the same tenacity as a tiny solitary ant. I'd ask Stendhal about the historic events he lived through, and I would hope he'd discuss with me *The Red and the Black* and *The Charterhouse of Parma,* his two novels that continue to this day to fascinate me.

MLG: I am surprised you haven't mentioned Pío Baroja.

JM: I would have loved to know him too. I've read his work since I was a child and, on occasion, I have said that his influence should be apparent in my work. But this is my very subjective view of the matter. It may very well be that this influence is not so noticeable to others. Influences are a mystery.

MLG: How do you come up with the topics for your books?

JM: Creating a book is a very mysterious process that for me almost always begins with images, not ideas. I have a visual memory, so all my personal memories are images. I have images of childhood, people I have known, events and so forth. I even devised images for stories they told me. Therefore, I generally start with an image, then another one comes up, and I discover certain possibilities in the contrast between them. For instance, I might juxtapose a childhood memory with a story someone told me, and those two images foster a third, and a galaxy comes into being. No matter how small, that galaxy begins to make up the story, and once you have a potential story, you have the beginnings of a novel. I could give you a more concrete example. I have been running some personal memories of mine every other Sunday in *El País,* which could very well end up as material for a novel. The plot concerns a madman I knew as a child who used to go around disguised as the Invisible Man, with his head in bandages, dark glasses, pajamas, and an overcoat. He would wander around the neighborhood and say he was the Invisible Man. I devised a story where this man would be accompanied by a boy, and they would walk around the neighborhood and comment on things. That boy could be me! So there you see how little by little a novel may take shape.

MLG: You go through this whole process before you sit down to write?

JM: Yes, I usually do. When I begin writing, I normally have an outline of the novel in my head. It may happen that, while writing the book, the initial ideas may be buried under other ideas that become more significant.

MLG: Do you already have the work in your head or do you develop it as you go along?

JM: I never have the whole book in my mind. Sometimes, even the story line isn't complete, nor are all the characters ever drawn at the outset. The work evolves as I write it, and many times I have to proceed without seeing where I am going. For instance, a character I considered very secondary may become very central all of a sudden, and vice versa—a focal character at the beginning of the writing process may have completely disappeared by the time the book is finished.

MLG: Do the characters dominate or does the author?

JM: The writer may assume that he is in control, but I think that it is really the material that is in charge. I believe that the author should let himself be carried by the flow of the book.

MLG: What's more important: the characters or the language?

JM: The language is the most essential thing; without it there would be no novel.

MLG: How do you use language?

JM: It depends on the material I am working on and the way the characters talk, given their social status and their verbal capabilities. But regardless of whether I use colloquial language or its literary counterpart, the problems of the novel begin and end with language.

MLG: Do you converse with your characters?

JM: I try to see them as real people, and I do talk to them in my head.

MLG: What's your relationship with them?

JM: Some characters are very closely tied to my personal life, and the events within it, while others are invented, products of the imagination that are nevertheless very real. The process has happened in reverse, because sometimes characters that have been drawn from real events and that you consider crucial might very well end up as mere footnotes. On the other hand, some characters born of the pure imagination, without support in reality, become very plausible. It all depends. There is everything here.

MLG: Do you have a favorite character?

JM: Yes, Manolo, the main character of *Ultimas tardes con Teresa.* Even the critics seem to like him the most. He is probably the man I would have liked to be. He is a projection of a dream of mine: that of a smart, penniless youth from Andalusia who comes to Barcelona. He has a romantic relationship with a rich, attractive, blue-eyed blonde Catalan girl, with her sports car and all that. This happens over the course of a single summer. I knew many youths like Manolo who had only their wits and good looks to go on. I think he is my favorite character.

MLG: So you find your characters among people you have known?

JM: I find them on the street and in life, otherwise things wouldn't jibe.

MLG: Do you combine realism and fantasy in your work?

JM: I am not very good with labels of this kind. Critics are knowledgeable about these things, but I don't know very much about realism, magical realism or pedestrian realism. What's more, it's a topic that I have always found incomparably boring; I don't know (and I don't want to know) about theories of the novel. Nevertheless, I would tell you that I think I belong to the realist tradition, very generally speaking.

MLG: How do you achieve realism in your work?

JM: By telling a good story. If you can do that, they'll believe anything you say, regardless of whether it is about flying elephants. Otherwise, they won't believe you even if you describe the simplest act, such as having a drink. Realism is measured by what the author can make you believe. A mediocre writer talking about real events may not make you believe in even the most commonplace daily occurrence, and it is due to a lack of narrative talent. So it boils down to narrative talent, which makes the reader believe what the author is writing.

MLG: What is writing for you?

JM: A way to escape from reality, modify and improve on it, manipulate and falsify it, and teach yourself something.

MLG: Is it a way of remaking history?

JM: No, it's a way of modifying it according to my personal idiosyncracies and neuroses, so that my dreams may become a part of the novel.

MLG: How do you feel when you write a book?

JM: Very tired and overwhelmed. It is far more pleasurable for me to read than to write.

MLG: Do you feel like a reader of your own work when you write?

JM: I like to keep an ideal reader in mind, who is anybody but myself, of course. I try to conceive an ideal reader who is very demanding and impatient, and who would immediately tell me when he gets bored. This is a pretty standard approach and one that is innate and automatic, meaning you don't spend your time thinking that you are the reader of your own work.

MLG: When do you usually write?

JM: Preferably in the morning, but there are also times when I can't write. There are times when I am not . . . I don't want to say inspired, because I don't believe in inspiration. I would say there are moments when I am not in the best frame of mind, and others when I am. When I am not in a really creative mood, I may work on some adaptation or another for television. Right now, for instance, I have put aside a novel that's half written, to work on an adaptation of *Un día volveré* for television, to be shown as a six-part series.

MLG: How do you feel about television and movie adaptations of your novels?

JM: Generally speaking, I am disappointed, because the adaptations are of a very debatable nature. Of course, when you sign over the rights to your novels and don't intervene personally in the making of the screenplays, you can expect terrible things to happen. By this I don't mean, however, that it is a sure guarantee of success if the author intervenes. Had I been involved in the picture-making, the movies could have turned out just as bad or even worse. These adaptations are all very bad, and not because they are not faithful to my books, which is really a secondary concern for me, as I don't believe you have to be completely faithful to produce a good adaptation. In fact, sometimes I think the opposite may be true: in order to be faithful to the book, you may have to betray and alter it in some way. But these movies they made are just plain awful; the first was *La oscura historia de la prima Montse,* then there was *Golden Girl,* finally *Ultimas tardes con Teresa.* A new picture has just been released of *The Fallen.* I am not the only writer who has experienced this, though. Most literary adaptations I have seen are bad, save for notable exceptions such as films directed by people like Buñuel or Visconti.

MLG: Going back to the actual writing of a book, what emotions do you have when finishing a book?

JM: Great relief and many doubts about whether the book has been well written. I am fairly pessimistic by nature, because I am never satisfied with the end result, especially when I compare it to my initial idea. The book always ends up being but a shadow of what I thought it would be.

MLG: Do you like to revise your work?

JM: Yes, I revise and I don't rush. I have published only eight novels. Rushing is bad in any situation, but it is fatal in literature.

MLG: Do you write many drafts?

JM: I first write by hand a couple of drafts before I type them, and then I continue to revise constantly. There have been instances when I have re-written chapters dozens of times. So I revise a lot, because my first drafts aren't very good, and they don't resemble the end product in the least. Eventually, I feel that the book is close enough to what I wanted, and I resign myself to it, even though I am never satisfied.

MLG: Do you reread your works?

JM: No, I glance through them sometimes to see if what I intended to be there is indeed there. But I never reread them in their entirety.

MLG: Do you read the translations of your novels if they are in a language you know?

JM: I lived in Paris for a couple of years, so French is the foreign language I know best, although I can only read it, not write it. I do occasionally read some chapters in French, to see how the translation is. But those are the only translations I'll look at because my English is very poor, and I know nothing of German. People have told me that the German translations were very bad, but there's nothing I can do about that.

MLG: When you read a French translation, do you still feel it's your own work or someone else's?

JM: Somebody else's, and that even happens with my works in Spanish after some time has passed.

MLG: Besides writing, what else did you do while you were in Paris?

JM: I worked at many things. Some friends of mine set me up as a Spanish teacher to the daughter of the well-known pianist Robert Casadesus and to the poet Pierre Emmanuel, who died a few years ago. Pierre Emmanuel just wanted to help me; he already spoke Spanish quite well. Then, when I was down to my last francs, I got a job as a lab assistant in the Department of Cellular Biochemistry at the Pasteur Institute, which was headed by Jacques Monod, who later became the director of the Institute and a Nobel Prize-winner. I later got a more lucrative job that took up less of my time; I translated movie scripts for French-Spanish coproductions. With the money I earned I would buy books, go to the theater and the movies. And I began writing a novel.

MLG: You have won, among others, the Biblioteca Breve Prize and an award for your short stories. How do you feel about receiving these prizes?

JM: I have also received the Planeta Prize and the Mexico International Novel Prize. Awards have nothing to do with literature. Literary prizes have more to do with promotion, distribution, and sales, which are also important factors, because books deserve to be promoted in the same way that soaps or detergents are. If a book is good, it will find its way whether it wins a prize or not, and if it is bad, it will disappear.

MLG: Do you prefer to write stories or novels?

JM: I have no preference; it depends on the material and how it stimulates me. I like writing stories a lot, but I haven't written many because I consider the short story an extremely difficult genre.

MLG: More difficult than the novel?

JM: I wouldn't go that far, but it is very difficult, at least for me.

MLG: Do you feel a special fondness for any particular novel of yours?

JM: For very subjective reasons, I am very fond of my first novel, *Encerrados con un solo juguete,* which is not my best. It is an autobiographical work, and it recounts a time in my life that was very special to me. The novel takes place in the house of some friends, where I spent many hours. I like that novel for many personal reasons which have nothing to do with the reader in the least. That's why I say my reasons are subjective, not objective.

MLG: *The Fallen* and *Ronda del guinardo* dwell on the postwar years when you were still a child. What does your childhood mean to you?

JM: It is basic for me. I am one of those writers who believe that childhood is paradise and the seat of our true selves. Later on, we are just like the living dead who have survived childhood. I have always believed this.

MLG: So maintaining the child in you is essential to your writing.

JM: In my case, this is true, although it may not be for others.

MLG: You wrote your second novel, *Esta cara de la luna,* in Paris.

JM: Yes, and I have always regretted doing that, because I wrote it in a hurry, as I desperately needed the money.

MLG: Can you say something about your third novel, *Ultimas tardes con Teresa?*

JM: When I first conceived that work, I was in Paris, working as a translator of movie scripts. The filming of one of the pictures (with the French actor Louis Jourdan) began in Paris but then moved to Barcelona, and I went along, thinking that I would just spend the summer there. When I visited the neighborhood where the action of *Ultimas tardes con Teresa* was supposed to take place, I realized that I would have to stay in Barcelona in order to write that work. And so I did, and I have remained here ever since.

MLG: What geometric form would you give your work?

JM: I had never thought about it. Since I have described much of this city, it could be like a map of streets and places; many of them no longer exist, but I have kept it alive in my mind. I once wrote a short novel describing the neighborhood where I lived forty years ago as a child. To answer your question, the form of my books might be that of a map of Barcelona as it used to be.

MLG: So the past is very important for you.

JM: In this sense, it is. But the past is not as important in other novels, which are closer to the present. The novel I am writing, for instance, takes place in the present, although there may be references to the past.

MLG: How do you come up with the titles for your books?

JM: They usually come up all of a sudden. I began several of my books without a title in mind, and the titles seemed to pop up as I reached the last few pages. Sometimes I really had to struggle to come up with one. On occasion, others have provided me with a title. Carlos Barral, for instance, suggested *Esta cara de la luna.* I had been considering "The Other Side of the Moon," but he thought that "This Side of the Moon" was a better title for the book. And I agreed with him. In the case of *Ultimas tardes con Teresa,* however, I had the title even before I started writing the book.

MLG: Do you believe that a writer must wear a mask?

JM: I have written more or less straightforward accounts, without wearing a mask, such as my short story "Teniente Bravo," which is also the title of my latest book. You need a good story to be able to do this, and a novel, of course, is a far more complex matter. With a novel, it is convenient to have little hiding places, recesses, several masks, if you want to label it this way. It is far easier to mask yourself, because it is very difficult to tell an enticing story without one. It could be a naked story otherwise. It is usually convenient to maintain some distance, but I wouldn't want to say that it is always true.

MLG: Do you hide behind your narrators and is that another form of a mask?

JM: That depends on the book. I generally mask myself and tell the story through others. In *The Fallen,* for instance, there are several narrators, primarily children.

MLG: Would language be another mask? Did you ever consider writing in Catalan?

JM: I was waiting for that question. A Catalan who writes in Spanish, what a traitor! I'm tired of having to explain the reasons why I write in Spanish and not Catalan, but here they are: after the Civil War ended, the political situation in this country meant that Catalan was completely abolished from the schools, so I learned Spanish. In my house, all the adventure novels and comic books that I read were in Spanish. So were the movies we saw at the theater. In an unconscious fashion, my mythical world as a child developed in Spanish, because that's the language I started writing in. A beginning writer does not imitate reality, because otherwise I would have written in the Catalan that my parents spoke to me. Instead, he imitates the books he reads. It is only later in life that he will cease imitating art and literature, and start copying life directly.

MLG: Are novels a reflection of life for you?

JM: Of course, but a beginning writer doesn't describe things. It doesn't occur to him to describe a chair or a man walking on the street; what he does is imitate what he reads—the novels of Sherlock Holmes for instance—and in the language they are written in, which in this case was Spanish. Therefore, I started writing in Spanish naturally, because my inner discourse was in Spanish. Now that Franco has fallen, it is possible to write in Catalan, but I am too old to change. I would even call it opportunistic for me to begin writing in Catalan now.

MLG: But you could do it?

JM: I could, I'd have to work on my grammar a little, because I don't know if I'd be able to write well, but I could, of course.

MLG: I wasn't planning on asking this question, but since we were speaking about the language, what does Spain represent for you?

JM: What am I going to say? Spain? Which Spain? There are so many. In the political sphere, Spain leaves a lot to be desired right now; it bores me. I acknowledge that there have been tremendous changes since Franco's time, but Spain doesn't mean anything to me on sentimental grounds. I don't believe in patriotism. My only fatherland would be childhood, as other authors have said. Spain as history is like a history book; you can look through it and it is relatively interesting, but that's it. My novels reflect part of that history. The influence of the Civil War is very obvious in some of my writings. But in others, the theme may be the dehumanizing aspect of living in cities as a result of the poor work of politicians or the toll of life itself. I dread the coming of 1992, when this country will turn into a very inhospitable, unsettling, and, I fear, ridiculous place. On top of everything else, we also have the Olympics to contend with that year. I think I will go away from Barcelona.

MLG: Could you compare your work to that of one of your Spanish or Latin American contemporaries?

JM: No, to none. I may have many friends among my colleagues, but my style is my own. As for the Boom, my first novel was published in 1960 before the Boom started with the works of Mario Vargas Llosa and Gabriel García Márquez.

MLG: What's the most important thing for you?

JM: I don't believe very many things in this life are important, but friendship is probably one of them. Boris, leave us alone!

MLG: Your dog seems to be barking in agreement. Do animals play a role in your work?

JM: A dog named Mao does play an important role in one of my novels, and animals do appear in my work.

MLG: Are you going to give Boris a role?

JM: If she behaves, maybe.

MLG: How does it feel to go from working at a jeweler's to being one of Spain's most important writers?

JM: As I should have said earlier, things haven't changed a great deal for me. I think from the outside it might appear that I have changed a lot, but speaking from the inside, I don't think that I have.

MLG: Who is Juan Marsé?

JM: I was born in 1933, so the postwar era began when I was seven years old and continued into the 1940s, when I started working at thirteen. Those years were crucial and fundamental in every sense, whether personal, literary, or whatever. Today, I am the same boy who started writing at thirteen; I am just a street kid. Like Juan Rulfo, who was a good friend of mine, I don't like to talk about myself, nor about my work, as I am sure you have noticed. I have nothing more to say, I think you've drawn everything out of me.

PABLO SOROZABAL

Carmen
Martín Gaite

Carmen Martín Gaite was born in 1925 in Salamanca, the provincial city she writes about in many of her novels. A member of the Generation of the 1950s, or "wounded generation," she began writing because it was for her a necessity as vital as breathing. In 1972, she received her doctorate from the University of Madrid, and her thesis, "Usos amorosos del siglo 18 en España" (Love Customs of Eighteenth-Century Spain), was the recipient of an outstanding award.

Carmen Martín Gaite has written more than twenty books, which include novels, short stories, and essays: *Entre visillos,* the 1957 Nadal Prize (*Behind the Curtains,* 1990); *Las ataduras* (The Strings), 1960; *Ritmo lento* (Slow Motion), finalist for the 1963 Biblioteca Breve Prize; *La búsqueda de interlocutor y otras búsquedas* (The Search for an Interlocutor and Other Searches), 1973; *Retahílas* (The Fastenings), 1974; *Fragmentos de interior* (Inside Fragments), 1976; *El cuarto de atrás,* the 1978 National Literary Prize (*The Back Room,* 1983); *El castillo de las tres murallas* (The Castle with the Three Walls), her first book of children's stories, 1981; *El cuento de nunca acabar* (The Never-Ending Story), 1983; *Usos amorosos de la postguerra española* (Love Customs of the Spanish Postwar Period), for which she received the 1987 Anagrama Essay Prize.

Martín Gaite has been a visiting professor at various American universities. During her stay at Barnard College in the fall of 1980, she turned to collage as yet another form of expression and as one more game with fantasy and reality. As she told me: "There is very little difference between truth and lies, dreams and reality."

Dialogues and tricks are the main axes around which her creative world revolves. While the characters talk, the novels are being written. As Martín

Gaite said, "A quiet and relaxed conversation is one of the most valuable things in life. We are all in search of an interlocutor." Her novels are written from the perspective of the insider looking out, for, as she claims, the women of her generation were conditioned to see the world from "behind the curtains."

In 1988, Martín Gaite was awarded the Prince of Asturias Prize.

With two black ribbons in her long, grayish hair, Carmen Martín Gaite could be mistaken for a young girl in a Renoir painting. But at closer range, I perceived a very intense and artistic woman. "I almost never reread my books," she told me, "and it is from you the critics that I discover things about my writings." She confided that, once she had an idea for a novel, the hardest thing was to give it a shape and that she constantly must contend with order and chaos. Very feminine, she talked about literature from a woman's point of view, the woman who writes it, the one who reads it, and the women characters who evolve in it. She had been in New York for a short time and yet her apartment looked as if she had lived there for years. There were pictures of her mother on the walls and she kept countless newspaper and magazine clippings, which she converted into precious material for her collages.

❖❖❖❖❖❖❖❖❖❖❖❖❖❖❖❖❖❖❖❖❖❖❖❖❖❖❖❖❖❖

MLG: Reading your books is like visiting you at home, since your way of writing is so similar to your way of speaking. Do you think that dialogue is a form of art?

CMG: Of course, it is an art, an escape and a consolation. A quiet and relaxed conversation is one of the most valuable things in life. It would be great to be able to converse with no time limit, without being surrounded by a series of threats that constantly fence us in, warning us that the dialogue may end at any time.

MLG: You have said that "children are the only human beings left who are free and masters of their time." What does childhood represent for you?

CMG: Childhood is very fundamental from a literary point of view. I believe that any novel we may consider important has implicit or explicit references to childhood because in it resides the root of all recollections. And when I say that children are the only people that have remained free, I am referring to their lack of responsibility, their lack of oppression, their relationship with time which is less tense than that of adults. Unfortunately, adults are determined to change children into time-making machines in order to plan their futures. I believe that when I was a little girl in Salamanca, childhood, that is to say the time of discovering the world, the time of wonderment and the time of play, was lived with greater intensity than it is today. Modern times oppress children because each day the sensation of danger and haste is intensified and this turns them into adults before their time.

MLG: When you speak about playing, do you also see the art of writing as a game?

CMG: Yes, without a doubt. It is often said that writing is a very laborious task and in some aspects it is, because of the problems that face the writer. But it is above all a game, like a bet that induces the author to laugh at these problems and overcome them. I believe that, when a writer has enjoyed the creation of the work, he always succeeds in amusing others. I hope that those who read my books enjoy themselves at least one-third as much as I enjoyed writing them. If one takes writing as an overwhelming obligation, the text reflects that compulsive attitude and it becomes more rigid and less flowing. Some men have said that writing is like giving birth, but men do not know what it is to give birth. I believe that a woman never would have thought of such an absurd metaphor.

MLG: You have written a book of essays entitled *La búsqueda del interlocutor*. Is it very important for you to find an interlocutor?

CMG: It is important for me and for everyone else. We are all in search of an interlocutor. Think of all the people who go to psychiatrists to tell them their problems, or who walk the streets speaking to themselves out loud. I dare say that, if one could find at a proper moment the perfect interlocutor, one might never pick up a pen. One writes adrift, as a result of disenchantment, at those precise moments when the real interlocutor fails to appear and one has to summon him.

MLG: In *The Back Room* why was the interlocutor, the person who came to visit you, a man and not a woman?

CMG: The interlocutor presented himself to my imagination as a man and not as a woman. Why? I don't know. Perhaps because that strange conversation, which we were holding during a stormy night, developed into a climate that, although camouflaged by fantasy, was nurtured by a certain flow of eroticism. There is a vein of sensuality that links me to that character dressed in black who visited me inopportunely. And for me, eroticism can only be conceived with a man.

MLG: When the unknown man dressed in black who visits you for no apparent reason offers you that small golden pillbox, it seems as if the novel sways toward the world of magic or the supernatural. What does the golden box symbolize?

CMG: Perhaps the box signifies the palpable trace of that impalpable man. Neither the reader nor I will ever know if the man has or hasn't really come to visit me. All we know is that by dawn he disappears as if by magic. But while he was with me, he offered me some colored pills which he carried in a small golden box, and he told me that if I took one it would revive my memory. When he left and I began to wonder if all this had been a dream, I saw that the little box had remained on the table as a reminder of his presence. This may mean that I really don't know whether he was there or not, and also that as the imaginary or real interview came to an end, the only remnant of it is what the small golden box contained: a symbol of memory.

MLG: *Retahílas* and *The Back Room* are written in the form of dialogues and both take place in the course of one night. Is this particularly significant?

CMG: I suffer from insomnia and it is at night that everything comes to me, whether it be good or bad. Perhaps this is the reason for having created literary conversations set at night. But I also feel that in some way conversation and night are good friends. At night there is less noise, there are fewer interruptions and no phone calls; the plumber will not come to fix leaky faucets, nor are you about to go out on sudden errands. Everything is quieter by night, less conditioned by the burdens of daily chores, and narration springs forth with greater ease. The night that I thought up *The Back Room* there was a storm with thunder and lightning. I was alone at home because my daughter had taken a trip to the mountains and she was late in returning. I began to suffer from an acute case of insomnia. I started feeling quite anguished and I was afraid. I thought that if I could speak to someone my anguish would be dispelled, but as I had no one at my side, it occurred to me to get up from bed and begin writing. As I sat there during the storm, it was already after one in the morning. I suddenly thought, "How pleasant it would be if someone came to see me, someone who would not be in a hurry, who would feel like listening to all that I need to tell!" And then I said to myself, "Why not?" In a book I am in charge and I can make things happen the way I want them to. I summon a visitor and there he is, I invent him and make him appear. Someone rang the doorbell and there he was, the man dressed in black. I don't know if it was real or not, but at least I believed it.

MLG: While you are speaking with your interlocutor you let us see how the text is being written, how the pile of notebooks is increasing, at the same time as the dialogue develops. What made you use the dynamic technique of the novel within the novel?

CMG: I cannot tell you. It just happened in front of my eyes, without my knowing how. The idea came to me in an explosive way, and the rest came as a result of that visit (because I believe that the man dressed in black actually came, or at least I'm not sure that he didn't come). The rest was out of my hands. When you cross the boundaries between what you are convinced exists and what you are not sure of, everything is possible. The notebooks grow by themselves, the man may sit by my side, and instead of being a mere interlocutor of my insomnia, he may take on a body and turn into a much better fictional character than I had thought of. Everything happened the way I am telling it. I cannot explain anything else.

MLG: Why did you call the novel *The Back Room?*

CMG: It refers to a real room from my childhood, the game room that was in the back of my Salamanca house. But it is also symbolic, because in the human mind there exists a back room where one stores up memories, where everything is piled up and the curtains are lifted from time to time, without our knowing why. With the visit from the man dressed in black the curtain was raised and with it my childhood memories came over me. So the title has a double meaning: on the one hand there is the allusion to childhood, on the other hand the allusion to memories, which the mysterious character brought to life with his unexpected visit.

MLG: In this novel you speak about the island of Bergai, which you invented with a friend of yours when you were a little girl. Could you discuss it?

CMG: I believe that what you are trying to do is trick me into telling you the plot of *The Back Room* and a plot cannot be summarized. Tolstoy once said that, if he were to tell what *Anna Karenina* was about, he would have to rewrite the novel. What it meant for me to invent with my friend from the Institute the island of Bergai is much better told in the novel. But it was my first literary experience with fantasy and the desire to isolate myself, to escape from reality.

MLG: When did you begin writing, and why do you write?

CMG: "Why do you write?" is a question that many people ask me and it leaves me perplexed, as if they were asking me why I eat or breathe. It seems to me so natural to put down my impressions, to make them permanent so that something of what I have seen and thought will remain. To give a specific date to the beginnings of this inclination for writing is also difficult for me. I always remember myself with a pen or a pencil in my hand, even when I was a little girl. It is not that I wanted to become a writer, I just wrote naturally. I have been writing since the age of twelve. My first novel was not published until I was twenty-nine, which shows that I was in no hurry. More important than seeing myself recognized as a writer with my picture appearing in newspapers, I wanted to write to amuse myself and imagine I was having a conversation with someone. I do not know with whom. Then, from this stage of putting down things without a definite purpose, I began to think, "Well, it is not bad, I am going to reshape it," and this is how the art of writing takes form. I enjoy writing best when I am working on a book, creating it. Once it is finished, when I see it in a bookstore display, it no longer seems to be mine. I see it as something foreign, distant, as if I had taken leave of it.

MLG: Do you like to play games to amuse your reader and yourself?

CMG: I like to play very much, but the unfortunate thing is that no one lets me. The concept of life as a game is about to disappear almost completely from present-day society. Everything is programmed, including idleness, vacations, trips. Everything is part of a system engulfed by organization, life has stopped being a pleasure and has become an obligation, or a symbol of social prestige. And literature is one of the few kingdoms that does not have a practical purpose. The only one who rules is the author, who establishes the norms. It is a pleasant kingdom where that playfulness is preserved in spite of the social code which tries to take away the substance of that spirit, to make it sterile and barren.

MLG: What do you believe is the most important and recurrent theme in your work? Is it, perhaps, one's search for identity?

CMG: It could very well be, but I don't know. I am very capable of analyzing the works of another writer, because I am a careful reader and I always try to foretell the motives and penetrate the riddles of someone else's thoughts. Indeed, I served as literary critic for three and a half years with *Diario 16,* one of the major newspapers of Madrid, and I think I was rather good at it. But with regard to my own writing—whether I do it well or not—it is the only thing I know how to do. To interpret or analyze the themes in my work is something that I consider out of my reach, but it is within the power of the critics.

MLG: Would you speak about the influence of the *novela rosa* (sentimental novel) on which young Spanish girls were brought up in the 1940s?

CMG: The *novela rosa* during the war and postwar years, in which we were beginning to change from children to young ladies, represents the receptacle of romantic illusions, dreams about everlasting love, and I think it left a deep imprint on us. Women are always more impressed than men by literary models of conduct. I think I made this very clear in my research work "Usos amorosos del siglo 18 en España." I speak in that book of the reason why women in the eighteenth century behaved in a particular way. I clarify the role that literature and the so-called sub-literature played in the lives of women.

MLG: What is your impression of the United States?

CMG: My impression of this country and especially of New York City, where I have lived, is too recent for me to sum up. It is a world so full of surprises, so filled with things different from those I am accustomed to, so fascinating and fast that it does not even leave time to jot down what it brings to mind. The impressions pour down upon me too quickly. Perhaps the most acute sensation is that events and images come too rapidly, without continuity. I am used to a slower rhythm, but here it has been broken. Here I would rather be a painter or a photographer than a writer. It is as if the word were crushed into tiny pieces and had become useless. Here there is no time either to write or to think carefully. Sometimes, when I take the subway, I feel as if images were riding on the express train and ideas on the local. Images run much faster than thoughts. And the local train remains behind, it does not reach me, I lose sight of it. I am on the express, riding in the train of images. In Spain, for me it is the other way around.

MLG: Are you writing a novel now?

CMG: I'm sorry, but I am not going to answer you, because I think it brings me bad luck. A Spanish writer and a friend of mine, Gonzalo Torrente Ballester, once told me that I like to speak of my books when I am seven months pregnant with them, as if I were afraid to have a miscarriage.

MLG: And you are not yet seven months pregnant?

CMG: No. I am pregnant with too many things at once.

MLG: Let's go back to *The Back Room*. Do you carry the small golden box with you?

CMG: Yes, I always have it.

MLG: Do you have it with you now?

CMG: I can't tell you where it is.

MLG: Another mystery?

CMG: Another mystery. Perhaps the most important.

Postscript

MLG: Time has gone by and, as if by magic, you have turned the months you spent in Manhattan into one of the most lovely books, which you illustrated yourself. What inspired you to write *Caperucita en Manhattan?* How did you dream up the character of Sara, the ten-year-old girl who seems to be a cross between Red Riding Hood and Alice in Wonderland?

CMG: For the past five years I had the idea in mind. As you well know, the world of magic has always attracted me. Even after *The Back Room,* I wrote two children's stories, *El castillo de las tres murallas* and *El pastel del diablo,* in which magic played an important part.

MLG: But what prompted you to set your new novel in New York and have a little girl engage in a conversation with the Statue of Liberty? Is it one more way of looking for a special interlocutor?

CMG: That's a long story! At first I thought of having a bag lady show Sara the true meaning of liberty. But when I suddenly found out that the sculptor Bartholdi had modeled the Statue of Liberty after his mother, I was so moved that I decided to bring back to life Madame Bartholdi. She befriends the little girl, but I don't want to say more. This book has a lot of suspense. It has been well received in Spain; I hope people will enjoy it also in New York, the Statue's own city.

Ana María Matute

MARIE-LISE GAZARIAN GAUTIER

Ana María Matute was born in 1926 in Barcelona, where she still lives. At the age of five, she wrote her first short story and illustrated it. At the outbreak of the Civil War, when she was only ten, she created the magazine *Shybill* and writing became a refuge for her. She wrote her first novel, *Pequeño teatro* (Marionettes), when she was seventeen. It was published eleven years later, in 1954, and won the Planeta Prize. That same year, her son Juan Pablo was born. As she says in the following interview, he was a moving force in inspiring her to write short stories. Since then, she has written more than fifty books, some of which have been translated into more than twenty languages. Her works include novels and short stories and children's books.

Some of her novels and collection of stories are *Los Abel* (The Abel Family), 1948; *Fiesta al Noroeste* (Fiesta in the Northwest), 1953, winner of the 1952 Café Gijón Prize; *Los niños tontos,* 1956 (*The Foolish Children,* 1961); *Los hijos muertos,* 1958 (*The Lost Children,* 1965), winner of the 1958 National Crítica Prize and the Miguel de Cervantes Prize; *Primera memoria,* 1960, winner of the 1959 Nadal Prize (*School of the Sun,* 1963); *Historias de la Artámila* (Stories of Artámila), 1961; *Los soldados lloran de noche* (Soldiers Cry by Night), 1964, winner of the 1969 Fastenrath Prize of the Spanish Royal Academy; *El polizón de Ulises* (Ulysses' Stowaway), winner of the 1965 National Children's Book Award; *Algunos muchachos y otros cuentos,* 1968 (*The Heliotrope Wall and Other Stories,* 1989); *La trampa* (The Trap), 1969; *La torre vigía* (The Watchtower), 1971; and *Solo, un pie descalzo* (One Bare Foot), 1983.

Ana María Matute is a corresponding member of the Hispanic Society of America. She was Visiting Lecturer at the University of Indiana, Bloomington, 1966-69, and at the University of Oklahoma, Norman, in 1969.

She was Writer-in-Residence at the University of Virginia, Charlottesville, 1978-79. The Mugar Library of Boston University has created the Ana María Matute Collection, to which she has given manuscripts and documents.

Matute has carried over the world of magic from childhood into adulthood. As she says in the interview: "I believe that reality is not only that which is visible; there is also an invisible reality. . . . It is that reality which saved me from my childhood loneliness, my adolescent loneliness and my loneliness as a woman." Listening to her was like going on a voyage beyond the scope of words or, as Manuel Durán so rightly said, "a lesson in words not uttered."

This two-part interview was conducted both in New York and in Barcelona. The places where we met are of little importance. What matters is the magnetic presence of Ana María Matute. Each time she managed to take me into her world of magic, where adults may act, feel, and talk as if they were twelve years old or less. When I came to her home, overlooking Barcelona, it was early afternoon; when I left, it was close to midnight. We seemed to exist outside of time, and the only real world around us was the one she talked about: a world made of paper, where goblins come and go, where trees have secrets to impart, and where entire cities are made of broken glass and planks of wood. She made me believe fairy tales do exist. There was a full moon, and as I was leaving her house, midnight struck. For a moment I thought I was Cinderella, but then suddenly the real Barcelona hit me and I came back to reality.

❖❖❖❖❖❖❖❖❖❖❖❖❖❖❖❖❖❖❖❖❖❖❖❖❖❖❖❖❖❖❖

Part 1

MLG: You wrote and illustrated your first story when you were five years old. When did you become a writer and why did you leave behind a career as an artist?

AMM: It is very difficult to say when I became a writer because I was so little when I began. Literature immediately attracted me as a means of expression that was easier for me than anything else, and I can say the same thing about drawing. In fact, I have not left it. I have always liked to draw and I continue to do so. I have illustrated the cover of my last book—badly, of course, but I did it.

MLG: Your literary output could be divided into three parts: novels and short stories for adults, stories for children and adults, and children's stories. What do you enjoy writing the most?

AMM: It depends on the moment. One does not enjoy one genre more than another. There are moments that force you into writing a story and moments that require a novel of you.

MLG: Manuel Durán of Yale once told me you were a poet who writes in prose. What does poetry mean to you?

AMM: Poetry for me is the highest literary expression. I would like to be a poet and I am grateful to Manuel Durán for saying I am one. I wish it were so.

MLG: You have never written poetry?

AMM: Never.

MLG: What prompted you to enter the magical world of children?

AMM: Children attract me and I worry about them. One cannot think of the future if one does not think about children, and even in societies where children are pampered there are great omissions. Children continue being lonely even when they are surrounded by material things, and I don't believe that we have yet found a system to make children "well-educated." It is a very difficult task, for which I do not feel qualified to find an answer. But as a writer, I like to point out the problem.

MLG: One of the most beautiful stories that I have ever read is "The Golden Tree," which takes us to another dimension. What made you reach that transparent world of angels without ever losing sight of the barren, deserted earth?

AMM: I believe that reality is not only that which is visible; there is also an invisible reality. That invisible reality is the one I have clung to since my childhood. It is that reality which saved me from my childhood loneliness, my adolescent loneliness and my loneliness as a woman.

MLG: Do you think you would have written so many stories with such sensitivity if you had not had a son who inspired you to tell them?

AMM: Of course when you have a son with enormous eyes who waits for you with "Mama, tell me a story," this stimulates you a lot to tell him precisely the story that you guess from his look he would like you to tell. But since I am a born writer (perhaps a bad one, perhaps average, perhaps even good, I don't know, time will tell), I would always have written.

MLG: Do you see the influence of *The Little Prince* by Saint-Exupéry, or perhaps of Gabriela Mistral, on your approach to the magical world of children?

AMM: No, we have three rather different ways of reaching out to children. Although I admire both of these writers, we are not alike.

MLG: Your stories about children who do not want to grow up resemble in one sense *Peter Pan* and Günther Grass's *The Tin Drum*. Do you think that in your writing and your own life you have been able to arrest time and capture it in the period of childhood?

AMM: It's not that I have done it, it's that I could not help it. One has to pay very dearly for it!

MLG: There is a moment in one of your stories when a child dies to childhood and wakes up to adulthood. This is symbolized by his mother sweeping ashes that represent the death of his childhood. Why do you keep the worlds of children and adults so far apart?

AMM: Because they are two totally different worlds. Childhood is a whole world, which is completely enclosed; that is, a child is not a projection of the future man, but the man is what remains, if anything remains, of the child he once was.

MLG: In your novel *La trampa,* one of your characters says, "I imagine that my true story begins in silence." Your work is a world of contrasts, in which the word becomes silence and silence turns into words. Can you explain why one hears the voice of silence in your work?

AMM: One of the things that always affects me is realizing that the best weapon of communication we humans have is the word, and that when we truly need to say something very important to another human being we discover that the words we know are useless. Then we have to look for another language, that which is behind words. I laugh a little because I make one of my characters, a sort of goblin, speak in what I have called a "non-language." This is the language that can be understood by every human being and even every nonhuman being, like cats and dogs and birds and flowers, for instance.

MLG: The protagonist of *School of the Sun* says, "I will try to make my imagination run like a small train through unknown forests and places." How did you achieve this equilibrium between reality and fantasy?

AMM: Through crying a lot, and feeling alone and isolated, because I have had to look for that invisible reality since I was a little girl. I stuttered and the other little girls laughed at me and I felt very lonely.

MLG: But no longer.

AMM: No, not as much.

MLG: The sun, the moon, the water, the tree, "The Golden Tree," even the entire forest, appear constantly in your work. What does nature represent for you?

AMM: Perhaps a way of expansion. As a little girl I always escaped to the forest alone. I remember vividly (although it sounds literary, it is real) that I had three friends who were trees: one was called "grandfather," the second one "the friend," and the third one, which was a little further away, was simply "the other." I had great conversations with them. Besides, they had holes into which I would peep, and I would see everything I wanted to.

MLG: And what did they tell you?

AMM: That is the quintessential secret.

MLG: In that forest you were also with all the goblins in the world.

AMM: As well as some I invented myself.

MLG: Do you believe in inspiration?

AMM: I don't know what inspiration is. There are those who say that it is working very hard and there are those who say that it arises in a sound, in a ray of light, or in darkness. I think inspiration is a state of mind that predisposes you to write. It's like a dike that suddenly bursts because the water cannot be restrained and jumps out in a cascade.

MLG: How do you capture the fantastic?

AMM: That's a mystery. You're speaking or listening to something and suddenly you hear a clicking. Then you are in another world, and from there on you can do whatever you want. It's like walking with your eyes closed, and then going into an overwhelming light.

MLG: Just as it happened in "The Golden Tree"?

AMM: Exactly. I had a very strange experience in the United States about the way students received "The Golden Tree." People have liked this story much more here than in Spain. Once, as I was visiting a university, a group of students gave me a lunch especially to speak about that story. In front of every plate they placed a card on which they had painted a golden tree, the centerpiece of the table was a golden tree, they all wore golden trees on their lapels, and we all spoke about the golden tree. I think in the end we all became golden trees. It was very moving and beautiful, because they were young people, they must have been nineteen or twenty at most.

MLG: Your work depicts the disintegrated world of the postwar years, but it also reflects a cosmic world in which your protagonists look up toward heaven with moonlight in their eyes. Many of your stories have that diaphanous element. Are you religious?

AMM: I believe in God. For a long time I did not, but now I do. It is not the God in whom I was taught to believe. That was not a God that was good for me. But there is a God for me.

MLG: On several occasions, you have spoken about the forces of good and evil. In *Los soldados lloran de noche* you said, "What does it matter to be good or evil, the world is planned in a different way, built with blows of the hammer, nail by nail, fitting another scheme." And in *La torre vigía* you wrote, "I shouted with my sword in the air that they were resolved to divide the world in two, since neither good nor evil has satisfied any man, to my knowledge." Do you have any solution to that moral and social problem?

AMM: None. The work of the writer is to expose the problem because for me writing is an inner search to find myself and reach others. How can I give solutions? If I had them, I would not write.

MLG: Then the purpose of writing is to awaken others?

AMM: Yes, to wake myself up and through that to awaken others, because if you do not know yourself, you cannot understand others. If you are not aware of your own shortcomings and do not understand the reasons behind them, how can you possibly understand other people's mistakes? It's almost impossible. It's like respect. If you don't respect others, they will not respect you either. It works both ways.

MLG: In the preface to your novel *Fiesta al Noroeste* you say, "Perhaps when I wrote this book I was committing without knowing it the crime of murdering hope." That statement is very strong. Are you a pessimist?

AMM: No, I only speak about my own experiences. I am not a pessimist, in general. I only explain what I feel. Besides, I said that while I was writing the book, many years ago.

MLG: Your first novel is called *Pequeño teatro* and throughout your work there appear puppets, carnivals, even machines to make people dream. Do you see the world as a puppet show?

AMM: I saw it like that when I was seventeen, which is when I wrote that book. My perception has changed somewhat since.

MLG: Are you interested in the art of caricature?

AMM: I was interested in it when I was a little girl because I was mischievous and I always drew caricatures of my teachers on the blackboard so that my classmates would laugh. By then I had overcome the stage of stammering. Now, I prefer drawing, painting and doing portraits. I am interested in people above all else, more so than landscapes.

MLG: Did the *novela rosa,* or sentimental novel, influence your work?

AMM: I have never read any.

MLG: Who is usually the narrator in your work?

AMM: It depends. For instance, in *Historias de la Artámila,* it is almost always the little girl I used to be with my brothers.

MLG: Like Juan Valera, you always describe the eyes, the hair, the hands, even the feet of your characters. Many of your characters have blue eyes. Why are you so attracted by that color?

AMM: I like blue eyes but I didn't realize I showed this preference in my work. I enjoy describing the physical appearance of my characters. I pay more attention to that "nonlanguage" which I mentioned before and which goes beyond words than to what people say. The "nonlanguage" is reflected a great deal in the eyes, the hands, and the feet. I am also a woman, and a friend told me once, "You live by colors." It's true, they impress me and seem very revealing. The greatest misfortune that could befall me would be not to see colors. Sometimes a color seems as important as a person or, at least, as some aspects of a person.

MLG: In your style of writing one also sees the art of painting. After all, you began writing and painting when you were five.

AMM: But I paint very badly. I do it because I enjoy it.

MLG: Do you see your work as an open book in which everything is explained or is it important for you that the reader make an effort to decipher it?

AMM: Everything cannot be explained in a book because then it would no longer be literature. It would be a manual, an explanatory booklet about how one handles something, and I don't believe that anyone has yet invented a perfect system for running one's life.

MLG: You have said in the preface to *Fiesta al Noroeste,* "Books are more mysterious for the author than for the readers."

AMM: Sometimes, yes. That issue takes on such proportions that I occasionally come to the end of the book full of doubts, wondering, "And for that I wrote this book?"

MLG: Who is the reader for you? Do you think about the reader when you write?

AMM: If while writing I thought someone was going to read that work, I do not know whether it would inhibit me. When I begin writing I no longer think of myself either. There arises another Ana María from within me, who writes and who is not the same as the one who later lives, eats, or speaks. It's another being who exists while writing. I can start writing only when the visible world around me disappears, when I no longer see the page or the typewriter. Of course, how can I think then about the reader? The reader is there in substance because, if I thought that no one would read me, I would not bother writing. But I am not such a narcissist. At the moment I am writing I think neither of the reader nor of the writer that I am. I think about the book. I become the book.

MLG: Do you pay more attention to the book as a whole, or to your characters?

AMM: When I am asked which is my favorite character from my books, I find myself at a loss because my characters do not really matter. They are there only in relation to my book. They matter to me because they are useful for the pursuit of the book but not in themselves.

MLG: So you can control your characters. They are not beings who enjoy their own freedom?

AMM: Not completely. Sometimes minor changes appear in form, but not in content.

MLG: Many of your novels are written in the form of diaries, for instance *School of the Sun.* Why?

AMM: That is not my concept of a diary. Of course, it is written in the first person. I have never written a diary and I believe it is impossible.

MLG: Why not?

AMM: Because it is not real. You can write facts, but you cannot write life.

MLG: Nowadays there is a tendency to speak about feminine and masculine reality when analyzing a literary work. Would it not be more correct to study the literary process of a writer, whether man or woman, for its own merits?

AMM: Definitely. But I have kept away from these things and I no longer comment on them. However, I believe there are books written by women and there are books written by men and that's that. And there are good books and bad books and that's the end of it.

MLG: You have said that writing, besides being a protest, is also a long unfinished question. You also indicated that writing is a solitary adventure. Could you share with us what writing is for you, at this particular moment?

AMM: It is a search of the inner defenses in order to reach others through my own intimate world. For example, the visible world is always a great source of wonder, as if I had suspended time when I was twelve years old.

That sense of amazement has never left me. To be able, through an interpretation of that wonder and through a sense of oneself, to understand
others, to reach a true communal humanity, to see others as your fellow
beings. I believe this is one of the major reasons impelling me to write. What
at a given moment may be interpreted as a selfish attitude, I believe is just
the opposite.

MLG: Could you share with us some of the moments you have experienced in the United States?

AMM: What I especially liked in the United States was the contact with
the students who came to my classes. It was a fabulous discovery for me and
I have learned so much with them that I believe I should have paid them
rather than them paying me.

MLG: Has the United States influenced your novels?

AMM: A section of *La trampa* takes place in the United States. It is not
that I intended to speak about that country, but the novel required that background because of the father's exile. I limited the environment to that of the
academic world of Spanish professors, exiled or nonexiled, who lived in the
United States. I can never speak of a country I am not familiar with, and in
order to know a country it is necessary to live in it for a long time and even
then it is not easy to know it completely. For that reason, I'll never write a
book about the United States because I think it would be very superficial.
This does not mean that others cannot do it, but I truly do not see myself as
capable of doing it. So when there is a passage involving another country in
my work, it always serves as background, never as a picture of that country,
never an exposition of what the country seemed to be. It is used simply as a
landscape, just as it may be necessary to depict a rococo drawing room, a
museum, or a tennis court.

MLG: Would you share with future writers some of your experier ces or
give them some advice?

AMM: Experiences, yes. They should not pay attention to those who do
not want them to be what they are. Let them continue. Advice, no. I do not
know how to give advice nor do I dare to. Besides, I think to advise is very
dangerous. I have received much advice and it has been of little use.

MLG: When you were in the United States did you teach a course on
Spanish literature or a seminar on your own work?

AMM: Both. One course was about novelists of my own generation in
postwar Spain, and another was about my own work since that was what
they had asked me to do. I felt a little anxious about that, but that was what
they wanted.

MLG: Did you read your works with them?

AMM: We read and we commented on them. Of course, no one could
speak to them about my work as I did, from within, without any compassion
for myself. I let myself be crucified by them, which was very good.

MLG: What is the meaning of the word for you? It is obviously important for you to correct and revise, since you write several versions of the same work.

AMM: I correct so much because I am searching for that "nonlanguage" behind words. Perhaps it can be found by placing a specific word, which in itself may not mean anything or may say something contrary to its meaning, exactly where it will be effective.

MLG: What do you do upon finishing a novel?

AMM: Close it and publish it. Unfortunately, publishers are always waiting for it in too great a hurry. I would correct my novels until the end of my life, but that can't be. If another novel comes immediately, I write it; if not, I'll wait for another ten years. There is no hurry.

MLG: When you finish your novel do you show it to someone?

AMM: It should be left alone. It's responsible for its own errors.

MLG: So when the novel is finished it acquires a life of its own?

AMM: Of course. But it does not exist if no one reads it and does not put something into it. The book belongs as much to the reader as to its author. The writer does not give anything ready-made, but only tries to awaken in the reader a curiosity, a question, a search. The continuation of that search is done by the reader. Sometimes the reader even finds the solution that the author has not found. This is beautiful. It would be beautiful for me to know it.

MLG: Who is Ana María Matute?

AMM: If I knew, I would behave much better. I would lead her to her goal and she would not stumble so much.

MLG: You once read me a verse by Luis Cernuda that I think symbolizes all your work.

AMM: "I believe in myself because someday I will become all the things that I do." This verse says one has to believe in oneself, but not to be vain. And no one can say it better than a poet. Cernuda's poem is priceless to me when I think of the strength one needs in order to write.

MLG: And that is what you have done and are doing. Your work is filled with love and a need for love. Upon reading your work one gets the sensation of a constant giving and receiving.

AMM: I hope so!

Part 2

MLG: Well, let us continue the conversation we began in New York.

AMM: Yes, we had a lot of fun.

MLG: A moment ago, we were discussing painting and how much you enjoy drawing.

AMM: A great deal, as well as painting. I generally draw all the characters of my work; I enjoy doing that a lot. I believe I am not the only one to do that. I draw my characters while I am writing about them.

MLG: Have you kept those drawings?

AMM: Yes. I have a few, although I have given some away and destroyed others or lost them. We lose so many things in this world, on top of our youth and our lives. In fact, losing all these things contributes to our loss of youth and life.

MLG: Do all your characters have blue eyes?

AMM: Most of them.

MLG: Even in your drawings?

AMM: Yes, even there. I enjoy drawing blue eyes a lot. As you pointed out to me in our last conversation, I have an obsession with blue eyes. I am fascinated by blue eyes. When I was young, and I used to have big, dark eyes, and people praised me for them, I would say to myself, "Why couldn't my eyes be blue?"

MLG: You paint in your work, but with words.

AMM: You would know that better than I. I am a very poor judge of my own work. You, the reader, can judge that better.

MLG: Since your son is now full-grown, do you feel the same sense of urgency to write children's stories?

AMM: I wrote children's stories while he was a child, but the strange thing is that he never read any of them. Well, I shouldn't say never, I thought he had not read them. But since then, I found out through an American friend of his—who used to be a student of mine in Charlottesville and is now a translator—that Juan Pablo had read my books and commented on them. The truth is that I wrote those books for him, and some of the characters are partially based on him. Anyway, as my son grew up, I became less interested in writing children's stories, although I have written one lately called *Solo, un pie descalzo,* which I think is my best. I won the National Prize for Children's Literature for that book, and I am very happy with it, but I think it is the last one of its kind I will ever write.

MLG: Are you writing anything now?

AMM: Yes, I am. I haven't written in many years, because of many ailments I have suffered and some blows life has dealt me. But I am now writing again, and I am almost finished with a book.

MLG: What is it called and what does it mean?

AMM: "Paraíso inhabitado" (Uninhabited Paradise). Loosely put, it is a book about wishes, and how when our wishes are granted, they don't seem quite as attractive anymore. That's what the book is about in very simple terms, although it is quite complex. But I won't say anything more. I am very superstitious and believe that if I talk about a book I am writing, I might jinx it. It is like opening a bottle of perfume and leaving it open: it all evaporates.

MLG: When is this book coming out?

AMM: Whenever I finish it. Don't you pressure me too. Everybody keeps calling, including my literary agent, and asking for it.

MLG: Many of your readers, as well. I visited a friend in Paris recently, and he told me that he was anxiously awaiting a new book from you. He asked me to beg you to publish a new book.

AMM: Hooray for that man! Anyway, my publishers and my literary agent, Carmen Balcells, are anxiously expecting that book, and they tell me it is going to be a success.

MLG: When do you write?

AMM: Whenever I feel like it. This is all very relative, because once I sink my teeth into a book, time stops moving for me, and I write continuously. If for any reason I have to stop (as I did with this book because of my illnesses), then it is very hard for me to get myself going again, although I did just that in this case. So, I can write any time, although I prefer mornings.

MLG: Does writing become an obsession?

AMM: Absolutely, it has always been, since I can remember. I lead an imaginary life which, of course, to me is real, and I set it down on paper. When I look back, I cannot help but conclude I have led a life set to paper. This did not prevent me from experiencing some beautiful moments very intensely, including a fabulous love that still glows. But when all is said and done, I have lived in and through books, and everything else falls into step. Unlike any of my other books, the first part of "Paraíso inhabitado" deals with my childhood. That's how I noticed that I have led a life made of paper. When I was a child, I didn't understand the world and it rejected me.

MLG: What was your mother like?

AMM: My mother was always very harsh and strict with me, and I always thought she didn't love me, although she probably did. My mother kissed me twice in my life.

MLG: Do you remember those moments?

AMM: Perfectly well; I could recount them to you in detail. The rest of the time she would blow a kiss in the air. I feared her and admired her. She made me feel very small. My father, on the other hand, was a dear.

MLG: What were you like as a child?

AMM: I was a very solitary, introverted child who got punished by being sent to a dark room quite frequently. But you cannot imagine how much I enjoyed myself in that room, and how I would look forward to being punished, because it was there that I discovered the light of darkness. All of this is in "Paraíso inhabitado." That room was where they put everyone's coats, including those of my brothers, who were studying at a Jesuit school at the time. I yearned for them, because they were very loving with me. Some of this is also recounted in a novelized form in *Solo, un pie descalzo*.

MLG: When did you start writing?

AMM: It was in that dark room that I started to write, because otherwise I would have died. Writing became a survival tool, and that explains why I have led a "life of paper."

MLG: You were very close to your brothers as a child?

AMM: My little brother and I were the youngest. I used to make up stories and tell him that we were going to escape in a wagon of puppeteers. I loved puppeteers, and sometimes when we went to our mother's country house in the summer, they would come with their wagons. I've written about this a lot in my books. Anyway, the puppeteers and the clowns would come, and I would tell my brother that we would escape one day, because we were not our parents' children; we had been adopted. This is one of the stories I used to tell my little brother, who is now a doctor.

MLG: And he believed you?

AMM: Blindly. We would console each other a lot like that.

MLG: Where was your mother's country home?

AMM: In a village that is now underwater called Mansilla de la Sierra. I have written a book, called *El río,* which details all this. It is the only work that is dangerously autobiographical, in which people and places are identified with their real names. It's not a novel, but a collection of literary columns of mine that used to come out in a weekly called *Destino.* I talk about the towns, rivers, and people of my childhood at my mother's country home, and of my return to that place after it became submerged. It was horrible. Once in a while, the water would go down and the church, our home, and everything else would reappear on the surface. I went through the same experience when my son was a young boy and we saw the town submerged. I am inside my books even though I may not want to be, but this one is a chronicle based on memories.

MLG: What did books mean to you as a child?

AMM: I loved reading *Sleeping Beauty* and the like. These stories were printed on special paper that was very thick and smelled spicy. The effect of those stories on me was almost sensual; they spoke of a fantastic, mysterious world that reached me through the smell and feel of those pages. I was fascinated by all this. Anyway, I am going to be saying a lot of silly things, so please cut me off.

MLG: You are the only writer in your family.

AMM: Yes, one mad person per family is enough, don't you think?

MLG: Can you picture your books visually and would you give them a particular form?

AMM: Yes, they ascend in a spiral shape.

MLG: Where to?

AMM: One never knows, because a book is never entirely finished. You can start a book, but you can never finish it.

MLG: Do you feel that each succeeding book is really the same one being written in a different form?

AMM: I am not sure, but there is probably a lot to this. Every person has obsessions, and writers perhaps more than other people. So it is quite common for an author to write the same book over and over from different angles. I hope that my work has evolved from *El pequeño teatro* to *Los Abel,* otherwise I would be horrified. Nevertheless, upon finishing each book, there is the sense that your initial will or intention has not been fulfilled and that it resurfaces again. For example, there are things within me—and I have been made aware of this by my readers and critics—such as my obsession with a lost paradise and childhood, the obsession of Cain and Abel, let us say. I know very well where that comes from.

MLG: From the Civil War, obviously.

AMM: That's it specifically. The obsession with Cain and Abel comes from the war between brothers that we suffered. There are other things as well, such as the absence of a mother in all my books. That's because, although I had a mother, she never made me feel she was there for me.

MLG: Do you still claim, as you did some years ago, that like Peter Pan you stopped growing at age twelve?

AMM: Yes, I am twelve years old. I've put on weight and become older, my hair has turned gray, but I'm still twelve years old, and still paying dearly for it.

MLG: Is writing a search for you?

AMM: Yes, without a doubt. And I still haven't found what I'm looking for. I have discovered many things along the way, but not what I was seeking. Even though it may sound pretentious, it is like the search for the Holy Grail. It is also like being close to an uninhabited paradise where no one has ever been.

MLG: Does reality hold a place in your life?

AMM: I have never discovered what it is. It has me perplexed. When people ask me to be more realistic, I invariably stick my foot in my mouth because I don't understand what it means. A goblin seems more real to me than the director of a bank. I understand a goblin, whereas I have never understood a banker. What is reality for me? I don't know.

MLG: What if I asked you about fantasy or imagination?

AMM: Those things seem normal to me. But don't forget that I lead a life of paper.

MLG: So fantasy is reality for you.

AMM: Yes, I do believe it is, because what some call reality causes them pain, while fantasy makes people happy, and also gets at the truth better sometimes.

MLG: Do you know other people who can feel as comfortable as you do in the fantasy world?

AMM: Once in a while I meet a person like that, and that's wonderful because we spend hours on end talking and laughing. But these people tend not to stay, they just come by and move along. They are sensitive, imaginative, insightful people, who can speak the "nonlanguage" that I talk about in one of my books. This nonlanguage has a special light about it, it has moondrops in its eyes, as I said in that work. After people actually went to the moon, the effect was ruined a little.

MLG: In what work did you dream up that expression?

AMM: That term comes from "El olvidado rey Gudu" (The Forgotten King Gudu), a two thousand-page book that I wrote long ago and which I haven't wanted to publish. It's finished, it only needs formal corrections. I have it here in my room, carefully kept with all its illustrations. The plot takes place in the tenth century and deals with a dynasty. I love that book because it dwells on things that I have always treasured. I dedicated it to the great authors I read as a child, like Hans Christian Andersen, the Brothers Grimm, Lewis Carroll, Barrie, and others; and also to everything I have lost or forgotten. I wrote it when I still lived in Sitges. That about sums it up, doesn't it?

MLG: Why don't you want to publish it?

AMM: Because it is some sort of a will, or testament.

MLG: Are you working on it now?

AMM: No, I have left it alone. It's been punished, because it was naughty.

MLG: The same way you got punished to the dark room when you were small?

AMM: Yes, so that it can gestate, because books gestate when they are left alone, they create offspring.

MLG: So the book has a soul and a life of its own for you.

AMM: Yes, absolutely. One day, while I was writing this book and thinking about the characters, I suddenly had a tremendous anxiety attack as I realized that my characters weren't real people. I felt like bursting into tears and crying out, "This cannot be! It cannot! They do exist! They told me to write this book!" I was so depressed that day, I thought I was going to die.

MLG: The book was in control.

AMM: Completely. At the risk of sounding romantic and literary, I would even say that I heard voices while writing that book. That's the only time this has ever happened to me. Can you believe that King Gudu is not even born until the second part of the book. But he has a very impressive lineage which I describe. The name of Gudu's mother, Queen Ardid (a nice-sounding name from Eastern Europe), means "trick" in Spanish, and she is like a magician. I also love a goblin who comes from the south. He really exists for me, I haven't made him up. I couldn't love those characters the way I do if they were not really alive. My goblin has nothing to do with the creatures you see on television nowadays. It really rankles me to see the way the real world of goblins is cheapened. I know that world perfectly well, since I was born there. Well, to go on with the story, the goblin is fond of grapes, then he turns to wine and gets drunk. He loses his characteristics as a goblin and falls in love with a human being. A bunch of grapes starts growing where he would have a heart (if goblins had hearts). People pick the grapes one by one and when they've eaten all of them, and only the stem is left, the goblin dies and turns to ashes.

MLG: So human beings are cruel.

AMM: Yes, they are, although they are also capable of wonderful things. Everything is explored in my book.

MLG: You tell this story like a fairy tale, I wish you wouldn't stop!

AMM: When my nieces were still little, they would sometimes come over, and instead of watching television, they would ask me to tell them the story of King Gudu. I would oblige and they turned into a captive audience. I would put on some music to accompany my story. Once, I played the soundtrack from some movie and I told them that the goblins danced to that music. A few days later, they went to see a movie and it happened to have the music I played them. They were so outraged that they left in the middle of the picture, claiming that someone had stolen the music for King Gudu from me! They weren't that young either, about ten or eleven years old. It got to such a point that their mother told me to stop putting ideas into their heads, because they were so preoccupied with them that they never did their homework.

MLG: Did you ever think of writing for television?

AMM: It doesn't interest me. My life is one of paper. They have adapted some of my works for the screen, such as *El polizón del Ulises,* but I was very disappointed when I saw it, because it didn't correspond to the images in my head. I had to endure instead of enjoying it.

MLG: Did you play any part in making that film?

AMM: No, and I almost didn't get paid for the rights to the story, our world being the way it is. They are currently adapting another one of my stories, and I really dread seeing what they have done with it.

MLG: Haven't they consulted you?

AMM: They haven't asked me anything. They pay you for the rights and that's it; they don't ask for your advice. I hate it when they change phrases in my stories or the color of a character's eyes! I say to myself, there is no way they should be allowed to do that! I struggled so hard to come up with just the thing for a character to say, and then they make him say something I would have never dreamed of, never! How stupid these people are!

MLG: If you could speak with an author from the past, whom would you choose?

AMM: I'd like to speak with many of them, for instance, Kafka, Andersen, and the anonymous author or authors of *The Knights of the Round Table*.

MLG: What would you say to them?

AMM: I would ask them many things. I'd love to talk with the Russians in particular: Dostoyevsky, Chekhov, Gogol, and Tolstoy. But perhaps more than anyone else, I'd love to talk with Proust.

MLG: What would you ask him?

AMM: I'd like to ask him if he was as solitary as I am, and if he too led a life made of paper.

MLG: When you read books other than your own, do you feel like continuing the story when you've reached the last page?

AMM: There are many times when it makes me sad to see a good story end. But no, I wouldn't want to continue it myself. It would lose all its charm. That's someone else's story, and although I may like it very much, I am not related to it at all.

MLG: What do you feel when you finish writing a book?

AMM: At first, overwhelming relief, and then great sadness. You know that the writing is done and that you must let it go. The book is now for others to read. I always leave an open door for the readers, so that they may speculate on what happened and what could transpire.

MLG: What does punctuation mean to you?

AMM: Well, I do like periods. I used a lot of suspension points in *La torre vigía,* for instance. That's one of my works I am proudest of.

MLG: Do you see the world through the eyes of a child?

AMM: Through the eyes of a frustrated eleven-year-old boy, because when I was that age, the other girls wouldn't let me play with them. I'm sorry if this may offend some feminists out there, but it is the truth.

MLG: Can you talk about the way children enjoy being with you and how you draw them into your magic world?

AMM: Yes, when I lived in Sitges, there was a group of eleven-year-olds who would come to my house, led by a redheaded boy called Amadeus, the son of an important American painter whose works are currently displayed in Madrid. These kids would come over and since I lived close to a carpenter, we would gather bits of wood and glass and anything we could find and build the most wonderful castles and cities you can imagine! You could see houses, roads, walls, and everything in our cities! That period of time in Sitges was one of the most wonderful in my life. Nowadays, it is impossible for me to look at anything without immediately visualizing it as part of the towns we built. I passed this on to my son, who now complains that he can't see a sponge without talking to it! Anyway, I loved to build staggered cities above the sea (which would have been impossible in real life), and I would construct little staircases for all the houses. At the top of the hill, I would always build the castle of the evil duke, who wasn't as evil as the butcher to whom he was pawning his castle in exchange for prime meat.

MLG: Does this appear in any of your books?

AMM: No, these whole cities were built with our hands. I would tell the children stories as we collected the material and put them together. We would sit down by the fireplace, and their parents marveled at the fact that their children would rather play with "la Matute" than watch television. I would also hide treasures, because there were always pirates in the seas adjacent to our towns. The great challenge was to find where the treasure was. I made a treasure chest and hid pieces of metal shaped into gold coins, and turned tiny specks of colored glass into rubies, emeralds, sapphires, and pearls. I've never cared much for jewels (although I had some very nice ones, which were stolen), but I've never seen an emerald as beautiful as the butt of a bottle, if you'll pardon the expression. The children who came over would bring me whatever they found to make our city more interesting. After a while, my husband told me that I was turning the house into a garbage dump and that I should tell the children to stop bringing all those strange things.

MLG: Have you kept any of those cities?

AMM: No, I always gave them away; some of the children still have them. They once showed me on television in the process of making one. I made minarets with the tops of onions, and I anxiously awaited for glasses to break so I would have the right color windows in my town. We would covet glass pieces, because you cannot imagine the worlds that lie behind a cut-glass fragment! The children would claim that the windows in the cities we built sparkled with multicolored iridescent lights. They really saw it that way and so did I.

MLG: Do you still own the house in Sitges?

AMM: No, I had to give it up. My husband Julio and I lived there for eight years, but it became difficult for his work because he had to travel so much, and the weather didn't agree with my health. That's when we decided to move to Barcelona. I will always miss the room where I used to write in Sitges, because it had glass on all sides and . . . I have never had a room to write in like that one, and I never will again. I became the friend of a palm tree I could see from that room.

MLG: Did you also speak with the sea?

AMM: No, you don't talk to the sea, it talks to you. The sea is very particular and you must treat it with respect, because it could kill us all if it wanted.

MLG: What would the sea say to you?

AMM: All sorts of things, the sea tells many things, and it scolded me a lot.

MLG: Does the wind also speak to you?

AMM: The wind is very important to me, and it is one of the few things that frighten me. The wind is used by other elements, like water, for instance. Have you ever listened to the water speak when you break its flow with your hand? You could write many stories about what it tells you. It talks to me as to everyone. What happens is that some of us understand what it is saying, while others don't.

MLG: Do animals talk with you too?

AMM: No, it's very strange. I respect animals a great deal and I wouldn't be able to stand someone mistreating one in front of me, but I will never have an animal in my home. When I was a little child, my father gave me a small bird, which promptly died. This made me so sad that I haven't been able to have an animal since. The same thing happened to my son, who loves dogs. Every time one of his dogs died, he would become so sad and upset that I haven't wanted anything more to do with animals. You have to take care of living things, because if you don't, they die, and that is horrible.

MLG: What has it meant to you to have a son?

AMM: Nothing in this world can compare with a son, especially one with whom you can communicate, because there are some with whom you can't.

MLG: What would take place between a mother made of paper and her son?

AMM: It was wonderful, because he was also very imaginative. He was my great companion and friend, on top of being my son. I can remember that when he hadn't yet learned to speak, he would squeeze my hand and look at me whenever I was sad. I have never had a conversation with anybody that could compare to that one, which was held without words.

MLG: The nonlanguage once again.

AMM: Yes. Juan Pablo is a pilot and he likes to parachute. When he first asked if he could do that, I refused, but finally I agreed. I think now I understand what it is like to fly, although I could never do it myself.

MLG: What is your husband like?

AMM: He is a businessman. I have gone all over the world with him. He has told me that as a child he used to play with a set of dominoes and dream that he was traveling the entire world in a jeep. He really wanted to go to China in particular, and when he grew up, that's just what he did. Do you know the color of his eyes? They are blue!

MLG: Of course, it couldn't be otherwise. Would you say that Ana María Matute is a very shy person?

AMM: Yes, in my books, I didn't want to use my name or have my photograph appear or even read any of the reviews of my works. My publishers of course refused, but after all these years, I still think that writing is a very private thing, and that as authors we allow others to read our innermost thoughts and to trample on our intimate secrets. How can we allow this? So I am very shy and it causes me great anxiety when others read my books, and great anger if I don't want them to look through my work. I am very egotistical about what I write, I want it for myself. It's mine, and nobody should come along and spoil it, irrespective of whether I think it is a good or bad work. It may be bad, but it is mine, it's the best part of me. It is very hard to put up with those moronic critics who don't understand anything. I can stand a critic who says one of my books is bad if at least he has understood it, but I can't bear someone who claims my work is wonderful and who hasn't comprehended even the smallest part in it.

MLG: Is that the reason why it is so hard for you to hand over your work to your publisher?

AMM: No. . . . Some people might say that if I feel this way, I should go hibernate in a cave, but I can't do that, because I want to communicate. And writing is communication. I write for others. I write for anybody who is sensitive and able to understand what I am talking about. It's the same thing as if someone came to me to discuss advanced mathematics; I wouldn't be able to appreciate it.

MLG: What is the most important purpose of literature then?

AMM: Communication with someone, which is so hard to achieve in life, and which I could not do as a child. That's why I started to write: I could not communicate, and if I had not invented my own world, I would have died. Although I understand the world a little better now (or it understands me), the basic situation has not changed. I believe that any writer, no matter how intellectual, cold or cerebral, wants to be understood, otherwise he wouldn't bother to write. It is not true that authors write for themselves. Like Kafka, if I couldn't have written, I would have exploded.

MLG: What do you consider most important in life?

AMM: To be true to oneself. You cannot be false, no matter what. Everyone is the way he is, and there is room for all of us. You should not be a fake, or ashamed of yourself, which shows your basic insecurity. Everyone is the way he is and that's it. Period.

MARIE-LISE GAZARIAN GAUTIER

Eduardo Mendoza

Eduardo Mendoza was born in 1943 in Barcelona, where he now lives after residing in New York from 1973 to 1982. While he was in New York, he served as an interpreter at the United Nations. He also had the opportunity to be present at the White House and serve as interpreter between Felipe González, Spain's prime minister, and President Ronald Reagan.

When he published his first novel, *La verdad sobre el caso Savolta* (The Truth about the Savolta Case), in 1975, six months before the death of Franco, he received immediate recognition. That book won the Crítica Prize for that year. Today, Eduardo Mendoza is considered in Europe, and especially in France, one of the most important writers. His novel *La ciudad de los prodigios,* 1986 (*The City of Marvels,* 1988), was a best-seller in Spain and was selected in France as the Best Book of the Year for 1988. He says jokingly about his success, "When I began writing I dreamed of becoming famous someday, but never of beginning success-fully, which is hard to follow. So I've had to live with it and not let my readers down." Two of his novels have been made into movies.

Eduardo Mendoza, like Laurence Sterne, turns to irony and parody. Rather than experimenting with language, he is constantly intertwining genres and experimenting with them. His detective stories represent a modern version of the traditional picaresque novel. Although not a historian, he uses history as material for literature and combines facts with imaginative fiction. He is primarily an author who writes about the history of a city and, in his case, the city he mostly turns to is Barcelona. However, in his latest novel, *La isla inaudita* (The Unheard-of Island), 1989, the city he describes is decadent Venice.

Among his other works are *El misterio de la cripta embrujada* (The Mystery of the Bewitched Crypt), 1979, and *El laberinto de las aceitunas* (The Olive Labyrinth), 1982.

Eduardo Mendoza is a tall, elegant man who tends to answer questions with a grin, followed by a joke, to avoid giving himself much importance. He looks at you with his beady eyes and laughs off his success. I had met him on several occasions while he lived in New York. This interview, however, took place in April 1988, when he was in Manhattan to take part in a symposium held at the Casa de España. We met over breakfast, and with great humility he spoke about his work. When I asked him what it felt like for him to see people reading one of his books, he answered, "I make sure they don't recognize me, because they might beat me up with their umbrellas. But seriously, what I really feel like doing is telling them to skip a particular paragraph because I don't think I did it justice."

❊❊❊❊❊❊❊❊❊❊❊❊❊❊❊❊❊❊❊❊❊❊❊❊❊❊❊❊❊❊❊❊❊❊❊❊❊

MLG: You lived in New York from 1973 to 1982. Do you think that the years spent there influenced you in any way?

EM: The ten years of my life spent in New York surely influenced me. I cannot pinpoint those influences in detail, but I can say that having lived in Manhattan, having been a part of its literary climate, having observed the type of novels that were being written, which blended very well with the Spanish literary tradition, must have influenced me.

MLG: During those years, you worked as an interpreter at the United Nations. When did you first realize that you wanted to be a writer?

EM: When I was four. The children's stories I would read, or the stories my mother would tell me, gave me a passionate desire to become a writer. These moments of my childhood have been the greatest influence on my life as a writer. Strangely enough, I don't remember any of the stories. There was nothing special about them, except that they made me discover at such an early age what my vocation would be. Of course, there have been other influences at every stage of my life. Cervantes and the picaresque novel had a very strong impact upon me, as well as Baroja, Valle Inclán, Stendhal, Tolstoy, and Dickens. These influences came to me one at a time. At this particular moment, I am somewhat confused. I don't know who is influencing me, or whom I am influencing. What I never thought was that I could make a living by writing. I always believed, and this is very much in the line of an ancient Spanish tradition, that you could not live by writing alone. So I held many jobs and, luckily, I enjoyed very much my work as an interpreter at the United Nations. I still do some interpretation sporadically. But writing is what I have always wanted to do, and it has become my way of life.

MLG: Did your mother, or any other member of your family, write?

EM: My mother read a lot, but she did not write. There were some writers in my family, but they had only an indirect influence upon me. I have an uncle who writes chronicles of a historical character.

MLG: What does writing mean to you, and why do you write?

EM: It is not so easy to answer this two-part question. When I get up in the morning, writing is the only thing I want to do. If I haven't been writing for a while, I become very nervous. If I get away from writing for a few days, if I take a vacation from writing, after a while I cannot stand it anymore. Writing is like a biological need, I write each morning like a hen that lays its eggs; if it didn't comply with its biological function, it would die. Why do I write? To create a world which will bring order to that world I carry within me.

MLG: Do you see the influence of journalism on your writings?

EM: No, I have never been a journalist, and I am not even a good reader of newspaper articles. Journalism does not interest me as a reproduction of reality. I resort to newspapers only to keep informed of what someone called "the pulse of an epoch." For instance, when I wrote *La verdad sobre el caso Savolta,* I turned to the papers of that particular period to see how people spoke in those days. But journalism as a style is not for me. I take my time when I write, I am not interested in relating current events, I only want to tell about the world shaping up in my head.

MLG: How did you come to write that novel?

EM: By a process of derivation. I began to write a novel, then I decided to develop a certain aspect of it, which led me to another, and so forth. With every novel that I write, I follow that same pattern. I start with an idea, then proceed by derivation and go from a main track to a secondary one until finally the novel is born.

MLG: Do you think that novelists repeat themselves in each of their works?

EM: There are many kinds of writers. For some, each new novel is a chapter added to his previous work. In my case, I attempt to make a mosaic and little by little I cover new territories. I am not an ambitious writer, I do not wish to write a complete novel, I want to leave something to say for the next one. I take one novel at a time and limit myself to what I set out to do.

MLG: How would you tie in your second book, *El misterio de la cripta embrujada,* with your first novel?

EM: My first novel introduces a series of possibilities, like a prologue to other books. It's an experiment I enjoyed very much doing, and I think my most interesting work. Movies were made of these two novels. As you know, one is seldom pleased with a novel put to the screen, it never exactly depicts the world as you envisioned it. The movie version of *El misterio de la cripta embrujada,* although technically inferior, came closest to the spirit embodied in the novel.

MLG: *The City of Marvels* received the Italian prize Grinzane Cavour and was cited in France as the 1988 Best Book of the Year. What made you write it?

EM: Invariably I follow the pattern of derivation. I began writing a page on a topic that was of interest to me, and then I realized that it needed a complementary angle, some kind of an explanation. So I did more thorough research and I ended up with the novel.

MLG: What do you feel when you know that you have reached the last page and your novel is ready to be sent out to the publisher?

EM: Mixed feelings, the satisfaction of knowing you have finished something that was beginning to become difficult, especially the end which is always turbulent, even unruly. A novel represents months, even years of obsession. When you write the final word, you feel an inner peace, a great relief. On the other hand, you experience a certain sense of loss because you know that you have come to the end of a particular journey. Even though it is hard for me to survive without writing, each time I finish a novel I impose upon myself a period of six months where I do not write anything, unless it is some brief account. I suppose I need that period to recharge.

MLG: You turn to history and change it into literature. Could you explain that?

EM: I believe that history is both a science and a literary form. In Spain, and in most of Europe, history lost its literary perspective. What I have done is rediscover our history, not for its scientific connotation, but as a literary means. For me, history is literature. I am not a historian; therefore, it is not the reason my novels are based on history. I am not primarily concerned with dates, but I am interested in recapturing our signs of identity. I am a narrator, who wants to tell a familiar story, the personal history of a given community, in this case, Barcelona, my city. Being a Catalan made it even harder to understand our past, because our personal history had deliberately been swept under a rug so that we would never know about it. In my novels I attempt to relate the past with a vision that we hold of it today. I lay aside important historical events, because they were not recorded by the collective memory, and stress other moments that are more relevant to our present. It is an evocation of the past from the perspective of the present.

MLG: Does parody play an important part in your work?

EM: The majority of questions I am asked about my work always leave me at a loss. It is not easy for me to answer because I work without an established scheme. My novels take a shape of their own, as they evolve step by step. Naturally, I never planned to write a parody of any other novel. But then I believe that 90 percent of novels are parodies of other novels. Isn't *Don Quixote* one? To some extent so is *The Divine Comedy*. Everything is a parody, you collect materials and shuffle them until they acquire a structure of their own. I have used some of the components of detective stories, the historical and political novels as well as novels of manners, and mixed them at random. When faced with different genres, I have applied a certain amount of distance and tried to assimilate them. For instance, I like detective stories. They entertain me. So I used their structure which has allowed me the freedom to move the way I wanted to. In a way, what I did was to write a picaresque novel and give it the body of a detective story.

When I began writing, people were experimenting with the novel, from a linguistic point of view. I thought I could probe into another kind of experiment, which would thin down the differences between genres by bending them. As I approached that slippery terrain between parody and keeping a straight face, I made sure that no one would know whether I was serious or joking.

MLG: You mentioned the political novel. Is your work political?

EM: I think every work is political, especially if you write about the life of a community. Again, I am referring to the community I know best, that of Barcelona. But it could be taken as a model for any other city. My novels are not representative of a party, but are derived from an ideological foundation.

MLG: Do you mind when critics see your work from just one particular angle?

EM: I have been invited to take part in symposia on the humorous novel, the historical novel, the picaresque novel, the detective story, and so on and so forth. I don't consider my writings to fit any of these categories, but each of these genres in some way describes a part of my work. So I guess I have to accept these distinctions as long as they are not taken as a limiting factor. It is all right to use them as a point of reference to position myself and other writers in the present-day Spanish narrative form.

MLG: Do you think your work has a special message?

EM: Messages are good for answering machines. All I want is to tell a story, put some order into the chaotic world I carry within me, organize it and give it a literary structure. That world is made of a multitude of ideas and emotions: worries, obsessions, memories, passions, fears, dreams. Sometimes I even wonder how people who do not write are not afraid that their heads will explode! Writing is a form of release, I extract these thoughts from my mind and give them the shape of a book. I don't offer any message to the world, I don't even claim that people should take an interest in my books. I tell my stories to a nameless interlocutor.

MLG: For whom do you write? Do you have a reader in mind?

EM: When I write, I don't think of a reader, I don't even think about myself. The only thing that counts at that particular moment of creation is the book. I don't visualize the readers of my work, I don't try to please them, I don't even know what they want. I look for an interlocutor, very much like myself, with a sense of humor and a level of intelligence not any worse than mine. It would be nice to be understood by someone. When I took my first book, *La verdad sobre el caso Savolta,* to a publisher, he rejected it. People did not write the way I did, publishers were not yet prepared for that type of novel. It is possible that the public would have been more ready for it and open to it.

MLG: What does language mean to you?

EM: It is an indispensable instrument, like a piano for a pianist. I am very fond of it. But we should also bear in mind that if the piano is necessary for the pianist to play, the musical score and his fingers are just as important.

MLG: How do you view a book?

EM: In two different ways. If I am referring to that material object called a book, I don't feel any respect for it. After I have read a book, I often throw it away, because I have no more need for it. If I look at it from an artistic point of view, I see it as something very fragile and delicate. The book jacket binds and holds together a personal world. No one knows exactly what the outside world is like. We all have a different idea of reality and we all live it as differently as the reality reflected in each book. Every book is a perspective on life. A person who comes from the south, or another from the north, will view the world differently. If you come from Mexico or from Canada, you will invariably have a distinct reaction to the climate, which will make you say that it is a nice day, or it is not. When I look at my books, I like to picture them as a crossword puzzle.

MLG: What kind of relationship do you have with your characters?

EM: Usually I like them and I think they like me. Some rebel and misbehave; they are like naughty and mischievous children. I always hold conversations with them, but if there is a problem or some kind of conflict, they somehow turn out to be winners. They have become independent of me and I lose out. To separate reality from fantasy would make for a very sterile form of writing. So my characters are born of fantasy, but are enriched by elements derived from reality. Onofre Bouvila of *The City of Marvels,* for example, is a character taken from real life, although he is not modeled after anyone in particular. He is a character who represents a thirst for power.

MLG: How do you come up with the titles for your books?

EM: With the greatest effort on my part. I have a very hard time finding the right titles for my books. I do not have them as I begin to write the books and, by the time I reach the end, it is even more difficult. It is like pasting on a tag to identify your work. Usually my good friend and publisher Pedro Joan Ferrer helps me resolve that problem. *The City of Marvels,* however, is my own title, but we worked at it for days until I finally came up with it.

MLG: Do you feel part of a generation?

EM: I do, but it has no effect on my writings. I don't get up in the morning saying, "I am part of a generation." But, of course, I share with some people similar experiences and training.

MLG: Did you begin writing after the death of Franco?

EM: As I said earlier, I have been writing all my life. What happened is that my first book only came out a few months before Franco's death. Since then, many other novels have been published. Naturally, my writings have evolved, I have polished my style, I am more in tune with my work, but basically I don't think I have changed.

MLG: Is there such a thing as a new Spanish novel?

EM: I don't believe so. It is only perceived as such by the rest of the world. This is how people view our cultural output from the perspective of the outsider. The Spanish novel is the same as ever, although it has gone through consecutive periods of evolution. For instance, we now have reached a plateau and we question many things. Times of crisis are very productive, we are ready to follow new paths, come up with new answers, experiment with an invigorating vitality.

MLG: What does Spain mean to you?

EM: I am a Spaniard, a Catalan from Barcelona, and no one can take that away from me. I am an integral part of that world. When I was living in New York, I was a Spaniard who happened to live there. There are no two ways about it. This is what I am.

MLG: Now that Spain has joined the Common Market, what is its relationship to the rest of Europe?

EM: It is true that today's circumstances have brought Spain into closer cultural contact with the rest of Europe. Our books are being read and translated, and we are finally part of Europe. This does not mean, of course, that our ties with Latin America are any less. Yet, in spite of our language identity with Latin America, we are physically very far apart, which makes it financially difficult for our books to be sold there.

MLG: Do you have any comments about 1992?

EM: It should be a reflection on a historical event, a restating of values, which are fundamental to our relationship with Latin America and, even more so, an opportunity to enable us to rediscover our own identity. To make of this important event a big party seems to me senseless and of no interest whatsoever.

MLG: Did any Latin American writer influence your own work?

EM: A direct influence as people, much more so than their books. For instance, their attitude toward writing has been of great fascination for me. My generation is deeply indebted to them; they had a tremendous impact on our literary experience. People like García Márquez, Vargas Llosa, especially Rulfo, came to Barcelona and brought with them an approach to literature different from our own. We have always enjoyed with Latin American writers an intense and fruitful dialogue.

MLG: Tell me, who is Eduardo Mendoza?

EM: That man facing you and being interviewed. A fellow who all his life has wanted to write and now, because of it, is surrounded by journalists and critics, nothing more. A good friend to his friends.

MLG: Like Don Quixote, or like Jorge Manrique's father?

EM: I wouldn't be so presumptuous. I am a man who writes and shuns any kind of public appearance. I have no interest in being seen on television, or having my picture taken, or being interviewed by the press. I am a man who wants to stand in the shadow of his own work.

Rosa Montero

Rosa Montero was born in 1951 in Madrid. A graduate of the Madrid Official School of Journalism, she turned to journalism in 1969. In 1977, she received the Journalism Prize of the Association of Motion Picture Writers; in 1978, the World Prize for Interviews; and in 1980, the National Prize of Journalism. She has written for some of the most important newspapers. Since 1977, she writes exclusively for *El País*. In 1981 and 1982, she was the editor in chief of the Sunday supplement of that newspaper. She has also written scripts for the Spanish National Television. As she explains in the interview that follows, journalism led her to fiction.

One of the most popular Spanish journalists, Rosa Montero has also made a name for herself as a novelist. She is the author of eight books, including two collections of interviews, a volume of women's stories, and five novels: *España para ti para siempre* (Spain Forever for You), 1976; *Crónica del desamor* (Chronicle of Indifference), 1979, her first novel, soon to appear in English; *La función Delta* (The Delta Function), 1981; *Cinco años de País* (The Last Five Years), 1982; *Doce relatos de mujer* (Twelve Women's Stories), 1982; *Te trataré como a una reina* (I'll Treat You like a Queen), 1983; *Amado Amo* (Beloved Master), the 1988 bestseller; *Temblor* (Tremor), 1990.

Montero has taken part in many symposia on the contemporary Spanish novel, as well as in discussions about Spain since the advent of democracy. In 1985, she taught two courses at Wellesley College, one on journalism as a literary genre, the other one on women's literature. Her work has attracted the attention of scholars in several parts of the world and is becoming a topic of dissertations. Although not a feminist, her novels are written from a woman's point of view.

I saw Rosa Montero for the first time when she took part in a symposium on Spanish writers at the Casa de España, in New York, in April 1988. She was the only woman panelist. The questions addressed to the male members of the panel dealt with literature or politics in general, while those directed at her seemed limited to female writing. In a very vivacious and graceful way, she complained that there was no reason she should always talk about female writing and that language did not have a sex. The day following the symposium, I met with her over breakfast in a restaurant near the hotel where she and other writers were staying. Although she is a renowned interviewer, she made me feel quite at ease. Montero is very open and direct. She does not mince her words and goes straight to the point. I could see that she had good training as a journalist. She volunteered information about her personal life and her experiences as a writer.

❖❖❖❖❖❖❖❖❖❖❖❖❖❖❖❖❖❖❖❖❖❖❖❖❖❖❖❖❖❖

MLG: In 1978 you won the World Prize for Interviews and in 1980 the National Prize of Journalism. Why do you think women have so much success as journalists?

RM: First of all, because there are more women in that profession than in other fields. That is to say, journalism is one of the liberal professions that have been most open to women. On the other hand, I think women have been successful because they have a special knack for it. For the most part, they are great observers, they tend to be inquisitive, they notice the smallest detail and are good with concrete things. And most of all, they relate well to people and show that they care. Men usually lean more toward the abstract, keep their distance and seem to be colder. Of course, I am somewhat following the stereotyped patterns expected of men and women.

MLG: Why did you choose to become a journalist?

RM: Because I love to write, I have always loved writing. When I was five, I suffered from tuberculosis and, as a result, I never attended school until I was nine. I stayed at home, and reading and writing became a sort of game for me. I wrote for myself and it was my own way of playing. When I turned fifteen and had to choose a profession, I said to myself, "I love to write, I am better at it than most girls my age, why not become a journalist and make use of words for a living?" I have always had a great curiosity for life, a longing for new experiences, an eagerness to travel, and I thought journalism could offer me all these things. I must confess now that I owe a lot to journalism. It has taught me many things, it has given me many opportunities.

MLG: You began writing as if it were some kind of a game?

RM: Absolutely! As a child and a teenager, I would start writing a story, which I never finished, to turn to another the next day. Each story was a game in itself, which I would discard when new plots and intrigues came to my mind. The fun part lay in thinking up all sorts of adventures with crimes and mystery. So I would write suspense novels and Westerns.

MLG: What made you write your first novel as an adult?

RM: It was pure coincidence. I began writing for *El País,* a newspaper which became so popular that it brought immediate fame to the journalists who were connected with it. I was asked by a small publishing firm to write a book that would consist of interviews with women. I said yes in a moment of weakness, signed the contract, and was given a small advance. Months went by, the deadline was getting closer, and I had done nothing about it. The topic bored me, I was tired of interviewing people, which was part of my job for the newspaper. Desperate, with a guilty conscience, I realized that I had to deal with the problem, and I sat down at my desk. The book that began to unfold had little to do with what I was expected to write. It was a fictitious story, an imaginary chronicle. When I finished the first draft, I told the publisher, "Look, if you're interested in this, it's yours; if not, I will give your money back, and that will be the end of it." It turned out that they loved it so much that they published it as their first novel in a new series they were just starting. So this is the story behind my first novel, *Crónica del desamor.* I imagine that, in any case, I would have written a novel at some stage of my life, but I must confess that to take that first giant step as a writer—even admit that you want to become one—is a frightening experience. And if you're a woman it's even worse. A novel demands respect, it is as important as if it were written in capital letters. How can you say, "I want to write a novel, I am capable of doing it"? So you repress your desire to write and you put it in the back of your mind.

MLG: Your first novel, then, had nothing to do with interviews?

RM: No, it is a testimonial novel, very youthful. It has nothing to do with interviews. It's a fictional work based on people I knew. It's a reflection on my own world. It had a great success that none of us could have foreseen. The publishing firm was small and had not publicized it. Yet, it became a hit through word of mouth, and now, ten years later, it continues to sell. It's been selling all along four thousand copies a year. And it's going to be my first novel translated into English.

MLG: How would you describe it?

RM: My intention was to write a fictitious chronicle that would be told in a realistic way. It is a sketchy testimonial, with which, I think, people identified. It was the first spark coming out of a young author. It may lack in structure what it has in spontaneity. I was under its spell while writing it. That book is responsible for bringing me success and opening for me the door to literature. Since then, all I have wanted to do is to write, and the book has given me the right to consider myself a writer. I am now the author of four more novels.

MLG: Why do you write and what does it mean to you?

RM: Writing is an existential adventure. It is a road to knowledge, to new experiences with life, an intense way of coming to grips with it. I have yet to find something that can offer me as much pleasure as the act of writing. It is what comes closest to a passionate love affair. When you are romantically involved with someone, you feel intensely alive and you believe you are eternal. Love gives you the power to defy death. When you are involved in the creative process, you sit at your desk in a trance. When I write, I am so intensely alive that death no longer exists for me.

MLG: What do you feel when you write?

RM: When I write, it is as if a two-way current has been released and a shock goes through my body. I have to contend with an obsession, which could be qualified as a love-hate relationship. I cannot live without writing, and yet it torments me and does not give me room to breathe. There are times when I go insane, when I want to run away from it all; there are times when I feel seduced and under a spell. It's a twenty-four hours a day love affair. The novel possesses you while you are working at it. When you can't stand it any longer, you know you have reached the end.

MLG: Did you ever experience the anguish of having to face the blank page and not be able to write?

RM: After my third novel, my writing came to a halt and I thought I would never write again. I experienced a mental block that lasted four years. I had an idea for a novel in my mind, but I could not really believe in it, nor get into my characters. After a while, I discarded those forty pages and that novel never came to be. Only after those four long, agonizing years did I finally break that silence. I started writing what I thought would be a short story when, suddenly, the plot began claiming more space and I realized I was writing a novel. It was my fourth novel, *Amado Amo.*

MLG: What does it take for you to believe in your story? How do you mix reality and fantasy to create that plausible novelistic world?

RM: I think that as writers, and especially as women writers, we have to relearn to let fantasy be set free. It is one more conquest that as women we have to achieve. In order to survive, women had to lay aside their imaginative power, so that men would not call them flighty and whimsical, and abide by the traditional accepted male values of logic and the abstract. This explains why women writers in the past turned to realism in their works. I feel that all writers, whether men or women, are like jesters who can bridge the boundaries imposed by society. Writers have the power to break through social barriers and their mission is to point out that it is possible to dream, to fantasize with the beautiful and the ugly.

MLG: Do you think that men and women write differently?

RM: Since we live in a sexist world, and the novel is an attempt to represent our views of the world, we can assume that men and women writers may depict it from their own perspectives. Our cultural and social backgrounds in the past were different, but less so now. However, I am not a feminist writer, and even less an activist. Going back to what I was just saying, the female writer has had to fight for many years to make her voice heard. In that process, she was forced to relinquish many of her feminine qualities. Her capacity for reaching out into the world of fantasy is one of them. What we must do now is come to the rescue of fantasy. This is what I have tried to achieve in my works. I believe that fantasy has been conquering more space with each of my books, together with humor. I have become removed from the immediate world to conquer another dimension.

MLG: Do you think that *Temblor,* your latest book, is representative of that new dimension?

RM: Definitely. It's my longest and most ambitious novel. It takes place in an imaginary world, in a time other than our own. It's a symbolic fairy tale story for grown-ups. It evolves around a ten-year span in the life of a young woman, from the time she was twelve to her twenty-second birthday. It reads like an adventure novel, but is really a metaphysical voyage into life. It deals with the passing of time, the anguish of living.

MLG: How did you evolve from *Crónica del desamor* to *Temblor,* how were you able to detach yourself from the reality that surrounds you?

RM: There are writers who find materials for their novels in their immediate world and then work hard to extract from its substance what makes it universal. The close at hand and personal turn into a reality that belongs to all. Proust is the perfect embodiment of this type of writing. There are other authors, like Flaubert, whose works stem from a reality totally alien to them. They have to struggle until they can make that reality their own. They must listen to the heartbeat of their characters, discover the essence of their inner beings. The challenge for these writers is to turn what is foreign to them, but universal, into something personal. Flaubert came to understand his feminine character so well that he identified with her and said, "I am Madame Bovary." I believe that every work of art essentially claims to be universal, no matter what road you choose to reach that universality. I have noticed that younger writers tend to use topics and characters totally different from their personal reality and that older writers lean toward the other approach. When you are young, it is often difficult to describe your own biographical world without becoming trapped in it and losing sight of the rest of the world. As for myself, going back to your question, I succeeded in depicting a reality which was not my own through long moments of struggle and even silence. For instance, in *Te trataré como a una reina,* my third novel, it took a tremendous effort on my part to plunge into the lives of characters so drastically different from those I knew. I would say it took blood and sweat out of me to become familiar with these characters I purposely chose to be illiterate, old, ugly, and fat. *Temblor* is in the nature of a legend.

MLG: In two of your novels you followed the Proustian approach, writing from your own reality, but with a sense of perspective.

RM: Yes, I have also followed his approach but, of course, without ever reaching his level. *La función delta* is about a woman in her sixties, dying of cancer in a hospital, who recalls a week in her life when she was thirty. The novel flashes back and forth between her present and her past. It is a meditation on love and death. Personally, I am very proud of *Amado Amo*. It deals with a topic that I know and I was able to achieve that distance which I deem necessary. I feel I have approached this work with a newly acquired maturity. Like my first novel, it is about a world familiar to me, its success and failure and alienation, but the vast difference is that I was able to write about it with a sense of perspective. I purposely chose a male protagonist who fails in his profession as well as in his personal life. Had I chosen a woman, it would have been less tragic and pathetic. We have been trained to accept defeat since the beginning of time.

MLG: Do you view the whole of your work as a single entity?

RM: Yes, it conveys a basic unity to which I would give the shape of a spiral staircase. However, it is not one that goes upward. I envision it as a spiral that descends toward the inner substance of life itself, and comes together with my relationship to the world and what it is all about. Obviously, every experience is different and no two novels are alike. My novels change drastically from one to another. Each piece of work is like a passage or road that leads to new adventures. All my novels take me in a direction that I cannot control; they guide me to a place that lies deep down in me, where my personal ghosts haunt me at the very core of my being. But one thing that is certain is that the underlying chord that beats throughout all my books is a web of obsessions—my fears and hopes.

MLG: What are some of those obsessions?

RM: Well, they're truly basic, the same as everyone else's. Since I am a nonbeliever and do not have ready-made answers to accept death with resignation, I reflect with melancholy on the absurdity of life. This includes the lack of balance between power and justice. I believe that these obsessions are at the core of all forms of art.

MLG: You just mentioned the word *death*. How do you cope with it?

RM: Death is what gives meaning to everything or what makes everything senseless. Death is the most important unknown data in a person's life. We all live in its pursuit or avoiding it, inventing things to do to fill the void, to forget that we must die, to give a meaning to the absurd.

MLG: Is your work political?

RM: I think everything is tied in with politics, even the way human beings relate to one another when they use influences to succeed. Yes, in the broader sense of the term, my novels are political.

MLG: How do you come up with the titles for your books?

RM: That depends. Normally it just hits me when I have reached the middle of the novel. In my last novel, however, I was at a loss and had to reach the last page to finally come upon the right title.

MLG: What kind of a relationship do you have with your characters?

RM: You start with an image that grows stronger and stronger until it shapes up into a character. Like a regular person, it begins to develop and, suddenly, to your great surprise you realize it has little to do with that image you had originally envisioned. You invent characters, but they evolve on their own, they create their own laws. In *Te trataré como a una reina,* I almost went crazy because my characters did not let me say what I wanted and kept on forcing me to speak about things I had not intended to mention. So I came to the conclusion that I had to be true to them, because they had a life of their own. It is an unequal match that is hard on you. You wrestle with them, but you know that they will always come out winners.

MLG: Of all your books, is there one that you like the most?

RM: The last one. I imagine most writers say that.

MLG: No, they sometimes look to their first book with a special fondness.

RM: I can say that I am very critical of myself. I take full responsibility for all my books. I have given my best on each occasion and I am pleased with the result. For me, my work is like a road; it is that spiral staircase we were talking about. I am convinced that each book I have published is better than the previous one. Critics and readers seem to agree on this. In any case, this has been my intent with each new book.

MLG: Why do you think *Amado Amo* was the best-seller at Madrid's 1988 Book Fair?

RM: No one knows the road to success nor its formula.

MLG: Is it important for you to know what people think of your books?

RM: It's a difficult question to answer, you know. When the book comes out, you go through a state of anguish. You want to know how it's doing, if people are reading it, if it's selling. But after two weeks have passed, you can rest if four or five people tell you that they like it. After a while, if a reader approaches me and tells me what he thinks of my novel, it makes me go through an uncomfortable, almost unbearable experience. I don't know where to hide as I listen to his comments.

MLG: Before the book is actually out, do you have a first reader?

RM: I write a first draft and then I rewrite it at least two or three times, and again I make many revisions. The act of writing is very personal; you are alone with your book and cannot be concerned with an abstract reader. That faceless being takes on for me some of the expressions of people I know and whose opinions I value. Yes, I like to show the manuscript to two of my friends. One is a journalist, the other a writer. I also show it to my successive boyfriends, but the poor souls are not reliable critics; they always say that it is well written.

MLG: Do you view your writings from the perspective of a reader?

RM: It would be lovely to say that we carry within ourselves a possible reader. I don't deny that it could be true, but it sounds rather clinical or analytic. When you write a novel, you are playing God. You experience a creative power and a sense of enrapture. Characters depend on you, it is a marvelous thing to invent new worlds, perhaps the most beautiful form of ecstasy. Maybe there is some kind of a feedback, whereby the author looks over his own shoulder and reads what he is writing. But what really counts is that creative force that whirls you into a frenzy.

MLG: How would you define the space that is self-contained in a book?

RM: That space, which is called book, is for me the voyage I have undertaken toward an unknown shore, that is to say, toward the vital adventure which becomes writing. When I put down the manuscript after having written the last sentence, I feel as if I had lived the lives of my characters, as if I had taken an active part in their problems, and I sense that I have grown older, wiser.

MLG: What does the written word represent for you?

RM: I don't know exactly. All I can say is that I am in love with it. The written word is fundamental to me. I like to rediscover it, reinvent it, reshape it, play with it.

MLG: So we are back where we started, playing games just like when you were a child.

RM: Playing is something very important to me, and I use the word *play* in its broadest meaning. I am a passionate woman who likes to gamble with life and who takes high risks. Words are the stakes I use in my games.

MLG: Carmen Martín Gaite also sees writing as a game. Is there any similarity between your work and hers?

RM: No, except that we are both very intense. I admire her greatly as a writer; she has a beautiful command of words.

MLG: Who is Rosa Montero?

RM: A woman of her times, like any other woman, with an inquisitive mind, an enormous capacity for life, and a genuine concern for people.

Antonio
Muñoz Molina

Antonio Muñoz Molina was born in 1956 in Ubeda, Jaén, into a rural society. More familiar to him were the oral traditions that he would overhear than television cartoons. Actually, television didn't reach his hometown until he was ten years old.

The first of his family to receive a formal education, he studied journalism in Madrid and received a Master's degree in art history at the University of Granada, where he has been living since 1974. Until 1988, he worked in Granada's City Hall as a municipal employee and organized concerts.

He has written articles for several major newspapers, including *ABC* and *El País.* Two volumes of his journalism came out in 1984 and 1986, *El Róbinson urbano* (The Urban Robinson) and *Diario del "Nautilus"* (Log of the *Nautilus*). His first novel, *Beatus Ille* (Happy the Man Who), 1986, was awarded the Icaro Prize. His second novel, *El invierno en Lisboa* (Winter in Lisbon), 1987, received the 1988 Crítica Prize and the National Literature Prize, placing him practically overnight in the ranks of the great Spanish writers. His latest work, *La Córdoba de los Omeyas* (The Córdoba of the Omeyas), 1990, is a historical study.

Muñoz Molina wrote the libretto for José García Román's new opera *El bosque de Diana* (Diana's Grove), which premiered in Madrid in the spring of 1990. Music plays an important part in his life and his work. He is particularly fond of jazz. In a way, his novel *El invierno en Lisboa* is a tribute to that world.

When I arrived in Salamanca to interview Gonzalo Torrente Ballester, his fear was that I would do a book on Spanish writers without including Antonio Muñoz Molina. "You should leave no stone unturned," he told me, "you must find Muñoz Molina's address and get in touch with him.

In time, this young author will become one of the most important writers."
So I followed his advice, went back to Madrid, found his telephone number
and called him in Granada. The interview that was to take place in Madrid
did not materialize. It was conducted over the phone, from New York to
Granada. With a warm southern voice, he talked freely about his work, as if
I were an old acquaintance. Since then, I have met him in person.

❊❊❊❊❊❊❊❊❊❊❊❊❊❊❊❊❊❊❊❊❊❊❊❊❊❊❊❊❊❊❊❊❊

MLG: Your first book received the Icaro Prize, and your second won the
Crítica as well as the National Literature prizes. How did you make the
transition from journalism to literature?

AMM: I didn't devote myself to journalism, strictly speaking. I was never
a reporter or an editor, but more of a literary columnist. So I wrote articles
with a literary bent—opinion pieces and creative writing—rather than
straightforward reporting.

MLG: When did you first realize that you were called to be a novelist?

AMM: I had always wanted to be a novelist, even before I started writing
for newspapers. I spent ten years working on my first novel, *Beatus Ille.* I
conceived it when I was twenty years old, but of course I wasn't ready to
write it then because the subject matter was too difficult. So it took me ten
years.

MLG: Did you take any notes during that ten-year period?

AMM: Yes, I did, I wrote drafts and chapters, and then destroyed them. I
should have a suitcase full of manuscripts, but I destroyed them all.

MLG: When did you realize your novel was ready to be published?

AMM: When I came up with a strong opening for it and had internalized
the point of view the novel would have. I also realized it was ready when the
structure became finalized, and when I saw that the work was advancing
with joy and the writing was inventive. When all these elements came
together after years of struggles, it became apparent that, instead of several
stories, I had one that was both coherent and realistic.

MLG: Do you still practice journalism?

AMM: Yes, I do. Right now, I am writing articles published in install-
ments in *ABC.* But I don't plan to continue, because I am afraid that through
these articles I may run the risk of parodying myself.

MLG: Journalism had an impact on your work as a novelist?

AMM: I have never considered myself a journalist, although I have
written articles for several newspapers. But as I just said, my articles were
always of a literary nature. So, as you can see, I ran no risk of contaminat-
ing my novels with the barbaric lingo displayed in journalism.

MLG: What did you do for a living prior to becoming a novelist?

AMM: I was a municipal employee in Granada's City Hall. What I did
for a living had nothing to do with my personal life. I was a writer, but I had

to earn my living any way I could. My job didn't compromise my stand on life because it was completely unrelated to me. But I must also confess that indirectly my work opened new alleys for me, which I put to good use in my novels. Let me give you an example. In Granada, jazz enjoys great popularity, no matter how strange it may seem being so far removed from America. We have some really excellent jazz players here. As part of my job as a municipal employee, I organized jazz concerts and festivals. This is one of the reasons I am so familiar with the atmosphere I depict in *El invierno en Lisboa.* For me, jazz belongs to the whole world, and I don't identify it as being strictly part of the American culture. In this world, there is a series of laments, and jazz is one of them.

MLG: What do you feel having won the Crítica Prize and the National Literature Prize?

AMM: Stupor. I was very surprised. I feel that these prizes actually mean less to me than to those who came to know me through them. Many people ask me, "How do you feel having achieved such rapid success?" and I reply, "I have been writing since I was twelve years old."

MLG: You started writing at twelve?

AMM: Of course! As I said, it took me ten years to write my first novel, and four of my books were published before *El invierno en Lisboa* garnered tremendous success. So the National Literature Prize makes me stuporous and giddy; it's like being drunk and then getting a hangover. I think most writers like to work alone and isolated, surrounded by a few friends. But when I won those awards, my house became like a beach overrun by tourists. For a couple of months, I had to hide myself, and I couldn't write.

MLG: Has your life changed since you won these prizes?

AMM: No, it hasn't changed because I didn't let that happen, and now these prizes are behind me. If my life had changed, I would have been unable to write. I have to be alone to write; I cannot be surrounded by admirers, critics, scholars, or anybody.

MLG: Is writing a solitary journey?

AMM: Yes, very solitary. Of course, this does not mean that I am isolated. I have a very broad definition of what constitutes friendship and love, and I very much enjoy being around my friends and the people I love. But when I write . . . You must know that when we speak about bullfighting, there comes the moment of truth when the bullfighter must face the bull alone. There is no public or anything else then; the bullfighter is alone. There is a similar moment of truth for the writer, and it is one of complete solitude.

MLG: Is writing for you a way of searching?

AMM: Yes, I think so. Writing is a means to make the unconscious conscious.

MLG: Isn't it also a way of finding oneself?

AMM: I don't believe so. Perhaps it is partly to discover oneself, or that hidden part of oneself. But rather it is for us to live many lives and take on many identities.

MLG: What do you feel when you write?

AMM: I feel that I am fulfilling some of my potential, and that I wouldn't be able to live otherwise.

MLG: Do you think your style of writing reflects the fact that you come from the south of Spain?

AMM: It has nothing to do with coming from the south, but rather with belonging to a rural society with a very rich language and a long oral tradition that hadn't yet been deformed by the uniform language television imposes. I was ten years old when television first reached our village and, from that point on, storytelling and all oral forms of tradition came to an end. Fortunately, I lived at the tail end of that vastly rich oral tradition. When I was a child, I can recall girls singing songs as they were playing that had come down from the fifteenth century.

MLG: Could you speak a little about your childhood?

AMM: I was born in Ubeda, a town of about thirty thousand inhabitants in the province of Jaén. My father was a peasant of modest means who had a piece of land which he cultivated, so we lived in the country. There were no books in my childhood, although there was this rich oral tradition I have mentioned. I was the first from my family to study formally. I had a perfectly happy if somewhat solitary childhood. From the street on which we lived, I could see the fields and the valley of Guadalquivir.

MLG: Did you also learn how to tell stories as a child?

AMM: To tell them and listen to them.

MLG: And live them.

AMM: Of course. Writing is the result of all that.

MLG: Why do you write?

AMM: Perhaps because I don't know how to do anything else.

MLG: That's the answer almost everybody gives.

AMM: Of course. I write because it is the only thing that allows me to be reconciled with myself and be myself.

MLG: Do you write whenever it strikes you?

AMM: Usually either in the morning or the afternoon.

MLG: Do you believe in inspiration?

AMM: I do not believe that a novel can be born without it, but I also think that inspiration has to be disciplined and controlled. However, no matter how hard you work, if there is no inspiration, what you are doing is worthless.

MLG: Does inspiration take on for you the magic spirit of García Lorca's elf?

AMM: Yes, partly. But I think you have to create the proper atmosphere to bring about an encounter with that elf. If you spend all your time hanging out on street corners and in bars, and never work, that magic spirit will never come to you.

MLG: What relationship do you have with your readers? Do you think of them when you write?

AMM: When I write, I try to imagine how I would react were I the reader.

MLG: Do you have a primary reader?

AMM: Yes, I have a couple of readers in whom I have absolute trust. I give them my manuscripts as soon as I finish them, and they have complete freedom to say whatever they want about them. My wife is one of them and so is my publisher.

MLG: Do you think the reader has an active role?

AMM: Definitely. I believe the reader is endowed with the qualities of a co-author; as he reads he puts in the ingredients that make the novel complete. I like to write elliptically. I don't want to spend a lot of time describing the characters—I want the reader to bring his input, which could be as much as half of the novel. I leave blank spaces for the reader's imagination to fill. I try to write novels that leave the readers wanting to know more and in which they have to reconstruct the story themselves. It's like giving them the music score and asking them to make their own orchestration.

MLG: In *El invierno en Lisboa,* for instance, you end the story without telling us what happened to Lucrecia and Biralbo. We could almost go on with the story ourselves to find out what really took place.

AMM: I could tell you an anecdote precisely related to that. Many people write me letters in which they tell me about my characters; what they have done without realizing it is continue my own novel. Recently I received a postcard from Portugal from someone who said he had seen Biralbo and Lucrecia in Lisbon.

MLG: What was your reaction to that?

AMM: I enjoyed it and thought it amusing. It has made me face the fact that once the novel is out it is no longer what I wrote, and it is no longer mine. It takes on new dimensions and belongs to the readers.

MLG: Can you tell me where Lucrecia and Biralbo are now?

AMM: I don't know, I really don't know.

MLG: They left, but you don't know where?

AMM: No, I haven't the faintest idea.

MLG: So they rebelled?

AMM: Yes, partly.

MLG: Do you feel a special fondness for your characters?

AMM: For some of them, not all.

MLG: Who dominates whom?

AMM: It is a curious relationship, because sometimes a character will not grow, despite one's best attempts to develop it. This is a sign that the character is not a good one. On the other hand, if one keeps discovering things about a character as the writing proceeds (in the same way that we discover new facets about a person the longer we know him), then the character is a good one.

MLG: Where do you find your characters? For instance, how did you come up with Lucrecia and Biralbo?

AMM: At the beginning of Montaigne's essays, he issues a little warning to the reader that runs as follows: "Reader, the only subject of my book is me." So, I come up with my characters in daily life, in movies, and, above all, in myself.

MLG: Do your novels have many autobiographical elements then?

AMM: Yes, except that they have been altered a great deal. I think all novels are fundamentally autobiographical. There is a relationship between a novel and reality that is similar to the association between dreams and reality; one feeds off the other. I don't know if I am making myself clear, but in my novels, there are autobiographical clues, although there are no direct autobiographical references.

MLG: Is there a constant interplay between reality and fantasy in your work?

AMM: Of course, because a novel is the result of that meeting between reality and fantasy. For instance, I know a man who interests me a great deal because he is so similar to my character Toussaints Morton in *El invierno en Lisboa.* I met this man and spent some time with him and I was struck by how much he resembles my character, although the poor man is neither a murderer nor an art smuggler. So the clash between reality and my own imagination produces a spark or a chemical reaction from which the character is born.

MLG: *El invierno en Lisboa* makes constant references to jazz. What effect has music had on your work?

AMM: A very substantial one, as it has on my life. I am the sort of man who likes to listen to songs continuously. We were listening to some boleros the other day, and I thought that literature had become so cold and technical that the truth could only be found in boleros. Music is like literature for me, although it has other ways of telling stories and stirring our hearts directly. That's why the characters in that story go crazy when they hear songs. There are always songs in my novels. It's not so much that I want to make direct references to music in my work, but rather that I want my writing to be musical and have a little swing.

MLG: Could we say that your writing has a special rhythm that might be compared to jazz music?

AMM: I would like to think so. I think that the principle which under-girds jazz is the same one that writing is based on: a mixture of discipline and improvisation. There is usually a fundamental melody in a jazz tune which then gives rise to improvisation. It is the same thing with literature: there is a fundamental idea with which one begins, but when the writing proceeds, many unexpected things spring up.

MLG: Do you play an instrument?

AMM: I wish I could; I would give anything to be able to play the piano.

MLG: Do you always write in the first person?

AMM: I have so far, and I think it yields a better result, although some of my tales are in the third person.

MLG: Who is that first-person narrator?

AMM: I don't know; that's one more thing I don't know. It's a being that was growing as the novel unraveled. As it developed, it turned into a character who holds the story together. Recently, one of my readers told me that the narrator was his favorite character because he tells the story and it is through him that we learn what other characters do and think. Of course, my narrator could also be lying!

MLG: Do you identify with the narrator?

AMM: Absolutely not. He is primarily a writing device.

MLG: Do you stand inside or outside your novel when you write?

AMM: Inside, of course. Flaubert explained this very well when he said that an author should stand like a god before his creation: omnipresent and invisible.

MLG: If you had to give your novels a geometric shape, what would it be?

AMM: I think I would give it the form of a labyrinth or a spiral that's almost closed, but which ends on a possible opening at the top.

MLG: How is a novel born?

AMM: By chance, from an image or event, or an expression you overhear. Things start to flow and images and characters come up. The novel is almost always triggered by trivial things. Henry James said something to that effect in one of his notebooks that all novels find their roots in the commonplace. The names of my characters are very important to me. First I look for a name, then I conceive the character. That's a very beautiful and exciting moment when I feel that something is growing in my imagination, although I am not quite sure what it is. The birth of a novel is a process very much like the formation of a pearl in an oyster shell. The beautiful gem develops in the pearl-bearing mollusk around a grain of sand or some other foreign matter.

MLG: What's your first novel about?

AMM: The plot is somewhat complex. Basically, it is an exploration of the life of a fictional poet from the Generation of 1927, who is very politically involved during the Civil War. After the war, he is jailed for seven years. Following his release in 1947, he decides to isolate himself from everything by returning to the village where he was born. He finds solace in solitude and takes up writing.

MLG: Why a poet from the Generation of 1927?

AMM: Because for Spaniards of my age who are interested in literature the Generation of 1927 represents the intelligence and cultural heroism we feel closest to. They are like our elders, like our parents. They exemplify the aesthetic, political, and moral postures that we thought important to recapture.

MLG: Are you a friend of Rafael Alberti, and did you pattern your character after him?

AMM: I am casually acquainted with him, but we are not close friends. He is one of the figures who inspired me to create my fictional character, which is a mixture of many things. I wanted a character who would seem alive and blend all of these things.

MLG: Why did you choose a title in Latin for that book?

AMM: It was a reference to Horace's "Beatus ille," taken from the *Epodes.* It goes somewhat like this: Happy the man who leaves behind the loud clamors of city life to seek refuge in country joys. Sometimes, I come up with my titles before I start writing. *El invierno en Lisboa* is an example of this. At other times, I find my title when I am halfway through the novel. That happened with *Beatus Ille.* I had to fight with the publisher to make him accept it. He thought that to have a title in Latin for a first work was to invite disaster. But I held my ground, and he finally agreed to it.

MLG: How can you explain the hold the Spanish Civil War has over you and many young Spaniards who didn't live through that conflict?

AMM: I could explain it by saying that as a child that war was very alive for me, because I saw with my own eyes those who had lost the war and were left traumatized by it. The fact that we should relive the past of our forefathers is in no way limited to Spain. William Faulkner wrote about the American Civil War, and he certainly did not experience it personally. The distance between his life and that war allowed him to write about it as if it were pure mythology. *Sartoris,* for example, is just another story.

MLG: Do you view the Spanish Civil War as a myth, or as something you experienced more directly?

AMM: It's like an epic poem for me. By the way, I should mention that Faulkner is a very important author to me.

MLG: *Beltenebros* represents the period of postwar Spain. How would you explain that book?

AMM: *Beltenebros* is about the anti-Franquist fight after the Civil War. It is based on real occurrences in Spain during the 1960s, when a clandestine group executed one of its members suspected of being a traitor.

MLG: What was the impact of that novel?

AMM: It's gone through several editions. It's the second or third best-seller in Spain.

MLG: But it hasn't yet received any kind of award.

AMM: I am going to tell them not to give me any, so as not to bore anyone.

MLG: You tackle the issue of drugs in *El invierno en Lisboa.*

AMM: There is now a fascination with drugs in Spain. But I am not very interested in the subject, because drugs frighten me and disgust me. I only mention it in passing in that novel.

MLG: What are some of the topics, besides those you've already mentioned, that appeal to you?

AMM: I like to write about love and friendship. *El invierno en Lisboa* is primarily about this. I also like to place characters in the position where they have to inquire about things around them.

MLG: What topics do you plan to tackle now?

AMM: I'll tell you a secret: the novel I have in mind now takes place in the 1930s.

MLG: Why does the past have a special hold on you?

AMM: The past is easier to interpret. It is easier to grasp its full meaning because it is farther away. This does not mean, however, that I avoid the present, and cannot deal with it. *El invierno en Lisboa* dwells in the present.

MLG: What do you feel when you finish a novel?

AMM: Relief. Usually, I feel very relieved, because the work involved is so long and tiring (you have to spend several hours a day for months, sometimes years). But I also feel empty when I am done, and, generally speaking, I will probably be depressed for a while.

MLG: Do you see some resemblance between your work and that of Latin American writers?

AMM: Yes, I always say that the new literature in Spain had been made possible by the work of Latin American authors. Speaking for myself, I wouldn't know how to write had it not been for the influence of Juan Carlos Onetti, Borges, and Bioy Casares.

MLG: It's interesting that you should choose authors who predate the so-called Boom.

AMM: The Boom concerns me very little, generally speaking.

MLG: What about writers such as Fuentes, Vargas Llosa, or Donoso?

AMM: I admire Fuentes a great deal, but you must know that one can admire an author without having anything to do with him. So there is no connection between those writers and me, whereas I feel an intimate relation with Borges, Bioy Casares, and Juan Rulfo, for instance.

MLG: What other authors have made an impact on your life and work?

AMM: The first one was Jules Verne. Cervantes and Galdós influenced me as well, as did the French and English novels of the nineteenth century. Among contemporary authors, I read and learned a lot from Dashiell Hammett and Raymond Chandler, for instance.

MLG: What about contemporary Spanish authors?

AMM: Among those writing now, I have to point to Juan Marsé.

MLG: If you could speak with a great writer from the past, whom would you choose?

AMM: Cervantes and Faulkner.

MLG: What would you say to them?

AMM: I wouldn't say anything. I would limit myself to listening to them.

MLG: What do you think Cervantes would tell you?

AMM: He would tell me wonderful tales, like those in his *Don Quixote*. He would speak about the meaning of life, despair, irony, and gentle emotions.

MLG: What about Faulkner?

AMM: Faulkner would spin fantastic tales about Southern gentlemen in Memphis and the like. It would be fabulous to spend an evening listening to him.

MLG: Is there such a thing as a "new Spanish novel"?

AMM: I don't believe in any such thing. I think that, speaking from a purely biological standpoint, you could say that a new generation of thirty-year-olds is writing novels. But the only new thing in Spain is the reader. There are beginning to be readers of novels in Spain, and they are a stimulating influence on Spanish novelists. A relationship such as this between readers and writers had not been seen in Spain since the times of Galdós.

MLG: Do you think there is a dramatic difference between the novels of your generation and the works of Camilo José Cela, Ana María Matute, Carmen Laforet, or Miguel Delibes, for example?

AMM: I think so. I think that our literature is less parochial and more connected to the rest of the world than theirs. It also has clues that are more easily accessible to anyone. Spain suffered terribly from its cultural and political isolation during Franco's dictatorship, but since the advent of democracy, it is starting to form part of a much broader world. I believe our works have a more universal appeal.

MLG: The themes of the Civil War and of dictatorship still prevail nonetheless.

AMM: The subject doesn't matter as much as how it is treated.

MLG: So what difference is there in the treatment, if the subject is more or less similar?

AMM: It can be similar in some cases, but the vast majority of authors of my generation do not write about the Civil War. Among us, only Julio Manzanares and I have dealt with it. My generation has a different way of looking at things. I don't know how to explain it to you.

MLG: How would you compare present-day Spain to the Spain of your childhood and youth?

AMM: I think today's Spain is a big disappointment. On the one hand, I cannot forget that we finally enjoy freedom, but, on the other hand, many of us who, in the 1970s, had such high expectations during the advent of democracy have been disillusioned by the current state of affairs. It seems that Spain is turning into a nation with little dignity and too much corruption. I don't like the direction it is taking.

MLG: What is your stand on the quincentennial celebration of the discovery of America?

AMM: I think that all of that is a very costly rhetoric, which may even be harmful. I think that we have to study our past and do without the rhetoric. Spain needs to firm up its ties with Latin America, and I don't think it is doing that. Spain is so busy with the Common Market that it is forgetting about Latin American countries. To require of Latin Americans to have a visa to enter into Spain and have a certain amount of dollars as well as their return ticket is, I think, scandalous and a sham. When Spaniards traveled to Latin America, and when they even emigrated there for political reasons, no requirements were ever made of them.

MLG: So Latin Americans won't enjoy the same privileges they were accustomed to?

AMM: They can come in, but with many difficulties. So I think it is hypocritical to talk about the quincentennial celebration, and the fact that we are brothers sharing a common history, if we are no longer capable of receiving them the way they receive us.

MLG: What does Latin America mean to you?

AMM: Some of my favorite writers are Latin Americans. That continent represents something that is different from us but yet looks familiar; it is a world completely unlike mine where they speak my language. As I said before, it makes me realize how universal Spanish really is. Spaniards have the tendency to believe that our language is a dialect spoken only in our own country. To hear Spanish spoken in Latin America is something not experienced by many Spaniards and it is very moving.

MLG: What kind of a Spaniard would you say you are?

AMM: I am a Spaniard, but a dissident one. Like most Spaniards, I follow in the footsteps of Cervantes, the Archpriest of Hita, Galdós, and Azaña and live on the fringe of my own country. I am a bit apprehensive about the new relationship with the rest of Europe.

MLG: You come from Granada. How would you describe yourself in relation to other regions of Spain?

AMM: I feel at home everywhere in Spain. I think that in my country too much of a fuss is being made about regionalism and whether one is from Andalusia or Catalonia. I think my fatherland is my language and all those people with whom I get along well. So I don't feel bad in any particular place, whether in Spain or outside of my country, because I find hospitality wherever I go. I feel comfortable wherever I am and I like to see new places and watch people and enjoy them.

MLG: What does language mean for you?

AMM: Language is my homeland. Language is very important for me, because it is both the present and the past. I speak the language others have spoken, I write with words that others have uttered, and in turn others will write with words I have used. I also think that Spanish is a wonderful tongue because it is so universal. When I was in Argentina last month I was struck by the fact that other people so far away from me spoke the same language I do. This is like a miracle and it seems to me the most valuable treasure.

MLG: Who is Antonio Muñoz Molina?

AMM: In one of my favorite novels, *Twenty Thousand Leagues under the Sea,* the main character is called Captain Nemo, or Captain Nobody. In the *Odyssey,* Ulysses saves himself from the cyclops by saying that his name is No one. That's how I would like to be called.

MLG: Why?

AMM: Because I'd like to be invisible, be able to move about incognito. I like to lead many different lives rather than be limited to just one. Perhaps that's one of the reasons I decided to become a novelist. Through my books I lead many lives. But it's not only that. I like to travel to unknown cities, where no one knows me for what I am, I am just another person, I am nobody. I check into a hotel and I go for a walk around the town.

MLG: So it must bother you to deal with people like me who chase you from New York to interview you over the phone.

AMM: Not at all, this has been a pleasant surprise.

Justo Jorge Padrón

Justo Jorge Padrón was born in 1943 in Las Palmas, Canary Islands. During his adolescence, he became an avid reader and was also attracted by the world of sports. For ten years he was the regional tennis champion and won over two hundred trophies. Although he went to Barcelona to study law and in 1966 became a lawyer, in 1973 he gave up his practice to write poetry. He belongs to the generation of poets of the 1970s.

In 1970, his first book, *Los oscuros fuegos* (Dark Fires), was awarded the Adonais Poetry Prize. His second book, *Mar de la noche* (Night Sea), received the Juan Boscán Award. His third book, *Los círculos del infierno,* 1976 (*The Circles of Hell,* 1981), won the 1977 Fastenrath Award of the Spanish Royal Academy and the Biennial Prize of the Swedish Writers Association. Borges said of that work, "He has succeeded to move me deeply and make me cry."

Padrón is also a specialist in Nordic poetry. Artur Lundkvist, president of the Nobel Committee of the Swedish Academy, said that he stands as "mediator between Nordic and Spanish literatures."

Among his other works are *El abedul en llamas* (The Birch Tree on Fire), 1978; *Otesnita,* 1979; *Obra poética 1971-1980* (Poetic Works, 1971-1980), which received the 1981 International Award of the World Art and Culture Academy and the Gold Medal of the French Cultural Commission of Brussels; *La visita del mar* (The Visit of the Sea), 1984; *Antología poética* (Poetic Anthology), 1988; and *Sólo muere la mano que te escribe* (Only Dies the Hand That Writes to You), 1989.

Currently, Padrón is secretary-general of the Fernando Rielo World Prize of Mystical Poetry. He is also the founder and editor in chief of the international poetry review *Equivalencias.* Padrón is also known for his translations and for his critical essays on poetry. He translated into Swedish the poetic work of Vicente Aleixandre and when the latter was awarded the 1977 Nobel Prize, he went to Stockholm to receive the award on his behalf.

During this interview he best expressed the role of the poet when he said, "The poet must be willing to sacrifice everything he owns in exchange for speaking the truth; this is why poets are such a thorn to many dictators."

The first part of the interview took place in the lobby of the Tudor Hotel in Manhattan, while Justo Jorge Padrón was in New York for the Fernando Rielo Mystical Poetry Award presentation held at the United Nations headquarters. A tall, handsome man, carefully dressed even when wearing casual clothes, he likes to be at his best. Soft-spoken, a characteristic typical of people from the Canary Islands, he enjoys reading his poetry aloud. A very persevering and intense person, he takes his role as a poet very seriously. Poetry, whether it be his or someone else's, represents for him the highest form of expression. My second meeting with Padrón took place in his modern apartment in Madrid, where he usually lives, although he often escapes to Las Palmas, where he prefers writing in his family home facing the sea. He spent the whole afternoon going carefully over the transcript of our interview. Every word, every comma mattered to him. He is very organized and has little to do with the stereotyped image of the bohemian poet, although there is something about him of the romantic hero.

❖❖❖❖❖❖❖❖❖❖❖❖❖❖❖❖❖❖❖❖❖❖❖❖❖❖❖❖❖❖❖❖❖

MLG: In the prologue to your *Obra poética,* you say: "When literature knocked at my door at the age of fourteen, converting me into an avid reader, it brought only novels under its arm." Could you explain this a little?

JJP: I owe my encounter with literature to a very casual happening. At the age of fourteen, as I was helping my father move a bookcase, the telephone rang in the adjoining room. He told me to wait for him and not touch anything. But I did not listen to him and tried to move that huge bookcase, trusting in my own strength. As a result, the books fell on me and all around me like an avalanche. I managed to put them back into place, except for one which I hid. It had lost its cover in the fall and it was in poor shape. Hours later, in the silence of the night, I turned to it and noticed its title. It was called *Pan,* and I assumed it referred to the basic nourishment, bread. A strange curiosity took hold of me and I began reading it. The magic of its pages slowly started casting a spell over me. I was being drawn into the Scandinavian forest, where strange, mysterious spirits invaded my private world. When I finished reading that book, I was shaking with an uncontrollable emotion and I looked for the name of the magician who had given a new direction to my life. He was Knut Hamsun, the man responsible for propelling me into the world of literature.

MLG: Eventually this love for literature had its reward. After practicing law for seven years, you totally dedicated yourself to poetry in 1973. What does the act of poetic creation mean to you?

JJP: When artistic creation manifests itself with overwhelming intensity, it forces the author to make a choice and follow his destiny. Therefore, although in my first years as a writer I was also a lawyer, I realized that it would not be long before I would choose the sole path of literature, as I understood the latter to be the real reason for my life. So I chose poetry, with all the risks and consequences it could have for my future as a poet and a person.

MLG: Do you continue to be an avid reader?

JJP: Of course, even though my readings are more focused now on poetry and on the theory of poetic phenomena.

MLG: What does the first word you set down on paper mean to you?

JJP: Henry Miller once said something very beautiful: "The word that a writer sets down on paper is that of a wounded angel; it is the word *suffering.*" My poetry, nevertheless, does not spring solely from suffering, as it also exhibits surprise and feeling in the light of the most wonderful experiences that I have had in my life. I am not just an agonizing or visionary poet; I am also a poet who sings about beauty when it most fully expresses itself.

MLG: What does beauty mean for you?

JJP: Beauty represents a promise of fulfillment in the future. If I can capture it and share it, it turns into a light, which is a vision of eternity.

MLG: Do you believe in inspiration?

JJP: Of course. I believe in artistic inspiration and in the role it plays for painters, musicians, and poets alike. But I also believe that, following a flash of inspiration or intuitive clarity, there comes a period where an artist must labor and show his capacity for discipline and rigor.

MLG: Do you like to polish your work then?

JJP: Baudelaire said that the first verse is given to us by the gods but all the following ones are the result of our own effort. Yes, I revise my poetry. I'm not only an artist but an artisan; I wrestle with words a lot in order to discover the truth they will embody in the future. The word for me is quintessential, it is the heart of things, it is the initial murmur or whisper, the concept of the world. Without the word nothing could exist, and we must make sure that it best express the inexpressible, the invisible side of our soul, the other side of the mirror, so to speak.

MLG: What do you feel when you start a poem and when you finish it?

JJP: I go through a state of euphoria and curiosity. When I write a poem, I really feel the truth of Baudelaire's saying, because I could not possibly have written it had it not been for some force or muse that gave me the idea for it. That idea makes a path for itself and I limit myself to cutting the branches that stand in its way, but I can never ride it as if it were a horse with reins. It is the poem that carries me, it thinks for me, and when suddenly it explodes or comes to an abrupt halt, that's when I realize that I am done.

MLG: How do you know when you have reached the point where the poem is just the way you want it?

JJP: Intuitively. I think the basic weapon I possess as a poet is intuition.

MLG: Do you show your poems to other people when you have reached that point?

JJP: I am open to opinions. In fact, before I publish a work, I like to gather the opinions of a few people whose judgment I trust for a poetic perspective.

MLG: Yes, but is it anything like Lorca used to do, calling his friends at any moment of the day or night, because he needed a reaction so badly?

JJP: No, I don't react that way. My reaction is more internal and contained. I prefer to show my friends a complete work rather than an individual poem.

MLG: But they could be read individually.

JJP: I think that a poem can only be read in conjunction with others, because sometimes a poem that is good in the context of a book is not as relevant individually. I am an author of works, not just isolated poems. I am interested in creating a poetic world through global ideas. Each poem contributes in elaborating that thematic world. It is as if each poem were a brick and the complete work a wall of bricks that mutually support and complement each other. So an individual poem may very well justify the unified vision of the complete work.

MLG: What difference is there between a poem and poetry?

JJP: In some sense, the poem is the dwelling of poetry, it is the structure that encloses that magical force that is the essence of poetry. Therefore, I see a very clear distinction between them. In other words, a poem is a castle; and the freshly scented air—or music or light—that permeates it is poetry.

MLG: How would you describe what poetry means to you?

JJP: To me, poetry is that peaceful state brought on by mystery and a gleaming brightness that leads to ecstasy. If I had to define poetry, I would say that it is an art form that uses metaphors and images to disclose profound reality, unseen by most people although it is in our midst. It is like an instant of our perception that brings the world to a standstill, allowing the poet to see its essential reality.

MLG: Your poetry is one of contrasts: you move from ecstasy to sorrow, from your inner world to the universe, from emotions to reason, and from darkness to light. Your poetry is both inventive and suggestive and it leads us to that magical world that is a mix of fantasy and reality. Can you speak to us about that third dimension that you have managed to create?

JJP: I would not like my poetry to be merely a way of remembering some intense moment of the past, either in my private life or in the collective one that all men share. I would like it to be occasion for fusing reality with magic to produce a moment of wonder—this is the mystery of poetry that I would call poetic revelation. In my book *La visita del mar,* I have incorporated new myths in the light of our present experience by giving them the perspective of man in our times, while at the same time leaving that encounter to express itself at the climax of its beauty.

MLG: Is there no distinction between reality and fantasy?

JJP: There is a very thin line between imagination and reality. When the imagination is not credible, then we can call it fantasy. As a poet I stand on the borderline between both worlds and partake of the real and the fantastic. The reader, caught unaware, may be swept away in a gentle and mysterious fashion to landscapes of the imagination. Upon reaching the last verse of the poem, he will come to realize that the poet has guided him through a new and unknown country. This exploring of unknown worlds within us is similar to the mystic experience.

MLG: Does your poetry harmonize with other art forms, such as painting and music?

JJP: Yes, my poetry is very much influenced by other artistic activities. When I was a young boy, I played the violin and the classical guitar, so poetry for me is a synthesis of all the arts. A good poem always displays a plastic quality and must as well be a musical expression. But it is also related to philosophy and other disciplines, including even the sciences. For instance, there is a definite architectural aspect to poetry. The poem has a very complex internal mechanism, like that of a fine clock, even though it's not visible to the eye. It's like a painting by Dali where you see a handsome blond boy lifting the skin of the sea to reveal a black hole. If we had a flashlight, we might be able to see the machinery that makes waves in that black hole. This is why both the arts and the sciences (in terms of the inner workings of the poem) are relevant to my poetry.

MLG: What impels you to write?

JJP: A feeling of destiny. Many of the good or bad things that have happened in my life would not have acquired poetic expression without that inevitable force which drives me to write. I feel compelled to write poetry as if it were a duty or an inner need that cannot be ignored.

MLG: Why does your writing have to be poetry?

JJP: Because I am a poet, obviously. When I was a boy, I wanted to be a novelist until I discovered that poetry was a more fascinating, more beautiful, and I could even say more dangerous art form. I have always been attracted by the risks and danger of the marvelous and the almost impossible, and this is the emotional tension that poetry demands of its subjects.

MLG: On one occasion you made a promise to your father: to be a poet to the world and to sing of beauty within the United Nations enclave. What did you feel when you finally spoke there?

JJP: It was a momentous occasion for me. I remembered that beautiful old verse by Federico García Lorca in which he spoke of being at the center of time. At the United Nations, I experienced emotions of particular intensity and relevance to my calling as a poet. I felt that I was not only speaking to those people who were sitting before me at that moment, but also that my words were transcending the United Nations enclave and, like a torch of goodwill, reaching out to all men and women.

MLG: During that address, why did you elaborate the fiction of transporting us to some future time?

JJP: As part of my talk on the stance of the poet in the technological era, I devised the fiction of a chronological trip to the future so as to bring our current reality into stronger and more intense focus. I wanted to make our reality accessible to any listener who might have been hearing my words for the first time. So, in my fictional trip, I envisioned a being from another century and another planet who would look at our world with virgin eyes and see it threatened by atomic destruction. For this reason, the words of that fiction were meant to warn us and to defend our sacred world, which is our duty.

MLG: Has the poet a special place in Western society?

JJP: Western society does not grant poets special roles such as leaders of the masses, snake charmers, or even mere magicians. The role of the poet in Western society is that of an artist who practices an almost hermetic, mis-understood art for the select few. Otherwise, how can you explain the fact that in countries such as France and Great Britain first-rate poets are pub-lished in a limited edition of one thousand books? This is an absolutely disgraceful situation. By contrast, when I was published in several maga-zines from the Soviet Union, I was told that these journals had a wide circulation of one million copies. Poetry plays an important role in Eastern bloc countries, where to some extent it has taken the place of religion. Poetry is also a provider of human dignity and human rights.

MLG: What does the world mean to you and how do you conceive the role of the poet in relation to the world?

JJP: The poet, in my opinion, has a threefold mission: his first mission is to be an exponent of beauty, a creator who brings a world of emotion out of nothing and who stuns and surprises us with its radiant light; his second mission is to be the critical conscience of the time and to be willing to sacrifice everything he owns in exchange for speaking the truth (this is why poets are such a thorn to many dictators who, to silence them, have them taken as prisoners or even killed); and his third mission is to be the guardian of the language. Our future world is threatened by a technical, pragmatic terminology—the language of computers. This type of language could become akin to a mere screw in a huge machine where man counts for nothing. For this reason, it is imperative that the poet preserve the sensitivity of feelings and reflection, so that he may always communicate universal thoughts with words that point to beauty.

MLG: You have said, "I am Man, I am all men." Is that the poet speaking or the man?

JJP: I think they are one and the same. I am the same man as poet that I am as man. In this quote you have taken from *The Circles of Hell,* I am just referring to my essential nature as a human being and a creator. With that statement I was also trying to define my hell, which has nothing to do with the Christian concept of hell, or Dante's, Rimbaud's, or Milton's in *Paradise Lost.* Unlike Sartre, who said that hell was "the other," I say that my hell is myself, because I am everyone else.

MLG: You usually use the first person plural. Why?

JJP: Because I wouldn't want to fall into the trap of a poetry that is exclusively intimate or exclusively self-enclosed, rotating around its own axis. I want to write a poetry that can represent all men and be useful to them. Naturally, this poetry stems from my own awareness, because it would be futile to try to get into the skin of another, although intuitively, and with the help of my imagination, I can enter into the circumstances of other beings and interpret them.

MLG: You have said, "Every true creator must begin with tradition and renew it. I have been unable to write realistic poetry." Do you consider your poetry surrealistic?

JJP: My poetry is neither realistic nor surrealistic. What I have attempted to do is to recover some forms of realism and some surrealist techniques to write a poem in which I can portray the feelings of man with words that are both new and part of a long tradition. This harks back to that old Horatian saying, "Old wine in new skins." In a way, that is what I am trying to do.

MLG: You have also said, "The poet must be born and die in each of his books." What do you do to renew yourself?

JJP: I have attempted to renew myself in each of my books, because the worst thing a poet can be is his own imitator. I have seen this happen in great poets, whose names I will not mention because of the quality of their work. What I am referring to are those instances where a great book is followed by three or four mediocre pastiches of previous works. I agree with Saint John of the Cross and Antonio Machado that once we have expressed to the world what we want to say, if we find no new outlet for our thoughts, it is best to remain quiet. Fortunately, I believe that I still have many things to say and, as long as they are expressed in a novel manner and remain faithful to my world, I will continue in the field of poetry.

MLG: Do you see an evolution in your poetry from *Los oscuros fuegos,* your first book, to your latest?

JJP: Yes, I can clearly discern two or three styles or, at least, varied thematic and stylistic directions. The first cycle could encompass *Los oscuros fuegos, Mar de la noche,* and *The Circles of Hell.* These three books represent a process of interiorization of my being that might be qualified as a meditation on human feeling and human suffering. This process finds its highest expression in my most important work of that era, *The Circles,* which is a cosmogony of contemporary man. A new cycle began in 1976, shortly after the publication of that book. It is represented by such works as *El abedul en llamas,* which appeared in 1978; *Otesnita,* in 1979;

and *La visita del mar* and *Los dones de la tierra,* in 1984. In these collections of poetry, the poet tries to capture a moment relative to eternity in a most essential and transcendent manner. The poems in this cycle are very lyrical and find their inspiration primarily in nature and love. The sea, for instance, is perhaps my oldest friend. I was born next to it and have lived close to it. When I go to sleep at night or wake up in the morning, I have the feeling that my room is a big ship welcoming the sea so as to furrow it. On another level, *La visita del mar* is a book of synthesis which brings together the thematic tendencies and tangential forces of my two literary periods.

MLG: What do your latest works represent?

JJP: In the last five years, I have written *Sólo muere la mano que te escribe* and *Los rostros escuchados.* Like my previous works, *Sólo muere* is a closely-knit series of poems that evolve around a single thematic scheme, that of the poet's passion for the word in a desire to express the inexpressible essence of poetry. The first part of the book recounts the origins of poetry. The second part contains visions and dreams woven around the poetic text. The third part reflects the elements necessary to the making of poetry. The fourth part is perhaps the most mysterious, with a metaphysical undercurrent. The last part, represented by a single poem, is an attempt at reaching a climax through poetic revelation. As for the collection *Los rostros escuchados,* I chose in that work to give vent to my poetic expression and let each instant freely determine its theme. I thought that it would give a fuller scale of tones and overtones to my poetry, with new possibilities of form and perception. I truly believe that this particular volume holds some of my best poems. It contains some metaphysical poetry, some magical humor, that is to say when humor blends with a type of realism that borders on magic. This magical humor with which I am exploring now may produce situations that are fantastic and, at the same time, plausible. The poems are aphoristic, with a dark tinge somewhat akin to the third part of *The Circles of Hell,* but with greater succinctness. *Los rostros escuchados* also contains some of my most lyrical poetry. In the section called "Cuaderno del Monte Lentiscal" (Mount Lentiscal Notebook), I sing to the extinct volcano of my childhood, amidst pine trees and flowers, and to my parents' house where I played as a child and where I now write as an adult. The final cycle is made up of erotic love poems, without doubt the best love poems I have written so far.

MLG: Is it necessary for you to preserve the child you once were in order to write?

JJP: Yes, even though poets may have the experience of older men, I think they always retain the ability of the child to wonder and be surprised. It is precisely because men are living paradoxes that paradoxes spur them on in their capacity for invention and creation.

MLG: *The Circles of Hell* won two major prizes in 1977, those of best Spanish and best European poet. The book has been translated into fourteen languages and has been the subject of over two hundred reviews. Is it also your favorite among your works?

JJP: One loves the things that protect us the most from life. Basically, what binds us to life the most or what saves us from life the most is that which we love the most. *The Circles of Hell* was born in a difficult and sad period of my life. During that time, perhaps the only hope I had left was that I would finish this book. When it was published, I had the strange sensation that, regardless of what I had written before it or would write after it, *The Circles* would justify me, not only as a man, but also as a poet. I had the rare conviction that my life had not been in vain. But perhaps I should not single out that book; I could select as well *La visita del mar* from among the nine books I have written and, for that matter, add *Los dones de la tierra.* María Zambrano said of the latter that it represented for her the first instance of a cosmogony written in Spanish poetry.

MLG: Do you have a favorite among your poems?

JJP: The last canto in *Los dones de la tierra,* which is called "Fascinación de las aguas" (The Fascination of the Waters). It is a very difficult poem, because in over 110 verses I try to capture music and philosophy through a lyrical interpretation of water. I recently heard Carlos Bousoño say that a great poet can be identified by a set number of poems, usually no more than ninety. Bousoño studied the works of Antonio Machado and Juan Ramón Jiménez and discovered that, curiously enough, they had both written about ninety poems. So I think that, if a poet can write more than twenty truly good poems in a lifetime, he has created an important body of work.

MLG: What place do love, the recovery of time past, personal and universal suffering hold in your poetry?

JJP: I think they lie at the core of my poetry. In my writings the heartbeat of time is felt. Man's passage on earth, with his passions, joy and sadness, utopias and self-destructive tendencies make up the intricate texture of the human soul and the contexture of poetry. I can say that my poetry is a struggle between the force of love and that of death.

MLG: Do you consider yourself part of a literary generation, that of the seventies?

JJP: I would say that any poet who participates in the dynamics of a creation that achieves clear relevance among critics belongs to a generation, etymologically and chronologically speaking. This does not mean, however, that the generation in question has only one style or poetic voice. Every poet is an individual and a creative force that represents itself. The generation of the seventies expressed itself in many ways. The Venetian School at the outset focused on the elegance of the word and, to some extent, on the imagination. A later tendency might be called that of substantive poetry, which tried to synthesize human emotions with philosophical concepts, the beauty of the language and the imagination. Together with many poets, I was an exponent of that tendency.

MLG: Could you mention some poets of the past or present whom you admire?

JJP: From the past, I admire Petrarch and Dante. I also admire the sixteenth- and seventeenth-century poets John Donne, Garcilaso, Góngora, and Quevedo. From the nineteenth century, I like the romantic poets Bécquer, Blake, Keats, and Hölderlin. I enjoy very much Lautréamont and Mallarmé, but Baudelaire attracts me most of all. There are many twentieth-century poets who interest me, such as my mentor Artur Lundkvist, the great Swedish writer, the Spaniards of the Generation of 1927, particularly Cernuda and Aleixandre, and Latin American poets like Pablo Neruda and Octavio Paz.

MLG: Artur Lundkvist, president of the Nobel Committee of the Swedish Academy, has said that you are "the essential mediator between Nordic and Spanish literatures." What has been the extent of Nordic influences on your work?

JJP: That is a question that interests me, and it interests me precisely because it is so difficult for me to answer. I am going to attempt to think out loud and say whatever comes to my mind. My work naturally reflects Spanish influences because I derive my sustenance from that tradition, culture, and language. On the other hand, the years that I have spent in Nordic countries have given me the option of looking at the world, and at culture and poetry, from another perspective. This new perspective is perhaps not so sensual, idealistic, or bloodthirsty as that of the Hispanic world, but the thinking it reflects is more subterranean, and the stance it adopts toward the inevitable things in life is cooler and more collected. Additionally, Nordic culture displays a more cosmopolitan vision and above all a burning pantheistic love toward the world and nature. A fusion of both the Hispanic and Nordic perspectives is in great part responsible for the person and poet I am today.

MLG: You have translated the works of many poets. Do you think translating is a good source of training for writers?

JJP: I think translation is the most humble of all literary genres. By translating, the poet not only touches the gaps in his creativity but also learns what is significant about marvelous poets from other latitudes. For me, it has been a bountiful source of learning. This is why I believe that, as long as I remain a translator, I will continue to learn that unassailable mystery that is at the heart of poetry.

MLG: In addition to being a poet and a translator, you are also the editor of *Equivalencias,* a bilingual poetry journal.

JJP: It is a magazine that I envisioned for a long time, and for which I had lobbied at ministries of culture and private foundations. I was lucky to find Fernando Rielo on my path, because with his great intelligence and generosity he understood the important task that this magazine might fulfill, not only in the Hispanic world but on an international scale. So, the magazine is being underwritten by the Fernando Rielo Foundation, which also sponsors an annual World Prize for Mystical Poetry.

MLG: How would you define yourself both as a poet and as a man?

JJP: As I have been saying all along, I am a poet who writes with passion and determination and who seeks in poetry the highest form of beauty. To answer the second part of your question, I shall let one of my poems, "Notice to the Traveler," taken from *The Circles of Hell,* speak for itself:

> Remember that even
> With the right eye or the left hand
> Or what remains of your limbs,
> You shall go forward
> And struggle with all your blindness
> Though it be for nothing more than to survive
> For you are only a man.

Julián Ríos

LAYLE SILBERT

Julián Ríos was born in 1941 in Vigo, Galicia, in the northwest of Spain. As a young man, he went to Madrid to study law, and later to France and England. In that early stage of his life, he turned to writing and by 1962 had published several short stories and been the recipient of the Gabriel Miró Prize. In 1970, when he was not yet thirty, he collaborated with Octavio Paz in London on *Solo a dos voces* (A Solo for Two Voices), a book of conversation with the Mexican writer.

An essayist and fiction writer, his passionate love affair with language no doubt began while he was living in London. *Larva: Babel de una noche de San Juan,* 1983 (*Larva: Midsummer Night's Babel,* 1990), the first of a projected five-volume cycle, is a masterful work in which he challenges both the Spanish language and the reader. The second volume, *Poundemonium,* 1986, evolves around the London of Ezra Pound.

His saga novel, or "roman fleuve" or "rivers" ("Ríos," his own name), shows the author as a polyglot who assimilates sounds and tongues. In each of his pages, he strips the conventional Spanish language to the core, conquers it, gives it multiple meanings and multidimensional readings through a multilingual interplay. His characters play along with him in this masquerade of words and guide the reader from the text on the right-hand page to commentary notes on the left-hand page. Juan Goytisolo has called his work "an authentic feast" and referred to him as the Spanish Joyce. He has also been compared to Rabelais, Quevedo, and Sterne.

Ríos has attracted much attention. The *Encyclopaedia Britannica* 1985 Book of the Year made the following remark: "Readers sympathetic to Ríos's baroque humor and tumultuous style discovered in *Larva* an instant postmodern classic, without doubt the most disturbingly original Spanish prose of the century." Ríos has coined many terms, some of which have an

English equivalent, to refer to what literature and life mean to him: "liberatura" (liberature), "escrivivir" (writ(h)ing), "lector/elector" (readirect), "escriatura" (offsprint). To translate him, one has to make continuous pirouettes and juggle the words. Of course, in that game many of his puns may be lost and the translator must seek new ones.

Ríos is also interested in the visual arts. He is the author of *Impresiones de Kitaj: La novela pintada* (Impressions of Kitaj: The Painted Novel), 1989, and two books on Antonio Saura.

I met Julián Ríos while he was in New York, staying at the Gramercy Park Hotel. My first question to him was "What would you call an interview?" to which he answered, "If we were in winter, I would call it winterview." Unfortunately it was autumn. His conversation was full of humor, making one pun after another on a multilingual scope. After lunch, we went for a walk around Gramercy Park. Then, we spent the whole afternoon in his room overlooking the park, which reminded him of London. A photographer came over and took some shots of him. The tall, handsome, bearded man stood against the window, pausing graciously for her, and talked about his interest in photography. The last section of his books is made up of pictures he has taken which focus on the unexpected. With these words he put an end to the interview: "Un grand merci de Gramercy." One more pun, one more verbal play from the man who has revolutionized present-day Spanish. And I understood why Juan Goytisolo had told me, "Julián Ríos is the man you must see!"

❖❖❖❖❖❖❖❖❖❖❖❖❖❖❖❖❖❖❖❖❖❖❖❖❖❖❖

MLG: Julián, I wish I could conduct this interview by mixing the thirty languages you use in *Larva* and playing with them the way you do. Do you think we can achieve a midsummer day's Babel in which words and ideas are created and re-created?

JR: I'd be happy if this interview didn't turn into mere babble on paper . . . Let's call it "A Babel of Many Stories."

MLG: To continue in your vein: do you think we need a series of footnotes so that this interview will be shaped after *Larva,* and become an "interlarview," or do you have your own term for an interview?

JR: No, I don't have a particular term for it. But as well as an interview, I would like this to be an interhear, so that both sight and sound work together.

MLG: You like to play.

JR: I do. To play is to live in a way. In *Homo Ludens,* Huizinga points out very well that man's nature is to play; although I have occasionally said in jest and in truth that those who play have to pay . . .

MLG: You must have played a lot as a child.

JR: Yes, all kinds of games, even verbal ones. Words were like toy guns that I liked to load and unload . . .

MLG: The 1985 Book of the Year of the *Encyclopaedia Britannica* called *Larva* "an instant postmodern classic, without doubt the most disturbingly original Spanish prose of the century." How do you feel about that assertion?

JR: We will have to wait until the year 2001, and I hope both you and I will have lived to the end of this Time Odyssey.

MLG: Many authors consider you one of the most innovative Spanish writers of the moment. Why do you think your works have been so popular?

JR: I think *popular* is an excessive word. I distrust popularity. I will say that a truly new work has to forge its own way and make its own readers slowly, a process I find interesting. I have said many times that my work has no need for speed, particularly when I see so many authors lose their heads and tales in the pursuit of best-sellers, "pest-sellers," and "bête-sellers." Every original writer has a unique vision of the world and of life, so his rendition of reality is new and unfamiliar and it is sometimes hard for people to accept. That's why I think that at the same time that I was suggesting a new way of writing, I was also pushing for a new form of reading. I don't know what my significance as a writer is, or how many readers I have, but I do know that my readers are the best readers. I am interested in quality far more than in quantity. And in the re-readers. Cyril Connolly very accurately pointed out that the difference between journalism and literature is that you read the latter twice; at least twice, I would add. A book starts to exist truly only after it is reread. In this sense, I have the most patient, extraordinary readers.

MLG: So writing and reading become "wriding."

JR: Yes, very well put. In some sense I think people write so that they may become readers. We should not forget that the writer reads his work twice; and I ask myself, doesn't the person who reads a book twice also write it? I think he does, undoubtedly. I cannot separate reading from writing because I believe that when you write you also read, and that you write in order to become a reader in the end. People have quoted Borges many times as saying that what he liked most was being a reader, and that reading was the most civilized of activities. My opinion, on the contrary, is that writing is the most civilized of all acts, because you do it only once, and it is an unrepeatable, limited action. Reading, meanwhile, is infinite and unending, so it can be a truly liberating act. This is the interesting point: reading is open to all possibilities, while writing is a finite act, so that when all is said and done, the only benefit a writer has is to become yet another reader.

MLG: You call your reader "lector/elector," a reader "readirecting" your play on words, as it were.

JR: That's right, the "lector" is the elector or selector, as I said in *Larva* and in interviews a few years ago. I think the "lector" elects with his eyes and with his hearing; he can elect multiple moments and directions, and he has all the electoral rights in the world. The writer doesn't have the vote, although he has a voice. That's why I think that when all is said and done, a book is no more than the sum total of its readers. This is much like Borges's mythical bird *Simurg,* from *Zoología fantástica,* the legendary king of the birds who is searched for by a flock of birds only to discover after many difficulties that they themselves, the survivors, are the *Simurg.* An ideal reader "readirects." My ideal reader is the sum total of all past, present, and future readers, myself included. Joyce was undoubtedly exaggerating when he said that his ideal reader needed to suffer from insomnia. Every writer wants to have readers who are awake and have their wits about them.

MLG: Is your ideal reader your accomplice?

JR: Yes, he is an active participant. Authors have called their readers all sorts of names: Cervantes termed them "curious"; Rabelais, "drinkers" and "syphilitics"; and Baudelaire, "hypocrites." I would be satisfied with having "curious readers," as Cervantes said, meaning people who are interested in getting into the text and its hidden nooks and crannies. I have a predilection for the curious "lector" or "predilector."

MLG: Do your readers have to go through a period of initiation to understand your work?

JR: No, absolutely not, but every reading is gradual. There are various levels or stories in any minimally complex work. I would like my tower of Babel or babble to have many stories, different floors and different tales. One can remain on the ground floor, go up to the second level, stay somewhere in the middle, or survey the view from the roof. The reader can glance over something quickly and in passing, like in a stroboscope, or he can stop and observe the details. For instance, when you look at the paintings of the Flemish master Brueghel or those of the meticulous Victorian painter Richard Dadd, you first see them from a distance, so as to catch their panoramic scope, and then you get closer to look at all the details you couldn't see from afar. I believe readers should do the same thing.

MLG: Rafael Conte speaks of "larvaddiction," suggesting that to read your work, readers have to become addicted to your language.

JR: More likely, the addiction is the result of the reading. I would say that what is good about a fiction is that it is like an affliction; there is an infection in the fiction. Every original fiction ends up producing "infiction" that infects the readers. I hope that some of my readers have caught my influential influenza, which is like a fluid case of the Spanish flu.

MLG: As a creator, you are also addicted to this "larvaddiction."

JR: I'm like a dealer trying to peddle drugs, but I'm also the first to become addicted, as I am a reader too. I don't see much difference between reading and writing, or the reader and the writer, because we are all pretty much the same, like that image of the *Simurg.* I wouldn't even separate literature from life; for me, to write is life, it is *escrivivir,* which in Spanish combines "writing" and living." A few years ago, the Parisian daily *Libéra-tion* asked writers from all over the world the old surrealist question, "Why do you write?" I remember a journalist from that newspaper coming to my house and telling me he needed an answer as soon as possible. This is more or less what I replied: For me, to write is *escrivivir,* it is the art of living more intensely.

MLG: So the work of a writer is his life.

JR: I would say there are two types of writers: those who are fated to write because it is as necessary and vital for them as breathing; and so-called authors who are mere salesmen and could be hawking any product really, it just happens to be writing.

MLG: When did you realize that writing was essential for you?

JR: I couldn't give you a specific date; it's something I became aware of gradually. Since I was a child, I have always written. It doesn't mean that what I wrote then was any good; I would just pen variations of the tales of the sea and shipwrecks (some of which I witnessed in real life) that I had read or heard as a child in Galicia.

MLG: Your two characters, Babelle and Milalias, live a life of literature more than a real life, isn't that right?

JR: There is a continuous process of osmosis between life and literature. In addition to these two characters whom we know by their "pen names," Babelle and Milalias or the man of a thousand aliases (his real name is Emil Alia), there is a commentator or scholiast named Herr Narrator, who is based on an old professor friend of theirs from London whose name is X. Reis. So on top of the double folly of wanting to live and write on the same plane, there is the madness of the character who echoes Babelle and Milalias, the commentator or "echommentator" Herr Narrator, who is twice crazy, since in German *Narr* and *Tor* both mean madman. My characters live to write and write to live, and many times they go off on adventures because they believe these can later be transposed into literature. This is unlike what happens in *Don Quixote,* where the main character reads books and tries to reenact them in real life. But there are some connecting links between Cervantes' work and mine. Babelle and Milalias are definitely a "Sanchixotic" pair, they are locked into a type of *folie à deux.* In their mad frenzy of writing and living, they become pawns in their own game. Milalias creates, destroys, and re-creates the manuscript of his mitobiographic novel with the help of Babelle. And in some instances, their fictions become so real for them that they can no longer distinguish what they lived from what they imagined.

MLG: Does the same thing happen to you?

JR: No, I always distinguish between my life and the life I describe in my books. We never get to rewrite our real lives, they never go into a second edition.

MLG: Is your work at all autobiographical?

JR: Basically, it isn't. I don't want to imply with this that I don't use elements of reality or things I have seen, heard, or lived, but I am not interested in recounting my life. I respect other authors who speak about themselves in their work, but I am more concerned with getting into the lives of others.

MLG: In your prologue to *Larva,* you address the reader as Cervantes does, calling him "sly." Would I be wrong in saying that you are baroque and very modern at the same time?

JR: I don't know . . . They have labeled me hyper-baroque, neo-baroque, baroque . . . Upon arriving here in New York, my friends took me to a restaurant named *Barocco.* As far as "sly reader" goes, I'd like to point out the following: unlike most novels, which begin on the first page, *Larva* starts on the dust jacket. This is only possible in a hardcover edition, of course. In the paperback edition, they had to include the "Supernumerary Note" in the preliminaries. I did this to target those readers who only read what's on the cover, and barely leaf through the book itself. I am basically winking at the serious reader with this, and playing a joke on the readers of book jackets, who are legion, even among critics. Some readers have told me that there have been people who read the book because they felt challenged by the cover, or even irritated that they had been found out as readers of book jackets. So they bought the novel, perhaps to their frustration, but that's the way it is.

MLG: You use the symbol of the clover repeatedly in *Larva.* Is it a four-leaf clover?

JR: It is. The pages on the right, which refer to a party held on the feast of Saint John, the longest night of the year, represent the first leaf. The pages on the left are the mirrors in which "language reflects itself," as Mallarmé said; they are the second leaf. The "Pillow Notes" are the third leaf. Finally, the fourth leaf of the clover is the "Index of Names" at the end of the book, which gives the readers some clues, although not all the names are mentioned, just some that are disguised in various phrases and phases, masked in that masque of masks which is *Larva.*

MLG: Why does the name Jorge Manrique not appear in that "Index of Names"? You could have played with his reference to "ríos" (rivers), which is also your name . . .

JR: Of course, "our lives are the rivers that flow into the sea." I did use that reference in *Poundemonium.* In *Larva* too, there is a play on words on Manrique's "sea that is death" and the Dead Sea. The "Index of Names" doesn't claim to be complete. It is a guide that gives some hints and sets certain rules for playing with words. For instance, if someone speaks about "Sterne-fried shrimp (with the usual trimmings)," then there is a veiled reference to *Tristram Shandy.*

MLG: *Larva* has been described, in *Quimera* of Barcelona, as "one of the most anticipated works of the last decade, an orgiastic text, a feast of words, a narrative and linguistic achievement that discovers new territories for the Spanish language." Do you see your work as challenging, controversial, explosive, and playful?

JR: I would like it to be all those things. Hopefully it is. I always keep the following quote from Wittgenstein in mind: "The limits of my language are the limits of my world." Without a doubt, by broadening the language I am expanding the limits of my world. That's why I often reiterate that I would like my language to be as *ancho* (broad) as Sancho, as long as his Don, if you will. To expand the language is fundamental for me. I want to take the language out of its bonds and bounds to make it more whopping.

MLG: Emir Rodríguez Monegal said you are a three-dimensional writer. Could you add the fourth dimension?

JR: I hope I can. I wish there could be many mentions and mansions in my language so that this fourth dimension, and if possible a fifth, will come out.

MLG: If you had to give geometric shapes to your books, what would they be?

JR: *Larva* has a visual leitmotiv (which appears very clearly on the spine of the hardcover edition), a mask which is both an upside-down eight, the symbol of infinity, and a Möbius strip. That continuous figure of eight/mask/strip shows us both its internal and external faces in a sort of Möbius striptease. . . . Someone also said *Larva* was like a Rubik's cube, because you can give it so many different spins. There is also the shape of a spiral. In any case, I let the readers decide which shapes are most appropriate; some might prefer a circle or vicious circle, others squaring the circle. In any event, I hope that my readers are not too "square" themselves.

MLG: *Larva* seems like a creature or "living screapture" which gains weight and acquires new dimensions every day. Do you think it will continue to grow in new directions?

JR: I most certainly do. I believe it's going to grow. Let me borrow the French *je crois* which means "I believe" and also "I grow." That's the way it is. *Larva* has five distinct parts, it is a five-volume set, and each segment is going to need room to dance its own rumba. The next is *Auto de Fénix*.

MLG: Which you have already written.

JR: Yes, I have written it, although I am still in the process of rewriting some chapters. It is a voluminous book of more than six hundred pages.

MLG: Are you working on anything else?

JR: Yes, on different things, but let's look at them one by one. Firstly, you have to let the reader chew on a work to get at its essence or marrow, as Rabelais said, or its "mas-medula," to pay tribute to Oliverio Girondo, the Argentine author of *La masmédula*. You have to allow the reader time to read and reread. We authors sometimes write too much and too quickly, and we offer readers too many things at once.

MLG: When do you write?

JR: At any moment, but I prefer mornings.

MLG: How do you manage to write books so different from *Don Quixote* and nevertheless create very strong intertextual links between Cervantes's work and the cycle of *Larva?*

JR: Irrespective of all the differences, *Larva* is a descendant of *Don Quixote.* Every author moves in a specific tradition, and the founding fathers of the tradition that attracts me are Rabelais, Cervantes, and Sterne. I like Rabelais because he is the founder of a Pantagruelian language that mixes all the codes, combining the highest with the lowest, the most technical vocabulary with slang, creating a verbal "melting potpourri." In the Western world there is no one with the linguistic richness of Rabelais, who was an explorer and colonizer of language. Unfortunately for literature, French literature in particular, he didn't have many followers. Of course, his high standards are difficult to emulate. The next founder, and "unfounder," of my parodic tradition is Cervantes, who initiates a critical dimension and an uncertainty principle in writing. The windmills are giants and windmills again and they stir up a dust whirlwind. Contrary to the chivalry novels (which continue to gallop to this day, long after their death, sometimes under labels such as "magical realism"), Cervantes's books introduce criticism and doubt; every story has a corresponding "mystory," and the benefit of the doubt, or the "benefiction," always remains. The third part of this exalted trinity is Sterne, who for the first time in the Western world explores the new space of the page. These three authors are the founders (both in the sense of originators and smelters) of my tradition, which begins with Apuleius' *Golden Ass.* Critics sometimes throw in my face vague terms such as avant-garde and experimentalism, and I reply that these are fine, but that they should keep in mind that I come from a tradition or "contradiction" as old as that of conventional novelists.

MLG: Can you mention some other writers who have influenced you?

JR: In addition to the founding fathers I have just talked about, I would mention Flaubert, Joyce, and Céline. It would take a long time to establish the relation of these relationships, wouldn't it? At the same time, people do not often take into account that what is truly distinctive and original about an author is precisely his influences, which are always relative, that is, from his relatives. They are his family. These influences could also be called affinities, often made on the intuitive level before the conscious or the elective one. However, I find it unfair and belittling to call for instance Guimarães Rosa "the Brazilian Joyce"; Carlo Emilio Gadda "the Italian Joyce"; and Arno Schmidt "the German Joyce." I think these comparisons belittle because every one of these authors is original. Although they may have familiar ties with great authors such as Joyce, they have their own national tongues and cultures, to which they have contributed. I feel very close and comfortable with all the writers I have mentioned, as well as many others from my own language, such as the authors of *Libro de buen amor, La Celestina, Tirano Banderas.*

MLG: You have said that *Larva* will be a five-volume work. Where does the "River Ríos" take its source? How do you manage to rouse up the "sly readers" by showering them with torrents of language?

JR: The undercover reader needs to pass under the volcano to see the source of the river of *Larva*. The starting point or origin for *Larva* is a passage (which will be included in *Auto de Fénix*) that was first published in 1973 in Mexico in Octavio Paz's magazine *Plural*. In a nutshell, in parentheses, that passage contains what *Larva* was to become.

MLG: In *Axolotl,* Julio Cortázar writes: "They were larvae, but larva means mask and also phantasm." Was this phrase the inspiration for your title?

JR: No, absolutely not. It is curious that the title has so many possible sources. I recall that, many years ago, a professor asked me if the title was a tribute to Valle Inclán, because in *La lámpara maravillosa* (The Marvelous Lamp), the author says that words are larvae which treasure the knowledge they have acquired under the rhythm of the sun. . . . I was ecstatic when I found out, because it is such a beautiful and accurate definition. And here I had spent so much time coining the word *palarvas,* which means both "words" and "larvae" in Spanish. I am a great admirer of the work of Julio Cortázar, and he was very encouraging with my first drafts of *Larva,* but the title didn't come from him or anyone specific. I am aware that larva also means mask, phantasm, and demonic possession. I think these three things define any sort of writing. I could also mention Descartes's "larvatus prodeo" or "I advance masked." I think there are a thousand possible connections. The good thing about the title is that it can come from many places, generally speaking, but from none specifically.

MLG: How do you arrive at your titles?

JR: Sometimes they come to me by themselves, while on other occasions I have to conquer them. For me, the title is the crucial element, because it generates writing more than anything else. In *Auto de Fénix,* for instance, all the chapters have titles, and the titles are significant in organizing the story. Sometimes, I play with the notion of the title in English as a sort of "tight tale," or a compressed story. The entire story is contained in the seed of the title, which harbors many possibilities. That's why I like to begin with a title, whenever possible. A title triggers me, while, without one, I cannot tell north from south or east from west. A title holds many surprises, and I think titles are what give literature its nobility.

MLG: From the first word of *Larva* to the last, one feels transported by the rhythm of the language and the chorus of voices that intertwine. If you were to compare that work to music, would it be a composition by Béla Bartók, a rock concert, or a dance of words, images, and ideas?

JR: I like Bartók a lot, and one of the "Pillow Notes" in *Larva* finds its inspiration in *The Miraculous Mandarin.* The critic Iury Lech compared the staccato rhythm of *Poundemonium* to Bartók's music. I wish it were so. But in terms of music, I would mention jazz because of its ability to give a musical phrase several interpretations or twists. I also like rock. Don't forget that an Irish rock group named Shamrock performs constantly in *Midsummer Night's Babel.* I make many allusions to popular songs in my work.

MLG: Do you speak out loud when you write?

JR: No, I am not a rapper. I always write in silence and hear what I write in my head. Once in a while, I read out loud to see if I have hit the target or not. But while I write, I listen with my inner ear, because just as there is an inner eye, there is also an inner ear, undoubtedly.

MLG: So you reread your work.

JR: I reread what I have just written and examine it, and often I don't need to read it out loud. When I do a public reading, I realize that the page is like a musical score. That's why I am against authors who think they can do without commas and periods; I think punctuation is a very valuable aid in indicating tones and pauses to the reader.

MLG: Why do you consider *Poundemonium* a bridge between *Midsummer Night's Babel* and *Auto de Fénix?*

JR: Because some shorter books such as *Poundemonium* are tributaries of larger works. *Poundemonium* was going to be a chapter in *Auto de Fénix,* but then it grew into an autonomous volume.

MLG: Why did Ezra Pound make such an impact on you?

JR: Because Pound or the "Signore Sterlina," as he said ironically, is a currency that doesn't lose value. I have always considered him an emblematic figure, and very generous in three ways: first, because he was a magnificent poet and he managed to recapture lost traditions while innovating new styles; second, because he was very generous intellectually and he stimulated his colleagues and young writers (the work of Joyce, for instance, might not have been possible or would have been considerably delayed without Pound's material help); and thirdly, because he was very important as a transmitter and translator of other cultures. He brought us closer to cultures distant from ours, such as those of China and Japan, and he helped us reclaim our own classical cultures and make them newly relevant, as well as bring dead languages back to life. When we read the work of Sextus Propertius or the troubadours through Pound's renderings, they come to life and they seem relevant to us. Like the Roman deity Janus, Pound has two faces, perhaps more, although not all of them were good ones. He could fall prey to obsessions, like his questionable political views, or his strange economic or "economystic" theories. In *Poundemonium,* X. Reis summarizes the best qualities of *il miglior fabbro* in a few lines. Pound made mistakes, but he was a generous soul, and both an innovator and a traditionalist. Not only did he give us astonishingly original, modern works, as Rimbaud wanted to, but he also gave new life to the books of the past. For this and many other reasons, my three characters who aspire to be writers, Milalias, "Rimbaudelaire" (his best friend from Belgium, so named because of his interest in Rimbaud and Baudelaire), and Reynaldo Rey, a Spanish reader in London, all look up to Ezra Pound as a sort of patron saint. Ezra Pound is their password and Pound is their "daimon."

MLG: That does explain the title for *Poundemonium,* daimon and demon.

JR: London is the pandemonium, the imaginary capital of hell. *Poundemonium* takes place on All Saints Day in 1972, the day following Pound's death, and the book gets its principal cue from the descent into hell at the beginning of Pound's *Cantos.* I think it was Shelley who said that London was a city very similar to hell. In this sense, London is the city of confusions, where all the languages are mixed, and it has a Babel-like, subterranean quality. Of course, *Poundemonium* is a play on words between Pound and pandemonium. Anyway, in my book, that descent into hell leads us on a pilgrimage through certain areas of London. The image of Ezra Pound is gradually evoked by visits to his old haunts—where he worked, lived, and socialized—before concluding with a special purifying bath when the main character returns home to his love, Babelle, at sunrise. It is a trip to the end of the night that aspires to daylight.

MLG: Are all your books going to take place in London?

JR: London—*my* London—is the center of the universe and a microcosm of the world. I am not interested in London as a British city, or in the London of the British Empire, but I am fascinated by London as a mix of foreigners or a "melting polis." It is a sort of global, planetary city, into which everything and everyone fits, and there are exiles and immigrants from all over the world.

MLG: Have you ever considered creating a fictional city?

JR: No, I find real cities fascinating and "stranger than fiction." I admire those authors who create fictional cities, but I think that all modern large cities are fantastical and full of fictions. Are we sure of what we see? Is that woman entering a cab being helped by a man, or is he forcing her in? Everything happens so quickly and in fragments in a city. Is what we see absolutely real? Let's not forget that Eliot referred to London or a part of it as the "unreal city." Modern cities are unreal and full of imaginary elements. Time and many generations have taken care of creating for me what I could not possibly have created myself.

MLG: You recently wrote a book on the American painter Ronald B. Kitaj called *La novela pintada.* What role does painting play in your work?

JR: I have always enjoyed working with painters and photographers. I like to establish what I call creative complicity with them, so that we can do together what is not frequently done when we are apart. Genres are not usually combined, let alone different arts. Painters and writers generally remain in their respective corners, and poets normally are not interested in music, novelists in sculpture, etc. I am interested in crossbreeding, mixing together diverse artistic forms, because very often we can learn the most from genres that differ from our own, yet which run on parallel tracks. An author may draw more inspiration from the work or the words of a painter than from a relationship with another writer, because we are hemmed in by our own field. So painting can open new doors to literature and vice versa. *Impresiones de Kitaj: La novela pintada* is an instance of "fiction painting" or novelized painting in action; words and images complement one another through a game of complicities, correspondences, and mutual reflections. It is definitely a book where you are expected to see images between the lines, and read between the images.

MLG: Why did you choose Kitaj?

JR: Primarily because of a set of elective and intuitive affinities. Kitaj is one of the great painters of our time. He has been very rightly praised here in the United States by critics such as John Russell and poets like John Ashbery, who considers Kitaj a painter with roots in the past who is nonetheless as modern as Jasper Johns or Frank Stella. Kitaj is a painter with an extraordinary and very modern capacity of figuration. His painting has sometimes been praised, and sometimes discounted, as "narrative," but it should be pointed out that ambiguity is its greatest trait. In Russian, Kitaj means Cathay, or China. *Kitaj* is a country with all sorts of ambiguities, even more than the seven varieties enumerated by William Empson. To have made this book with Kitaj has truly been an encyclopedic adventure, not only through the world of painting, but other distant worlds, such as those of film, Judaism, and baseball. A painting by Kitaj is a dispenser of allusions and it can contain veiled references to literature, painting, and history. This *Novela pintada* on Kitaj is like a detective novel, in a way, because it is full of searches and it touches all the bases. I call Kitaj an "allusionist" instead of an illusionist. I think that all the great writers and artists of our time are "allusionists" because they are able to make many allusions through a single work.

MLG: Do you also play with words in that work?

JR: Of course, constantly, as much in the English original as in the Spanish version or perversion. There are even plays on words in the titles of the various chapters of this "painted novel" or untainted painting. For instance, one of the chapters is titled "The Grand Jewry," with double meaning for "Jewry" and "jury." There is wordplay because the three characters of *Larva* also take part and because, whenever a word is in play, it ends up saying more than it means. I'd like to point out that people sometimes think that playing with words is just fun. It is fun, but it also has the effect of revealing unseen corners of reality and illuminating them. For instance, Freudian slips allow desire to express repressed thoughts. Wordplay also allows you to emphasize without being emphatic, to underscore something to great effect with economy. Let us remember that the first stone of the Church is laid with a play on words. Additionally, unlike realism, which often gives us a simplistic rendering of life, wordplay allows us to see the complexity of reality. Sometimes wordplay is almost like a cubist painting where you can see several different angles or perspectives on the same plane. I really like to be able to show various facets of the same reality simultaneously.

MLG: Who is Albert Alter, the painter who appears in *Larva?*

JR: He is a character in the *Larva* cycle and an occasional collaborator of mine. He has done some covers for the magazine *Espiral,* when I was its director, and he designed the cover of the first edition of *Poundemonium,* as well as a series of sketches that appear at the beginning of that edition under the heading of "Sketches for *Faces in the Crowd.*" Albert Alter is an important character in *Larva,* and his significance is going to grow in the remaining volumes of that cycle. He is a Jewish painter of Dutch origin who lives in a studio on the docks of London, on a street called Artichoke Hill. He meets with his painter friends in his studio, and they will eventually take the name of the "Artichoke" or "Arty choke" group. My fascination with painting appears through the character of Albert Alter. The characters of *Larva* frequently go to exhibits. Babelle and Milalias, for instance, go to the Tate Gallery to see Richard Dadd's famous painting *The Fairy Fellers Master-Stroke,* a somewhat mythical work which they examine and scrutinize because it is really detailed, although from afar all you see is a woodcutter with his ax raised in a clearing in the forest. But when you get closer, you begin to see many diminutive fairy-tale characters and other things through the cracks in the grass. Babelle and Milalias find a great likeness between Dadd's woodcutter and Albert Alter. So Albert Alter is my alter ego somewhat.

MLG: In that case, could I say that all your characters are your doubles?

JR: Yes and no. I think that every author, when it comes right down to it, can say about his character that "Madame Bovary, c'est moi," not only in the sense of she is I ("c'est moi") but she is moved ("s'émoit"). At the same time, I think that most writers try to come out of themselves to some extent, and that they are very aware that "I" means others, as Rimbaud said, so they try to find those others. The funny thing is that I appear as myself only once in *Larva,* and that I enter into the novel in the only way possible, through a refractive process. Reality and fiction occupy different spheres, as we know, and go their separate ways. When all is said and done, the world of the real cannot enter into the world of literature without distortion. At the end of *Larva,* there is a scene in Reis's room in the Maide Vale neighborhood of London in which he speaks to a bearded stranger with round-rimmed glasses. Milalias, who is on his way to visit his beloved mentor, X. Reis, overhears their conversation in Spanish. Reis and the bearded man, who are sitting having a drink together, comment that they have the same name, because the stranger says that his dentist's nurse mispronounces his name as "Mr. Rayos." Reis retorts that his last name, of Portuguese origin, is also often mispronounced by Britishers as Rays, as in X rays. So the two of them joke that they must be the same character as they are both rays. And this is where refractive rays enter into the picture. The main character of my novel sees me, the author, in the form of a fictional character, Mr. Rays, because I have to be distorted in order to get inside the book, I can't join the action as Mr. Ríos. So the character sees me and doesn't recognize me (the same might happen if we were to meet our own creator) and he asks himself, "Who the devil is this Mr. Rays?" So, somewhat differently from Hitchcock, I try to enter into my fiction, but I have to do so as yet another character, Mr. Rayos, who is not quite like Mr. Ríos, Milalias, Reis, Albert Alter . . . Those characters are far more interesting than I am, because they are fictional, while I am real, and thus less interesting.

MLG: If you are a double for your own characters, how do you feel about appearing as a character in a novel by Carlos Fuentes?

JR: Fuentes told me that I will appear in his next novel [*La campaña*] as an ex-Jesuit priest called Julián Ríos, who has a fondness for wordplay. Like Whitman, Fuentes likes all the flow of rivers, and I'm sure that his Padre Ríos or Father Rivers will earn the generous epithet Fuentes gave me, "Rivers of fun!" In *Tallien,* a novel written by my American friend Frederic Tuten, there is also an old seaman named Julian Rios who is a friend of Tallien. These are just winks my accomplice writer friends give me. It's not as if I were really a character in their novels. On the other hand, characters never believe they are characters. I recall the indignant comment of the librarian Richard Best when he found out that he appeared as a character in Joyce's *Ulysses:* "I am not a character in a novel, I am a living being." But today, he is only alive in the pages of *Ulysses.*

MLG: What relationship do you have with your characters?

JR: I try not to fall into the trap of Balzac's literary tradition of calling the doctor in your novel to cure you. Valéry condemned this tendency. I see and hear my characters as if they were made of flesh and blood, but I have to accept that they are made of words.

MLG: Is the main character of your novels the word?

JR: Never. Words are at the service of facts and things. Sometimes readers are blinded by the verbal fireworks of certain authors, and they don't see the path that the words are tracing. The important thing for me is what I have to say and what the words are saying. Whenever the American translators of my work were tempted to remove something from my story in order to achieve a wordplay, I always refused, concluding that "the tale is the head of my novel." The tail of a tale is very important, sometimes more so than dazzling wordplay. I haven't forgotten Hamlet's famous soliloquy that literature is words, words, words. How these words are arranged is also significant, of course, because a new world or reality can spring from this.

MLG: Why is dialogue so important in your work?

JR: Dialogue is one of my names for literature, I can't understand literature without dialogue. I have written a book of what I term critical dialectic called *La vida sexual de las palabras,* and its subtitle is "Conversations in the Library of Babel." In *Larva,* at one point Babelle dreams that she is seated at a swiveling round table in a magnificent library with Milalias and Reis, or his double, Herr Narrator. She sees them both as older men, and herself as a little girl, like Lewis Carroll's Alice. And they have a feast of books; they can read whatever they want in that dream, unlike in real life, where Babelle and Milalias feel deeply frustrated when they go to the British Museum and see a Japanese man reading a manuscript which they will never be able to read. The three characters in *Larva* use dialogue constantly to read and comment on very diverse books.

MLG: Joyce's *Finnegans Wake* is the source of all books for you. Do you think *Larva* is a novel which represents all novels?

JR: *Larva* is a novel that can only represent itself, and just barely, but I do agree that the aim of all great books is to stand for all works. Joyce used to say that if they burned Dublin down, they could rebuild it on the basis of *Ulysses.* My highest ambition would be to write a book that would permit all of literature to be rewritten if they burned down every library in the world. This is impossible, of course, but authors write to seek the impossible and they have to remain impassible about doing so. The book of all books, the total work, is the synecdoche of literature. All books end up being that ideal work, a literary *Simurg* in the hand. It is still difficult to accept that literature comes from literature, as well as from life and experience. Any minimally complex book brings out previous works. In this sense, *Finnegans Wake* would be a magnificent example of a work that lifts the curtain on almost all Western literature.

MLG: Why do you place photographs and maps of London in all your books?

JR: Since I am interested in typography, how am I not going to be fascinated with topography, as these are the places where the characters move? I have always loved maps and books with maps. I think the first things I learned how to read were maps. As a child, I would spend hours on end looking at the atlas.

MLG: So you like geography.

JR: Yes, I do. But more than geography itself, what I liked was that all those places I had never visited—and maybe never will—triggered my imagination. I liked the names of the places more than the places themselves. That's why in *Larva* there is a scene in which a character stands before a huge book with the following palindrome, "salta ese atlas" (jump over that atlas), "bounding over the binding." The palindrome refers to the world, once again a circular world, and don't forget that *Larva* depicts itself as an *orbilibro* or "orb-book." Novalis suggested, "Find the universe in a book," and Mallarmé said, "The world exists to become a book." There is some playing with this inordinate ambition in *Larva;* Milalias almost says as much while reading the daily *Le Monde.* In any event, I love maps and they have always held me enthralled. And photographs too. Many of the photographs of London in *Larva* and *Poundemonium* are "historical," in a manner of speaking, because they show places of little touristic interest that have changed considerably or disappeared altogether since my books came out. Perhaps the only evidence that will remain of them are the humble photographs in my novels. In some instances, even the signs over the pubs have changed. For example, there is a pub that is very important in *Larva* and *Auto de Fénix,* the World's End—not at the end of the world but of the touristy King's Road—which had a beautiful emblem showing an old man with a scythe on his shoulder sitting next to a signpost with the word *finis* inscribed. This is the finis or end that is going to conjure up the phoenix in *Auto de Fénix* or auto of finis, so to speak. Anyway, this lovely sign has now disappeared and been replaced with an emblem of a bloody vessel falling off the end of the world. So the photographs of the World's End and some other places in *Larva* are now all that remain of those places.

MLG: Like Cortázar, you trace a sort of textual path for your readers: from the pages on the right, you send us to the notes on the left, and later to the "Pillow Notes." Should we read your books lying down?

JR: At least, I hope I haven't made you lie too much. Lying down would be the ideal position, as long as your ignorance is not facedown. . . . I was not joking the many times that I have said that *Larva* should be read in bed and, if at all possible, with four hands, regardless of the type of couple involved. That would be the ideal way to read it, because Babelle and Milalias sometimes read their favorite works in this fashion. The movement from the right to the left of the text is designed to break the linear pace of the novel and reveal its complex web of interconnections. Sometimes, people who are reading *Larva* for the first time ask me where to begin. As with almost all works, I think that my novel can be read in many ways, and there is no set of instructions to follow. You might read *Larva* without looking at the pages on the left, and following the narrative conventionally, as with most novels. As I said before in reference to Brueghel, you can look at the panorama or take in the details. Once again, it depends on which side of the clover or cover you want to clutch the book by. On the one hand, there is the narrative action, like taking a moment to see what's happening when you first arrive at a party, but eventually being drawn in and meeting some of the characters there. Then there is the aspect of the reality and concreteness of the writing. We mustn't forget that *Larva* is a book of books, it is a work which the characters attempt to live and write at the same time. So the act of writing is significant, and this is reflected in the pages on the left, which send us to the anecdotes that support the verbal thought and action at the party and back to the beginning. So *Larva* can be read in many ways.

MLG: Nevertheless, you would like to impose on us the triptych order of your chaotic world.

JR: Chaos is not really chaos when you look at it with a modicum of care. Sometimes, what seems confusing to us isn't really, is it? Ezra Pound loved an inscription at the base of a statue of William Shakespeare in Leicester

Square that says: "There is no darkness, but ignorance." Many times, what seems chaotic or dark to us is nothing but the shadow of our own ignorance in the face of something we don't know or don't understand. So I don't impose a way of reading on my readers. I would like the motto of *Larva* to be Thélème's assertion: "Fay ce que vouldras," or "Do as you will." The author should not be authoritarian. In *Larva,* I allow readers to have their own say, or essay the approach that they want. Since I have been wrapped up in the work for fifteen years, I occasionally allow myself to voice an opinion as a reader to the reader and tell him what particular path I think he should follow to understand better a particular paragraph. You could also be very strict and look up a note every time the text makes reference to it. This is a way of underscoring the fact that we sometimes read too fast and that we should take more time to look at the landscape.

MLG: So it is a form of mutation?

JR: A mutual-action.

MLG: A mutation or metamorphosis?

JR: Yes, a *motamorphose* (word-metamorphosis). In a journal called *Texture,* put out by the French department of the Universidad del Pais Vasco, they made a directory of Spanish authors, with labels for each. Under my name, they put the term *motamorphose,* or metamorphosis of words. The term is based on a play of words in *Larva,* "métamorphose des mots."

MLG: You look at your readers as handymen who have to work with you in reading/writing the book. It is as if they are your co-authors.

JR: Of course, they become co-authors and have to work with what is at hand. Handymen are persons who have to improvise a little, they don't need all the tools in the world. The readers or "bricolecteurs" can read creatively even with limited means or knowledge. This interests me a great deal.

MLG: Where does your dizzying passion for words, almost to the brink of madness, originate?

JR: From words, words, mirror words. From patch/page work. In *Larva,* Babelle says Milalias has a "délire de lire" (a delirium of reading), "a page agape." I too am a page of honor of the Page. As Novalis used to say and Octavio Paz has repeated, the author is a servant of the language. "Amo idioma": Master Language. I would even add that the writer talks back to his master, particularly over academic norms. Writers are therefore in a vicious or virtuous cycle from which they can never escape, because they have chosen the world of the word that begins anew every time. How can I not be fascinated by words, since they are all that I have as an author? If I were a movie director or a photographer, I could count on the collaboration of actors and models, people of flesh and blood. But characters in a literary work are made of words, no more and no less. Words on the page. People tend to think that words are abstract. Writers often envy painters for their ability to use plastic materials and dip their fingers into the paint. But for me, words are also tactile and plastic; they have an inherent sensuality. As a writer, I attempt to show the sensual, physical, material aspects of words.

MLG: So the word has a body.

JR: It has a body and his bodyguard and servant the writer knows how to handle the word hand by hand. "Amo idioma" (I love language). A living offprint/offspring is born from this struggle and fond embrace between the author and his words. This is the difference between a living author, who writes with a dynamic language, and a scribbler, who writes with a dead language in which words still seem to be buried in the dictionary, lifeless and without personality.

MLG: Why did you choose to bring the ghost of Don Juan into your novel? Was it to seduce and conquer the Spanish language?

JR: Of course, I would say that the aim of the masked Don Juan is to seduce with his words, and not just people, but other languages as well. This is without taking into account the sexual, promiscuous adventures of the character in a then very promiscuous post-swinging London. All the tongues that appear in *Larva* usually belong to ladies, and Milalias attempts to seduce both the women and the tongues they speak. In one chapter, in tribute to his Spanish language, Milalias says, "All languages are going to become languages of my language," which can be interpreted in many ways. So there, all the tongues are disguised in Spanish. For instance, when Finnish and Japanese women speak, they do so with Finnish and Japanese words disguised in Spanish. As far as I know, this linguistic transvestism has never been done in any language, and this is what separates me radically from Joyce. My aim is not so much to babelize, babble and mix languages, but rather to give all languages the appearance of being Spanish, as we are at a costume ball and the tongues are masked in a masquerade of words. The Peruvian writer and critic Julio Ortega, a professor at Brown University, once said that if Hispanophiles from twenty or thirty different countries could gather to read excerpts of *Larva* in Spanish as well as in the subtext of their own native tongues, the laughter would be heard all the way to Tokyo. For instance, when a Japanese girl calls Don Juan *ganso,* she is not only calling him "stupid" but also an "inventor," which is what the word means in Japanese. This is the fantastic side of words, they are layers of masks on a many-sided polyhedron.

MLG: In *Midsummer Night's Babel,* the devil reminds Don Juan that he sold "his soul for a bunch of words." Are these words your novel?

JR: I think that any book is a pact with the devil, in some sense. I think demons possess the true writers, and that we do sell our souls for a bunch of words, otherwise we wouldn't spend our lives stringing words together. Writing is also a rebellious act. The writer, as Blake said of Milton, is of the devil's party.

MLG: Then it cannot be deus ex machina but diabolus ex machina.

JR: And Deus as well. One of the Italian wordplays in *Larva* is

"Diobolo," which means god and the devil at the same time. To be able to reconcile all extremes is the supreme ambition of any author; we don't want the light and darkness, high and low, and the other dichotomies of the Manicheans to stand any longer. I think that the best modern literature is complex precisely because there are no set boundaries, and one is not sure which is the light and which is the shadow, what is good and what is bad. . . . This is what is both fascinating and disturbing about the modern world, don't you think?

MLG: What is literature—or "liberature," as you like to call it?

JR: "Liberature" is the term used by the characters of *Larva,* and it refers to the significant desire of writers to transform what is repressed, to express what we repress so that it doesn't oppress us anymore, and I don't just mean psychological repressions. It appears that writing was invented to control slaves, but, as we know, it eventually became a tool of liberation. We write to seek greater freedom, in many ways. The great writers have been great liberators of energies, taboos, and all sorts of things. That's why I like to speak of "liberature," meaning a literature that strives for freedom.

MLG: Do you seek the universality of tongues within the Spanish language?

JR: Every author is hemmed in by his mother tongue. When a writer has a truly original vision, the language is born anew in his writing. At the same time, a language always goes further than itself. I think that basically every writer inscribes himself in a tradition that goes further than his own language or national culture. When I mentioned Wittgenstein earlier, I noted his comment that the desire of the writer is to increase the boundaries of his language. Juan Goytisolo has also said that the important thing for an author should be to make the language richer than when he first found it. I also share Carlos Fuentes's vision of gaining ground from the sea in the name of literature; this is the task of any genuine author. So, any great writer is basically an explorer of language who charts the new tongue and discovers new territories for it.

MLG: The writing in *Larva* sometimes seems coded. For instance, you tell us in Morse code that nothing is certain and everything allowed. Could this be a definition of what the process of writing means for you?

JR: I think that if a novelist follows his own narrative game, he eventually achieves a state where everything is permitted. The phrase you just mentioned contains a more or less legendary allusion to the Ismaili sect of the Assassins, which existed in the eleventh and twelfth centuries. One of the founders of this sect, Hasan ibn-Sabbah, also known as the Old Man of the Mountain, used to intoxicate his followers with hashish in his fort at Alamut, in the north of Iran. When they were completely intoxicated or asleep, he had them moved to a secret garden in the castle, where some girls (the most beautiful in the world, according to Marco Polo) would tend to their needs, offering them fruit, attention, and more hash, until they once again got intoxicated. Then Hasan ibn-Sabbah would have them moved back to their grungy quarters and the harsh reality of a razed landscape. When they awoke, the Old Man of the Mountain would appear at the right moment and tell them that they had had a divine vision of the heavenly paradise awaiting them if they followed his orders and executed the enemies of his sect and died for their ideals. After having such realistic "dreams," the "assassins," or eaters of hash, would become fanatics and stop at nothing to do their master's bidding. The saying that nothing is certain and everything allowed (which some chroniclers claim Hasan ibn-Sabbah uttered before dying) alludes to the play of mirrors between reality and fiction. Fiction is not reality but it is truer than nature, it is a lie that becomes the truth, and makes that everything is permitted. Because everything is permuted, or transmuted. Everything is allowed in literature when one has talent and the ability to tell a tall tale tellingly, and to allow words to release their inner meanings. Everything is admitted in literature when it becomes "liberature."

José Luis Sampedro

José Luis Sampedro was born in 1917 in Barcelona, although he spent his childhood in Tangiers, where his father, a military doctor, headed a hospital. From 1933 to 1935, he studied in Madrid at the Official Academy of Customs and became a civil servant. From 1944 to 1947, he studied economics at the University of Madrid.

Sampedro has led a busy life as an economist and has written many books on that subject. He taught economics for many years, served as consultant for Spain's Banco Exterior, was vice president of the Fundación Banco Exterior, and headed the Central Customs Office. He also was a visiting professor at Bryn Mawr, the University of Liverpool, and the University of Salford.

Yet, he found time to write fiction and establish himself as a novelist and playwright. Now that he has retired from his work as an economist, he devotes all his time to creative writing. In 1950, he was the recipient of the National Prize for Drama for his play *La paloma de cartón* (The Cardboard Dove), which premiered in 1952. His other play, *Un sitio para vivir* (A Place to Live), 1958, is a defense of ecology, twenty years ahead of its time.

Sampedro looks to writing as a labor of love. When the setting or the time is different from his own, he researches carefully every step to be taken. He spent nineteen years working on his novel *Octubre, octubre* (October, October), 1981, which he describes as a testament he wanted his only daughter to have. A deeply sensitive man, he expresses in *La sonrisa etrusca* (The Etruscan Smile), 1985, the emotion that a grandfather feels as he holds his grandchild in his arms. His other works include *Congreso en Estocolmo* (A Congress in Stockholm), 1952; *El río que nos lleva* (The River That Carries Us), 1961; *El caballo desnudo* (The Naked Horse), 1970; *La vieja sirena* (The Old Siren), 1990.

Although his literary production is not extensive, his works have a universal appeal and have made a tremendous impact on readers. In 1990, he was elected to the Spanish Royal Academy.

José Luis Sampedro lives in a top-floor apartment in Madrid, with a large terrace adorned with plants. As I arrived, he was listening to classical music. He led me into a bright living room where he showed me his owl collection and also explained that he finds it more comfortable to sit in an armchair to write than to sit at a desk. A tall, bearded man, there was something warm and kindly about him that gave the interview the personal tone of two people discovering they had many things in common. As I was about to leave, he took me to his study so I could see for myself that he keeps all his manuscripts, including every single draft. In another room, someone was typing the last pages of his novel *La vieja sirena,* which, as he explained, had undergone the metamorphosis of "monster" to "dragon," that is to say, had passed the draft stage and turned into the final copy.

❊❊❊❊❊❊❊❊❊❊❊❊❊❊❊❊❊❊❊❊❊❊❊❊❊❊❊❊❊❊

MLG: You don't like to sit at a desk when you work.

JLS: It's not that I don't like it, I'm just more comfortable sitting in an armchair with a board across it, so that I can write. It is easier on my back.

MLG: I hear music in the background, and I can't help noticing your collection of flutes.

JLS: I was listening to Kreisler performed by Itzhak Perlman, while I was waiting for you. When I work, I don't listen to music because I find it too distracting, but music is essential to my life and is reflected in my work. When I was young, I played the piano a little, but when I was really starting to make progress and getting good at it, the Civil War came along, and I had to stop. Afterward, I had to make a living and life took its course. As for the flutes, I bought them during my trip to Latin America. I spent three months in Chile while Allende was in power, working for the United Nations Conference on Trade and Development. Chile in those days was a wonderful, moving place, particularly for a Spaniard still living under Franco's dictatorship. So while I was there I traveled to neighboring countries and bought these flutes. I have never studied musical composition, but I am an enthusiastic amateur and can sight-read. When I write, I think in terms of musical composition. I combine phrases, wondering whether I should try to harmonize or write counterpoint.

MLG: Rhythm is very important to you, therefore.

JLS: Extraordinarily so. For *Octubre, octubre,* for instance, I drew some flow charts that went up or down, chapter by chapter, according to the intensity of the emotions felt by the characters. This would allow me to notice if two adjacent chapters were both sentimental, and whether I should interject a more realistic chapter in between. In this way, I would avoid being monotonous or repetitious. I'm very careful with things like that. I have some records of Beethoven sonatas I bought in London that show the additions and subtractions Beethoven made when he composed. I conceive literary composition in the same way: I begin with a subject, a character, or an idea, and if I see that it is not growing, I combine it with others, I introduce additional elements. It's very hard to explain, but it resembles musical composition more than anything else. The various characters can be compared to instruments; some are trumpets, others violins, or double basses.

MLG: If I were to ask you to give a geometric form to your works, I imagine you would rather turn to music.

JLS: Yes, that's so true. I would be more inclined to use a musical simile than a geometric one. I think that a literary work resembles a symphony more than anything else. Music and literature are diachronic arts, so time comes very much into play, unlike more static forms such as painting, sculpture, or architecture. *Octubre, octubre* would be a symphony, while *La sonrisa etrusca* would be a trio between Hortensia, the grandfather, and the grandchild.

MLG: I see you have a big library. Which books have influenced you over the years?

JLS: I have read a lot, in phases. I would like to read more philosophy now. But let me turn to my childhood years for a moment to explain some of these influences. I spent my childhood in Tangiers, which was then quite an international town, and a world very unlike Spain. I lived there until I was thirteen and it forms the crucible for my earliest memories. That place was like a paradise for me, because of the beaches in summer and the cosmopolitan atmosphere. Although we lived with other Spaniards in a colony, there were students in my school who were French, English, and so on. My father, who was a military doctor, had been sent to Tangiers to head a hospital. My mother, born in Oran, Algeria, to a Spanish immigrant and his Swiss-Italian wife, learned to speak Spanish when she was eighteen. My mother and grandmother used to speak French at home. And I have no problem with the language myself. My mother was a very sensitive woman who, in her days, had written some articles under the name of Colombina. She would narrate little things or describe street scenes. I found that out after her death. She loved Pierre Loti, and it was because of her that I read *Aziyadé, Ramuntcho,* and *An Iceland Fisherman,* among other things. Anyway, you were asking me what books have influenced me, and that's impossible to summarize. There are so many writers that I like that my list would be endless. I could say, though, that D. H. Lawrence greatly influenced me in the early 1940s.

MLG: If you could speak with some writer from the past, whom would you choose?

JLS: I don't know, perhaps with Quevedo, because in terms of handling the language, there is no one like him in Spanish literature, although I don't know whether I would like him so much as a person. I'd probably also want to speak with Cervantes, the man, not the author, because as an individual his life is very moving and worthy of compassion and admiration.

MLG: What would you ask Cervantes?

JLS: I would ask him if he was happy. But do you know with whom I would like to speak today?

MLG: With whom?

JLS: Ernesto Sábato. I consider him the most important writer of our time. I barely know him, but I agree with almost everything he says about life, philosophy, technique, and anti-technique. I sent him *La sonrisa etrusca* and he replied with a little note that I treasure. In it he wondered how a Spaniard could know so much about a peasant from southern Italy, because that's where his father came from. I found his words very encouraging.

MLG: Could we now perhaps turn to your work, and would you define it for me?

JLS: I have been writing for over fifty years. Some people think that I am merely an economist who began writing late in life, but I have been doing so since 1935. How would I define my work? I wouldn't really know what to tell you. I write because I can't help it or avoid it. My work only gained prominence in 1980, when *Octubre, octubre* was published. Until that time, I wrote because I felt I needed to, not to earn a living, although I was given some very good reviews. So I write to invent a world and share it with others. My concerns are not stylistic in the least, but I am interested in constructing my phrases well and in saying things as effectively as possible. I work very slowly; *Octubre, octubre* took me nineteen years to write, and the novel I have just finished, *La vieja sirena,* has been a long journey.

MLG: Why did you call it that?

JLS: In olden times, mermaids were not conceived as having the body of a fish, but of a bird. The Nereids or sea nymphs were the ones who had fish bodies, but calling the book "The Old Nereid" seemed a little awkward and I didn't think it would appeal as much because of its erudition. In any event, the plot deals with a sea woman who becomes a real woman, although— unlike other stories written along these lines—the fact that she turns into a woman is not my main concern. As I have said, my literature has no stylistic goals and does not claim to be avant-garde; I just want to tell a story as simply as possible, and I struggle to achieve this simplicity. In *La sonrisa etrusca,* for instance, I worked hard so that people might see that my words were transparent and that there was a clear meaning behind each one of them. I try to make what I wanted to say very obvious, and I exert myself to achieve this.

MLG: This is what Ana María Matute calls the "nonlanguage."

JLS: I didn't know that, but I think it is a wonderful term. Another important factor in my case is that I have always operated separately from the literary world (I haven't made my living as a writer), and what they call the "movida" (hip happenings) in Madrid nowadays. If I lived the "movida," of course, I wouldn't have time to write. So I have been isolated, a sort of furtive author who has published a novel or a play every seven or eight years, although novels are what I do best. Anyway, I am very happy with the life I have led. It is perhaps true that I would have written more had I devoted myself exclusively to being a writer, but earning my living with another profession has allowed me to write only the works I really liked.

MLG: What did you do for a living?

JLS: I am a retired professor of economics at the University of Madrid and I was a visiting professor in London and in the United States, at Bryn Mawr College. So I made my living as an economist. If I had chosen writing to earn my daily bread, I would have had to write newspaper articles and engage in technical writing, so to speak. But this way, what I have written truly came from the inside, and I am happy about that.

MLG: Is your life as an economist reflected in your writing?

JLS: Yes, but only indirectly in terms of human concerns. My literary work isn't related to the world of an economist, a banker, or a university professor, because I am not very interested in those topics.

MLG: How do you come up with titles in general, and *Octubre, octubre* in particular? I am interested in that work because I was born in October.

JLS: In some cases, I have the title before I start writing, while in others I really have to struggle to come up with one. Since it took me nineteen years to write *Octubre, octubre,* I played around with a lot of different titles before settling on that one. I like it because it is very effective, direct, easy to remember, and symbolic. October is an ambivalent month: on the one hand, it is revolutionary (Red October and all that), while on the other it is also melancholic because it represents the onset of fall and winter. This dichotomy is also present in the novel, which is concerned with two different options for human salvation: going up toward the sun or down toward the night. It seemed like a good title therefore.

MLG: I sense that you would want to say something more about that work, and that it means something very special to you.

JLS: Yes, it is a very long and complex novel. It considers two possible alternatives for human salvation: that of passion—violent, physical love—and that of the spirit as shown by a character who leads a mystical life. But the action is rather complicated, and the novel is the most difficult I have ever written. The mystical character, for instance, has been trying to write a novel all his life, and his work is superimposed on mine, along with my thoughts and reflections. Excuse me for digressing here, but I must say that you inspire me to speak of things that I don't usually discuss, like the fact that *Octubre, octubre* was written as a will. I wanted my only daughter to know what her father was like. That novel, therefore, is a self-portrait into which I poured everything I could over a period of nineteen years.

MLG: What was your relationship with that author within the novel? Did you find him saying things you wouldn't want to utter?

JLS: We are both strong, but we never had to struggle against each other. There are four characters in that work: a human couple called Agata and Luis, who are the primary characters, Miguel, the spiritual protagonist I just spoke of, and myself. Agata and Luis lead a passionate, erotic, but complicated life. There are also a series of secondary characters, who are not really secondary. It is difficult to summarize the novel. The plot takes place in Madrid for the most part, but there are some digressions to seventeenth-century Istanbul, during the reign of Suleiman II. I have been very pleasantly surprised that such a relatively complicated work (although I have read many novels that were far more difficult) has been so successful. It is now in its twelfth printing, and young people read it a lot and say they like it.

MLG: How did you come up with the plot for that novel, and was it a labor of love over those nineteen years?

JLS: Your question elicits many things. It's a very strange story. The novel prior to *Octubre, octubre* was called *El río que nos lleva;* it is an adventure novel, and it took me nine years to write. After I finished it, I resolved to write a simple novel in which I would confine myself exclusively to the love between two characters. I would leave everything else out and concentrate on these two characters as though they were in a test tube. I would confine them to a wedding bed like those they used in the Renaissance, with drawn curtains all around, and watch how their love grew. My original locale for the novel was a house in Madrid, but I found I couldn't really write the work that way. I then thought of adding political elements to the book, but this debased the love story, although I did leave a chapter chronicling some demonstrations during the time of Franco in the novel. Anyway, at that point, I decided to give the male character a belief in reincarnation, so that he would have a psychological basis for continuing to live and not kill himself. I don't support or reject the notion of reincarnation in the novel, but the character thought he had been a slave in the harem of Suleiman II in Constantinople. I did a lot of research on this period, although most of it may not be apparent in the book. After all this, I still found the novel lacking a spiritual dimension. Although I don't follow any particular religious creed, I do believe that the spirit plays an important role in one's inner life, so I added the mystical character I referred to before. The novel I first envisioned as short and simple became extremely complicated. That's the way it goes.

MLG: What is the story behind *La sonrisa etrusca?*

JLS: The first few pages of a copy of that work that I am going to give you explain how that novel came about. But to give you a brief account of the inspiration for that book, I should tell you that I have a daughter and a newborn grandson living in Strasbourg. This last Christmas, when the child was fourteen months old, I went to visit them. I am a light sleeper, so when the baby would wake up crying at two or three in the morning, I would go to comfort it, since my wife and I were in the adjacent room. When I went in there, I noticed that the city was covered with a fresh coat of snow and that there was a stunning moon in the night sky. As I was tending to the baby, I became overwhelmed by the startling beauty of the scene, and I began thinking what would become of that child, and if he would ever have the chance to know me. So I wrote a five- or six-page short story called "El abuelo" (The Grandfather). As it grew and became more complex, I changed the title to *La sonrisa etrusca*. The plot concerned a grandfather who had been raised in a traditional rural culture, and his son and daughter-in-law, who were far more modern, and who had adopted different ways of raising a child. To be completely truthful, I wasn't particularly keen on the child being put in his own room at such an early age. After considering Spain and Greece, I settled on Italy as the book's locale, and decided to make the Etruscan terra-cottas a symbol for the novel. I think there are two astounding smiles in the universal statuary: the ineffable expression on the Buddha's face, and the smile of the Etruscan terra-cottas, where the dead were represented as eating grapes and being merry on their own graves. I found this an extraordinary celebration of life, and that's how the novel came about. It has been very successful and there is a German translation of that work and a Portuguese one is in preparation.

MLG: Why do you think that novel has been so successful?

JLS: People say it has a lot of warmth. In any case, this is what I tried to convey. The plot deals with an old man from Calabria who was a partisan during the war, and a shepherd at other times. He never knew his parents, and he made his money working in the fields. He had always been a man of great vitality and enormous energy, and he was quite a womanizer. But now he has fallen prey to cancer, and so his son, a chemist married to an archaeologist, brings his father to Milan, where he lives, to have specialists take a look at him. When the old man arrives in Milan, he discovers that he has a grandson, which he didn't know. I have noticed that men from the country often don't acknowledge the existence of their children until they are full grown and start to till the soil and help out on the farm. While they are small, they consider them as belonging to the realm of women. A relationship develops between this child, who cannot yet speak, and his grandfather. The old man soon objects to the way the baby is being raised: for instance, he doesn't want the baby to eat baby food bought at the pharmacy, because he thinks it should drink "firewater" and eat as they do in the village, so that it may grow strong. The grandfather also disapproves of the baby sleeping in a room apart from his parents. So he wages a type of cold war on his son and daughter-in-law, and at night, he goes to the baby's room, cuddles it, and tells it stories. He wants to be a father and a mother to that child. There is a very touching scene where the mother and grandfather are buttoning the baby's shirt. While she is on the tenth button, he is still struggling with the first, his big, strong peasant hands incapable of such a delicate task. But meeting the child's needs is so important to him that he locks himself in his room with the shirt and practices until he masters buttoning it. One day, while strolling through the park with the baby, he meets a widow who is also from the south, and a platonic love develops between them. That's when the grandfather realizes that although he has made love to many women in his lifetime, he didn't really know any of them, not even the girl who loved him and understood him during the war. To go back to your question, I think that people have identified with the novel because it is deeply human.

MLG: I hope it will soon be translated into English. People would love it here. Have other of your novels been translated?

JLS: *El río que nos lleva* has been translated into Russian and into Romanian, although I didn't request the latter. Some of my works on economics have been translated into English.

MLG: How did you arrive at the title *El río que nos lleva?*

JLS: In 1930, I was thirteen years old and lived in the beautiful town of Aranjuez. In those days, I would see American lumbermen who had cut trees down in the Sierra of Cuenca floating them downstream on the Tajo River. These people were so rugged and primitive that I felt compelled to write about them, although I was only thirteen at the time and had no intention of becoming a great storyteller. I would take long walks and dream about being a good second-rate writer. I looked at writing as something very important and my standards were very high. When I say second-rate, it's not false modesty on my part. After fighting on the losing side of the Civil War, I decided I would write *El río que nos lleva.*

MLG: What did you think of the movie that was made of that novel, starring the son of Gregory Peck?

JLS: It's not a great movie, but it was fairly well done and quite decent. I know something about movies because in 1935 I was already a member of a film club in Madrid. Madrid in those days of the Republic was home to real culture, although this may be the nostalgic opinion of an old man. Films are a completely different form of expression than novels. They must capture the essence of the novel and add another dimension. They cannot be a mere reproduction of one's work. I was fortunate that the screenplay for *El río que nos lleva* was written by the excellent Uruguayan scriptwriter Antonio Larreta, with whom I got along very well. The movie itself was filmed with great simplicity and without any tricks in the province of Cuenca. All of the actors did their own stunts, and they worked quite well as a team. The film also didn't star famous actors, something I liked, because they tend to detract from the characters they play. More specifically, the public focuses its attention on big stars, but does not see the characters for themselves.

MLG: Why have you kept your first two attempts at writing from being published?

JLS: Neither of my first two novels has ever been published. The first was called "La estatua de Adolfo Espejo," and I haven't wanted it published because I consider it very amateurish. The other one is titled "La sombra de los días," and they can publish it when I am dead and they can deem me a genius. The first of my works to be published was *Congreso en Estocolmo*. It is an account of a scientific meeting held in Stockholm, and it went into two or three editions. *El río que nos lleva* came next, followed by *El caballo desnudo* and *Octubre, octubre*.

MLG: What happens to an author when he is in the middle of one work and an unrelated theme crops up?

JLS: I am always writing two or three novels at the same time, until one of them decides that it will take precedence over the others. Basically, I play with the ideas in my head and on paper until one of them absorbs me more than the others. When that happens, I forget everything else and immerse myself completely in a particular work.

MLG: Are you inside or outside the book when you write?

JLS: Completely inside. I do a tremendous amount of research precisely so that I can get inside the book. My golden rule when writing is that if I don't believe my own story, I cannot expect anyone else to. The convincing trickster is he who believes his own story. So I have to believe my own tale, and I could show you all the research I do to get to this point, although most of it doesn't show up in the final draft of my books. For instance, to speak about a neighborhood in Madrid, I felt the need to have all the plans for that area dating back to the seventeenth century. I copied all of them and super-imposed them, so that when I say something was at a particular spot, it most certainly was there. Likewise, in *La sonrisa etrusca,* when I say that tram X went up street Y, it most assuredly did, because I have to believe it.

MLG: So details are very important for you.

JLS: Yes, the smallest of details, such as a broken tooth, a run in a stocking, a broken heel, and so on, are what make the commonplace real.

MLG: Through the use of details, don't you also transform fantasy into reality?

JLS: Yes, what is fantastic is more credible that way because you can hold on to it, it's not lost in the ether. For instance, in my novel *El caballo desnudo,* I tell a rather satirical story about a woman in Madrid in 1917 who sees a naked horse on the street. She's so scandalized by the sight that she decides to create the League for Animal Morals, with the purpose of clothing animals so as to avoid outraging people. This is all fantastical and a bit grotesque. So fantasy and reality are combined here.

MLG: Do you have a favorite among your works?

JLS: It's like having children—you love them all for different reasons. Without a doubt, the most important work I have written is *Octubre, octubre.* The work is perhaps too ambitious and somewhat uneven, because it is difficult to sustain the quality over six hundred pages, but to date, it is my most significant book, although *La vieja sirena* may supplant it. *La sonrisa etrusca,* meanwhile, is the novel that I wrote the best, in the sense that it corresponds most closely to what I wanted to say. It's been very successful—there have been fourteen printings since it came out in 1985— although I don't think it is as important as *Octubre, octubre.* I love *El río que nos lleva* because it deals with a topic that is so ferociously Iberian and Hispanic. *El caballo desnudo* is my criticism of Spanish morals, and it was published during Franco's time. *Congreso en Estocolmo* is a first work, and although it may be a little naive, some people like it a lot. What do you want me to say? I love all my works, and each for different reasons.

MLG: Do you see writing as a craft or a profession?

JLS: I often read novels with great premises that are wonderfully written but that haven't been worked out sufficiently. I may not be a good writer, but I am a thorough craftsman, and I delve deeply into my subjects. In *Octubre, octubre,* I quote Saint John of the Cross, who says, "Let us enter more deeply into the thickness." For me, a writer is like a miner who goes down the shaft to extract minerals from the earth. I too descend into myself to uncover what is inside and bring it out. Writing is a way of life. Many years ago, I read an interview with Victoria Ocampo, the Argentine author whom I admired very much, in which they asked . . .

MLG: I knew her.

JLS: Good for you, I wasn't so lucky. In an interview, they asked her what she thought of herself, and she replied that she was a human being seeking to express herself. I try to do the same. Why do I feel the need to write? At my age, my only ambition as an author is to be minimally genuine; I couldn't care less about the rest. I tell you most truthfully: all of my books are love letters, some to specific people, others to the general public. I write because I need to express myself and communicate with others; without people, we are nothing. You could see my works as mendicant literature, a plea for others to like me.

MLG: Well, I can tell you your readers feel very close to you. By the way, do you think about them when you write?

JLS: Once in a while I may have a specific reader in mind, but I usually think in terms of a group of readers that shares my predilections. I don't become a reader myself. I am like a madman, speaking to myself.

MLG: Who is your primary reader?

JLS: Usually, I am. I don't talk about my novels with anyone until they are finished. Once the manuscripts were completed, my wife, who died two years ago, was the first to read them. The only exception to this scheme was *La sonrisa etrusca.* I wrote that work with relative ease chapter by chapter over a period of three years, and in that case I read each chapter to my wife as it came out; don't forget that it dealt with our grandchild. But generally speaking, I don't discuss my works with others, because I don't want to be influenced, and I need to be alone.

MLG: Do you find writing to be a solitary journey?

JLS: Undoubtedly, but let's make sure what we are talking about. I write alone, but I am surrounded by many external elements. It's like walking through a garden alone picking the flowers that others have grown.

MLG: You are quite a poet.

JLS: In part. I started out writing poetry, like almost everyone else. I have 100 or 150 poems I wrote in my distant youth that haven't been published. Actually, I gave six or seven of them to a painter friend of mine who had them published together with his engravings. On more than one occasion, I have been told that my prose is quite lyrical.

MLG: The way you speak is equally lyrical and warm.

JLS: Yes, I do think I am warm, and perhaps lyrical in this sense. You're speaking to me about things that are very close to my soul. As I told you at the beginning, writing is my life; I don't do it to earn a living.

MLG: When you were a university professor, how did you find the time to write?

JLS: I would get up at 5:30 A.M. and start writing at 6:15 until about 8:00 or 8:30, because everything was quiet during those two hours and my wife was sleeping. At 8:30, I had to leave for work and this was sometimes very frustrating for me. Nevertheless, I continued writing whenever I could: during the summers, when I was on vacation, on weekends. Like many other authors, I also carried a little notebook everywhere I went, jotting down anything that struck me. That's how my books were written. They were all published before I retired from the university, except for the last one.

MLG: Do ideas just strike you when you start writing?

JLS: Sometimes, a novel starts with one or two characters; on other occasions, it begins with a situation. *Congreso en Estocolmo,* for instance, was based on a trip I took to Sweden in 1950 to attend a meeting of economists. For a Spaniard in 1950, Sweden was like another planet, and I wanted to write about it. On the other hand, *La sonrisa etrusca* started with the old man and his grandson. The premise for a book can vary, therefore.

MLG: What are your personal views on the role of characters in a book?

JLS: I try to create them because they are fundamental to the plot. Like Flaubert, I believe that I am Madame Bovary. Occasionally during a colloquium they will ask me if a particular work was autobiographical, and I will reply that all novels are autobiographical. What occurs is that those works don't talk about what actually happened to the author, but what he would have liked to transpire or not transpire, as the case may be. I cannot envision any other way of inventing novels than with my sweat and blood.

MLG: Do you control your characters or do they become independent of you?

JLS: Sometimes they resist what I want them to do. I had to rewrite *Octubre, octubre* four times, because the characters refused to accept the endings I proposed. I don't want to give the impression that my characters have a life of their own, but when you create them, you limit them and their options, and they cannot realistically do certain things that you might want them to. This is the negative aspect of resisting the author's will to which I was making reference. When I finished that novel and took it to the publisher, the pile of everything I had written stood more than four feet tall, and I am not exaggerating.

MLG: Do you destroy all those drafts or do you keep them?

JLS: I have kept them all. I don't destroy anything. Let them destroy things when I am dead, if they want.

MLG: Could I assume then that you like to polish your work?

JLS: Not "polish," I don't very much like that word, because I don't strive for the beauty of a phrase, just its maximum effect. What I mean is that I turn a phrase over in my head until I'm sure it says what I want it to say. I don't much care if the words are elegant or ugly.

MLG: Do your characters lean toward dialogues or monologues?

JLS: Toward both. My paragraphs vary in terms of narration and length depending on which character is in them. In *Octubre, octubre,* for instance, Agata speaks in very short phrases, with many periods, and she tends to jump from topic to topic. You may get mad at me for saying this, but I have found that women do skip around when they talk, without necessarily digressing. Luis, meanwhile, speaks in long paragraphs and his language is far more baroque. As the novel progressed and Agata and Luis became closer, Agata's language became more like that of Luis and, in turn, he began talking like her. At the end of the novel, their two monologues merge into one, and they speak together.

MLG: A little like Don Quixote and Sancho who end up speaking like the other.

JLS: Exactly.

MLG: Would you ever devise a novel where characters play no role?

JLS: At a colloquium held in Madrid recently, I was on a panel with Montserrat Roig, the author, and some young critic. After we described the way we wrote, the critic remarked somewhat condescendingly that our approach was very traditional in comparison to those authors who devise novels without characters. Although I don't accept it for myself, I acknowledge the fact that some novels are conceived without characters. But I was completely flabbergasted by the example he quoted. He said that Miguel Delibes's *Five Hours with Mario* was an instance of a novel without characters. This is absolutely untrue, that novel is full of characters. I am not much concerned with the sophisticated terms critics use today, I can only talk about the technical problems I encounter while writing. In my latest novel, *La vieja sirena,* I have the following characters: the first is that of the narrator, namely I, who tells the story, which takes place in third-century Alexandria, in the present tense. Then there are the inner thoughts of a couple of characters, also told in the present. Finally, there is a third-person narrative told in the past tense recounting the memories of the characters. Occasionally, I will combine the first- and third-person narratives with the present and the past in order to give a different perspective. In that particular novel, there are more dialogues than monologues.

MLG: Could you explain what going through the last writing stage of a novel entails?

JLS: Let me use my last novel, *La vieja sirena,* as an example. When I reached the stage of what I call the monster, I knew the first draft of the novel was completed. I call it that because you have to reckon with it. In this case, the monster was 510 pages long. Once you have the monster, you know you are ready to deal with the dragon, which is slowly taking on a shape of its own.

MLG: Does that mean that you have reached the point where you can transfer the dragon onto the typewriter or the computer?

JLS: Not quite. I have to resist doing that. I still have to take the monster apart and put it together again, so that in that process the dragon will emerge with a definitive shape. I imagine that many authors would probably be tempted to publish the book in its primary form, but not I. The reason for it is that I come up with notions that I feel must be included at the beginning, which propel me to reconstruct the whole symphony. I have all the themes and the melodies, but I must incorporate the chords and the counterpoints. So the process of composing is endless. The book in its final form has 600 pages and I hope it is not inferior to my other works. I would like to think that it will trigger various levels of reading and open new avenues. No, I don't work with a computer, I sold mine because I never learned to tinker with it long enough. I am an old man, although I don't discard the possibility of getting used to a word processor. I managed just fine without it so far with all my books. We'll see about the next novel.

MLG: Nature must mean a lot to you. Your terrace has a beautiful array of flowers. Does nature also play a part in your books?

JLS: It depends. In *Congreso en Estocolmo,* for example, Nordic nature is enormously important. Someone reminded me yesterday that I wrote that book forty years ago. People are particularly fond of a scene where an old reindeer is approached by a young doe, but he is so aged that he dies. Several characters witness the biological tragedy of his death, and there is a lot of discussion about the woods and lakes of Stockholm. Nature does play a role, and so do animals, as symbols of that nature.

MLG: I can't help but notice that you have quite a collection of owls. What do they represent for you?

JLS: Those are just whims. I don't have many paintings, although I do own many books about them. I like owls because they are very decorative and because they are the only ones that can beat eagles after dark. It's a very peaceful bird, a good provider for its offspring. I also keep stones and things

I have picked up here and there. I'm old and I find pleasure in these objects, because they remind me of things I've seen and places I've been. But I am not an art collector. They are just memories for me. I don't like classifying objects, as they do in museums, nor do I like traveling with a camera or anything of the sort. I think you have to let life select your memories and create a museum of your past. I've a fairly good memory.

MLG: I would like to ask you a question which has nothing to do with you as a writer. What is your personal opinion on the festivities of the discovery of America?

JLS: They've tried to involve me with that trifling event. I would like Spain to stop glorifying its dubious history in America, and turn its sights to 1993. It could represent the beginning of a new culture we would refer to as Greco-Roman, not Ibero-American, because that has all sorts of negative connotations. I think there are two different types of culture in Europe: one that is Anglo-Saxon—but not Nordic, because that is something else—and very pragmatic, and one that is Mediterranean. The first one extended to the United States, while the second went to what is called today Latin America. Mediterranean culture has Greek and Roman roots, and it is not solely concerned with producing and consuming. It likes life and knows how to enjoy it. I would like to think that at a time when money and technology are destroying so many cultures, several will survive into the twenty-first century. I would hope that they be Anglo-Saxon, Hindu, Islamic, Asian, and Mediterranean. By Mediterranean I imply whatever lies between the Aegean Sea and Patagonia. I find it more important to devote ourselves to this notion of culture than spending our time with small talk about the past. I also fear that the 1992 celebrations are not going to amount to very much; there will be a few exhibits, spectacles, shows, and a Disneyland atmosphere. It would be far more significant if the six smallest nations in Central America agreed to unite, because they cannot subsist on their own in our technological age. That this small request be entertained would be far more important than anything else.

MLG: I feel there is very little difference between José Luis Sampedro, the man and the writer.

JLS: It's possible that there may not be, it's possible. What I will tell you is this: I am seventy-two years old, but my curiosity is still extraordinarily alive. I consider myself a craftsman in the highest sense of the term. I have labored long and hard and with great determination to be what I am today. In terms of keeping my vitality, I do what I can.

MLG: You're doing a good job. You were born on February 1, the same as my mother, and your granddaughter was born on October 4, and I on October 3. I feel there is some kind of an invisible link.

JLS: One thing is very clear: within ten minutes of meeting someone, you know if they speak the same language you do, and I think you talk in the same musical key as I do—G minor.

Gonzalo Torrente Ballester

MARIE-LISE GAZARIAN GAUTIER

Gonzalo Torrente Ballester was born in 1910 in El Ferrol, La Coruña, an important military port of Galicia. As a young man he graduated with a master's degree in history from the University of Santiago de Compostela, where he later served on the faculty. He also taught language and literature in other universities. In 1947, he moved to Madrid where he became drama critic for the daily *Arriba*. In 1964, he went back to Galicia and lived for two years in Pontevedra. From 1966 to 1972, he taught Spanish literature at the University of Albany in New York.

During those busy years as professor and critic, Torrente Ballester found time to write plays and then turned exclusively to novels. *El señor llega* (The Master Comes), 1957, the first volume of the trilogy *Los gozos y las sombras* (Pleasures and Shadows), received the 1959 Novel Prize from the Fundación Juan March. In 1960 and 1962, respectively, appeared *En donde da la vuelta el aire* (Where the Air Turns) and *La Pascua triste* (The Sad Easter), the other two volumes of that trilogy; a very popular television adaptation was made of the latter.

Among his other works are *Don Juan,* 1963; *Off-side,* 1969; *La saga/fuga de J. B.* (The Saga/Fugue of J. B.), winner of the 1972 Crítica Prize; *Fragmentos de Apocalipsis* (Fragments of Apocalypsis), 1977; *Las sombras recobradas* (Recovered Shadows), 1979; *La isla de los jacintos cortados* (The Island of Cut Hyacinths), 1980; *Los cuadernos de un vate vago* (The Notebooks of a Lazy Poet), 1982; *Hombre al agua* (Man Overboard), 1987; *La otra orilla: las manos son inocentes* (On the Other Bank: The Hands Are Innocent), 1988; *Filomeno, a mi pesar* (Filomeno, despite Myself), for which he won the 1988 Planeta Prize; *Crónica del rey pasmado* (Chronicle of the Astounded King), 1989.

Torrente Ballester won the 1985 Miguel de Cervantes Prize. One of

273

today's most prominent novelists, he is humble about his work and displays a great sense of humor. Married twice, he has four children by the first marriage and seven by the second. He now lives in Salamanca.

When I arrived at the Gran Hotel of Salamanca, where Gonzalo Torrente Ballester had arranged to meet me, I found him sitting in a comfortable arm-chair reading a newspaper, his eyes hidden behind thick, dark glasses. He was wearing a blue shirt and a plaid tie, with a navy double-breasted jacket and gray pants. He told me that he made it a habit to spend his mornings there. When I sat down across from him, before I could say anything, he asked, "What's your opinion on tobacco?" It was his way of asking me, "Do you mind if I smoke?" When I told him I didn't mind, he took out a Davidoff Havana cigarette and lit it. Then the interview proceeded. He was interview-ing me, deciding for me who should or should not be in my book. There was a flow about his conversation which, he said, he owed to his fifty years of teaching. He spoke in a clear, very direct fashion, with a typical Galician humor, punctuating the last word of most sentences with laughter. As the interview ended, we walked out together on the beautiful plaza, and we were stopped by his youngest son who happened to pass by at that very moment.

GTB: Your book of interviews sounds very interesting, but you should include some young writers in it as well.

MLG: I can't fit them all into one volume!

GTB: These young writers are going to feel very bad about that. For instance, you should include Muñoz Molina; you must find him any way you can, because among younger writers (those forty years old or less) he is going to be a great novelist. You should leave no stone unturned in your search.

MLG: I will do just that the moment I get back to Madrid, I promise. But let me first enjoy the beautiful city of Salamanca, its Gran Hotel, and your stimulating company. You are one of Spain's foremost novelists, but you are also known for your essays, reviews, and drama.

GTB: I used to write all those things, but now I devote myself exclusively to novels.

MLG: Why?

GTB: Keep in mind that I am a fairly old man and that while the theater has evolved a great deal, I haven't followed it. I will even say that the current forms of theater don't interest me, and consequently not only have I stopped writing for the stage (I wrote all of my plays half a century ago), but I don't even go to the theater anymore.

MLG: Your novels, nevertheless, reflect all the literary genres. Might one say that you are a direct descendant of Cervantes?

GTB: I would like to think so.

MLG: If you could speak with him, what would you say?

GTB: I would ask him to give me his secret.

MLG: But I think you have already discovered it.

GTB: No, I circle around it, but I haven't yet arrived at its essence.

MLG: Is your sense of reality and fantasy derived from Cervantes or from Latin American authors?

GTB: From neither.

MLG: It's your own?

GTB: No, it is something that has been around in Europe for centuries. You don't have to go to Latin America to discover fantasy; it was created in Europe, not Latin America.

MLG: And who invented it?

GTB: A number of anonymous authors from long ago who told the tales of King Arthur and the Round Table.

MLG: You were born in Galicia. Do you think that you have inherited that spirit of adventure and imagination that Galicians are known for?

GTB: I hope so. If the fatherland of writers is their childhood, then the clues to my personality lie in my boyhood. One of my best books, *Dafne y ensueños,* is a narration of my childhood that combines real and fantastic elements.

MLG: Why that title?

GTB: Because there is a more or less imaginary character called Dafne, and because it is a book that mixes the real with the fantastic. It has some ten chapters, and I alternate those chapters we could call autobiographical with those in which aspects of my autobiography are transformed and become fantastic, always within limits. The action takes place over a ten-year period.

MLG: Do you consider yourself a romantic?

GTB: Half romantic, half rationalist. Keep in mind that I am a Gemini, I was born on June 13, and I have always had at least two personalities that were nurtured by the world in which I lived, where both the fantastic and the rational coexisted. I was born in a city called Ferrol, built in the eighteenth century, where the right angle predominates, and the streets run parallel or perpendicular to each other, forming perfect squares. Perhaps that's why mathematics was emphasized so much when we were children. If you find this surprising or contradictory in someone with Mediterranean blood, all I can tell you is that you need humor to resolve this dilemma. If I didn't have a sense of humor, I would have had to jump out of the window, kill people, or take drastic steps like that. Humor is the means to neutralize tragedy. Fantasy, meanwhile, is another outlet, one which feeds the creative process.

MLG: What is reality for you?

GTB: Everything.

MLG: How do you feel about fantasy?

GTB: I need it and accept it. It has been a part of me since I began to have memories. I believe personality is formed in childhood and destiny is determined then. Life is the struggle against reality from which destiny results.

MLG: How would you describe fantasy?

GTB: Fantasy consists in displacing a real element from its proper sphere and placing it in a sphere that is not its own. Reality is a very complex thing, everything is real, each thing is in its own reality. The Pythagorean theorem is not in the same reality as this newspaper I am showing you, for instance. If I were to place this newspaper into the Pythagorean theorem, that would be an illustration of the fantastic. Let me give you an example: the dragon is a fantastic figure comprised of elements which, taken separately, are real—its claws are those of a tiger, its body that of a lion, its tail that of a serpent, and its heads are those of dogs. All these real elements that belong in other spheres are combined into a new fantastic object which is the dragon. So the technique of fantasy is to take objects out of their proper spheres in reality and place them in other areas of reality to make up a new object.

MLG: Do you achieve this by turning to detail?

GTB: That depends on the technique of the author or painter.

MLG: Do you paint?

GTB: No, very badly, it's not my field.

MLG: I have noticed that in the homes of the many writers I have interviewed there are a lot of paintings. I imagine you love art as well.

GTB: Well, it is one thing for me not to be able to paint and quite another to appreciate art. I love the arts but I am very clumsy at painting or drawing, or playing music for that matter. Among the plastic arts, my favorite is architecture; I am very interested in architecture.

MLG: Nevertheless, you chose to write. What made you become a writer?

GTB: That is something that happened so long ago that the only thing I can tell you is that I was eleven years old when I made a bet with a school friend that I would write a novel, and that's what I did. I became so enthusiastic about writing that I have been doing it ever since.

MLG: Do you consider writing a solitary endeavor?

GTB: Yes, although one has to depend a lot on others, because they provide the raw materials. I don't consider myself the subject of the book, and my books are never personal confessions, they are always worked out in relation to experience, and experience is always the result of dealing with reality. I need others, therefore, as a starting point for inventions that later do not resemble reality although they proceed from it. You will find that everything that I have written has a reference to reality.

MLG: Are you like García Lorca, who would hide in the garden to see what was happening in the house next door, and use that reality as a springboard for his fantasy?

GTB: I never did precisely that. My personality and my world are totally unlike García Lorca's. Otherwise I would have been a poet and not a novelist.

MLG: Have you ever written poetry?

GTB: I wrote as much poetry as was necessary when my novels called for a poem. But no, I was never a poet, I never sang about my loves or tribulations, nothing like that.

MLG: Could we nonetheless say that your prose is poetic?

GTB: Sometimes. Of course, the fact that I haven't written verse does not mean that I am insensitive to lyricism . . .

MLG: Or to rhythm.

GTB: Or to rhythm fundamentally. Every prose writer has to find a rhythm for his work.

MLG: What do you feel when you write?

GTB: Nothing. The need to write.

MLG: When do you write?

GTB: I write when I feel like it, when I have something to tell. Nothing more, nothing less. I am not a systematic worker, nor do I worry if I die before I can finish a novel. What's written is there, and what wasn't will be swallowed up by the other world.

MLG: Do you think of the reader when you write?

GTB: No, but I recognize that each reader has the right to read the work the way he wants to. A book is written from one point of view but may be read from another. There are points of agreement between me as an author and you as a reader because we are contemporaries, but there are also great differences. The reader judges and lives those differences from the perspective of his personality, not mine.

MLG: So the reader becomes a co-author.

GTB: Obviously, but each one of us is going to take the novel in a different direction. You will not interpret it the same way as the waiter who served us our coffee would.

MLG: It is like looking at a painting; each one sees it from a different perspective. I think Cervantes taught us this.

GTB: We should have learned it from him, because he is in all those perspectives. These different interpretations are the basis of everything that is being done today, particularly in Germany, where the point of view of the reader is based on that reality.

MLG: A TV series was based on your book *Los gozos y las sombras.* Did you like this visual interpretation of your work?

GTB: Yes, it was good and it provided a new dimension to my novel. As a result of the series, people began buying the novel, which had been around for over twenty years, although it had gone unnoticed. One of the few critics who bothered to read the book when it first came out in Spain said it was too old-fashioned to be of interest to anybody. However, it enjoyed great popularity in Buenos Aires, where it went into a fifth edition. Because of that work alone, I was better known in Argentina than in Spain. Since the movie, of course, a million and a half copies of the book have been sold in Spain.

MLG: Can you detach yourself from your work and become just another reader?

GTB: Yes, I become my own reader because I have to pass judgment on my own work and look at it with a critical eye. I then revise my work to the best of my ability. But when I write, all I am thinking about is the novel that I have before me. I am not interested in whether people are going to like it or not, or if a particular effect is going to be successful or not.

MLG: Do you have a primary reader of your work?

GTB: My primary reader is my wife, because she types the manuscript for me. But we don't really talk about the book. The most I will ask is whether she likes it, and she always replies that she does, even though it might not be a good book.

MLG: Do you reread your books?

GTB: No, never.

MLG: What about your books in translation?

GTB: Well, I do read the fragments that translators send me for approval. But I don't read them all, because there are many languages I don't know.

MLG: When you read a fragment in a language you know, what do you feel?

GTB: What I look for first is the accuracy of the translation and then its literary quality. At this time, for instance, I am happy with the French translations as they are very well done.

MLG: Are there any in English?

GTB: The British have been waiting to see how well my books would do in France before translating them. But my work is going to come out in Swedish, Danish, and German. The Germans do things so slowly that by the time my books come out in Germany I may be dead! I was just in Germany and they told me that the first of three volumes they are going to translate will come out in 1991. The other two will be published six months later, so everything will be done by 1992, and who knows if I'll still be living then.

MLG: Do you stand inside or outside the book during the creative process?

GTB: Outside, outside. Otherwise I wouldn't be able to write. If I were inside the work, I wouldn't be able to see things and steer the book, and I would run the risk of being dragged . . . I work with the elements that I invent and organize, and then I set them down on paper.

MLG: So when you sit at your desk, do you know exactly what you are about to write? Do you have a definite plan?

GTB: Yes, yes, yes.

MLG: Do you take notes?

GTB: Presently I don't, but I used to record my thoughts.

MLG: Do you write by hand?

GTB: No, I write on a typewriter and revise by hand.

MLG: There are writers who say that when they write they become the book.

GTB: Not I, I don't turn into the book. And if I did, I wouldn't write it.

MLG: What does the book mean to you?

GTB: Well look, something that has to be done, something that can be done. It requires of me to draw a line between what could be and what will be. I follow a path that leads back to the *Iliad,* which represents three different aspects of creativity: invention, composition, and expression. What Quintilian and Aristotle used to say continues to be true—one has to invent, combine, and write. Of course, every writer will carry out these processes in a different manner; for instance, some authors already have the novel in their heads before they write it, like me, while others start with only a vague intuition that becomes clearer as they write.

MLG: When you write, do you control the characters or do they control you?

GTB: I hope I control the characters inasmuch as they can be controlled, because there is always an unconscious element that works involuntarily and appears when I write.

MLG: What is writing for you?

GTB: I haven't always written for the same reason throughout my life. Right now I write because it is the only thing I know how to do. I suppose that at other times in my life it was an outlet, a mode of expression, or a necessity. Currently it is a game. It can be a sad game or a happy one, a conscious or unconscious one, but it is always a game in the sense of the objective manipulation of some data, like in a game of cards, for instance.

MLG: Do you enjoy playing with words?

GTB: No, I don't play with words a lot. I like to play with images, with characters, with inventions . . . that is to say, with all the imaginative elements.

MLG: What does the written word mean to you?

GTB: It is a necessary instrument which helps us attain the rhythm of the prose. The ordering of words according to their sound naturally determines the rhythm of the prose.

MLG: What do you feel when you finish a book?

GTB: The need to continue revising it, which would lead to its destruction. There comes a time when you should no longer revise because you might destroy. At least in my case, a book never leaves me satisfied, there are always other things that could have been done, eliminated, added, transformed, but of course at a certain point one can no longer do that because the work would be destroyed. When I reach that moment I say, very well, that's it.

MLG: Since we were speaking about architecture, what geometric form would you give to your books if you had to?

GTB: I have given geometric forms to many of my books. I could tell you, for instance, that my first book, *El viaje del joven Tobías,* which was written over fifty years ago, has the design of a six-pointed star, while *Don Juan* has the form of the Gothic arch of a cathedral. *La saga/fuga de J. B.* is in the shape of a spiral, or a fugue, a musical fugue. I always look for a well-balanced or unbalanced structure according to the theme of the book. I seek the ideal form as determined by the materials, and every set of materials will produce a different form. My basic problem is to discover which one.

MLG: I have asked that question many times, and you are one of the few authors to answer it so directly.

GTB: Of course, because it is a fundamental problem for me. If you study all my narrative works patiently, you will see that there are many different forms there, and even formulas. The danger lies in trying to accommodate everything to fit one particular formula. This is what happened with novels in the nineteenth century, and why they are all virtually the same.

MLG: You have mentioned *La saga/fuga de J. B.* What led you to write such a wonderful book?

GTB: *La saga/fuga de J. B.* derives from a novel that I never wrote which would have been called "Campana y piedra" (Bell and Stone). Both *La saga/fuga* and *Fragmentos de Apocalipsis* are drawn from the raw materials for that book. It would have been an impossible work to write as it would have run to three thousand pages. So, little by little certain aspects of that novel became independent and gave way to other works. So far, two books have come from it, and it might give rise to more. If you read the middle section of *Los cuadernos de un vate vago,* you will find an account of the creative process that led to *La saga/fuga,* which was conceived and partially written in the United States over a period of three years. It started becoming independent of "Campana y piedra" in 1966 or 1967, and by the time I wrote the first chapter in 1970, the whole book was already thought out in my head.

MLG: Could you explain the creative process?

GTB: The creative process has two aspects: that of inventing the materials, and that of organizing them. I invented the materials easily and I began to write, and all of a sudden I had 400 pages that were useless, so I destroyed them, I burned them in the fireplace of my house in McKownville near Albany.

MLG: Wasn't that painful?

GTB: Yes, it hurt but I had no other choice, otherwise the novel wouldn't have been written. I needed a form that would allow me to manipulate simultaneously materials far removed from each other in time. When I first wrote the story, I started the action in 1000 B.C., which was a mistake. So I had to look for another approach, and I found that letting a character with a very different mind-set from mine tell the story worked much better than my telling it. He could tell it, I could not. Once I discovered this, writing the story became easy, but up to that point, I had a very hard time.

MLG: You are very objective about your own work, which means you are an excellent critic.

GTB: Don't forget that I was a professor of literature for forty years during which I had to explain what literature was, and this forced me to be critical. I was also a professional critic for many years, although nowadays I scrutinize only my own work. One has to be both just and implacable with oneself. It is very painful for me to have to eliminate things, but it has to be done because sometimes there is no alternative. This does not mean that I don't make mistakes, but at least I don't make them on purpose.

MLG: Sometimes there are several narrators in your works.

GTB: In *La saga/fuga* there is only one. His name is José Bastida and he narrates in the first, second, and third persons. But it is always he who narrates; his mental makeup is always the same.

MLG: Many critics and readers make the mistake of equating the narrative "I" of a novel with the "I" of the author.

GTB: Yes, sometimes it is a mistake and sometimes it is not. The "I" of *Jacintos cortados,* for instance, is not I, although it has elements of me. On the other hand, the "I" of *Dafne y ensueños* is I.

MLG: Your titles have a very poetic quality. What are the dynamics involved in coming up with your titles?

GTB: Some are a starting point, others an ending point. For instance, *Quizás nos lleve el viento al infinito* is the last sentence of the novel. Another example is *Donde da la vuelta el aire,* which is an expression I overheard in the street. I borrowed *Mi reino por un caballo* from Shakespeare because it suited the narration. *La isla de los jacintos cortados* came to me as I wrote the novel. In that work I mentioned twice a fictional place called "the island of cut hyacinths," and I thought it would be a pretty name for the book.

MLG: What about *La saga/fuga?*

GTB: In the notes to that book, you will find that *La saga/fuga* was first called "The Saga of J. M.," after General John Moore, who was a prominent figure in Galician history. But when I changed the action to a seaport, I could no longer use a general, so I had to invent an admiral, and I took the initials for the admiral's name from a brand of whisky, J&B. And all the characters came to be called J. B.

MLG: What about *Los cuadernos de un vate vago?*

GTB: It is a transcription of my notes; you might call it a diary of my work, including complete accounts of *La Pascua triste, La saga/fuga,* and *Fragmentos de Apocalipsis* as well as partial descriptions of *Don Juan* and *Off-side.*

MLG: Is it a play on words?

GTB: "Vate" is the Latin word for poet, and "vago" means a person who doesn't work very hard.

MLG: Nevertheless, you work a lot!

GTB: No, not really.

MLG: The theme of the Civil War is a recurrent one in your work, as in that of most Spaniards in the postwar era.

GTB: Political elements are a part of reality and so one has to use them sometimes, although never in an ideological or pragmatic manner, but quite simply as literary material. You will note that my description of the Civil War is nonpartisan. In the daily life of Spaniards, the Civil War is still felt as an undercurrent, and it sometimes surfaces in a literary form.

MLG: Is that what gave rise to your novel *El golpe de estado de Guadalupe Limón?*

GTB: Yes, the Civil War and the fact that there are two myths surrounding it. In my opinion, this is a crucial issue and one that is very infrequently discussed. The first myth won out over the second, the myth of Franco while he was living beat out the myth of Primo de Rivera, who was already dead. That's because Franco was alive and in power. This gave me a certain sensitivity toward myth, and it is one of the recurring themes in my work, which was first expressed in *Guadalupe.* The fact that the novel takes place in South America instead of Poland or Scotland is the result of my years as a professor of Latin American history. It has nothing to do with Valle Inclán's *Tirano Banderas.*

MLG: Why are myths so important?

GTB: Because we are living in the midst of myths. We are moving at a very frantic pace. An analyst of our current situation might detect ten or twelve myths of great significance in the political, social, economic, and historic realms.

MLG: Myths that become obsessions?

GTB: Sometimes, of course, but they serve to control the masses in any case. The myth is always something that symbolizes or represents a living reality, a hope, a memory, a desire, or whatever. *Perestroika* is a current myth, for instance.

MLG: Do you limit yourself to historical myths, or are you also subject to personal myths?

GTB: I am demythified. I am like the psychoanalyst who has to undergo analysis himself before he can practice. I am concerned with the problem of the myth on an intellectual level, and it is a recurrent subject in many of my novels; for instance, *Guadalupe Limón, Fragmentos de Apocalipsis,* and *Jacintos cortados.* The myth is the central theme of those three novels.

MLG: There are many writers who say they wear a mask. Isn't that a form of demythologizing?

GTB: There are some who wear masks, but I don't, I don't need them. I live in Salamanca, in relative isolation, and I don't involve myself much with anything. A mask is an instrument, a device to get along in society. I don't feel comfortable with a mask, I would rather be sincere. This is simple and objective, like me.

MLG: What impresses me is to see how little difference there is between you and your work. You are a very sincere, very authentic person.

GTB: But are you so sure that my work is sincere? I never intended it to be sincere or insincere.

MLG: You seem to be very religious. What can you say about your concept of God and the role of the writer before God?

GTB: I don't know if the word "concept" is the most appropriate in this case because God does not fit into a concept. He fills up one's personal totality. So the writer's stance before God is primarily a personal one, which has nothing to do with literature. Another approach to God might be called propagandist, for lack of a better word. Authors such as Graham Greene and Brownson, both Catholics, utilize this notion of God in their works. Finally, there is another approach to God, which is my own, and that is that the religious problem is a real one, and as such, one that can be fictionalized. Yes, I am religious. When I write a novel, however, I don't take sides. I don't write a book to invite anybody to believe in God, although there can be some character in the novel who may have some religious problems, while another does not.

MLG: Speaking of religion, do you see any resemblance between your work and that of Miguel de Unamuno?

GTB: No. I read much of Unamuno's work between the ages of twenty and twenty-three, but there is a radical incompatibility between us. I don't believe in tragedy. I am a Galician and Galicians don't believe in tragedy.

MLG: Which writers did influence you then?

GTB: My roots as a writer lie in Cervantes and the British novelists of the eighteenth century, particularly Sterne and Swift.

MLG: What about Chesterton?

GTB: Yes. He is a much more recent writer, obviously, but I read him early on in my life. He fell between my readings of Sterne's *A Sentimental Journey* and *Tristram Shandy*.

MLG: Has French literature influenced you?

GTB: Yes, especially in the areas of the theory of literature and criticism. Rabelais in particular has left a definite imprint on my work, notably in *La saga/fuga*. I am an avid reader of Baudelaire, but since I am not a poet, he has not influenced my writing. I enjoy reading French literature.

MLG: If you could speak with an author from the past, whom would you choose?

GTB: That would depend on the day, because one does not have the same interests every day. Nevertheless, I would have loved to speak with those two authors I just mentioned, Sterne and Swift. I never spoke with Chesterton, but I attended one of his lectures in Madrid around 1925. I would also have to say that I would have liked to hold a conversation with Pirandello, whose works I have read at great length and who has influenced me quite a bit.

MLG: Do you think critics are aware of those influences on your work?

GTB: When critics discuss some book of mine, they always look for incorrect references, because they are young people who have been raised on other works. Their point of reference is different from mine. For instance, they never mention that I have been influenced by Rabelais because they have never read him. They claim Joyce has influenced me, while the truth of the matter is that it is Rabelais who has. Of course, I have read Joyce and continue to read him. They all have read Latin American writers, but they are not familiar with the British writers of the eighteenth century. I'll tell you a funny story that happened to me in Cambridge, which illustrates what I am saying. I had been invited by a professor to lecture on *La saga/fuga*. After a three-hour session with his graduate students, I said to them: "In *La saga/fuga* there are some very concrete images that come from a contemporary British author. Let's see if by the time I return here next year you've discovered who he is." I came back the following year and they still hadn't found the answer. So I told them it was Chesterton and I gave them as homework to look for the specific book that had influenced me. I haven't gone back to Cambridge since then, but I often wonder whether they were able to come up with the title. Why didn't they think of Chesterton? Because he is a writer who is no longer read. Borges used to be an avid Chesterton reader, and so am I.

MLG: Do you see any parallels between your work and that of writers of the Boom, which would justify some of the comments those critics made?

GTB: Latin American literature is very imaginative. But as I said before, this is not something new. In fact, to produce good literature one has to write well and be imaginative. What happens is that writers from Spain are generally unimaginative, with the exception of Cervantes and authors from Galicia, like Cunqueiro. So when critics stumble across a writer like him, they look for references in Borges. Cunqueiro and I were very good friends, and I can tell you that he never read Borges. But there are many similarities between them, especially in the fact they both borrowed very little from reality. I differ from Cunqueiro in that I always start from something real, regardless of the many literary elements in my writings. Cunqueiro, on the other hand, didn't root himself in reality, he moved in a world of literary fantasies with which he worked marvelously well. He should have been on your list, but unfortunately he is dead. He would have been material for an amazing interview. He was such an eloquent and dazzling man.

MLG: How do you perceive your role as a critic?

GTB: My critical stance comes from my experience as a writer, not just from reading books. I think my best work of criticism is a small book called *El Quijote como juego,* which is based on my experience as an author, and is not the result of my systematic study of Cervantes or my scholarship about him. That's what critics very often lack: the inner experience of being an author and looking at the structure of a work from that point of view. The critics draw on a doctrine or a theory and, of course, they are very often wrong. This does not mean that there are not useful materials out there, especially in regard to terminology, where they are discovering adequate terms. Occasionally, they also come up with real insights, such as that the narrator of a novel need not be the author. To my thinking, this is the case with the *Quixote,* as with my *La saga/fuga.* I am not the narrator, just the writer. In *El Quijote como juego,* I point out that the narrator of *Quixote* knew the story inside out, because he had read it in Cide Hamete Benengeli's manuscript. Cervantes, on the other hand, did not know the story, he invented it as he went along. Even though this may sound like a paradox, it is very clearly stated in the book.

MLG: You used to be a history professor at the University of Santiago de Compostela before the war. Why did you choose to be a historian?

GTB: Because I liked it, I have always liked it and I continue to do so. There are historical references in all of my books, so the world of history exists for me.

MLG: As a novelist, do you play with history or remain faithful to it?

GTB: It depends, there are times when it is convenient for me to be faithful to it, and others when it isn't.

MLG: Would you care to comment on the five hundredth anniversary celebrations of the discovery of America, to be held in 1992?

GTB: I would like the truth to come out of that event. The discovery of America is a very controversial issue, of course, with many aspects that have been decried and many exalted. But I think we should strike a balance between the two, because the variables involved are the same as in other cases of colonization. What happened in America with Spain happened in Spain with Rome, more or less. But there are many political passions and many rivalries at play. Some place more emphasis on the discovery of America, others on its colonization. I'm afraid that nothing is going to come of this, however. A few speeches will be delivered, a few trips will be taken by some gentlemen who will attend the requisite banquets, empty talk will dominate the day, and it will all have been in vain. I think it should mainly be an event for historians.

MLG: Your vision of the world is all-encompassing. How do you bring together cosmic, scientific, and historical elements?

GTB: I'd like to be able to do so, because what I see happening now is increasing rupture, which contrasts with the ideal of the unity of vision of the era of humanism. I consider myself a humanist, but I can't achieve this unity by myself, as I have within me the same rupture as the outside world. Physics goes one way while cosmology goes another. I suppose that some-day they will come up with a single science. But I don't think it will happen immediately, in spite of the fact that it is a necessity and that many people are striving to establish it. When I was growing up, things hadn't yet come to this chaotic point and we still had ideas in common, a joint notion of reality. This notion has gradually been destroyed by technology, but I hope it can be rebuilt. We have a right to know what sort of world we live in. Right now, they give it to us in fragments, perhaps because of political, economic, or social priorities. But since I believe things are going to get better, I think there will come a time when the Renaissance ideal of the universal man will be achieved. This man, of course, will have more knowledge and a clearer view of reality than was possible during the Renaissance. But I don't think we can ever attain a stable and definite vision of reality. I believe reality cannot be measured. Although we increase our knowledge bit by bit, we never know enough. What we learn today will rectify what we learned in the past, while future knowledge will correct what is known today. In the final analysis, what matters is that a few men continue to have these concerns, and tell us what they are thinking and discovering.

MLG: What's your response to the state of our planet?

GTB: Let's say that I am disenchanted.

MLG: Why?

GTB: I think that at my age all people are disenchanted, I am no different from them. I am not completely disillusioned because, in spite of my age and my experience, I continue to be an incorrigible optimist. Nevertheless, my optimism is tempered by many reservations. There is no doubt that if one is interested in the future of the world, one has to acknowledge that there are presently many factors to make one fear for the future, such as the absolute control states have over individuals. There is a place where my file, and everybody else's, is kept, and where all the good and bad things that we have done have been recorded.

MLG: What are your thoughts on the pollution of our environment?

GTB: Let's see if nature still exists fifty years from now. I fear it is not going to fare so well. This is one of the most serious things that is happening and one of the most stupid. People can see only the short-term gains and don't realize that profits today mean a catastrophe for tomorrow. But people have always been stupid, there is nothing that can be done about that.

MLG: In the course of our conversation, I felt I was in the presence of a great humanist.

GTB: Please don't call me great. I am not that ambitious, I am just a simple storyteller who likes to play. What would I do if I couldn't play?

MLG: I can see you don't take yourself seriously.

GTB: No, God forbid. I don't take myself seriously at all. Is the interview over already? If you have something left to ask I am in no hurry. I don't think we have been talking nonsense, at least.

MLG: Who is Gonzalo Torrente Ballester?

GTB: Would you please give me five minutes so I can go make a phone call? Don't worry, I'll tell you who I am when I return. . . .

MLG: Did they give you the answer over the phone?

GTB: The answer could be the following: I am a man who has lived longer than he thought he would and whose legs are beginning to fail him, although not his head. So I live more with my head than with my legs, and since I have a lot of free time because I am retired, I am beginning to concern myself a lot with things I didn't have the time for earlier. For instance, I am concerned with cosmic, biological, and historical matters. Sometimes I write, but I don't write with a lot of enthusiasm, because nothing stirs enthusiasm within me. I try to have fun while I write, without great expectations that what I am doing is very important. It is enough for me that it be a worthy effort, because I don't believe that my creative talents today are what they were fifteen or twenty years ago. But I still write things and my only concern is that they be reasonably good, so no one can accuse me of having written them poorly. I hope I've been successful. If I have time, I will visit some cities and see some landscapes that I don't know. If I am lucky, I will also meet some interesting people. I am not aroused by many, but some are thought-provoking. My attitude is that of a man who waits. That's all.

MARÍA ESPAÑA

Francisco
Umbral

Francisco Umbral was born in 1935 in Madrid. As he himself tells it, he is the author of over seventy books and perhaps one million articles. A regular columnist for *El País,* he began his journalistic career in Valladolid writing for *El Norte de Castilla,* where Miguel Delibes worked and guided him. He says of him, "Delibes taught me how to write articles."

Umbral is known for his articles, chronicles, interviews, criticism, essays, biographies, memoirs, short stories, and novels. All his works are marked by a style and personality that are definitely his own. His fiction and nonfiction are closely related to his biography.

In 1975, Umbral received the Nadal Prize for his book *Las ninfas* (The Nymphs), with which he closed the cycle of four novels about childhood and youth. Winner of the César González-Ruano Prize for Journalism, he has been described as one of the most striking exponents of new journalism in Spain. Since Mariano José de Larra in the nineteenth century, no one had turned journalism into a literary genre. Like Larra in the romantic period, he has become the chronicler of the Madrid of his time, that of the Franco years, the period of transition, and the democratic Spain of today. But as he states in the following interview, he is also a chronicler of himself and of his forefathers.

Among his numerous books are *Lorca, poeta maldito* (Lorca, the Accursed Poet), 1968; *Amar en Madrid* (To Love in Madrid), 1972; *Diario de un español cansado* (Diary of a Tired Spaniard), 1975; *La noche que llegué al Café Gijón* (The Night I Came to the Café Gijón), 1977; *Diario de un escritor burgués* (Diary of a Bourgeois Writer), 1979; *España como invento* (Spain as Invention), 1984; *Memorias de un hijo del siglo* (Memoirs of a Child of the Century), 1986; *El día en que violé a Alma Mahler* (The Day I Raped Alma Mahler), 1988; *Mortal y rosa,* 1975 (*A*

Mortal Spring, 1980), his only novel translated into English, is a poignant account of the death of his only son.

One of Spain's most popular and prolific writers, Umbral nevertheless stands as a lonely man.

Over six feet tall, elegant, with a white scarf around his neck like a doomed romantic hero and poet, Francisco Umbral stood out among other writers in the Café Gijón. He had come from his home outside Madrid, where he now lives, to be interviewed. José Luis Castillo Puche introduced us. I sat down at a table between Umbral and his wife. A well-known photographer in her own right, she remained silent throughout the interview. Amidst the noise of the Café Gijón, with writers and journalists holding animated conversations, Umbral talked about himself and the many masks he wears, which reveal the inimitable presence of a man who is at the same time sardonic and sensuous, delicate and lonely.

❉❉❉❉❉❉❉❉❉❉❉❉❉❉❉❉❉❉❉❉❉❉❉❉❉❉❉❉❉❉❉

MLG: Since we are having crumpets here, what does the Café Gijón mean to you, on both the personal and historical levels?

FU: Well, from the historical standpoint, it is a café that is one hundred years old and has been frequented by all Spanish authors since the time of Galdós. Personally, I first came to this café in 1960 and I virtually lived in it for ten years, until 1970, when I stopped coming. I have returned since, and one of my books is dedicated to the Café Gijón. It is a collection of memories about the people, painters, writers, men and women who used to gather here and talk about their work. It is a long book of memoirs.

MLG: Let me begin with a very broad question: how would you define your work?

FU: It's primarily autobiographical, like an autobiography made into a novel, and it is very much alive.

MLG: Do you see some similarity with Larra?

FU: It's a comparison that's been drawn so many times in my life that it tires me a little, quite frankly. But, yes, there is a relation, not only because of the book I wrote about Larra, but also owing to the fact that we can both be considered chroniclers of Spanish society as seen from Madrid. He was critical of the society of his time, as I am of mine. The only difference is that he was brilliant and I am not.

MLG: Do you feel like a chronicler of your time?

FU: Yes, among other things.

MLG: What other things?

FU: I am also a chronicler of myself, my life, and the life of my family going back two or three generations, which I have also recounted in my novels. It is like a family saga in which different subjects are tackled.

MLG: You have written novels, biographies, essays, memoirs. With what genre do you feel most comfortable?

FU: It doesn't matter. I always do the same thing, I am always Francisco Umbral. I am comfortable in any genre.

MLG: So Francisco Umbral always comes out, whether in an article or a novel?

FU: Always. I think my writing style is quite unmistakable.

MLG: Do you ever feel like an accursed poet, to borrow the title of your book on Lorca?

FU: No, because I am neither accursed nor a poet. I even wrote a book called *Diario de un escritor burgués* (The Diary of a Bourgeois Writer), so I don't feel very damned. I have never been a poet or written verses.

MLG: Don't you feel your prose is somewhat poetic?

FU: The critics always say that there is poetry not only in my writing, but also in my way of seeing the world. That's what the critics say, and I guess it's possible.

MLG: What is your way of viewing the world?

FU: It is poetic, lyrical, and ironic. The world either provokes a poetic feeling or an ironic grin from me. Although I am very involved in politics and everything else, I feel sometimes that I am just a spectator. Like Larra, in a way, I find myself outside society.

MLG: What about loneliness? Do you partake of the image of the bilious romantic poets of the nineteenth century?

FU: Loneliness is inevitable, loneliness is now becoming my best companion. But it does not spring from a literary mood, its roots lie in my own biography. I think I was born with it, it is something genetic. I was an only child and I rebelled against my parents.

MLG: It would be wrong then to see you as a romantic?

FU: I am very fond of the French and English romantics, and their Spanish counterparts. The study of rebels and cursed people has been a central concern of mine. It's quite probable that they have left their imprint on me. So have such writers as Barbey d'Aurevilly, Baudelaire, Lautréamont, Rimbaud, and Verlaine. But I love the twentieth century, especially the 1920s. I was commissioned by the publisher Seix Barral of Barcelona to write some memoirs of our century.

MLG: Do you see writing as a solitary journey?

FU: Yes, of course. It is solitary as a job, because I cannot write with people around me, like in a newsroom or here in this café. But it's not lonely on the inside, particularly if you are writing a novel, a biography, or some memoirs, because then you are living intimately and speaking directly to the characters in your work. So all the characters in the book keep me company, even though I might look alone from the outside.

MLG: Are your characters also lonely?

FU: In novels, as in life, everyone is alone. We meet up, live together and fraternize, but we are all alone.

MLG: Is there no communication possible, either for people or for characters?

FU: What does exist is communication of a conventional sort. More than dialogues, you have monologues where two people speak not with each other, but at each other. Their voices are kept on two separate tracks and never meet. I believe in body language more than in spoken language. Body contact is the greatest form of communication to which we can aspire, and therein lies the significance of sex and also of sports. This is not a mere anecdote, but a profound observation, which the ancient Greeks knew and believed in. I don't play any sports, but sometimes I think I would have liked to be a soccer player. Writing, of course, is another form of communication, and I think I am pretty good at it.

MLG: How do you feel about your characters? Do they become people and do you communicate with them?

FU: They don't need to become people, because I always begin with real persons I have known; if I write about my great-grandfather, I do so from memory. So the characters don't need to become persons, because they were real people when I started writing about them.

MLG: Does that mean that imagination has no part in the makeup of your characters?

FU: Of course, imagination plays a big part in my writing. Literature transforms those people into characters, the way it transforms a blank page into a poem. In my books, I give a poetical dimension to those people.

MLG: Nevertheless, I assume, for instance, that the people who used to come to the Café Gijón and have read your book about it recognized themselves.

FU: Yes, of course, the people from that time recognized themselves, as did the waiters and the owner of the café, who still runs this place. I tried to get deep under the skin of people; I researched them and their work, whether they were painters, musicians, poets, novelists, journalists, or just plain people who don't do anything. The people I praised were flattered, those I didn't felt uncomfortable. But literature transforms everything it touches, that is its function. It plays magic tricks.

MLG: Do you turn some of your characters into objects?

FU: I love to write about the dead, because they represent the ultimate object. They are objects with a biography. I like it, but not because of necrophilia. It's just that I think a beautiful woman is prettier when she has just died than when she was alive. She has become a pure object, the best object. I have rendered people as objects many times. I like to define people physically, and find a few adjectives that will forever transform them into objects.

MLG: Why do objects hold such attraction for you?

FU: Because all objects are beautiful. This chair is attractive, even though it is common. I could write an entire book about this bottle, for instance, or about the teacup you are holding in your hand. I believe a story can be told through objects, even more so than through people. I see the world as a painter would, in terms of colors, forms, and movement. The smaller the object, the better, almost as if I were Japanese, because they know the art of miniature. I don't see the world as a sociologist or philosopher. Take the Café Gijón, for instance: it is a self-enclosed space suitable for painting or writing. Better yet, it is a mirror in which you see the people reflected. All you have to do is put a frame around that mirror and you get a great painting. I am very tactile and more sense-oriented than mental. I think I've been quite influenced by Pablo Neruda and Ramón Gómez de la Serna in this respect. For that same reason, I like the French *nouveau roman* and the "New Wave" invented by Malraux, where the camera delights in lingering over objects more than people.

MLG: I've noticed writers are very fond of paintings. Do you own many?

FU: I am an avid enthusiast of painting. I have many friends who are painters and who have given me some of their works or made portraits of me. I also have a Roman sculpture of the Virgin as a pregnant adolescent, which I bought in the flea market in Madrid for one million pesetas.

MLG: Going back to your characters, do you have a favorite among them?

FU: I am not always a character in my books, but I am my favorite character.

MLG: Is the narrator the author himself?

FU: Marcel Proust (who wrote all of his work in the first person, as you well know) explained this very well when he said there is a split between author and narrator, and that the two shouldn't be confused. The Proust who wandered around Paris and attended the soirees of princesses and counts is different from the narrator of *Remembrance of Things Past.*

MLG: What about in Umbral's case?

FU: The same is true, although I wouldn't compare myself to Proust.

MLG: Since your work is so intricately tied to yourself as a person, what biographical data would you care to mention?

FU: I was born in Madrid in 1935, I studied and worked in Valladolid, where I got married. In 1960, I returned to Madrid, and since then I have devoted myself to literature and journalism. I have written seventy-five books and perhaps one million articles. I live with my wife in a town called Majadahonda in the outskirts of Madrid. We live in a chalet with a garden. During the mornings, I write; in the afternoons, I read; and in the evenings, I go down to Madrid, either alone or with company, to be sociable, and that's it. Once in a while, I travel to the provinces or abroad to give a lecture or two, but it seems I do it less and less. I have traveled all over the world, I have seen a lot of Europe, some of the United States, especially New York.

MLG: You have received several literary awards.

FU: Some prize or other. I don't take part in literary competitions anymore. I won the César González-Ruano Prize, which is one of the most important journalistic awards in Spain. I won that some years ago for an article I published in *El País*.

MLG: You mentioned the years you spent in Valladolid. Did Miguel Delibes have an impact on you as a writer?

FU: We are very close friends and I have learned a great deal from him, but more as a journalist than a novelist. He taught me how to write articles. In the late fifties, I wrote a lot for the newspaper he directed in Valladolid. He made a journalist out of me. But my style is quite different from his. He writes in a very sober, clipped Castilian Spanish, while I am far more baroque, I think. As an adolescent I tried to write in many different modes, and I didn't like any of them until I discovered Spanish baroque literature. I then found that I could write in that style with great ease, so I saw that my roots as a writer lay there.

MLG: Do you write articles every day, and do you consider journalism as a good discipline for creative writing?

FU: I have been writing a couple of articles a day for the past thirty years. Journalism is the best training. I would compare it to a pianist who rehearses in the morning so that he can give a good concert that night. It's something you can't let go, your fingers become accustomed to it. I love journalism with a passion. It takes me about fifteen minutes to write an article, and thirty to forty-five minutes for two of them. It gives me the rest of the day to work on whatever I want or on nothing at all.

MLG: When you sit down at your desk in the morning, do you know whether it's the journalist or the writer who is going to take charge?

FU: That depends on what is required. I wake up early in the morning and write, no matter what the circumstances, even if I am sick. If I have an article to write, then that's the first thing I do. If I have to give a lecture the following day, that's what I'll write. These things are determined by my working calendar. I write books whenever I feel like it, at my own pace.

MLG: When did you realize that writing was a necessity for you?

FU: It was the first thing I comprehended fully. Only later did I realize that I was a child, a seven-year-old, that I had a family and all of that. But before that, I already knew I was a writer.

MLG: Why do you write and what do your books represent?

FU: They represent nothing whatsoever. I write because I like to and because they pay me and I can eat, but literature has no use. Its glory and greatness lie in the fact that it is totally useless. I think literature is seduction, and I want to seduce my readers. It's like with a woman: it is better to seduce her than to make her fall in love with you. The writer should be a seducer; if he is not capable of it, he should cease writing, as he will be very boring.

MLG: What do you feel when you write?

FU: Pleasure, entertainment, and the feeling that I like it more than anything else and I am having a good time. I want to share this feeling with others, I don't want to keep it to myself.

MLG: How do you come up with the subjects for your novels?

FU: They just come to me. What you cannot do is sit and wonder what you are going to write about. The novel develops within you on the basis of a particular time in your life, whether it be one year or ten years, when you lived in a particular place and devoted yourself to a particular work. That world develops in you until it is sufficiently clear that you can write about it. So the subjects for my novels usually come from my own life and recollections of things past. I think that life, just like books, is made up of chapters. When you feel that a particular stage in your life has come to an end (because you stopped coming to the Café Gijón, or you are no longer poor or love ended or someone close to you died), all these things are material for your books. When you have a clear sense that a stage is complete, all you have to do is take that chunk of life and give it the form of a novel.

MLG: How would you define the time-frame of a book, between the first and last pages?

FU: It is an unreal time, which never corresponds to real time, whatever that may mean (and we don't know what it does—it's certainly not the time our watches keep). So it is a time you have to create. Perhaps the greatest problem in writing a novel is creating your own time or times. It is very fashionable to play with several time-frames nowadays, and I do the same in some of my books: sometimes the present or the past prevails, or the action takes place in a single night with linear time. The book begins and ends with that night, but there are many flashbacks in between.

MLG: What do you feel when you write a novel?

FU: I feel the novel. Norman Mailer called the novel "the great whore," and that's because it slowly wraps itself around you. When you start writing, you may not be very enthusiastic, but if the book looks like it is going to work (and if it doesn't, you have to throw it away), then it slowly wraps itself around you. The novel gradually becomes more complex and complicated, and it starts to branch out into other worlds, until the author eventually feels that the novel has completely enclosed him.

MLG: In the preceding situation, does the author stay inside or outside the book?

FU: When I write, I become involved in the world I describe, which explains why I invariably end up as one of my characters. This phenomenon has nothing to do with being narcissistic. If I stood outside that creative world, I could not feel passionate and be interested. Some critics tell me that I am too cerebral and intellectual, and therefore cold. I don't believe it to be so. Television may be a cold medium of communication, but my books are not. I think they are a display of warm emotions. I believe everything I have written is alive. When I write, I am completely trapped inside my books,

I barely exist outside that labyrinth. The book releases me only when it is completed.

MLG: What goes through your head when you finish a novel?

FU: I just start another one.

MLG: Do you have a favorite work among your books?

FU: Always the last one, because as the years go by and I become more proficient in my work as a writer, it is logical to assume that each succeeding book is better than the previous one, because it is the product of increased wisdom. Cervantes wrote *Don Quixote* very late in life, and if he had been slightly more lax, he wouldn't have written it at all. Everything he wrote before is pretty poor, both his prose and his plays. So he learned how to write only late in life. Therefore, I believe in tardy authors. Even though I have been writing since childhood, I believe that writers mature late in life.

MLG: Do you see an evolution in your own work?

FU: It is inevitable, whether I want it or not. The work evolves in the same way that my hair is turning gray. Of course, there is an evolution; what is important is that it be a good one.

MLG: But if you always like your latest work, that must mean that you like all of them.

FU: With the passage of time, I tend to prefer some over others, because time gives me the perspective I need to evaluate the flaws and virtues of each of my books. But if I have to choose, I will always prefer my latest work.

MLG: Which one is that?

FU: A book that came out recently called *El fulgor de Africa*. It is a novel that recounts Spain's last colonial war in Africa during the 1920s, when part of Morocco was still in Spanish hands. It is a historical novel in the sense that I talk about things that happened before I was born, in 1935. Prior to this book, I had always written about events I had lived through, so in this instance I had to turn to history properly speaking, as well as my family's memories.

MLG: Do you like to play with history and transform it?

FU: Yes, I do, but it's not my specialty. Perhaps I will not write another historical novel, but yes, I do find it fascinating. Other writers have done it before me like Marguerite Yourcenar with Hadrian, Robert Graves with Claudius, and it is a popular trend nowadays.

MLG: How do you come up with the titles for your novels?

FU: I need to find the title first. I usually have an idea in my head, and when I find a title I like (which might take me some time), then I know what I have to do. The title is like an outline which helps me give a shape to the book.

MLG: If you had to give your books a geometric shape, would they all have different forms?

FU: The shape that appeals most to me is the globe or the sphere. I would like the self-enclosed worlds of a book to be shaped like a honeycomb, and I say this not only as a writer, but also as a reader. If a novel takes place in Paris, I don't like to see the characters appear in New York all of a sudden because they are on a business trip. If a novel takes place in New York, like Tom Wolfe's *Bonfire of the Vanities,* then let it remain in New York, and not shift to California.

MLG: What about Cortázar? Didn't he do precisely that in *Hopscotch?*

FU: I enjoy his work, but I dislike that novel because it shifts from Paris to Buenos Aires. I like the part that takes place in Paris, but not the other half. Cortázar wasn't a novelist anyway, he was a short story writer, a narrator of brief tales. His short stories, like those of Borges and García Márquez, are complete, self-enclosed worlds.

MLG: For you it is important to maintain a connecting point between the beginning and the end of a novel?

FU: I speak both as a writer and a reader when I say that; for my taste, I prefer everything to be self-enclosed and for the characters to remain constant. I don't like it if in the last five pages of a novel a new character appears.

MLG: Many writers carry their personal obsessions to their work. Is it your case?

FU: I don't think I have any obsessions, generally speaking, although I am somewhat obsessed with age and with death now. Maybe it's a little too soon for that, but lately I have been thinking about it. As the Greeks or whoever said, "Either I am or death is." When I die, I won't witness my own death, so death does not exist for me. Only the death of others exists for me because I can attest to it. I don't have any obsessions, just fixed memories, usually of an autobiographical nature (love and family). Azorín used to say that memory is personality, and I work almost exclusively from memory. So more than obsessions, what I have are fixed memories, which provide me with my material. Every day I realize how unfathomable our memories are; we have more things stored up inside us than we know, and until we write about them, we can't really discover them.

MLG: Given all of this, what does childhood mean to you?

FU: Childhood is inexhaustible, as many writers have said. I don't always write about childhood, so as not to repeat myself or be pigeonholed as limited, but I could write forever about childhood.

MLG: Your work reflects both gentle and violent elements. How would you explain these opposite elements?

FU: Violence and gentleness form a very deliberate contrast in my work and, I think, in my personality. There is a book by the name of *Violencia y ternura,* which was written by Oscar Bayo, a very famous Spanish doctor and essayist, and a distant disciple of Freud and psychoanalysis. I think that violence and gentleness are keys to my work, and I have always employed the rose and the whip in them. It is a choice between a rose and a whip.

MLG: How do you relate to the rose, and what does the whip stand for?

FU: The rose can make me think of a girl, a boy, of a woman I have fallen in love with, while with the whip I chastise life and the world, because I am very critical. Writing provides me with my greatest weapons. A writer must be a critic, and a journalist even more so. After I have written a metaphor that looks a little too quaint and pretty, for instance, I like to apply the whip to my prose. I do the same thing when I write articles. After a poetic phrase I come down with thunder. In my novels as well as in my journalistic prose the technique I follow is the same. In novels this swing from gentleness to violence is achieved at a slower pace; in articles it has to be more abrupt, as everything is condensed into two pages. I believe that the word that best describes my writing technique is efficiency.

MLG: Camilo José Cela uses a similar technique of violence and gentleness. Do you see some resemblance between your explosive blasts and his?

FU: I admire him a great deal. He is a true master in violence and gentleness. His gentleness is expressed with tremendous sobriety; it is a macho gentleness that never falls into sentimentality. His voice is truly original, while he has said of me that I am a copycat. I have learned a great deal from him. He is the single most important writer in Spain today, as he has been for the last fifty years, following his debut after the Civil War. Both Cela and I are constantly ironic.

MLG: Since we've just discussed the impact of gentleness and violence on your work, how would you relate to love and hate?

FU: I don't much believe in either of them. I find hate very tiring. What a pain and a bother it is to hate. I don't know if a lot of people hate me, because they don't tell me. As for myself, I don't hate anybody. I think it is unhealthy to hate.

MLG: Do you think you approach literature from an intellectual standpoint?

FU: Yes, I do adopt an intellectual and critical approach to the study of ideas and style. This is the case, for instance, in my essays, studies, and biographies of Lord Byron, Valle Inclán, and Ramón Gómez de la Serna.

MLG: But at the same time there is a great human element in your writings, with a display of emotions.

FU: Of course, no one is an instrument with only one string. I suppose I have several vibrating strings. If I had only one, I would be a very poor writer. The strings are flexible in range and tone; I pluck one chord, then another, and several together later still.

MLG: Your wife is a photographer.

FU: Yes, she is a photojournalist, but she has given up on that, because we live in the country, and while I can write there, she cannot constantly be taking pictures of flowers. She should come to Madrid more often.

MLG: Could I label you a photographer with a pen, who takes shots of people and landscapes the way your wife did with her camera?

FU: Not exactly, because that would presuppose that my literature is realistic, and I don't think I am a realist. Maybe I am a realist occasionally, but I think this might be attributed to what I was saying earlier about lyrically transforming whatever I touch. I undertake a lyrical transformation through my style, so I am not strictly speaking a realist, I am a photographic writer.

MLG: Now that you live in the country, what does nature mean to you?

FU: Nowadays a lot, before nothing, because I am a man of the city, and I had never seen nature, other than those trees over there. But now I live in the country, so I like nature a lot. I am trying to find the formula to write a non-urban book, because all my books have urban settings. I have written half a novel that takes place deep within a forest, but I have abandoned the book somewhat, because I don't think I have mastered the subject of nature as I have that of the city.

MLG: Are you involved with another novel as well?

FU: I am writing a novel called "Madrid 650," which is about the Madrid of the slums, where juvenile delinquency and absolute misery reign. It is the third-world Madrid. My novel is going to be quite long, I think.

MLG: Why do you think that your novel *A Mortal Spring* has had such a popular appeal?

FU: Critics in Spain, the United States, and other countries insist that it is my best work. They have insisted so much since the book came out in 1975 or 1976 that I now believe it. Professors, critics, reviewers, readers, and everyone else says it is my best book, so I think they must be right.

MLG: I know that work has a special meaning for you.

FU: It is a novel about the death of my only son. I had been planning to write a novel about that child, and while I was working on the book he got sick and died. In any case I would have written about him; unfortunately, life gave me the end for it.

MLG: What does your first novel, *Travesía de Madrid,* represent for you?

FU: It represents my rediscovery of Madrid, after I came back from Valladolid in 1960. I wrote that book in 1965. It is a chronicle of those five striving years when I was poor and had no other refuge than this place, the Café Gijón, those days when a cup of coffee went for one peseta.

MLG: Do you care to mention some other novels?

FU: My first best-seller was *El Giocondo,* a novel set in Madrid in the 1970s about homosexuals. I received the Nadal Prize, the award most coveted by novelists in Spain, for *Las ninfas,* a book about adolescence.

MLG: *Amar en Madrid, Diario de un escritor burgués, Diario de un español cansado, La guapa gente de derechas,* and *Crónicas antiparlamentarias* are collections of some of your numerous articles. Do you plan to gather your million articles in book form?

FU: Ten or fifteen of my books are collections of articles. The publishers have asked to put together some more anthologies.

MLG: Do you see some changes in your work from the time of Franco to the onset of democracy?

FU: In terms of journalism, of course, because I can now write with absolute freedom, whereas under Franco I wrote what I could. Many of my articles were censored. But my books are not usually political, so they weren't affected.

MLG: How did censorship affect your work? Did you have to use the literary ruse of symbols?

FU: All sorts of ruses, yes, beginning with a profound understanding of the language. A Spanish author of that time whom I deeply admired, César González-Ruano, once said that since the censors had forbidden the use of the word *thigh,* writers were forced into discovering forty ways of saying it without actually using that word. When you have a rich vocabulary and you know how to say things, it is not necessary to use a particular term; you can find another word to suggest the same thing. So instead of referring directly to a woman's thigh, you resort to tricks, which are often more effective.

MLG: Is the musicality of words important to you?

FU: It's fascinating. I write because I have music within me.

MLG: Does this music influence you when you write, or are visual elements more important?

FU: Music is apparent in the way things happen and in the verbs, while sculpture and painting come into play in the way adjectives are employed.

MLG: Do you like to paint or draw?

FU: I like to draw a lot, and my subjects are always women.

MLG: What does the written word mean to you?

FU: Everything. The word represents everything in literature. A writer who is not a master of his own language and syntax, as the structuralist would have it, would be better off working in a bank than writing. Unfortunately, there are many authors today who don't know their own language.

MLG: Do you know of any author who writes in your vein?

FU: Yes, columnists from Madrid and the provinces do copy my journalistic style.

MLG: How do you know?

FU: I can see it immediately, because I have a very peculiar style.

MLG: Is language more important to you than characters?

FU: It is the only thing for me, there is nothing else. How do you create a character if not with language? You must select the appropriate words, nouns, adjectives, verbs that best describe the movements of your characters, whether serene or brusque. With painting you use colors, and with literature you use words. A writer has nothing else but to work with words.

MLG: How do you feel about translations? Can they render your style in another language?

FU: Translations interest me, although they almost always disappoint me, because I cannot recognize my work any longer. For instance, they gave *Mortal y rosa* [Deadly and Rosy] the horrible title *A Mortal Spring*. The title is ridiculous and the cover very ugly. Fortunately, it was a hard-cover book, so I just threw away the jacket and kept the book. It's a fairly good translation, but it has lost my music, which cannot be rendered in another language. A writer of style is far more difficult to translate than one who tells a story. Like a poet, a writer concerned with style depends exclusively on language, and the quality of his writing is usually lost in translation.

MLG: What does a book mean to you?

FU: I have always been a great fan of books. I love to touch them, even smell them. They are the objects I love most. When my own books come out, I am very fond of them for the first few days, and I manhandle them a lot. But afterward, I forget about them and never read them again.

MLG: If you could speak with an author from the past, whom would you choose?

FU: Baudelaire, Proust, and Spanish writers from the seventeenth century, particularly Quevedo, who is a great master and a far better writer than Cervantes ever was.

MLG: What would you say to Quevedo?

FU: I wouldn't say anything to him; I'd limit myself to asking questions and listening to the replies. I don't think Quevedo would let me speak anyway, because he talked a lot and very well. He spoke the way he wrote, with literature.

MLG: Do you see some resemblance between your work and your personality and that of another author?

FU: I believe it would be Quevedo.

MLG: What about present-day writers?

FU: I don't find any connection with them. I like Valle Inclán, who was from the Generation of 1898, and I also enjoy contemporary North American writers such as Norman Mailer and Tom Wolfe. Among living authors, those are the two I prefer.

MLG: What about Latin American authors?

FU: García Márquez and Borges.

MLG: Why Borges?

FU: Because he is fashionable, because he interests me as he interests everybody, because he is a great writer. But he hasn't influenced me at all, except perhaps in the way I place my adjectives. He was an intellectual, who used to say that he didn't write books based on life, but based on other books. He didn't really live his own life, since he was blind and lived tied to his mother's apron. I am not like that, I am a chronicler of life, even though I have read many books (although not as many as Borges).

MLG: Many writers say they wear masks. What about you?

FU: Yes, I wear a mask, but underneath my mask, I am the same person.

MLG: Can't you take it off?

FU: If I take it off, I will still be the same.

MLG: Are you wearing a mask right now?

FU: I always wear it, but my disguise is myself.

MLG: You also wear it at home?

FU: Not abandoning yourself to yourself is the most important thing. I wear it even when I am alone, so as not to lose myself. Baudelaire said that you have to be consistently sublime.

MLG: But if your disguise is the same as you, you are not really concealing anything.

FU: If you ask anyone in Madrid, they will say that Umbral wears a mask. Nevertheless, it is just myself. Everyone disguises himself as himself, even at masquerade parties. You disguise yourself as you would have liked to be, or as you are. The mask doesn't hide, it reveals.

MLG: And what would you have liked to be?

FU: Francisco Umbral.

MLG: What is Francisco Umbral like?

FU: He is a man who delights in frivolity. I am very frivolous. I am frivolous when it comes to frivolity. I think frivolity is the apex of culture and civilization. A people without frivolity cannot be considered truly civilized; the Spartans and the Nazis couldn't be frivolous, for instance. Frivolity is the sign of a very mature civilization.

MLG: Who is Francisco Umbral?

FU: I would say Francisco Umbral. Borrowing from Borges when he said that "Quevedo is not a man, he is a vast and powerful literature," I could say, "Umbral is a vast and powerful literature." He is a writer who is over fifty years old, who is 1.90 meters tall, and who has written seventy-five books and perhaps one million articles.

Manuel Vázquez Montalbán

LAYLE SILBERT

Manuel Vázquez Montalbán was born in 1939 in Barcelona at the end of the Civil War. As a young man, he received his master's degree in philosophy and letters from the University of Barcelona and also graduated from the Madrid Official School of Journalism.

Vázquez Montalbán is known for both his poetry and his prose, which includes novels, plays, and essays. His work, like that of most Spaniards, is deeply marked by the Civil War and the postwar years. He turns to these obsessions with a definite ethical approach, and makes comparisons between those who fought the war and those who lived under Franco's dictatorship (his own generation). In 1962, he was sentenced to jail for political reasons, just as his father had been during the Civil War. His novels are collages that make use of his childhood memories, as well as memories of his family who lived through the Barcelona of the Republic and then experienced the horrors of the Civil War.

In his novel *Yo maté a Kennedy* (I Killed Kennedy), 1972, he introduced his character Pepe Carvalho, a detective around whom he builds a series of suspense novels and that allows him to view the Spanish society of his time and to discover the rest of the world. With this cycle of detective stories, Vázquez Montalbán brought Anglo-Saxon black humor to Spanish fiction.

The author of numerous books, he has been translated into many languages. Among his poetic works are *Una educación sentimental* (A Sentimental Education), 1967; *Praga* (Prague), 1982; *Memoria y deseo* (Memory and Desire), 1986; *A la sombra de las muchachas sin flor* (In the Shadow of Flowerless Young Girls), 1973. Among his narrative works, the following should be mentioned: *Recordando a Dardé* (Remembering Dardé), 1969, and the Carvalho series: *Tatuaje* (Tatoo), 1974; *La soledad del manager,* 1977 (*The Angst-ridden Executive,* 1990); *Los mares del sur,* 1979 (*Southern Seas,* 1986), winner of the Planeta Prize and the International Prize for Detective Stories, Paris, 1981; *Asesinato en el Comité Central,* 1981 (*Murder in the Central Committee,* 1985); *Los pájaros de Bangkok* (The Birds of Bangkok), 1983; *La rosa de Alejandría* (The Rose of Alexandria), 1984; *El pianista,* 1985 (*The Pianist,* 1989); *El balneario* (The Spa), 1986; *Asesinato en Prado del Rey y otras historias sórdidas* (Murder at Prado del Rey and Other Sordid Stories), 1987; *Los alegres muchachos de Atzavara* (The Happy Young Men from Atzavara), 1987; *El delantero centro fue asesinado al atardecer* (The Center Forward Was Murdered at Nightfall), 1988. His latest novel, *Galíndez,* 1990, is the story of Jesús de Galíndez, the Basque exile who was kidnapped from his New York home in 1956 and murdered by agents of dictator Trujillo.

A chronicler of his time and that of the preceding generation, he turns politics and history into literature. When asked by the French newspaper *Libération* what writing meant to him, he answered, "I write because I want to be tall and handsome and rich. I only succeeded in becoming tall and handsome."

Manuel Vázquez Montalbán met with me after taking part in a symposium on Spanish writers held at the Casa de España in New York in April 1988. Like the Cuban Guillermo Cabrera Infante, he kept a straight face and displayed a dry sense of humor. Wearing a black leather jacket and black pants, he had something about him that made me think of his own character, the detective Pepe Carvalho. It was as if Carvalho were ready to take on New York and solve old and new mysteries. He talked about the personal ghosts and obsessions that drive him to writing. He also spoke about Jesús de Galíndez and Muriel Colbert, the characters in his latest novel.

❖❖❖❖❖❖❖❖❖❖❖❖❖❖❖❖❖❖❖❖❖❖❖❖❖❖❖❖❖❖

MLG: You have written poetry, essays, novels, and detective stories. What do you enjoy writing most?

MVM: I enjoy all these genres, otherwise I would not cultivate them. A writer selects one genre or another in terms of his obsessions that determine the particular choice. On the other hand, according to the Spanish critic José María Castellet, there is a common thread that runs through my work and binds these genres together. There is a tendency in all of my books, whether they are novels that belong or not to the Carvalho cycle, or whether they are collections of poetry, to write a chronicle type of literature. Let me explain: a chronicle in the sense that literature reflects the conflict between people and society, between the soloist and the chorus, or the single entity and the composite of people that make up that society. A chronicle that, very much like a collage, assembles cultural and subcultural characteristics. For that reason, I have no problem going from one genre to another. In poetry, I uncover a language laboratory, where I can experiment with words and their derivatives, go back to the roots of language itself. I turn to poetry as a cleansing exercise, to free myself from the toxic substance of daily living. In novels, characters and the lives they lead are at the core of things.

MLG: What are some of the obsessions that inhabit your world?

MVM: One of my obsessions is the use of memory as a source for knowledge, but a falsified or distorted source. One's memory is never the same as the memory of someone else who has gone through the same experience. In the case of Spain particularly, memory plays an important part in our own present, because it is our only link with a dramatic period in our history—the hidden memory of the Spain of the wounded, those who were defeated in the Civil War. Those of us who were the children of the defeated have had to struggle to recover that concealed past. This struggle entailed what we could call a political move. Another theme that fascinates me is the relationship between the conqueror and the conquered on all levels of life; the professional, the economic, even the love relationship between two people. I am interested in this topic from a Calvinistic outlook, with its concept of predestination so much exploited by modern society. And the questions that always arise are of an ethical nature: how does one determine who is the loser and who is the winner, what determining factor turns a person into one or the other category? Why do human beings follow certain lines of conduct, why are they ready to fight or even die for them, while others settle for very little and accept the misery that life has to offer? I like to juxtapose the present with the past to resolve that ethical question: what gave our fathers the power of endurance as they faced the challenge of the Civil War, a power we seem to be lacking? I think these are some of the obsessions that appear constantly in my work. They probably are a key element in my writing.

MLG: Do you consider yourself a chronicler of your time?

MVM: Yes, but that's very relative. All things considered, I think I feed on what surrounds me, but then, of course, I filter that substance and turn it into literature. It can never be totally testimonial; you either falsify reality or, on the other hand, when you make every effort not to write testimonial novels, you realize, as years go by, that what you have written is a reflection of your time. There are writers who have looked upon testimonial literature with disdain, denying ever writing from such a perspective, and fifty years later critics categorize their works as such. I prefer to be more aware of what I do, more in command.

MLG: Do you think that reality is more important to you than fantasy?

MVM: No, I wouldn't say that. In literature, reality always manifests itself as fantasy. Otherwise, it would be the same as journalism. Journalism is the exact reproduction of reality—although that too would depend, if we refer to Tom Wolfe's new journalism. When a writer confronts reality, he never intends to reproduce it as such; reality is filtered through the language he uses, through his subjective ways of recalling events, and through his creative imagination. For that reason, fantasy is a necessary recourse and it plays a significant part in creative writing.

MLG: What does language mean to you?

MVM: For me it is everything. It is the very substance of writing. Of course, it does not imply that I view language from a purely linguistic approach, turning literature into a constant exploration into words. I believe that language is functional, it is a necessary tool, it is the raw material with which every writer has to work to mold it into a style that best expresses his obsessions. There are writers, however, who turn language into an obsession and who make their novels a verbal display, a liberation of the verbal energy, or what Kandinsky sought in painting, the release of the pictorial mass. It is not so in my case. The criteria I follow in my handling of language is very simple: to select for each of my novels a language that fits it most.

MLG: Do you like to polish your style? Do you go over each of your works?

MVM: I revise constantly, especially when I work with poetry. I may end up with many versions or variations of the same poem, until I finally select one for publication. I also experience moments of forced silence, when I come to a standstill and feel I have reached a dead end. For the past five years, for instance, I have had to put aside a book of poetry, called *El viaje,* because I was unable to find the exact three verses that would describe a dialogue between Saint Augustine and a child. As the saint is walking on the beach, his attention is stirred by a child who is digging a hole in the sand and filling it with water. He tells the saint that he is emptying the sea. A discussion unfolds whereby Saint Augustine tells the child that what he is doing is an impossible feat, to which the child responds that what the saint is doing— explaining the work of God—is in no way a more plausible task. I gave the book to the publisher only recently, although I wrote it five years ago. The last three verses, as I had them, did not convince me, they did not convey what I had wanted to express.

MLG: Are you religious?

MVM: No, I am not. This work is a metaphor about our lifelong attempt at understanding the world. This search into life may be undertaken through political or religious channels. At the end of his journey, when the poet has attempted to say all he could in his book, he realizes that it is an impossible quest, that it is almost a useless game to want to explain the world. He must accept that in part he has failed.

MLG: Is writing an attempt at understanding and then explaining the world?

MVM: When, a long time ago, a reporter for the newspaper *Libération* asked me that same question, I answered, "I write because I want to be tall and handsome and rich. I only succeeded in becoming tall and handsome!"

MLG: Arrabal made a somewhat similar statement.

MVM: I was unaware of it. In the moment of truth there is always a narcissistic component that makes you give the best image of yourself through literary tricks; it is a way of compensating for what your reality lacks. When a man decides to become a plumber, a banker, or a politician, it is because he wants to exercise those professions. The person who commits himself to writing does so because he needs to modify life with his words. That means that there is something that does not function properly, most likely in life itself, and words then become the filter that corrects the imperfection. I think that writing entails a need to seduce and every writer goes about it in his own way, following his own linguistic code. Language, then, becomes that handsome face, that perfect anatomy. Writers, painters, sculptors display their own patterns of seduction, like the compulsive character who exposes himself to attract attention in public parks.

MLG: Why do you write?

MVM: I have nothing else to do. Some people are teachers, engineers, or bricklayers. I know how to write, it's the only thing I am relatively good at. For me, writing is a way of being in touch with myself and with others. It is a way of communicating with that inner reader that lives within me and branches out into the outside world.

MLG: Can writing be a form of escape?

MVM: It can be so initially, but you come to realize after a while that it is a false form of escape. On the contrary, in the process of writing you are in constant contact with your personal ghosts and feel that inner anguish. You may think that you have released them and that you have been set free, but what you actually accomplished is to reinforce those obsessions and give them food on which to thrive.

MLG: When did you feel for the first time this passion for writing?

MVM: As a seven-year-old boy, I already felt the need to write. This passion continued during my adolescent years until finally, when I entered the university, I showed some of my writings to one of my teachers. It was then I realized that I would dedicate my life to writing.

MLG: Do you consider writing a profession?

MVM: I have never held an office in my life, except for a very brief time as a teacher. In other words, I have always lived from my writings, alternating between journalism and literature. During the period where I was barred from journalism because of political reasons, I had to write wherever I could in order to survive. Writing then took on for me the most diverse forms, from fashion magazines, advertising lingerie, to magazines about gardening and furniture. In that sense, yes, I would say I developed some kind of a trade. Literature, however, is altogether a different matter. As a writer, you enter at your own pace into an intimate relationship with your work.

MLG: Do you think that the writer plays a special role in society?

MVM: A writer has a gift for words and is its sole possessor. This in itself, I believe, gives him a certain role to perform, in a society where there are people who work with their hands and others with their heads. Let every writer do what he wishes, as long as his writings do not become dogmatic. Personally, I feel a sense of responsibility toward the language that I use.

MLG: Are your books political?

MVM: It has never been my intention to use literature for political reasons, but literature, no matter what, always reflects political tendencies. Eliot's poems were political; there is nothing more political than a poetry sealed hermetically. Poetry instills and transmits ideas, envisions new worlds and restructures old ones. The reader not only receives an emotional or sensory message when he reads, he also absorbs strong ideological beliefs.

MLG: How would you describe your own poetry?

MVM: It's a poetry that could partly be compared to that of the poets of the 1930s or to the Generation of '27; for instance, the poetry of Cernuda. It's a poetry of experience, a personal chronicle which, with an ironic over-tone, blends in a collage form the cultural and subcultural elements of our society. I don't really belong to any generation and this has left critics slightly puzzled.

MLG: Since writing takes for you the form of a chronicle, when do you know that you are going to resort to poetry or turn to a novel?

MVM: That depends on the preoccupation that takes hold of me and also on the interior rhythm. These two factors will determine what I express and how I express it.

MLG: What made you write detective stories, and how did the character of Carvalho come about?

MVM: In 1970, I wrote an experimental and rather intellectual novel called *Yo maté a Kennedy*. It was a reflection on a Spain divided into victims and executioners. Pepe Carvalho is Kennedy's bodyguard and the person responsible for his death. He is his assassin. I experimented with the character, he interested me, and I decided to create a cycle of novels that would evolve around him. It was my intent to write a chronicle of our time and use Carvalho as the perfect filter that could capture all the components of history.

MLG: Do you identify with him?

MVM: To some degree, but he has a mind of his own. You create a character, but he becomes independent of you. You talk to him and want to make him say things that are irrelevant to his personality. The writer is never totally free when he engages in a dialogue with his characters. The characters, in turn, are stronger than the author, they are self-governing. The author's chance in that battle for power between himself and his character is to kill or betray him.

MLG: Do you see some similarity with Unamuno?

MVM: Not only with him, but also with Pirandello and Kierkegaard. For me, emotion and reason are two opposite poles necessary to knowledge. But perhaps reason is more important, as long as it does not turn into a robot-like machine.

MLG: How would you explain the fact that Carvalho has turned into a universal figure?

MVM: All over the world we share the same obsessions. Differences between peoples and nations seem to be disappearing.

MLG: *Southern Seas* received the 1979 Planeta Prize. What can you say about that novel?

MVM: It's the novel in which the Carvalho cycle reaches its most intricate form. It's also one of the first cases where a detective story was awarded a prize based on its literary merits and regardless of its genre. That award gave me great satisfaction, because it proved to me that one should not separate literature into different categories. There is no such thing as white, black, pink, or fuchsia colors as far as literature is concerned; what matters is whether it is good or bad literature.

MLG: Is *Los alegres muchachos de Atzavara* a moral biography of your time?

MVM: It is a biography of the period of transition, which we have all experienced. We looked at the old as something that had to die and turned to the new until, with the passing of time, we came to realize that all we had done was change one standard for another. So the idea is that it is necessary to change, but at the same time whether we change or not makes no difference. At the moment of truth things change very little.

MLG: Do you belong to that transition period?

MVM: No, but I have observed that generation. Through my writings I have tried to make a photocopy of it. I have described, with a certain amount of irony, people who with the death of Franco proclaimed their freedom in all aspects of life, to the point of announcing publicly that they were homosexuals. Yet, when they finally could enjoy that newly discovered freedom, all they wanted to do was return to a normal kind of life. So they got married, with a church wedding at that.

MLG: I note a certain sense of sarcasm. Irony plays an important part in your work.

MVM: Irony is to me like an antidote or a vaccine against pessimism. Things never turn out exactly as we would like, especially when you have lived long periods dreaming of utopias. I was discussing precisely this idea with a friend of mine, a Portuguese writer, and his thought on the subject was that he used literature to counteract the effect of utopias; I am not so ambitious, I am satisfied with irony. Without it, I surely would fall into depression. Irony helps you maintain your lucidity and sharpen your critical sense. It makes you face your biological failure—death—and bounce back when you feel unfulfilled.

MLG: Do you see a difference in your work since the death of Franco and the rebirth of democracy?

MVM: The difference lies in the fact that I now dare describe scenes as never before and make characters say what could never have been uttered. But my language and my personal stand have remained basically the same. It's just that certain topics could never have been discussed before. For instance, denouncing repression, all the machinery or wheels of power, descriptions of the police force and the military. I would never have dared to attack them openly in my books, because I knew that during the Franco regime they would have put an end to my writing.

MLG: Is your work autobiographical?

MVM: Not really, although in all my novels, in the Carvalho cycle as well as in *The Pianist,* there are personal elements taken from my own experience.

MLG: What made you write *The Pianist?*

MVM: It is a tribute to the people who fought during the Spanish Civil War and saw their lives and dreams destroyed. These people had an enormous capacity for sacrifice because they truly believed in their cause. I tried to compare their moral anguish to that of the people of my generation who had to struggle under better conditions against a dictatorship and contend with it. Yet, we seem to fall short of their courage and endurance. So I question whether our moral values and our loyalty to our cause lacked the stamina displayed by our fathers and grandfathers. I also ponder on the role of the artist, to what extent is he above good and evil, and how involved his relationship is with history. The artist, modeled in part after Dali, comes out triumphant. As you see, I resort to history and politics to transpose them into literary material.

MLG: Your latest novel is called *Galíndez,* based on the life of the Spanish Basque who was kidnapped in the 1950s. My classmate at Columbia University drove him to the subway that night and was the last person to see him alive.

MVM: Once more I find my challenge in history. Galíndez was a Basque who lived in exile in New York and was kidnapped by a Trujillo commando. The novel evolves in two periods of time: the past, when Galíndez was alive, and the present, when Muriel Colbert, a young American teacher, receives a grant to do research on him. She becomes so fascinated by his personality and his life that she begins to identify with him.

MLG: How do you come up with the titles for your books?

MVM: I follow different paths. It may be suggestive of a song, like the old traditional Spanish song of the fifteenth century that goes, "You are like the rose of Alexandria, colored by night and white by day," which is of course symbolic of the myth of the double conduct of women, the myth of "Belle de jour." My collection of poems, *Una educación sentimental,* is a parody of Flaubert's *L'Education sentimentale. A la sombra de las muchachas sin flor,* another book of poems, is a parody of Proust. As you see, there are many ways of coming up with what you believe is the right title.

MLG: Do you go through a particular emotion when you finish writing a book?

MVM: A great amount of fear, I am tremendously afraid of the result. To such a point that I cannot reread any work of mine until at least ten or fifteen years have gone by. But even then I do not read it with a sense of peace; I always look at my books with apprehension.

MLG: How does it feel to see your books in translation?

MVM: To think that a reader very different from you can appreciate your work, in a language which is not your own, is in itself a small miracle. You thought you were writing to be understood by your own people and suddenly you wake up to the reality that you are reaching a far greater audience. It makes you realize that the world is becoming more and more homogeneous and that writers, publishers, and readers can communicate now in a much easier way than ever before.

MLG: If you had to give a geometric shape to your work as a whole, what would it be?

MVM: It would have to be a polyhedron. But I should also add that most of my novels evolve in a circular fashion, whereby the starting and closing points come together.

MLG: Did the granting of the Nobel Prize to Camilo José Cela have an impact on Spanish letters?

MVM: You know, writers are a strange breed; they are rather envious of the success of others. Those who are his friends were pleased, the others were not. I think that this honor should be considered as a recognition of Spain, now that we are a democratic nation.

MLG: How were Spanish writers viewed outside of Spain during the Franco regime?

MVM: For many years, we had to put up with the suspicion that the Franco regime had contaminated all cultural output. This drew around us an isolation, as if every book written in Spain were placed in quarantine. The rest of the world seemed to say that some nations give rise to great writers and others to none. We were the country that had witnessed the birth of literature, with Cervantes, and its death with the shots that took the life of García Lorca.

MLG: How would you explain the great popularity the Spanish novel is enjoying in France today?

MVM: It's the astonishment that I suppose one feels when confronted with the arrival of someone new. As you are face-to-face with that person you know nothing about, you suddenly discover in the course of the conversation that you have many things in common. Our novels are telling them things that they needed to hear. Our cultural efforts had purposely been kept hidden from them and the only knowledge they had of us was either related to bullfighting or to our struggle against repression. In fact, Spain had already begun a revival of the narrative form in the late 1950s, in spite of the Franco regime. The novels from the 1960s to the present are what they have discovered today, now that we have joined the ranks of other democratic nations.

MLG: Do you think Spain is going through a cultural "Boom"?

MVM: I wouldn't say that. But what has taken place is the following: Spain has returned to a normal democratic way of life. Our country has recovered its heterodox cultural past, hidden by the Franco regime, and has become aware of a new creative growth in today's novel. The same thing is taking place in the picture industry. Film directors like Manuel Gutiérrez Aragón and Almodóvar have introduced topics that could not have been discussed before. Another important change is having given a cultural autonomy to all the regions of Spain. So, rather than a cultural "Boom," I would say that Spain has returned to a cultural life under a democratic government.

MLG: How would you describe the present-day Spanish novel?

MVM: Its roots lie in the novels of the late 1950s, or early 1960s, when writers broke away from traditional realism. They began reading the great European literature of the two world wars, and the literature from both North and South America. The Spanish novel has not become what it is today overnight. It is in no way a miracle. It had to go through a long process to reach that stage. I think every writer has been using his obsessions as creative material. These preoccupations are basically the same, the difference lies in our capacity to deal with them.

MLG: Is there a difference between novels that come from Barcelona and those from Madrid?

MVM: I don't like to fall into the habit of making sweeping generalizations. There are, however, some differences. Our novels—the novels from Barcelona—are usually more concerned with telling a story. That would seem to be the case for Marsé, Mendoza, and myself. We turn history into literature, we reflect on the historical past, on the social and political aspect of things, without losing touch with the present. The novels from Madrid, on the other hand, are much more concerned with structure, with verbal display. They are less interested in the characters and their story, and much more in the form.

MLG: How do you view the Spain of this new decade in relationship to the rest of the world?

MVM: I'll tell you something that may sound ironic, I think that Spain is beginning to look like Japan, with its stress on achievement. Materialistic values, like economic security, technological advances, are becoming more and more prevalent. This is the new philosophy which is being emphasized today. I don't know how Spaniards, who were so fond of the cosmological and sensory vision of the earth, typical of the Mediterranean, will learn how to cope with this new set of optics. I hope they learn to synthesize these two outlooks on life.

MLG: What is your reaction to the celebration of 1992? Should it be considered a festive event?

MVM: I think the best thing we can do is forget about the celebration of the conquest of America, because it was an imperialistic feat of arms, and keep history in the background as a point of reference. We should look toward the future and start anew. All the people who share Spanish as their common language should join together to help one another in the fight for democracy, for a new sense of emancipation, for better living conditions.

MLG: One more question: who is Manuel Vázquez Montalbán?

MVM: I don't know, that's the type of question I stopped asking myself a long time ago, so I wouldn't have to listen to my own lies. But if you insist, let me answer it this way. I imagine I am many people all in one. It is up to others to select that particular aspect which is of most interest to them. It may raise, of course, the problem of personality. What makes up the personality is an enigma that has tormented philosophers for the past century. We shouldn't really worry much about it, though. The important thing is to realize that other people take from our personality the trait that is best suitable to them.

Selected Bibliography

I. WORKS BY THE AUTHORS

RAFAEL ALBERTI

El adefesio (Fábula del amor y las viejas). Buenos Aires: Editorial Losada, 1944. Plays.

A la pintura. Buenos Aires: Imprenta López, 1945. Poems.

El alba del alhelí (1925-1926). Santander: Edición para amigos de José María de Cossío, 1927. Poems.

Antología poética (1918-1936). Buenos Aires: Editorial Pleamar, 1943.

Antología poética (1924-1940). Buenos Aires: Editorial Losada, 1942.

La arboleda perdida (Libro primero de memorias). México: Editorial Séneca, 1942. Memoirs.

La arboleda perdida: libros I y II de memorias. Buenos Aires: Compañía General Fabril Editora, 1959. (*The Lost Grove*. Trans. Gabriel Berns. Berkeley: University of California Press, 1976.) Memoirs.

La arboleda perdida: libros III y IV de memorias. Barcelona: Seix Barral, 1987. Memoirs.

Baladas y canciones del Paraná (1953-1954). Buenos Aires: Editorial Losada, 1954. (*Ballads and Songs of the Paraná, 1953-1954*. Van Nuys, CA: C'est moi-même, 1988.) Poems.

Cal y canto (1926-1927). Madrid: Revista de Occidente, 1929. Poems.

Canciones del alto valle del Aniene y otros versos y prosas (1967-1972). Buenos Aires: Editorial Losada, 1972. Poems.

Coplas de Juan Panadero (Libro I). Montevideo: Edición Pueblos Unidos, 1949; *Coplas de Juan Panadero (1949-1977), seguidas de Vida bilingüe de un refugiado español en Francia (1939-1940)*. Madrid: Editorial Mayoría, 1977. Poems.

Del mar de Cádiz. Antología de su poesía gaditana. Cádiz: Fundación

Municipal de Cultura, 1981.

Entre el clavel y la espada (1939-1940). Buenos Aires: Editorial Losada, 1941. Poems.

Un fantasma recorre Europa. Madrid: La Tentativa Poética, 1933. (*A Spectre Is Haunting Europe: Poems of Revolutionary Spain.* Trans. Ira Jan Wallach and Angel Flores. New York: Critics Group, 1936.) Poems.

Fustigada luz (1972-1978). Barcelona: Seix Barral, 1980. Poems.

García Lorca. Antología poética (1918-1936). Buenos Aires: Editorial Pleamar, 1943.

Los hijos del drago y otros poemas. Granada: Excma. Diputación Provincial de Granada, 1986. Poems.

El hombre deshabitado. Madrid: Editorial "Plutarco," 1931. Play.

Imagen primera de . . . Buenos Aires: Editorial Losada, 1945. Prose.

Libro del mar. Barcelona: Editorial Lumen, 1968. Poems.

Lope de Vega y la poesía contemporánea seguido de "La Pájara pinta." Paris: Centre de recherches de l'Institut d'études hispaniques, 1964.

Lo que canté y dije de Picasso. Barcelona: Editorial Bruguera, 1980.

Marinero en tierra (1924). Madrid: Biblioteca Nueva, 1925. Poems.

Numancia: tragedia: adaptación y versión actualizada de la destrucción de Numancia, de Miguel de Cervantes. Buenos Aires: Editorial Losada, 1943. Play.

Obras completas. Poesía. Madrid: Aguilar, 1988. 3 volumes.

Obras de Rafael Alberti. Barcelona: Seix Barral, 1978. Anthology.

Los ocho nombres de Picasso y No digo más de lo que no digo (1966-1970). Barcelona: Kairós, 1970. Poems.

Ora marítima. Buenos Aires: Editorial Losada, 1953.

The Other Shore: 100 Poems. Trans. José A. Elgorriaga and Martin Paul. Ed. Kosrof Chantikian. San Francisco: Kosmos, 1981. Bilingual anthology.

The Owl's Insomnia: 16 Poems. Selected and trans. Mark Strand. New York: Atheneum, 1973. Bilingual anthology.

Poesía. Ed. Aitana Alberti. Madrid: Aguilar, 1972. Poems.

Poesía (1924-1937). Madrid: Editorial Signo, 1938. Poems.

El poeta en la calle: poesía civil (1931-1965). Paris: Editions de la Librairie du Globe, 1966. Poems.

Un poeta español en el Río de la Plata. Roma: Instituto Italo-Latinoamericano, 1969.

Retornos de lo vivo lejano (1948-1952). Buenos Aires: Editorial Losada, 1952. Poems.

Roma, peligro para caminantes. México: Joaquín Mortiz, 1968.

Selected Poems. Ed. and trans. Ben Belitt. Berkeley: University of California Press, 1966.

Selected Poems of Rafael Alberti. Trans. Lloyd Mallan. New York: New Directions, 1944.

Sobre los ángeles (1927-1928). Madrid: Compañía Iberoamericana, 1929. (*Concerning the Angels.* Trans. Geoffrey Connell. London: Rapp & Carroll, 1967; Chicago: Swallow Press, 1967). Poems.

Trece bandas y cuarenta y ocho estrellas. Poemas del Mar Caribe. Madrid: Impresor Manuel Altolaguirre, 1936. Poems.
Versos sueltos de cada día: primer y segundo cuadernos chinos (1979-1982). Barcelona: Seix Barral, 1982. Poems.
Verte y no verte. A Ignacio Sánchez Mejías (1935). Mexico: Miguel N. Lira, 1935.

FERNANDO ARRABAL

Baal Babylone. Paris: Editions Julliard, 1959. (*Baal Babylon.* Trans. from the French by Richard Howard. New York: Grove Press, 1961.) Novel.
Carta a los comunistas españoles y otras cartas. Murcia: Editorial Godoy, 1981.
Cérémonie pour une chèvre sur un nuage. La Louvière: Daily Bul, 1967. Play.
Echecs et mythe. Paris: Payot, 1984.
L'enterrement de la sardine. Paris: Editions Julliard, 1961. (*The Burial of the Sardine.* Trans. from the French by Patrick Bowles. London: Calder & Boyars, 1966.) Novel.
Extravagante croisade d'un castrat amoureux, ou, Comme un lys entre les épines. Paris: Ramsay, 1989; *La extravagante cruzada de un castrado enamorado.* Barcelona: Seix Barral, 1990. Novel.
Fêtes et rites de la confusion. Paris: Eric Losfeld, 1967.
La hija de King Kong. Barcelona: Seix Barral, 1988. Novel.
El hombre pánico: El cementerio de automóviles: Ciugrena: Los dos verdugos. Madrid: Taurus, 1965. Plays.
Inquisición. Granada: Ed. Don Quijote, Edición de A. Berenguer, 1982. Plays.
Lettre à Fidel Castro. Paris: Christian Bourgeois, 1983.
Lettre au Général Franco. Paris: Union Générale d'Editions, 1972.
Mis humildes paraísos. Barcelona: Ediciones Destino, 1985. Poems.
Le New York d'Arrabal. Paris: André Balland, 1973.
La piedra iluminada. Barcelona: Ediciones Destino, 1985. (*The Compass Stone.* Trans. Andrew Hurley. New York: Grove Press, 1987.) Novel.
La pierre de la folie. Paris: Editions Julliard, 1963. Poems.
Sur Fischer: initiation aux échecs. Paris: Editions du Rocher, 1974. Essays.
Théâtre I (Oraison, Les deux bourreaux, Fando et Lis, Le cimetière des voitures). Paris: Editions Julliard, 1958. (*The Automobile Graveyard, The Two Executioners.* Trans. Richard Howard. New York: Grove Press, 1960; *Plays. Vol. I. Orison, The Two Executioners, Fando and Lis, The Car Cemetery.* Trans. Barbara Wright. London: Calder & Boyars, 1962.)
Théâtre II (Guernica, Le labyrinthe, Le tricycle, Pique-nique en campagne, La bicyclette du condamné). Paris: Editions Julliard, 1961. (*Plays, Vol. II. Guernica, The Labyrinth, The Tricycle, Picnic on the Battlefield, The Condemned Man's Bicycle.* Trans. Barbara Wright. London: Calder & Boyars, 1967; *Pique-nique en campagne / Pic-nic on the Battlefield.* A bilingual edition. Columbus, OH: Logan Elm Press, 1983.)

Théâtre III (Le couronnement, Le grand cérémonial, Cérémonie pour un noir assassiné). Paris: Editions Julliard, 1965. (*Plays. Vol. III. The Architect and the Emperor of Assyria; The Grand Ceremonial; The Solemn Communion.* Trans. Jean Benedetti and John Calder. London: Calder & Boyars, 1970.)

Théâtre V (Théâtre panique, L'architecte et l'empereur d'Assyrie). Paris: Christian Bourgeois, 1967. (*The Architect and the Emperor of Assyria.* Trans. Everard d'Harnoncourt and Adele Shank. New York: Grove Press, 1969; *Plays. III. The Architect and the Emperor of Assyria; The Grand Ceremonial; The Solemn Communion.* Trans. Jean Benedetti and John Calder. London: Calder & Boyars, 1970.)

Théâtre VI (Le jardin des délices, Bestialite érotique, Une tortue nommée Dostoïevski). Paris: Christian Bourgeois, 1969. (*Garden of Delights.* Trans. Helen and Tom Bishop. New York: Grove Press, 1974.)

Théâtre VII (Et ils passèrent des menottes aux fleurs, L'aurore rouge et noire). Paris: Christian Bourgeois, 1969. (*And They Put Handcuffs on the Flowers.* Trans. Charles Marowitz. New York: Grove Press, 1973.)

Théâtre XIV (Extravagante réussite de Jésus-Christ, Karl Marx et William Shakespeare, Lève-toi et rêve). Paris: Christian Bourgeois, 1982. Plays.

Tormentos y delicias de la carne: homenaje a la conjura de los necios de John Kennedy Toole. Barcelona: Ediciones Destino, 1985. Plays.

La torre herida por el rayo. Barcelona: Ediciones Destino, 1983. (*The Tower Struck by Lightning.* Trans. Anthony Kerrigan. New York: Viking, 1988.) Novel.

La vierge rouge. Paris: Acropole, 1986; *La virgen roja.* Barcelona: Seix Barral, 1987. Novel.

JUAN BENET

El aire de un crimen. Barcelona: Editorial Planeta, 1980. Novel.

El ángel del señor abandona a Tobías. Barcelona: La Gaya Ciencia, 1976.

Artículos. Ediciones Libertarias, 1983.

Barojiana. Madrid: Taurus, 1972.

5 narraciones y 2 fabulas. Barcelona: La Gaya Ciencia, 1972. Short stories.

Cuentos completos. Madrid: Alianza Editorial, 1977. Short stories.

Del pozo y del Numa. Barcelona: La Gaya Ciencia, 1978. An essay and a legend.

Dionisio Ridruejo, de la falange a la oposición. Madrid: Taurus, 1976.

Edad Media y literatura contemporánea. Madrid: Trieste, 1985. Criticism.

En el estado. Madrid: Alfaguara, 1977. Novel.

En la penumbra. Madrid: Alfaguara, 1989. Novel.

Herrumbrosas lanzas. Madrid: Alfaguara, 1983-86.

La inspiración y el estilo. Madrid: Revista de Occidente, 1966. Essays.

Londres victoriano. Barcelona: Editorial Planeta, 1989.

Una meditación. Barcelona: Seix Barral, 1969. (*A Meditation.* Trans. Gregory Rabassa. New York: Persea Books, 1982.) Novel.

La moviola de Eurípides y otros ensayos. Madrid: Taurus, 1981. Essays.

Nunca llegarás a nada. Madrid: Editorial Tebas, 1961. Short stories.
Otoño en Madrid hacia 1950. Madrid: Alianza, 1987.
Saúl ante Samuel. Barcelona: La Gaya Ciencia, 1980. Novel.
Sobre la incertidumbre. Barcelona: Ariel, 1982.
Sub rosa. Barcelona: La Gaya Ciencia, 1973. Short stories.
Trece fábulas y media. Madrid: Alfaguara, 1981. Short stories.
Una tumba. Barcelona: Editorial Lumen, 1971. Novel.
Un viaje de invierno. Barcelona: La Gaya Ciencia, 1972. Novel.
Volverás a Región. Barcelona: Ediciones Destino, 1967. (*Return to Región.* Trans. Gregory Rabassa. New York: Columbia University Press, 1985.) Novel.

ANTONIO BUERO VALLEJO

Caimán: relato escénico en dos partes: Las cartas boca abajo: tragedia española en dos actos y cuatro cuadros. Madrid: Espasa-Calpe, 1981. Plays.
Casi un cuento de hadas. Madrid: Ediciones Alfil, 1953. Play.
El concierto de San Ovidio. Barcelona: Aymá, 1962. (*The Concert at Saint Ovide.* Trans. Farris Anderson. University Park: Pennsylvania State University Press, 1967.) Play.
Diálogo secreto: fantasía en dos partes. Madrid: Espasa-Calpe, 1985. Play.
La doble historia del doctor Valmy: relato escénico en dos partes. Philadelphia: Center for Curriculum Development, 1970. Play.
En la ardiente oscuridad. Madrid: Ediciones Alfil, 1951. Play.
Historia de una escalera. Barcelona: J. Janés, 1950. Play.
Hoy es fiesta. Madrid: Ediciones Alfil, 1957. (*Today's a Holiday.* Trans. James Dunlop. Lanham: University Press of America, 1987.) Play.
Lázaro en el laberinto. Madrid: Espasa-Calpe, 1987. Play.
Las Meninas: Fantasía velazqueña en dos partes. Madrid: Escelicer, 1961; New York: Scribner, 1963. (*Las Meninas: A Fantasia in Two Parts.* Trans. Marion Peter Holt. San Antonio, TX: Trinity University Press, 1987.) Play.
Mito (Libro para una ópera). Madrid: Ediciones Alfil, 1968.
Un soñador para un pueblo. Madrid: Ediciones Alfil, 1959. Play.
Soto, Apuleyo; El buey de los cuernos de oro; El país de luna grande; Una casita roja. Madrid: Editorial Fundamentos, 1981.
El sueño de la razón. Madrid: Escelicer, 1970. (*Three Plays: The Sleep of Reason, The Foundation, In the Burning Darkness.* Trans. Marion Peter Holt. San Antonio, TX: Trinity University Press, 1985.) Plays.
Teatro español actual. Madrid: Fundación Juan March, 1977.
La tejedora de sueños. Drama en tres actos. Madrid: Ediciones Alfil, 1952. Play.
El terror inmóvil. Madrid: Escelicer, 1954; Murcia: Universidad de Murcia, 1979. Play.
El tragaluz. Madrid: Ediciones Alfil, 1968. Play.

José María Carrascal

La aventura americana. Barcelona: Editorial Planeta, 1982.
El capitán que nunca mandó un barco. Barcelona: Ediciones Destino, 1972. Novel.
Cuatrocientos años triunfales. Barcelona: Plaza & Janés, 1982.
Mientras tenga mis piernas. Barcelona: Ediciones Destino, 1975. Novel.
La muerte no existe. Madrid: Breogan, 1974. Novel.
USA superstar. Barcelona: Ediciones Destino, 1973. Novel.
Groovy. Barcelona: Ediciones Destino, 1973. Novel.

José Luis Castillo Puche

El amargo sabor de la retama. Barcelona: Ediciones Destino, 1979. Novel.
América de cabo a rabo. Madrid: Ediciones Cid, 1959. Travelogue.
El cíngulo: Como ovejas al matadero. Barcelona: Ediciones Destino, 1971. Novel.
Con la muerte al hombro. Madrid: Biblioteca Nueva, 1954. Novel.
El Congo estrena libertad. Madrid: Biblioteca Nueva, 1961. Travelogue.
Conocerás el poso de la nada. Barcelona: Ediciones Destino, 1982. Novel.
Estudio de la pintura de Toral. Madrid: Espasa-Calpe, 1987.
Hemingway: entre la vida y la muerte. Barcelona: Ediciones Destino, 1968. (*Hemingway in Spain: A Personal Reminiscence of Hemingway's Years in Spain by His Friend.* Trans. Helen R. Lane. New York: Doubleday, 1974.)
Hicieron partes. Madrid: Escelicer, 1957. Novel.
Jeremías, el anarquista. Barcelona: Ediciones Destino, 1975. Novel.
El leproso y otras narraciones. Murcia: Ediciones Mediterráneo, 1981. Short stories.
El libro de las visiones y las apariciones. Barcelona: Ediciones Destino, 1977.
Misión a Estambul. Madrid: Ediciones Cid, 1954. Novel.
Los murciélagos no son pájaros. Barcelona: Ediciones Destino, 1986. Novel.
Oro blanco. Madrid: Ediciones Cid, 1963.
Paralelo 40. Barcelona: Ediciones Destino, 1963. Novel.
El perro loco. Madrid: La novela popular, 1965. Novel.
Ramón J. Sender, el distanciamiento del exilio. Barcelona: Ediciones Destino, 1985. Essay.
Sin camino. Buenos Aires: Emecé Editores, 1956. Novel.
El vengador. Barcelona: Editorial Planeta, 1956. Novel.

Camilo José Cela

Album de taller. Barcelona: Ambit, 1981.
El asno de Buridán. Madrid: El País, 1986.
Balada del vagabundo sin suerte y otros papeles volanderos. Madrid: Espasa-Calpe, 1973.
Barcelona. Barcelona: Alfaguara, 1970.

La bola del mundo: escenas cotidianas. Madrid: Organización Sala Editorial, 1972.

El bonito crimen del carabinero. Barcelona: J. Janés, 1947. Short stories.

La Catira. Barcelona: Editorial Noguer, 1955. Novel.

El ciudadano Iscariote Reclús. Madrid: Alfaguara, 1965.

La colmena. Buenos Aires: Emecé Editores, 1951. (*The Hive.* Trans. J. Cohen. New York: Farrar, Straus and Young, 1953; reprint: Farrar, Straus and Giroux, 1990.) Novel.

Cristo versus Arizona. Barcelona: Seix Barral, 1988. Novel.

Cuaderno del Guadarrama. Madrid: Arión, 1960.

Cuatro figuras del 98: Unamuno; Valle Inclán, Baroja, Azorín, y otros retratos y ensayos españoles. Barcelona: Aedos, 1961. Essays.

La cucaña. Memorias. Libro primero. La rosa. Barcelona: Ediciones Destino, 1959.

Cuentos para leer después del baño. Barcelona: La Gaya Ciencia, 1974.

Diccionario del erotismo. Barcelona: Grijalbo, 1982.

Diccionario secreto. Madrid: Alfaguara, vol. 1, 1968; vol. 2, 1971.

Enciclopedia del erotismo. Madrid: Sedmay, 1976.

El espejo y otros cuentos. Madrid: Espasa-Calpe, 1981. Short stories.

La familia de Pascual Duarte. Madrid: Editorial Aldecoa, 1942. (*The Family of Pascual Duarte.* Trans. John Marks. London: Eyre & Spottiswoode, 1946; Trans. Anthony Kerrigan. Boston: Little, Brown, 1964.) Novel.

Gavilla de fábulas sin amor. Palma de Mallorca: Papeles de Son Armadans, 1962. Text with illustrations by Picasso.

Judíos, moros y cristianos. Barcelona: Ediciones Destino, 1956.

Madrid. Madrid: Alfaguara, 1966.

La Mancha en el corazón y en los ojos. Barcelona: EDISVEN, 1971.

María Sabina. Palma de Mallorca: Papeles de Son Armadans, 1967. (With English and Spanish text. Trans. Theodore S. Beardsley, Jr. and Luz Castaños. Dobbs Ferry, NY: General Music Publishing Co., 1981.) Music: Leonardo Balada. Opera.

María Sabina, El carro de heno: o, El inventor de la guillotina. Madrid: Alfaguara, 1969.

Mazurca para dos muertos. Barcelona: Seix Barral, 1983. Novel.

Mesa revuelta. Madrid: Ediciones de los estudiantes españoles, 1945.

Mis páginas preferidas. Madrid Editorial Gredos, 1956.

El molino de viento y otras novelas cortas. Barcelona: Noguer, 1956. Novellas.

Mrs. Caldwell habla con su hijo. Barcelona: Ediciones Destino, 1953. (*Mrs. Caldwell Speaks to Her Son.* Trans. Jerome Bernstein. Ithaca: Cornell University, 1968.) Novel.

Nuevas andanzas y desventuras de Lazarillo de Tormes. Madrid: Ediciones La Nave, 1944. Novel.

Nuevas escenas matritenses. Madrid: Alfaguara, 1965-66. 7 volumes.

Nuevo viaje a la Alcarria. Barcelona: Plaza & Janés, 1986.

Obras completas de Camilo José Cela. Barcelona: Ediciones Destino, 1962.

La obra literaria del pintor Solana. Madrid: Alfaguara, 1967.

Oficio de tinieblas 5. Barcelona: Editorial Argos Vergara, 1973. Novel.

Pabellón de reposo. Madrid: Afrodisio Aguado, 1943. (*Rest Home.* Trans. Herma Briffault. New York: Las Américas, 1961.) Novel.

Poemas de una adolescencia cruel. Barcelona: Ediciones del Zodíaco, 1945.

Recuerdo de don Pío Baroja. México: Ediciones de Andrea, 1958.

El reto de los halcones: antología de la prensa apocalíptica española en la apertura (febrero de 1974-junio de 1975). Madrid: Ediciones Júcar, 1975.

Rol de cornudos. Barcelona: Ediciones Noguer, S.A., 1976.

San Camilo, 1936. Madrid: Alfaguara, 1969. Novel.

Al servicio de algo. Madrid: Alfaguara, 1969.

El solitario. Palma de Mallorca: Papeles de Son Armadans, 1963.

Los sueños vanos. Los ángeles curiosos. Barcelona: Editorial Argos Vergara, 1979.

Los vasos comunicantes. Barcelona: Bruguera, 1981.

Viaje a la Alcarria. Madrid: Revista de Occidente, 1948. (*Journey to the Alcarria.* Trans. Frances M. López-Morillas. Madison: University of Wisconsin Press, 1964; reprint: New York: Atlantic Monthly Press, 1990.) Travelogue.

Viaje a USA: o, El que la sigue la mata. Madrid: Alfaguara, 1967.

Los viejos amigos. Barcelona: Editorial Noguer, Colección El Espejo y La Pluma, 1960.

Vuelta de hoja. Barcelona: Ediciones Destino, 1981.

A vueltas con España. Madrid: Seminarios y Ediciones, 1973.

CARMEN CONDE

Acompañando a Francisca Sánchez; resumen de una vida junto a Rubén Darío. Nicaragua: Editorial Unión, 1964.

A este lado de la eternidad. Madrid: Biblioteca Nueva, 1970. Poems.

Ansia de la Gracia. Madrid: Ediciones Adonais, 1945. Poems.

Antología de poesía amorosa contemporánea. Barcelona: Editorial Bruguera, 1969.

Antología poética. Madrid: Espasa-Calpe, 1985.

Brocal. Madrid: Editorial La Lectura, 1929. Poems.

Brocal y Poemas a María. Madrid: Biblioteca Nueva, 1984.

Cancionero de la enamorada. Avila: Diputación Provincial, Institución Gran Duque de Alba, 1971. Poems.

Cita con la vida. Madrid: Biblioteca Nueva, 1976. Poems.

Cobre. Madrid: Editorial El Grifón, 1953. Novel.

Corrosión. Madrid: Biblioteca Nueva, 1975. Poems.

Cráter. Madrid: Biblioteca Nueva, 1985. Poems.

Creció espesa la yerba. Barcelona: Editorial Planeta, 1979. Novel.

Derramen su sangre las sombras. Madrid: Ediciones Torremozas, 1983. Poems.

Derribado arcángel. Madrid: Revista de Occidente, 1960. Poems.

Desde nunca. Barcelona: Libros Río Nuevo, 1982.

Días por la tierra: antología incompleta. Madrid: Editorial Nacional, 1977. Anthology.

Empezando la vida, memorias de una infancia en Marruecos, 1914-1920. Tetuán: Ediciones "Al-Motamid," 1955.

Gabriela Mistral. Madrid: E.P.E.S.A., 1970.

En manos del silencio. Barcelona: J. Janés, 1950. Novel.

En un mundo de fugitivos. Buenos Aires: Editorial Losada, 1960. Poems.

Menéndez Pidal. Madrid: Unión Editorial, 1969.

Mientras los hombres mueren. Milano: Istituto Editoriale Cisalpino, 1953. Poems.

Mujer sin Edén. Madrid: Ediciones Jura, 1946. (*Woman without Eden.* A bilingual edition. Trans. José de Armas and Alexis Levitin. Miami: Ediciones Universal, 1986.) Poems.

La noche oscura del cuerpo. Madrid: Biblioteca Nueva, 1980. Poems.

Obra poética (1922-1966). Madrid: Biblioteca Nueva, 1967.

Once grandes poetisas americohispanas. Madrid: Ediciones Cultura Hispánica, 1967. Anthology.

Las oscuras raíces. Barcelona: Garbo, 1953. Novel.

Los poemas de Mar Menor. Murcia: Universidad de Murcia, 1962.

Poesía femenina española 1939-1950. Barcelona: Editorial Bruguera, 1967. Anthology.

Poesía femenina española viviente. Madrid: Ediciones Arquero, 1954. Anthology.

Por el camino, viendo sus orillas. Barcelona: Plaza & Janés, 1986. 3 volumes. Memoirs.

Soy la madre. Barcelona: Editorial Planeta, 1980. Novel.

El tiempo es un río lentísimo de fuego. Barcelona: Ediciones 29, 1978. Poems.

MIGUEL DELIBES

Un año de mi vida. Barcelona: Ediciones Destino, 1972. Novel.

Aventuras, venturas y desventuras de un cazador a rabo. Barcelona: Ediciones Destino, 1977.

El camino. Barcelona: Ediciones Destino, 1950. (*The Path.* Trans. John and Brita Haycraft. New York: John Day, 1961; London: H. Hamilton, 1961.) Novel.

Cartas de amor de un sexagenario voluptuoso. Barcelona: Ediciones Destino, 1983. Novel.

Castilla, lo castellano y los castellanos. Barcelona: Editorial Planeta, 1979.

La caza de la perdiz roja. Barcelona: Editorial Lumen, 1963.

La censura de prensa en los años 40 y otros ensayos. Valladolid: Ambito, 1985. Essays.

Cinco horas con Mario. Barcelona: Ediciones Destino, 1966. (*Five Hours with Mario.* Trans. Frances M. López-Morillas. New York: Columbia University Press, 1988.) Novel.

Con la escopeta al hombro. Barcelona: Ediciones Destino, 1970. Nonfiction.
Diario de un cazador. Barcelona: Ediciones Destino, 1955. Novel.
Diario de un emigrante. Barcelona: Ediciones Destino, 1958. Novel.
El disputado voto del señor Cayo. Barcelona: Ediciones Destino, 1978. Novel.
Dos viajes en automóvil: Suecia y Países Bajos. Barcelona: Plaza & Janés, 1982.
Las guerras de nuestros antepasados. Barcelona: Ediciones Destino, 1975. Novel.
La hoja roja. Barcelona: Ediciones Destino, 1959. Novel.
El loco. Madrid: Editorial Tecnos, 1953.
Mi idolatrado hijo Sisí. Barcelona: Ediciones Destino, 1953. Novel.
Mi querida bicicleta. Madrid: Editorial Miñon, 1988.
Mi vida al aire libre: memorias deportivas de un hombre sedentario. Barcelona: Ediciones Destino, 1989.
La mortaja. Madrid: Alianza Editorial, 1970. Short stories.
Un novelista descubre América (Chile en el ojo ajeno). Madrid: Editora Nacional, 1956.
El otro fútbol. Barcelona: Ediciones Destino, 1982.
Parábola del náufrago. Barcelona: Ediciones Destino, 1969. (*The Hedge.* Trans. Frances M. López-Morillas. New York: Columbia University Press, 1983.) Novel.
Las perdices del domingo. Barcelona: Ediciones Destino, 1981.
La primavera de Praga. Madrid: Alianza Editorial, 1968.
El príncipe destronado. Barcelona: Ediciones Destino, 1974. Novel.
Las ratas. Barcelona: Ediciones Destino, 1962. (*Smoke on the Ground.* Trans. Alfred Johnson. Garden City, NY: Doubleday, 1972.) Novel.
Los santos inocentes. Barcelona: Editorial Planeta, 1981. Novel.
Siestas con viento sur. Barcelona: Ediciones Destino, 1957. Short stories.
La sombra del ciprés es alargada. Barcelona: Ediciones Destino, 1948. Novel.
S.O.S. Barcelona: Ediciones Destino, 1976.
El tesoro. Barcelona: Ediciones Destino, 1985.
377A, madera de héroe. Barcelona: Ediciones Destino, 1987. (*The Stuff of Heroes.* Trans. Frances M. López-Morillas. New York: Pantheon Books, 1990.) Novel.
USA y yo. Barcelona: Editorial Destino, 1966.
Viejas historias de Castilla la Vieja. Barcelona: Editorial Lumen, 1964.
Vivir al día. Barcelona: Ediciones Destino, 1968.

LIDIA FALCÓN

El alboroto español. Barcelona: Fontanella, 1984.
Cartas a una idiota española. Barcelona: Editorial Dirosa, 1974.
En el infierno: Ser mujer en las cárceles de España. Barcelona: Ediciones de Feminismo, 1977. Nonfiction.

El juego de la piel. Barcelona: Editorial Argos Vergara, 1983. Novel.
Es largo esperar callado. Barcelona: Pomaire, 1975. Novel.
Los hijos de los vencidos (1939-1949). Barcelona: Pomaire, 1979. Memoirs.
La razón feminista. Barcelona: Fontanella, 1981-82. 2 volumes. Nonfiction.
Rupturas. Barcelona: Fontanella, 1985. Novel.
El varón español a la búsqueda de su identidad. Barcelona: Plaza & Janés, 1986.
Viernes y trece en la Calle del Correo. Barcelona: Editorial Planeta, 1981. Novel.

JUAN GOYTISOLO

Algo sobre temas de hoy. Madrid: Speiro, 1972.
Campos de Níjar. Barcelona: Seix Barral, 1959. (*The Countryside of Níjar and La Chanca.* Trans. Luigi Luccarelli. Plainfield, IN: Alembic Press, 1987.) Travelogue.
La Chanca. Paris: Librería Española, 1962. Travelogue.
El circo. Barcelona: Ediciones Destino, 1957. Novel.
Coto vedado. Barcelona: Seix Barral, 1985. (*Forbidden Territory.* Trans. Peter Bush. San Francisco: North Point Press, 1989.) Memoirs.
Crónicas sarracinas. Madrid: Editorial Ruedo Ibérico, 1982. Essays.
Duelo en el paraíso. Barcelona: Editorial Planeta, 1955. (*Children of Chaos.* Trans. Christine Brooke-Rose. London: MacGibbon & Kee, 1958.) Novel.
En los reinos de taifa. Barcelona: Seix Barral, 1986. (*Realms of Strife: Memoirs, 1957-1982.* Trans. Peter Bush. San Francisco: North Point, 1990.) Memoirs.
España y los españoles. Barcelona: Editorial Lumen, 1969. Essay.
Estambul otomano. Barcelona: Editorial Planeta, 1989. Essay.
Fiestas. Buenos Aires: Emecé Editores, 1958. (*Fiestas.* Trans. Herbert Weinstock. New York: Knopf, 1960.) Novel.
Fin de fiesta. Barcelona: Seix Barral, 1962. (*The Party's Over: Four Attempts to Define a Love Story.* Trans. José Yglesia. New York: Grove Press, 1966.) Short stories.
El furgón de cola. Paris: Ruedo ibérico, 1967. Essays.
La isla. Barcelona: Seix Barral, 1961. (*Island of Women.* Trans. José Yglesias. New York: Knopf, 1962; published in England as *Sands of Terremolinos.* London: Cape, 1962.) Novel.
Juan sin tierra. Barcelona: Seix Barral, 1975. (*Juan the Landless.* Trans. Helen R. Lane. New York: Viking, 1977.) Novel.
Juegos de manos. Barcelona: Ediciones Destino, 1954. (*The Young Assassins.* Trans. John Rust. New York: Knopf, 1959.) Novel.
Libertad, libertad, libertad. Barcelona: Editorial Anagrama, 1978. Essay.
Makbara. Barcelona: Seix Barral, 1980. (*Makbara.* Trans. Helen R. Lane. New York: Seaver Books, 1981.) Novel.
Obra inglesa de Blanco White. Buenos Aires: Ediciones Formentor, 1972. Essays. (Preface.)

324 Interviews with Spanish Writers

Paisajes después de la batalla. Barcelona: Montesinos, 1982. (*Landscapes after the Battle.* Trans. Helen R. Lane. New York: Seaver Books, 1987.) Novel.
Para vivir aquí. Buenos Aires: Sur, 1960. Short stories.
Problemas de la novela. Barcelona: Seix Barral, 1959. Essays.
Reivindicación del Conde don Julián. México: Editorial J. Mortiz, 1970. (*Count Julian.* Trans. Helen R. Lane. New York: Viking, 1974.) Novel.
La resaca. Paris: Club del Libro Español, 1958. Novel.
Señas de identidad. México: J. Mortiz, 1966. (*Marks of Identity.* Trans. Gregory Rabassa. New York: Grove Press, 1969.) Novel.
Sociedad de masas y derecho. Madrid: Taurus, 1968.
Space in Motion. Trans. Helen R. Lane. New York: Lumen Books, 1987. Essays.
Las virtudes del pájaro solitario. Barcelona: Seix Barral, 1988. (*The Virtues of the Lonely Bird.* Trans. Helen R. Lane. London: Serpent's Tail, 1991.) Novel.

CARMEN LAFORET

Gran Canaria. Barcelona: Editorial Noguer, 1961. (*Gran Canaria.* Trans. John Forrester. Barcelona: Editorial Noguer, 1961.)
La insolación. Barcelona: Editorial Planeta, 1963. Novel.
La isla y los demonios. Barcelona: Ediciones Destino, 1952. Novel.
La llamada. Barcelona: Ediciones Destino, 1954. Novellas.
Un matrimonio. Madrid: Mon, 1956. Novel.
Mis páginas mejores. Madrid: Editorial Gredos, 1956.
La muerta. Madrid: Ediciones Rumbos, 1952. Novel.
La mujer nueva. Barcelona: Ediciones Destino, 1955. Novel.
Nada. Barcelona: Ediciones Destino, 1945. (*Nada.* Trans. Inez Muñoz. London: Weidenfeld and Nicolson, 1958; *Andrea.* Trans. Charles F. Payne. New York: Vantage Press, 1964.) Novel.
La niña. Madrid: Ediciones Cid, 1954. Short stories.
Novelas. Barcelona: Editorial Planeta, 1957.
Un noviazgo. Madrid: Editorial Tecnos, 1953. Novel.
Paralelo 35. Barcelona: Editorial Planeta, 1967; rpt. as *Mi primer viaje a USA.* Madrid: P.P.P. Ediciones, 1985.

JUAN MARSÉ

Confidencias de un chorizo. Barcelona: Editorial Planeta, 1977.
Un día volveré. Barcelona: Plaza & Janés, 1982. Novel.
Encerrados con un solo juguete. Barcelona: Seix Barral, 1960. Novel.
Esta cara de la luna. Barcelona: Seix Barral, 1962. Novel.
El fantasma del cine Roxy. Madrid: Almarabu, 1985.
Historia de España, vista con buenos ojos. Barcelona: Punch Ediciones, 1975.

Imágenes y recuerdos, 1929-1940; la gran desilusión. Barcelona: Difusora
Internacional, 1971.
La muchacha de las bragas de oro. Barcelona: Editorial Planeta, 1978.
(*Golden Girl.* Trans. Helen R. Lane. Boston: Little, Brown, 1981.) Novel.
La oscura historia de la prima Montse. Barcelona: Seix Barral, 1970. Novel.
Señoras y señores. Barcelona: Punch Ediciones, 1977.
Si te dicen que caí. México: Organización Editorial Novaro, 1973. (*The
Fallen.* Trans. Helen R. Lane. Boston: Little, Brown, 1979.) Novel.
Teniente Bravo. Barcelona: Seix Barral, 1987. Novel.
Ultimas tardes con Teresa. Barcelona: Seix Barral, 1966. Novel.

CARMEN MARTÍN GAITE

Las ataduras. Barcelona: Ediciones Destino, 1960. Novella and six stories.
El balneario. Barcelona: Ediciones Destino, 1955. Novel.
La búsqueda de interlocutor y otras búsquedas. Madrid: Nostromo, 1973.
Caperucita en Manhattan. Madrid: Ediciones Sirvela, 1990. Novel.
El castillo de las tres murallas. Barcelona: Editorial Lumen, 1981. Children's
story.
El cuarto de atrás. Barcelona: Ediciones Destino, 1978. (*The Back Room.*
Trans. Helen R. Lane. New York: Columbia University Press, 1983.)
Novel.
El cuento de nunca acabar: apuntes sobre la narración, el amor y la mentira.
Madrid: Trieste, 1983. Nonfiction.
Dos relatos fantásticos. Barcelona: Editorial Lumen, 1985.
Entre visillos. Barcelona: Ediciones Destino, 1958. (*Behind the Curtains.*
Trans. Frances M. López-Morillas. New York: Columbia University Press,
1990.) Novel.
Fragmentos de interior. Barcelona: Ediciones Destino, 1976. Novel.
Ocho siglos de poesía gallega: Antología bilingüe. Madrid: Alianza Editorial,
1972.
El pastel del diablo. Barcelona: Editorial Lumen, 1985. Children's story.
El proceso de Macanaz: historia de un empapelamiento. Madrid: Editorial
Moneda y Crédito, 1970; reissued as *Macanaz, otro paciente de la Inquisi-
cion.* Madrid: Taurus, 1975. Nonfiction.
Retahílas. Barcelona: Ediciones Destino, 1974. Novel.
Ritmo lento. Barcelona: Seix Barral, 1963. Novel.
Usos amorosos de la postguerra española. Barcelona: Editorial Anagrama,
1987.
Usos amorosos del dieciocho en España. Madrid: Siglo Veintiuno de España
Editores, 1972.

ANA MARÍA MATUTE

Los Abel. Barcelona: Ediciones Destino, 1948. Novel.
A la mitad del camino. Barcelona: Rocas, 1961.

Algunos muchachos y otros cuentos. Barcelona: Ediciones Destino, 1968.
   (*The Heliotrope Wall and Other Stories.* Trans. Michael Scott Doyle. New
   York: Columbia University Press, 1989.) Short stories.
El arrepentido y otras narraciones. Barcelona: Rocas, 1961; revised edition:
   Barcelona: Editorial Juventud, 1967. Short stories.
En esta tierra. Barcelona: Editorial Exito, 1955. Novel.
Fiesta al Noroeste. Madrid: Afrodisio Aguado, 1953. Novel.
Los hijos muertos. Barcelona: Editorial Planeta, 1958. (*The Lost Children.*
   Trans. Joan MacLean. New York: Macmillan, 1965.) Novel.
Historias de la Artámila. Barcelona: Ediciones Destino, 1961.
Libro de juegos para los niños de los otros. Barcelona: Editorial Lumen, 1961.
Los mercaderes. Barcelona: Ediciones Destino, 1959. Novel.
Los niños tontos. Madrid: Ediciones Arión, 1956. Short stories.
Obra completa. Barcelona: Ediciones Destino, 1971.
Paulina. Barcelona: Garbo Editorial, 1960. Novel.
Pequeño teatro. Barcelona: Editorial Planeta, 1954. Novel.
El polizón de Ulises. Barcelona: Editorial Lumen, 1965. Children's story.
Primera memoria. Barcelona: Ediciones Destino, 1960. (*School of the Sun.*
   Trans. Elaine Kerrigan. New York: Pantheon, 1963; *Awakening.* Trans.
   James Holman Mason. London: Hutchinson, 1963.) Novel.
El río. Barcelona: Editorial Argos, 1963. Short stories.
El saltamontes verde. El aprendiz. Barcelona: Editorial Lumen, 1960.
   Children's story.
Los soldados lloran de noche. Barcelona: Ediciones Destino, 1964. Novel.
Solo, un pie descalzo. Barcelona: Editorial Lumen, 1983. Children's story.
El tiempo. Barcelona: Editorial Mateu, 1957. Short stories.
La torre vigía. Barcelona: Editorial Lumen, 1971. Novel.
La trampa. Barcelona: Ediciones Destino, 1969. Novel.
Tres y un sueño. Barcelona: Ediciones Destino, 1961. Three short novels.

EDUARDO MENDOZA

Barcelona modernista. Barcelona: Editorial Planeta, 1989.
La ciudad de los prodigios. Barcelona: Seix Barral, 1986. (*The City of
   Marvels.* Trans. Bernard Molloy. San Diego: Harcourt Brace Jovanovich,
   1988.) Novel.
La isla inaudita. Barcelona: Seix Barral, 1989. Novel.
El laberinto de las aceitunas. Barcelona: Seix Barral, 1982. Novel.
El misterio de la cripta embrujada. Barcelona: Seix Barral, 1979. Novel.
La verdad sobre el caso Savolta. Barcelona: Seix Barral, 1975. Novel.

ROSA MONTERO

Amado Amo. Madrid: Editorial Debate, 1988. Novel.
Cinco años de País. Madrid: Editorial Debate, 1982. Interviews.
Crónica del desamor. Madrid: Editorial Debate, 1979. Novel.

Doce relatos de mujer. Madrid: Alianza Editorial, 1982. Short stories.
España para ti para siempre. Madrid: A.Q. Ediciones, 1976. Interviews.
La función Delta. Madrid: Editorial Debate, 1981. Novel.
Te trataré como a una reina. Barcelona: Seix Barral, 1983. Novel.
Temblor. Barcelona: Seix Barral, 1990. Novel.

Antonio Muñoz Molina

Beatus Ille. Barcelona: Seix Barral, 1986. Novel.
Beltenebros. Barcelona: Seix Barral, 1989. Novel.
La Córdoba de los omeyas. Barcelona: Editorial Planeta, 1990. Nonfiction.
Diario del "Nautilus." Granada: Colección de bolsillo de la Diputación Provincial de Granada, 1986. Articles.
El invierno en Lisboa. Barcelona: Seix Barral, 1987. Novel.
Las otras vidas. Madrid: Mondadori, 1988.
El Róbinson urbano. Pamplona: Pamiela, 1984. Articles.

Justo Jorge Padrón

Antología poética (1971-1988). Islas Canarias: Biblioteca Básica Canaria, 1988.
Los Círculos del Infierno / The Circles of Hell (1973-1975). A bilingual edition. Trans. Louis Bourne. Luxembourg: Euroeditor, 1981. Poems.
Mar de la noche. Barcelona: Instituto Catalán de Cultura Hispánica, 1973. Poems.
Obra poética 1971-1980. Barcelona: Editorial Plaza & Janés, 1980.
On the Cutting Edge. Selected Poems. Trans. Louis Bourne. London: Forest Books, 1988.
Sólo muere la mano que te escribe; Los rostros escuchados. Madrid: Espasa-Calpe, 1989. Poems.
La visita del mar, 1980-1984; Los dones de la tierra. Madrid: Espasa-Calpe, 1984. Poems.

Julián Ríos

Impresiones de Kitaj: La novela pintada. Madrid: Mondadori, 1989.
Larva: Babel de una noche de San Juan. Barcelona: Edicions del Mall, 1983. (*Larva: Midsummer Night's Babel.* Trans. Richard Alan Francis with Suzanne Jill Levine and the author. Elmwood Park, IL: Dalkey Archive Press, 1990.) Novel.
Poundemónium: homenaje a Ezra Pound. Barcelona: Edicions del Mall, 1986; expanded edition: Madrid: Mondadori, 1989. Novel.
Solo a dos voces. Barcelona: Editorial Lumen, 1973. A conversation with Octavio Paz.

JOSÉ LUIS SAMPEDRO

El caballo desnudo. Barcelona: Editorial Planeta, 1970. Novel.
Congreso en Estocolmo. Madrid: Editorial Aguilar, 1952. Novel.
Estructura económica; teoría básica y estructura mundial. Barcelona:
    Ediciones Ariel, 1969.
Las fuerzas económicas de nuestro tiempo. Madrid: Ediciones Guadarrama,
    1967. (*Decisive Forces in World Economics.* Trans. S. E. Nodder. New
    York: McGraw-Hill, 1967.)
Octubre, octubre. Madrid: Alfaguara, 1981. Novel.
*Perfiles económicos de las regiones españolas / Economic Profiles of the
    Regions of Spain.* Madrid: Seminario de Investigaciones Económicas,
    Banco Urquijo, Sociedad de Estudios y Publicaciones, 1964.
El río que nos lleva. Madrid: Ediciones M. Aguilar, 1961. Novel.
La segunda ampliación de la C. E. E. Madrid: Servicio de Estudios
    Económicos. With Juan Antonio Payno as co-editor and the assistance of
    Fuencisla Rico Martín and Emma Rodríguez Pinar. Banco Exterior de
    España, 1982. (*The Enlargement of the European Community.* Ed. Lyn
    Gorman and Marja Liisa Kiljunen. London: Macmillan, 1983.)
La sonrisa etrusca. Madrid: Alfaguara, 1985. Novel.

GONZALO TORRENTE BALLESTER

Compostela. Madrid: Afrodisio Aguado, 1948.
Crónica del rey pasmado. Barcelona: Editorial Planeta, 1989. Novel.
Cuadernos de La Romana. Barcelona: Ediciones Destino, 1975.
Los cuadernos de un vate vago. Barcelona: Plaza & Janés, 1982. Novel.
Dafne y ensueños. Barcelona: Ediciones Destino, 1983. Novel.
Ensayos críticos. Barcelona: Ediciones Destino, 1982. Essays.
Filomeno, a mi pesar. Barcelona: Editorial Planeta, 1988. Novel.
Fragmentos de Apocalipsis. Barcelona: Ediciones Destino, 1977. Novel.
El golpe de estado de Guadalupe Limón. Madrid: Ediciones Nueva Epoca,
    1946.
Hombre al agua. Madrid: Amarabu, 1987. Novel.
La isla de los jacintos cortados: carta de amor con interpolaciones mágicas.
    Barcelona: Ediciones Destino, 1980. Novel.
Javier Mariño, historia de una conversación. Madrid: Nacional, 1943.
Lo mejor de Gonzalo Torrente Ballester. Barcelona: Seix Barral, 1989.
Obra completa. Barcelona: Ediciones Destino, 1977.
Off-side. Barcelona: Ediciones Destino, 1969. Novel.
La otra orilla: las manos son inocentes. Madrid: Espasa-Calpe, 1988.
Panorama de la literatura española contemporánea. Madrid: Ediciones
    Guadarrama, 1956. Criticism.
La Princesa Durmiente va a la escuela: historia de humor para eruditos.
    Barcelona: Plaza & Janés, 1983. Novel.
El Quijote como juego y otros trabajos críticos. Madrid: Ediciones

Guadarrama, 1975. Criticism.
Quizá nos lleve el viento al infinito. Barcelona: Plaza & Janés, 1984. Novel.
El retorno de Ulises. Madrid: Nacional, 1946.
La saga/fuga de J. B. Barcelona: Ediciones Destino, 1972. Novel.
Santiago de Rosalía de Castro: apuntes sobre la vida en Compostela en tiempos de Rosalía de Castro. Barcelona: Editorial Planeta, 1989. Essay.
Las sombras recobradas. Barcelona: Editorial Planeta, 1979. Short stories.
El viaje del joven Tobías. Madrid: Ediciones Jerarquía, 1938.
Yo no soy, evidentemente. Barcelona: Plaza & Janés, 1987.

FRANCISCO UMBRAL

A la sombra de las muchachas rojas: crónicas marcianas de la transición. Madrid: Cátedra, 1981.
Amar en Madrid. Barcelona: Editorial Planeta, 1972. Articles.
Los amores diurnos. Barcelona: Kairós, 1979. Novel.
Los ángeles custodios. Barcelona: Ediciones Destino, 1981. Memoirs.
Las ánimas del purgatorio. Barcelona: Grijalbo, 1982. Memoirs.
Un carnívoro cuchillo. Barcelona: Editorial Planeta, 1988. Novel.
Carta abierta a una chica 'progre.' Madrid: Ediciones 99, 1973.
Crímenes y baladas. Cuenca: Editorial Olcades, 1981.
Crónicas antiparlamentarias. Madrid: Ediciones Júcar, 1974. Articles.
Crónicas post-franquistas. Madrid: A.Q. Ediciones, 1976. Articles.
El día en que violé a Alma Mahler. Barcelona: Ediciones Destino, 1988.
Diario de un escritor burgués. Barcelona: Ediciones Destino, 1979. Articles.
Diario de un español cansado. Barcelona: Ediciones Destino, 1975. Articles.
Diario de un snob. Barcelona: Ediciones Destino, 1973.
Diccionario cheli. Barcelona: Grijalbo, 1983.
Diccionario para pobres. Madrid: Sedmay Ediciones, 1977.
España como invento. Madrid: Ediciones Libertarias, 1984.
Las españolas. Barcelona: Editorial Planeta, 1974.
Las europeas. Andorra la Vella: Editorial Andorra, 1970. Novel.
Fábula del falo. Barcelona: Kairós, 1985.
El fetichismo. Madrid: El Observatorio Ediciones, 1985.
El fulgor de África. Barcelona: Seix Barral, 1989.
Las giganteas. Barcelona: Plaza & Janés, 1982.
El Giocondo. Barcelona: Editorial Planeta, 1970. Novel.
La guapa gente de derechas. Barcelona: Luis de Caralt, 1975. Articles.
Guía de la posmodernidad: crónica, personajes e itinerarios madrileños. Madrid: Ediciones Temas de Hoy, 1987.
El hijo de Greta Garbo. Barcelona: Ediciones Destino, 1982. Novel.
Iba yo a comprar el pan . . . Madrid: Sedmay Ediciones, 1976. Articles.
Larra, anatomía de un dandy. Madrid: Biblioteca Nueva, 1976. Biography.
Lorca, poeta maldito. Madrid: Biblioteca Nueva, 1968. Biography.
Los males sagrados. Barcelona: Editorial Planeta, 1973.
Memoria de un niño de derechas. Barcelona: Ediciones Destino, 1972.

Memorias de un hijo del siglo. Madrid: Ediciones El País, 1986.
Miguel Delibes. Madrid: E.P.E.S.A., 1970. Biography.
Mis mujeres. Barcelona: Editorial Planeta, 1976.
Mis paraísos artificiales. Barcelona: Librería Editorial Argos, 1976.
Mis queridos monstruos. Madrid: Ediciones El País, 1985.
Mortal y rosa. Barcelona: Ediciones Destino, 1975. (*A Mortal Spring.* Trans.
   Helen R. Lane. New York: Harcourt Brace Jovanovich, 1980.) Novel.
Museo nacional del mal gusto. Barcelona: Plaza & Janés, 1974.
Nada en el domingo. Barcelona: Seix Barral, 1988.
Las ninfas. Barcelona: Ediciones Destino, 1976. Novel.
La noche que llegué al Café Gijón. Barcelona: Ediciones Destino, 1977.
Las respetuosas. Barcelona: Editorial Planeta, 1976.
Si hubiéramos sabido que el amor era eso. Madrid: Ediciones Literoy, 1969.
   Novel.
Sinfonía borbónica. Barcelona: Ediciones Destino, 1987.
Spleen de Madrid. Madrid: Organización Sala Editorial, 1972. Articles.
Teoría de Lola y otros cuentos. Barcelona: Ediciones Destino, 1977.
Trilogía de Madrid. Barcelona: Editorial Planeta, 1984.
Valle-Inclán. Madrid: Unión Editorial, 1968. Biography.
Las vírgenes. Madrid: Editorial Azur, 1969. Short stories.

MANUEL VÁZQUEZ MONTALBÁN

A la sombra de las muchachas sin flor; poemas del amor y del terror. Barce-
   lona: Ediciones Saturno, 1973. Poems.
Los alegres muchachos de Atzavara. Barcelona: Seix Barral, 1987. Novel.
Asesinato en el Comité Central. Barcelona: Editorial Planeta, 1981. (*Murder
   in the Central Committee.* Trans. Patrick Camiller. London: Pluto, 1985;
   Chicago: Academy Chicago, 1985.) Novel.
El balneario. Barcelona: Editorial Planeta, 1986. Novel.
Cancionero general, 1939-1971. Barcelona: Editorial Lumen, 1972.
100 años de canción y music hall. Barcelona: Difusora Internacional, 1974.
100 años de deporte, del esfuerzo individual al espectáculo de masas. Barce-
   lona: Difusora Internacional, 1972.
Como liquidaron el franquismo en dieciseis meses y un día. Barcelona:
   Editorial Planeta, 1977.
Coplas a la muerte de mi tía Daniela. Barcelona: Ediciones Saturno, 1973.
   Poems.
Crónica sentimental de España. Barcelona: Editorial Bruguera, 1971. Essays.
Cuestiones marxistas. Barcelona: Editorial Anagrama, 1974.
El delantero centro fue asesinado al atardecer. Barcelona: Editorial Planeta,
   1988. Novel.
Los demonios familiares de Franco. Barcelona: DOPESA, 1978.
Diccionario del franquismo. Barcelona: DOPESA, 1977.
Una educación sentimental. Barcelona: Saturno, 1967. Poems.
Galíndez. Barcelona: Seix Barral, 1990. Novel.

Historia y comunicación social. Madrid: Alianza Editorial, 1985.

Informe sobre la información. Barcelona: Editorial Fontanella, 1963. Essays.

Joan Manuel Serrat. Madrid: Júcar, 1976.

Manifiesto subnormal. Barcelona: Kairós, 1970. Essays.

Los mares del sur. Barcelona: Editorial Planeta, 1979. (*Southern Seas.* Trans. Patrick Camiller. London: Pluto, 1986.) Novel.

El matarife. Madrid: Almarabu, 1986.

1974: España se queda sola. Barcelona: Punch, 1974.

1975; el año del ¡ay, ay, ay! Madrid: SEDMAY, 1976.

Mis almuerzos con gente inquietante. Barcelona: Editorial Planeta, 1984.

Los pájaros de Bangkok. Barcelona: Editorial Planeta, 1983. Novel.

La palabra libre en la ciudad libre. Barcelona: Gedisa, 1979. Essays.

La penetración americana en España. Madrid: Editorial Cuadernos para el diálogo, 1974. Essays.

El pianista. Barcelona: Seix Barral, 1985. (*The Pianist.* Trans. Elizabeth Plaister. London: Quartet, 1989.) Novel.

Pigmalión y otros relatos. Barcelona: Seix Barral, 1987. Short stories.

Praga. Barcelona: Editorial Lumen, 1982. Poems.

Recordando a Dardé y otros relatos. Barcelona: Seix Barral, 1969. Short stories.

La rosa de Alejandría. Barcelona: Editorial Planeta, 1984.

La soledad del manager. Barcelona: Editorial Planeta, 1977. (*The Angst-ridden Executive.* Trans. Ed Emery. London: Serpent's Tail, 1990.) Novel.

Tatuaje. Barcelona: J. Batlló, 1974. Novel.

La vía chilena al golpe de estado. Barcelona: Saturno, 1975.

Yo maté a Kennedy; impresiones, observaciones y memorias de un guardaespaldas. Barcelona: Editorial Planeta, 1972. Novel.

II. CRITICAL WORKS ON THE AUTHORS

A. IN SPANISH

Albert Robatto, Matilde. *La creación literaria de Juan Goytisolo.* Barcelona: Editorial Planeta, 1977.

Alvar, Manuel. *El mundo novelesco de Miguel Delibes.* Madrid: Editorial Gredos, 1987.

Argente del Castillo Ocana, Concha. *Rafael Alberti: Poesía del destierro.* Granada: Universidad de Granada, 1986.

Arniz, Francisco M., ed. *Homenaje a Rafael Alberti.* Barcelona: Península, 1977.

Bache Cortés, Yolanda. *Pascual Duarte y Alfanhui.* México: Universidad Nacional Autónoma de México, 1979.

Bartolomé Pons, Esther. *Miguel Delibes y su guerra constante.* Barcelona:

V. Pozanco, 1979.

Bayo, Manuel. *Sobre Alberti.* Madrid: CVS Ediciones, 1974.

Bellver, Catherine G. *Rafael Alberti en sus horas de destierro.* Salamanca: Colegio de España, 1984.

Berenger, Angel and Joan. *Fernando Arrabal.* Madrid: Editorial Fundamentos, 1979.

Café Gijón: 100 años de historia. Madrid: Ediciones Kaydera, 1988.

Cardona, Rodolfo. *Novelistas españoles de postguerra.* Madrid: Taurus 1976.

Cela Conde, Camilo José. *Cela mi padre.* Madrid: Ediciones Temas de Hoy, 1989.

Cortina, José Ramón. *El arte dramático de Antonio Buero Vallejo.* Madrid: Editorial Gredos, 1969.

De la Peña, Jesús. *La publicidad en la obra creativa de M. Vázquez Montalbán.* Valencia: Publicación de la Universidad, 1971.

De Paco, Mariano. *Estudios sobre Buero Vallejo.* Murcia: Universidad de Murcia, 1984.

Devoto, Juan Bautista. *Antonio Buero Vallejo. Un dramaturgo del moderno teatro español.* La Plata: Elite, 1954.

Díaz de Castro, Francisco J. *Juan Marsé, ciudad y novela.* Palma de Mallorca: Universidad de Palma de Mallorca, 1984.

Doménech, Ricardo. *El teatro de Buero Vallejo.* Madrid: Editorial Gredos, 1979.

Dowd, Catherine Elizabeth. *Realismo trascendente en cuatro tragedias sociales de Antonio Buero Vallejo.* Chapel Hill: University of North Carolina, 1974.

Eternidad yacente. Estudios sobre la obra de Rafael Alberti. Granada: Universidad de Granada, 1985.

García Domínguez, Ramón. *Miguel Delibes: un hombre, un paisaje, una pasión.* Barcelona: Ediciones Destino, 1985.

Giménez, Alicia. *Torrente Ballester.* Barcelona: Barcanova, 1981.

Giménez-Frontín, José Luis. *Camilo José Cela: texto y contexto.* Barcelona: Montesinos, 1985.

González-Grano de Oro, Emilio. *El español de José L. Castillo-Puche.* Madrid: Editorial Gredos, 1983.

González Lanuza, Eduardo, *Rafael Alberti.* Buenos Aires: Ediciones Culturales Argentinas, 1965.

González Martín, Jerónimo Pablo. *Rafael Alberti.* Madrid: Ediciones Júcar, 1980.

Gullón, Agnes. *La novela experimental de Miguel Delibes.* Madrid: Taurus, 1980.

Gullón, Germán and Agnes. *Teoría de la novela.* Salamanca: Taurus, 1974.

Homenaje a Camilo José Cela. Cuadernos Hispanoamericanos 337-338 (Julio-Agosto 1978).

Homenaje a Gonzalo Torrente Ballester. Salamanca: Biblioteca de la Caja de Ahorros, 1981.

Homenaje al profesor Sampedro. Ciclo de conferencias. Madrid: Fundación Banco Exterior, 1987.

Ilie, Paul. *La novelística de Camilo José Cela.* Madrid: Editorial Gredos, 1963.

Illanes Adaro, Graciela. *La novelística de Carmen Laforet.* Madrid: Editorial Gredos, 1971.

Inclán, Josefina. *Carmen Conde y el mar.* Miami: Ediciones Universal, 1980.

Juan Goytisolo. (Proceedings of round table conference held at the University of Wisconsin-Parkside.) Madrid: Editorial Fundamentos, 1975.

Lázaro, Jesús. *La novelística de Juan Goytisolo.* Madrid: Alhambra, 1984.

Levine, Linda Gould. *Juan Goytisolo, la destrucción creadora.* México: Joaquín Mortiz, 1976.

—— and Gloria Feiman Waldman. *Feminismo ante el franquismo: Entrevistas con feministas de España.* Miami: Ediciones Universal, 1980.

López Martínez, Luis. *La novelística de Miguel Delibes.* Murcia: Universidad de Murcia, 1973.

Mactas, Mario. *Las perversiones de Francisco Umbral.* Madrid: Anjana, 1984.

Marbán, Jorge A. *Camus y Cela: el drama del antihéroe trágico.* Barcelona: Ediciones Picazo, 1973.

Marrast, Robert. *Rafael Alberti en México (1935).* Santander: La Isla de los Ratones, 1984.

May, Barbara Dale. *El dilema de la nostalgia en la poesía de Alberti.* Bern: P. Lang, 1978.

Monleón, José. *Rafael Alberti y Nuria Espert.* Caracas: Editorial Ateneo de Caracas, 1979.

Navajas, Gonzalo. *La novela de Juan Goytisolo.* Madrid: Sociedad General Española de Librería, 1979.

Pajón Mecloy, Enrique. *Buero Vallejo y el antihéroe.* Madrid: E. Pajón Mecloy: Distribuye, Breogan, 1986.

Palabras para Larva. Edición al cuidado de Andrés Sánchez Robayna y Gonzalo Díaz-Migoyo. Barcelona: Edicions del Mall, 1985.

Pérez, José Carlos. *La trayectoria novelística de Juan Goytisolo: El autor y sus obsesiones.* Zaragoza: Ediciones Oroel, 1984.

Prjervalinsky, Olga. *El sistema estético de Camilo José Cela.* Madrid: Editorial Castalia, 1960.

Rey, Alfonso. *La originalidad novelística de Delibes.* Santiago de Compostela: Universidad de Santiago de Compostela, 1975.

Richmond, Carolyn. *Un análisis de la novela "Las guerras de nuestros antepasados" de M. Delibes.* Barcelona: Ediciones Destino, 1982.

Roma, Rosa. *Ana María Matute.* Madrid: E.P.E.S.A., 1971.

Romero, Héctor René. *La evolución literaria de Juan Goytisolo.* Miami: Ediciones Universal, 1979.

Salcedo, Emilio. *Miguel Delibes, novelista de Castilla.* Valladolid: Consejería de Educación y Cultura, 1986.

Salinas de Marichal, Solita. *El mundo poético de Rafael Alberti.* Madrid:

Editorial Gredos, 1968.

Sanz, Santos. *Lectura de Juan Goytisolo.* Barcelona: V. Pozanco, 1977.

Schaefer-Rodríguez, Claudia. *Juan Goytisolo: del "realismo crítico" a la utopía.* Madrid: Ediciones J. Porrúa Turanzas, 1984.

Sherzer, William M. *Juan Marsé: entre la ironía y la dialéctica.* Madrid: Fundamentos, 1982.

Sobejano, Gonzalo. *Novela española de nuestro tiempo.* Madrid: Editorial Prensa Española, 1975.

Spand, Kurt. *Inquietud y nostalgia: la poesía de Rafael Alberti.* Pamplona: Ediciones Universidad de Navarra, 1973.

Suárez Solís, Sara. *El léxico de Camilo José Cela.* Madrid: Alfaguara, 1969.

Tejada, José Luis. *Rafael Alberti, entre la tradición y la vanguardia.* Madrid: Editorial Gredos, 1977.

Tejerina, José María R. *Camilo José Cela y la medicina.* Palma de Mallorca: M. Alcover, 1974.

Torres Monreal, Francisco. *Introducción al teatro de Arrabal.* Murcia: Editorial Godoy, 1981.

Umbral, Francisco. *Miguel Delibes.* Madrid: E.P.E.S.A., 1970.

Velloso, José Miguel. *Conversaciones con Rafael Alberti.* Madrid: Sedmay Ediciones, 1977.

Verdú de Gregorio, Joaquín. *La luz y la oscuridad en el teatro de Buero Vallejo.* Barcelona: Ariel, 1977.

Vernon, Kathleen. *Juan Benet.* Madrid: Taurus, 1986.

Zamora Vicente, Alonso. *Camilo José Cela; acercamiento a un escritor.* Madrid: Ediciones Gredos, 1962.

B. In English

Arata, Luis Oscar. *The Festive Play of Fernando Arrabal.* Lexington: University Press of Kentucky, 1982.

Blackwell, Frieda Hilda. *The Game of Literature: Demythification and Parody in the Novels of Gonzalo Torrente Ballester.* Chapel Hill: Albatros Ediciones, 1985.

Brown, Joan Lipman. *Secrets from the Back Room: The Fiction of Carmen Martin Gaite.* University, MS: University of Mississippi Romance Monographs, 1987.

Cabrera, Vicente. *Juan Benet.* Boston: Twayne, 1983.

Camilo José Cela Number. *Review of Contemporary Fiction* 4, no. 3 (Fall 1984).

Díaz, Janet. *Ana María Matute.* New York: Twayne, 1971.

———. *Miguel Delibes.* New York: Twayne, 1971.

Donahue, Thomas John. *The Theater of Fernando Arrabal: A Garden of Earthly Delights.* New York: New York University Press, 1980.

Forrest, Gene Steven. "The Novelistic World of Juan Goytisolo." Diss., Vanderbilt University, 1969.

Foster, David William. *Forms of the Novel in the Work of Camilo José Cela.*

Columbia: University of Missouri Press, 1967.

Juan Goytisolo / Ishmael Reed Number. *Review of Contemporary Fiction* 4, no. 2 (Summer 1984).

Halsey, Martha T. *Antonio Buero Vallejo.* New York: Twayne, 1973.

Henn, David. *C. J. Cela: La colmena.* London: Tamesis Books, 1974.

Herzberger, David K. *The Novelistic World of Juan Benet.* Indiana: The American Hispanist, 1976.

Inclán, Josefina. *Carmen Conde and the Sea.* Miami: Ediciones Universal, 1980.

Jentsch-Grooms, Lynda. *Exile and the Process of Individuation: a Jungian Analysis of Marine Symbolism in the Poetry of Rafael Alberti.* Valencia: Albatros Hispanófila, 1986.

Jiménez-Fajardo, Salvador. *Multiple Spaces: The Poetry of Rafael Alberti.* London: Tamesis Books, 1985.

Johnson, Roberta. *Carmen Laforet.* Boston: Twayne, 1981.

Jones, Margaret E.W. *The Literary World of Ana María Matute.* Lexington: University Press of Kentucky, 1970.

Kirsner, Robert. *The Novels and Travels of Camilo José Cela.* Chapel Hill: University of North Carolina Press, 1966.

Manteiga, Roberto C. *The Poetry of Rafael Alberti: A Visual Approach.* London: Tamesis Books, 1979.

————, David K. Herzberger, and Malcom Alan Compitello, eds. *Critical Approaches to the Writings of Juan Benet.* Hanover, NH: University Press of New England, 1984.

McPheeters, D.W. *Camilo José Cela.* New York: Twayne, 1969.

Nantell, Judith. *Rafael Alberti's Poetry of the Thirties: The Poet's Public Voice.* Athens: University of Georgia Press, 1986.

Nicholas, Robert L. *The Tragic Stages of Antonio Buero Vallejo.* Chapel Hill: University of North Carolina, 1972.

Orenstein, Gloria. *The Theater of the Marvelous.* New York: New York University Press, 1975.

Pauk, Edgar. "Miguel Delibes: Development of a Writer (1947-1969)." Diss., Yale University, 1970.

Pérez, Genaro J. *Formalist Elements in the Novels of Juan Goytisolo.* MD: J. Porrúa Turanzas, 1979.

Pérez, Janet. *Contemporary Women Writers of Spain.* Boston: Twayne, 1988.

————. *Gonzalo Torrente Ballester.* Boston: Twayne, 1984.

Podol, Peter L. *Fernando Arrabal.* Boston: Twayne, 1978.

Popkin, Louise B. *The Theatre of Rafael Alberti.* London: Tamesis Books, 1975.

Pritchett, Sharon Kay. "Linguistic Structure, Theme and Technique in the Poetry of Manuel Vázquez Montalbán." Diss., University of North Carolina at Chapel Hill, 1979.

Rogers, Elizabeth Senicka. "Human Values and Themes in the Novels of Miguel Delibes." Diss., University of Illinois at Urbana-Champaign, 1970.

Schwartz, Kessel. *Juan Goytisolo.* New York: Twayne, 1970.

Servodidio, Mirella and Marcia L. Welles, eds. *From Fiction to Metafiction: Essays in Honor of Carmen Martin Gaite.* NE: Society of Spanish and Spanish-American Studies, 1983.

Six, Abigail Lee. *Juan Goytisolo: The Case for Chaos.* New Haven: Yale University Press, 1990.

Ugarte, Michael. *Trilogy of Treason: An Intertextual Study of Juan Goytisolo.* Columbia: University of Missouri Press, 1982.

Wesseling, Pieter. "The Poetry of Rafael Alberti: Traditionalism and Revolution." Diss., University of Wisconsin, Madison, 1970.

Index

With rare exceptions, compound Spanish surnames are indexed under the first (paternal) name; hence Federico García Lorca is indexed under García, even though he is often referred to by Lorca only.